W9-BQY-981

Introduction to Unix and Linux

JOHN MUSTER

McGraw-Hill Osborne

New York / Chicago / San Francisco
Lisbon / London / Madrid / Mexico City / Milan
New Delhi / San Juan / Seoul / Singapore / Sydney / Toronto

The McGraw·Hill Companies

McGraw-Hill Osborne
2100 Powell Street, 10th Floor
Emeryville, California 94608
U.S.A.

To arrange bulk purchase discounts for sales promotions, premiums, or fund-raisers, please contact
McGraw-Hill/Osborne at the above address. For information on translations or book distributors
outside the U.S.A., please see the International Contact Information page immediately following the
index of this book.

Introduction to Unix and Linux

234567890 FGR FGR 019876543

Book p/n 0-07-222796-6 and CD 1 P/N: 0-07-222797-4 and CD 2 P/N: 0-07-222798-2
parts of
ISBN 0-07-222695-1

Publisher
    Brandon A. Nordin

Vice President & Associate Publisher
    Scott Rogers

Acquisitions Editor
    Christopher C. Johnson

Project Editor
    Julie M. Smith

Acquisitions Coordinator
    Athena Honore

MLA Project Director
    Nate Hinerman

Copy Editor
    Andy Saff

Proofreader
    Karen Mead

Technical Editors
    Douglas K. Horton, Hagerstown Community College
    Walter Merchant, ECPI College of Technology
    Dennis Rice, DeVry University
    Michael J. Riha, Thomas Nelson Community College
    Erik van Renselaar, New England Institute of Technology

Indexer
    Valerie Perry

Computer Designer
    Kathleen Fay Edwards, Lucie Ericksen

Illustrator
    Melinda Moore Lytle, Michael Mueller, Lyssa Wald

Cover Design
    Greg Scott

Series Design
    Peter F. Hancik

This book was composed with Corel VENTURA™ Publisher.

About the Author

Students consistently report that John Muster obviously loves teaching students. Helping students learn is at the center of his work—in the classroom, in the Teacher Education Seminar, in the books and media he develops, and in the programs he supports. His scientific work began in astronomy, then educational psychology. He focuses on how people learn complex skills or content, and how to develop materials, exercises, events, problems, and ways of guiding students that support their growth and success. For the last twenty years he has explored how to facilitate learning of UNIX and Linux through several major projects funded by the United States Treasury, Anderson Consulting (Accenture), Sun Microsystems and Apple Computing. These projects form the body of work on which this text is based.
In addition to research and consulting, John Muster teaches and conducts educational development at the educational center of silicon valley, the University of California's Extension Division, where he was given the Honored Teacher Award. His undergraduate and graduate education took place at Otterbein College, Ohio State University, and the University of California, Berkeley.

This book was carefully developed and written for you.
We hope that you enjoy successfully teaching yourself UNIX/Linux.

John Muster
Berkeley, CA 2002

Contents

Acknowledgments

For more than 20 years I have thoroughly enjoyed writing, teaching UNIX/ Linux, listening to students' questions and suggestions, solving problems, consulting, revising the chapters, teaching, revising…. The evolution of these exercises was possible because I have had the good fortune to be engaged with committed students at the University of California and at corporate education facilities around the world. Thank you for your challenges, comments, and ideas.

Additionally, the fundamental research into how students master content such as this would not have been possible without the generous support of the Lubrizol Foundation, the Department of the Treasury, Accenture, Sun Microsystems and Apple Computing.

Nate Hinerman is a remarkably competent project director who made completion of this text possible. He kept track of details without loosing sight of the big picture, facilitated teamwork by providing mutual support, kept lines of communication open and active, and was remarkably productive. Isaac Chellin brought gifted artistic talent, cutting-edge technical skills, and a cooperative design approach to the development of both the illustrations and the related web pages. Marcelo Carvalho was tireless in his testing, evaluating, and checking of the materials. Thomas Brightbill's programming, web design, and communication skills led to the development of the current internet site with its support for this text.

I want to thank the talented group of academics who reviewed this book and provided feedback that made this a better book: Walt Merchant (ECPI College of Technology), Eric van Reneslaar (New England Institute of Technology), Doug Horton (Hagerstown Community College), Dennis Rice (DeVry University) and Michael Riha (Thomas Nelson Community College).

From my earliest days, I have enjoyed watching the lights go on as people make sense out of what they are studying. Through the years of physics and computer science education I have enjoyed interacting with committed colleagues who have shared that same joy—and have affected how this book works. Thank you Phil Barnhart, Lelia Braucher, Orin Braucher, Catherine Cavette, Marjorie Conrad, John Coulter, Gene Eakins, Lillian Frank, Harold Hall, Nate Hinerman, Peter Kindfield, John Laubach, Albert Levy, Mel Mayfield, Marguerite McKinney, James Miller, Walter Mitchell, Catherine M. Muster, John T. Muster, Bob Place, Siggy Selquist, Lyle Strand, and David Waas.

In the last analysis, it's the relationships. Catherine, Cassy, extended family, dear friends: thank you for the unending support, encouragement, and affection.

Introduction

About This Book

If you want to know general facts about Mount Everest, get a good reference book or encyclopedia. If you want to really experience Mount Everest, find a good guide, an experienced Sherpa to lead you through all the right steps to the summit.

This book is a Sherpa, not a reference text. Although command summaries and tables are included, this book is fundamentally a guide designed to help you really learn the skills needed to master the UNIX/Linux environment. Through carefully developed, hands-on interactions with a UNIX/Linux system, you are guided through a grand, stimulating journey from the absolutely basic system features to a rich mastery of the details employed by experts.

If you are looking for a quick reference text, put this book back on the shelf. There are many good reference texts available. This book stands alone. It is a learning guide. It is a Sherpa.

Getting the Most from this Text

Learning UNIX can be reasonably easy—if you approach it the same way you learned to ride a bicycle. Your parents did not set up the overhead projector in the living room and show you 50 minutes worth of slides in rapid succession, explaining the intricacies of micro-human bicycle propulsion. And you did not learn how to ride your bike by reading the manual either.

You got on your bike. Someone steadied it and at the precise moment that it was needed, gave you the specific, appropriate information that supported your mastering the needed skills: "turn the handlebars this way"; "to stop, just start peddling backwards"; "lean into the curve; avoid that rock."…

The same is true as you master UNIX/Linux skills.

Get on to a UNIX or Linux system. Open the book to the beginning of the first chapter and start peddling. The key is to actually do each exercise on a live UNIX/Linux system so you can see how it responds and exactly what you must do to get results. As you work through the chapters of this book, you will enter commands, will read about what is happening, and will then enter more commands. Instructions in the chapters guide you carefully from the most tentative, initial steps; to exploring the essential features; to mastery of basic and advanced user and programming skills.

Each step is specified; the implications are discussed as you investigate each feature.

This book can be your UNIX tutor—your Sherpa—as you climb and teach yourself UNIX.

If you're an experienced user, start at the beginning and quickly pass through a topic if you have done it several times before. Be sure to create all files as instructed because they are needed in later exercises. Wade in until you are in deep enough to swim, then carefully do each exercise. Most people, unless they are very experienced, find new skills even in the first chapters.

After the basic skills are mastered, you explore more complex features built on the basics. You carefully construct your knowledge of UNIX, adding each piece as it is appropriate.

When you are asked to enter a command, the first step is preceded with an icon that looks like Please put arrow icon here If there are several steps, they are numbered.

Explanations generally *follow* the keyboard exercise. If results are puzzling, read on.

UNIX is a collection of powerful programs, the foundation for modern operating systems, the ultimate user-hostile interface, a Tinkertoy for adults, a fascinating and enjoyable programming environment...

Log on and let us guide you as you have fun and master UNIX/Linux.

Resources for Teachers

Teachers are our heroes to whom we give our thanks and for whom we have created a powerful collection of time-saving teaching tools that are available on CD-ROM, including:

- An Instructor's Manual that maps to the organization of textbook
- ExamView® Pro testbank software that generates a wide array of paper or network-based tests, and features automatic grading
- Hundreds of questions, written by experienced IT instructors
- Wide variety of question types and difficulty levels, allowing teachers to customize each test to maximize student progress
- Engaging PowerPoint® slides on the lecture topics

## CHAPTER 1

Logging On to the System

SKILLS CHECK

Before beginning this chapter, you should:

- Have access to a working UNIX/Linux system
- Have the login name and password for a normal user account, not *root*

OBJECTIVES

After completing this chapter, you will be able to:

- Discuss why UNIX/Linux is important in today's technical world
- Log on to a UNIX/Linux system to accomplish work
- Log off, ending a session
- Start a terminal window from a graphical interface

Whether you are a total newcomer to the world of UNIX/Linux or have used some commands and programs, welcome to a thorough examination of the features and programs of the system. This first chapter examines why mastering UNIX/Linux is important in today's technical world, and guides you through accessing and leaving the system. After the brief summary of the role of Linux and UNIX in our world, you will start entering information and commands at the monitor and keyboard on your system.

1.1 Why Study UNIX/Linux?

In this ever-changing technical world, why should you bother learning about UNIX/ Linux? After all, it's a computer system largely developed in ancient times: the 1970s and 1980s.

Why should anyone take the time to learn UNIX/Linux?

Not just because it is *there*, but because it is *everywhere*.

If tomorrow morning all UNIX/Linux computer systems ceased to function, we would be living in a very different world.

Without UNIX or Linux, there would be:

- **No Internet** Most Internet servers and essentially all of the fundamental computing structures run on a UNIX or Linux computer.
- **No Modern Films** Most of the special effects are generated on UNIX/Linux systems.
- **No Stocks and Bonds Sales** Nearly all transactions are handled by UNIX/Linux systems.
- **No ATMs or Banking** Many of the actual ATMs and most of the communication networks are running on UNIX/Linux systems.
- **No Electronic Games** The development of many electronic games occurs in UNIX/Linux environments.
- **No Military** The general infrastructure for communications, programs, smart devices, and critical data is managed on UNIX/Linux systems.
- **No Operational Government** Tax liens, records, communications, and more are stored on UNIX/Linux machines.
- **No Functioning Universities** Records, research, communication, development, publications, and more depend on applications provided by UNIX/Linux systems.

- **No Large Corporations** Data, research, file serving for desktops, e-mail, and an enormous portion of publishing run in UNIX/Linux environments.

What would be left? We could still use your existing desktop computer systems to do word processing and run other local applications, if we had any electricity to run the computers—but that would be difficult because both the electricity production and delivery grid are largely managed through UNIX/Linux systems.

UNIX/Linux has become the fundamental foundation for our modern computing world, but it is not just running on huge machines. We can explore and utilize UNIX/Linux on personal computers, then apply those skills in industry, government, university, and small business situations. So the task is to become a proficient user. But first, we have to log on to a system that is running Linux or UNIX.

1.2 Logging On to a System

This first chapter examines accessing and leaving a running system. We will begin exploring standard features of UNIX/Linux in Chapter 2, after you master logging on to your system. Chapters 2 and 3 guide you on a tour of system features, and the chapters that follow examine the system in depth.

One of the primary features of the UNIX computing environment is that it can serve many users at the same time. A single system can often handle tens to thousands of individual users, a cost-effective solution. When a system's administrator adds a new user to a system, a unique *account* associated with a *login* name is created. The *login* name, often called the *username*, is unique to each user. For security reasons, entry onto a UNIX/Linux system is granted only when a user provides both a *login* name and the associated *password* that match an established user on the system.

Obtaining Needed Resources

Depending on your situation, one of the following three conditions is true.

- You have a system, but Linux is not installed,
  or

- You have access to a running Linux system, complete with the user login name *root,* and you have the password for the *root* account,

  or

- You have an account on either Linux or UNIX and the username you are to use is a regular username and password, not *root*.

  Depending on which of the preceding situations is true, you will need to accomplish different tasks.

- If you have a system, but Linux is not installed, you must first install Linux on the computer and create a user account. Proceed to Appendix A which provides guidance on the needed steps. After installing Linux and creating a regular user account, you should return here to explore logging in and out. If you were given the information to log on using an account named *root*, you need to create a regular user account before continuing. The user named *root* is granted the extensive powers needed to administer the system. Because this account carries substantial authority over system events and operations, you can hurt or destroy a system by issuing the wrong commands. It is dangerous to log on using the *root* account. You should do so only to accomplish specific tasks, and then only very carefully. Add yourself as a user by following the instructions in Chapter 13 and return to the following steps to explore logging in and out.

- If you have the login name and password for a regular user on the system, you are ready to proceed.

Logging On

Because many system administrators modify the login process to fit local needs, some of the steps listed in the following exercises may not fit your particular situation. If you note that certain steps do not fit your situation and cannot determine what to do, find an accomplished user who can show you how to get on the system. Once you are logged on, you should find that the steps described in this text are compatible with the system

1. Make sure that both the monitor and the computer are turned on.

At this point, the screen displays a *login:* banner in a plain terminal like one of the following:

```
Red Hat Linux release 7.2 (Enigma)
Kernel 2.4.7-10 on an i686
login: _
```

If your screen display is like the preceding, the system is interacting with your monitor as though it were just a character-based terminal, not a graphic one.

The alternative display of the *login:* banner is in a graphical window similar to the following:

```
 Session   Language   System    Sun Aug 18, 05:53 PM

              Welcome to ume
 _____

   Login:
        [                                          ]

              Please enter your login
```

If your system is displaying a graphical login banner, it is using the graphical features of the monitor.

At this point, the system is waiting for any one of the many legal users to type their username and password.

2. In response to the login prompt, identify yourself by entering the name of your account, your *login name,* or your *username.*

   Because both UNIX and Linux are case-sensitive, you must enter the login data exactly as it was set up. On most systems, the login name and often the password are in lowercase letters.

3. After entering the exact account name information, press ENTER.

   Whether or not you entered the login name correctly, you are asked for a password with the following prompt:

   `Password:`

4. Enter your password exactly as you created it, or as it was provided to you. Pay careful attention to case and easily confused characters such as *1* (one) and *l* (*el*).

For security reasons, as you type your password, it is not displayed on the screen. Often there is no confirmation that you are entering anything at all, although sometimes the screen displays * or # to let you know that the system registered a key.

5. After you type your password, press ENTER

If you typed both the username and password correctly, you are successfully logged in.

After you log in, the screen clears. If there are no icons but instead the display consists of just one or a few lines of text such as the following, you are in a character-based terminal window:

```
Red Hat Linux release 7.2 (Enigma)
Kernel 2.4.7-10 on an i686
login: nate
Password:
Last login: Mon Aug 19 17:18:07
bash-2.05$
```

```
$
%
login@SystemName  $
```

After logging in, if you are presented with a full graphical environment—probably complete with a menu bar at the top, some icons on the screen, and a *Task Bar* at the bottom—you are in a graphical window.

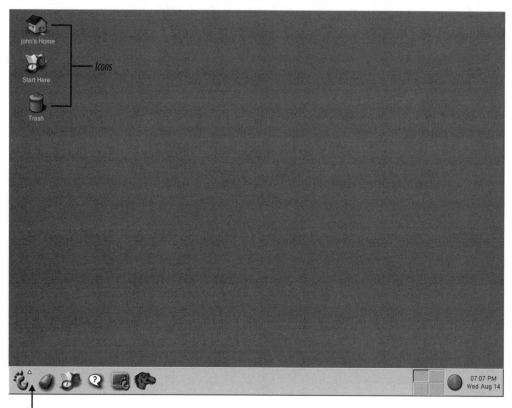

Although the various graphical windows from Red Hat, SuSe, and Sun look somewhat different, they all provide the same functionality.

Correcting Login Errors

If you provide a valid set of corresponding login and password entries, you are moved on to the next step. However, if either the login or password you supplied is incorrect, an error message appears, such as:

```
Login incorrect
```

Following are some common mistakes made when entering either the login or password that result in an incorrect login:

- Users confuse the numeral *1* and the letter *l* (el), or confuse the numeral *0* (zero) and the letter *O* (oh).
- Users make simple typing mistakes.
- Users employ BACKSPACE to correct an error. (Although many modern systems permit making corrections, many others do not.)
- Users type in uppercase letters.
- The information is wrong.

Terminal Window: Interacting with the System

The last line displayed on the terminal window is the prompt, which is something like:

```
$
%
Login@SystemName$
```

If logging in results in a terminal window, you are ready to start issuing commands to UNIX or Linux.

➥ Confirm all is well by entering:

date

and press ENTER.

The output of the **date** program, the current date and time, is displayed.

Logging Off from a Terminal Environment

If you are in a terminal rather than graphical environment, exiting the terminal logs you off the system.

➥ 1. To log off from a terminal environment, enter:

exit

The session ends and a new login banner is displayed.

2. At this point, scan through the next section to become familiar with the graphical windows, read the conclusion, and start the second chapter, which explores UNIX/Linux using the terminal.

Graphical Window: Starting a Terminal Window

The remaining exercises in the following chapters of this book explore how you work with the system by issuing commands in a character-based terminal, or in a terminal window if you are provided with the graphical environment.

If you are in the graphical world, a terminal window may appear on the screen as part of the default desktop setup. Usually no terminal window is presented, so we have to start one.

1. Examine the *Task Bar* at the bottom of the screen. An icon that looks like a monitor or terminal is probably included.

2. With your mouse, click the terminal icon.

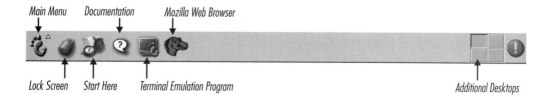

A terminal window is displayed on the screen.

If the terminal window was displayed when you logged in, or if you just started it, you will need to make it the active window to issue commands.

3. Click the mouse anywhere in the terminal window.

4. Once the terminal is active, type:

   date

   and press the ENTER key.

The current date and time are displayed. This terminal window is used for the exercises that follow in this text.

Logging Off from a Graphical Window

When we are in a graphical environment, logging off the system is accomplished through the menu bar.

1. Click on the leftmost icon, probably one of the following:

Menu Bar

A menu is displayed:

Log out ——→

2. To end this session, click on the *Log out* option.

Chapter Review

Use this section to review the contents of this chapter and test yourself on your knowledge of the concepts.

Chapter Summary

- People who can enter an accepted username and password are granted access to the system.
- If you are using a character-based terminal, after you log in, the terminal is available for entering commands.
- In a graphical environment, we must start a terminal window by clicking on the appropriate icon in the menu bar.
- In a character-based terminal, exiting the terminal exits the session.
- In the graphical environment, we must select *Log out* from the *Applications Menu* to exit the session.

Assignment

1. Describe the kinds of environments that use UNIX/Linux extensively and environments that use it much less.
2. Why should users log on as a regular user and not as the user *root*?
3. Try to log in but provide a space in the middle of your login name. What error message results and when is it displayed?
4. Try to log in putting a space in the password. What error message results?
5. How do you exit from a terminal window or character based terminal?

Touring Essential Programs

2

O B J E C T I V E S

After completing this chapter, you will be able to:

- Run programs to obtain system and user information
- Communicate instructions properly to the system's command interpreter
- Navigate to other directories in the filesystem
- Use standard programs to create, examine, and manage files
- Access the online manual pages that describe specific commands and files
- Search the online manual pages by keyword or regular expression
- Identify and access useful Internet sites

One effective way to visit a major city for the first time is to begin by going to the top of one of its highest buildings. From that lofty perch, we can easily identify the major features and see how streets are laid out. Next, we could briefly visit the major features of the city using the transportation system. Such a quick tour of the highlights would show how the major systems work and would give the visitor a foundation for later, more in-depth investigations of the most interesting parts of the city.

In the same way, this chapter and the one that follows take you on a guided, hands-on, whirlwind tour of a UNIX/Linux system. You will master fundamental skills that will enable you to get around the system, use essential tools, identify the major features, and take advantage of the system's underlying design structures. Each feature is explored through hands-on, direct interaction with a functioning system. After you finish this introductory tour, the book's remaining chapters guide your further, in-depth exploration of the individual features.

The secret to mastering the wealth of skills included in this text is to enter the commands, read the associated explanations, and do the exercises. Hundreds of thousands of people have carefully followed the paths laid out in this text and have become proficient users of the UNIX system and its major features.

2.1 Surveying the Development of UNIX and Linux

UNIX was initially developed in the 1970s by a group of young inventive scientists at Bell Laboratories. They created an operating system that consisted of several things:

- A main program to control the central processing unit (*CPU*), and all other hardware. This underlying program is called the *kernel*.
- A collection of user and system programs often called *utilities*.
- A structure for keeping and locating data in files on the hard drive, called the *filesystem*.

Soon after the initial development, the operating system code was then licensed to the University of California at Berkeley, where graduate students and faculty members completed significant additional development, adding many programs and rewriting the operating system to permit systems to communicate in a network environment.

Several computer manufacturers started making UNIX computers and workstations. They added new features and modified aspects of the system to meet their particular needs. As a result, versions of UNIX running on Sun, HP, IBM, and so forth are slightly different.

In recent years, Linus Torvalds and a host of Internet accomplices wrote Linux, a UNIX look-alike operating system that is available for free in its basic form for download, or at low cost from several distributors. Today the UNIX/Linux operating systems run on equipment of essentially any size made by nearly all computer manufacturers.

In Linux, the fundamental programs employ the same code, but different distributions (including Red Hat, SuSe, Mandrake, and Lindows) add special features and installation programs. As a result, UNIX/Linux is not simply a "single" operating system. Rather, the term *UNIX* includes many slightly different flavors of the same general operating system. From the user's perspective, the various flavors are essentially identical because nearly all user commands work the same in recent versions.

2.2 Issuing Commands to Execute Utilities

In UNIX/Linux, the operating system includes an ever-expanding set of individual program utilities that users run or have executed. One program interprets your requests and executes the needed programs. This first section examines how to interact with the command interpreter to execute programs.

1. Log on to your UNIX or Linux system as a regular user, *not* as *root*.

2. If you are in the graphical environment, start a *terminal window.*

Meeting the Shell

Once you have successfully logged on, you may receive some informational messages, the screen may clear, one or more windows may be displayed, and a mouse may or may not be active.

At this point, you are using either a character-based terminal or a graphical terminal window. A prompt is displayed to the left of the cursor. The prompt may be customized for your site, or it may be one of the default prompts, such as:

```
$
%
login@hostname
```

where *login* is your username, and *hostname* is the name of your machine.

The prompt is displayed on your screen by a program called the *shell*, which reads your instructions (*commands*) and interprets them to the remainder of the system.

Issuing a Command to the Shell

After you have successfully logged on, the shell displays its prompt on the screen, which is the shell command interpreter's way of asking what you want to do next. The cursor is at the shell prompt. It is at the prompt that user and programmers give instructions that start and manage the wealth of programs available in UNIX and Linux systems. Although a graphical interface is available to accomplish many tasks, the fundamental and complete way to interact is by way of commands issued at the prompt.

1. Enter the following lowercase command:

   whoami

   and press ENTER.

   When you press ENTER, the command line you typed is sent to the shell, which interprets your instructions and executes whatever programs you specify.

   In this case, the **whoami** program runs. Its output, which is your login name or username, is displayed on your screen.

2. Type the following:

   WHOAMI

   and press ENTER.

An error message indicating that the command could not be found is displayed. UNIX and Linux are case-sensitive. Essentially all commands are in lowercase.

Obtaining Date and System Information

All UNIX and Linux systems keep track of the current date and time, which are then available to both users and programs as needed.

➥ 1. Type in:

date

and press ENTER.

The output of the **date** program, displayed on your screen, is the current date and time.

2. To see the system you are on, enter:

hostname

and press ENTER.

The name for the system is displayed.

Clearing the Screen

Another useful command instructs the shell to clear away whatever text is on the screen.

➥ At the shell prompt enter:

clear

The data on the screen is cleared, and the prompt is displayed at the top of the screen or window.

Making Corrections While Entering a Command Line

Typing is an inexact science. Our fingers often do not go where we intend. In this exercise, you will make an error entering a command and then correct it.

➥ 1. Type the following four letters, but do *not* press ENTER:

dzte

2. Try using the BACKSPACE key to move the cursor back.

On some systems, pressing BACKSPACE does not move the cursor but enters control characters on the line. If such is the case with your system, proceed to step 5.

3. Enter the command correctly:

   date

   Press ENTER.

4. Whether or not BACKSPACE worked in step 2, again enter:

   dzte

5. Try backing up and retyping to correct the error, using each of the following:

   DELETE

   CTRL-H   (Hold down CTRL and press H one time.)

At least one of these keys works to move the cursor back and erase whatever you type.

Determining Who Is on the System

At the shell prompt, we can ask that programs be executed. In a multiuser environment, it is often important to find out whether a colleague is logged on.

At the shell prompt, type the following lowercase command:

who

and press ENTER.

A list of users currently logged on is displayed.

The command line you just entered instructs the shell to execute a program or utility named **who**. The **who** utility determines who is currently logged on and formats a display of information concerning those logged-on users. In this instance, that data, the *output* of the **who** program, is sent to your screen. If you are the only user, only one line of data is displayed. If you are on a multiuser system, several login records are displayed.

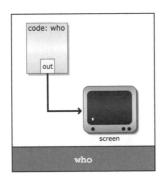

The output that **who** generates is in the following form. The data in your output contains information about the user(s) currently logged on to your system, such as:

```
anna      tty4      Apr 24 17:58
kyle      tty6      Apr 24 14:11
marty     pts1      Apr 23 21:13    (purdy.muster.com)
cassy     pts2      Apr 23 14:31    (thamzin.muster.com)
```

Identifying the Fields in the Output of *who*

Each line in the output of **who** contains data about one of the users who is currently logged on. Each line consists of several *fields* separated by one or more spaces. For instance, the components of the entry for *cassy* are as follows.

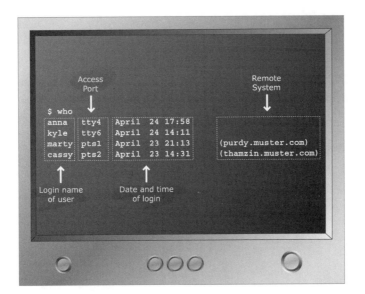

Each terminal or monitor is attached to the computer through a wire connected to a *port*—a physical location on the back of the computer. Each port has a designation that usually begins with the letters *tty* and a number. A terminal connected through a network uses an electronic or pseudo port named *pts*. When you issue the **who** command, the shell executes the **who** utility, which searches specific system files to determine the login name, port, and time each user logged on. The **who** utility then formats the information and outputs it. In this case, the output comes to your screen. The date and time of logging in are the last fields.

After **who** has completed its work, it exits and tells the shell that all went well. The shell then displays a new prompt, indicating that it is ready for your next instruction.

Using the Shell to Execute Programs

The procedure that you just followed in entering the **who** command is the way we work in the UNIX/Linux environment:

A. After we log on or start a terminal window, a program called the *shell* is started. The shell displays a prompt indicating that it is ready to receive instructions.

B. We type in a command and press ENTER.

C. The shell makes sense out of what we request (or complains if it cannot).

D. The shell then has whatever utility we requested run or executed, such as **date**, **cal**, or **ls**.

E. The utility's code is followed, producing whatever output it creates.

F. When the end of the code is reached, the shell is told that program is finished and it then terminates.

G. Upon receiving information that the last program has terminated, the shell displays another prompt and waits for your next instruction.

The interaction cycle is depicted in Figure 2-1.

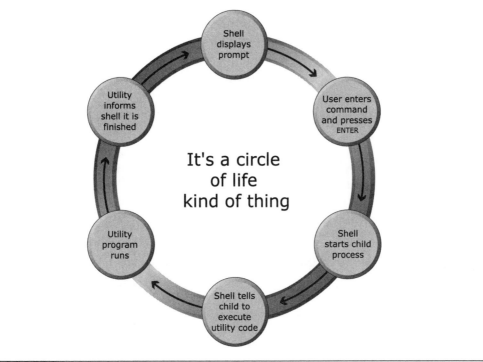

FIGURE 2-1 How the shell works

Passing Information to a Utility

Most distributions of UNIX and Linux include a program that outputs a 12-month calendar. In this exercise, you will display a calendar and examine how to use a shell command to pass information to the program requesting a particular year.

1. At the prompt, enter the following command:

   cal

   followed by ENTER

   The shell runs the **cal** program, which outputs the current month's calendar.

2. Now request a specific year's calendar by entering:

   cal99

   followed by ENTER

The shell reports that the command **cal99** is not found. We know from experiencing the previous command that **cal** is a legitimate utility, but evidently **cal99** is not.

The problem is that the shell is programmed to communicate much like humans. For example,

Thissentenceishardtoparsebecausetherearenospaces!

is easier to comprehend when displayed as:

This sentence is hard to parse because there are no spaces!

In human communication, spaces are used to identify each string of characters that forms a word. Likewise, for the shell, we need to provide spaces to identify each word or token on a command line.

3. Include a space between the **cal** utility and the information that we want to pass to **cal**, called its *argument*:

>   **cal** *99*

followed by ENTER

December 31 is not a Friday on this calendar. If you did not celebrate too much, you might remember that the great party held on December 31, 1999, was on a Friday evening. The output displayed on your screen cannot be for the year 1999. When you provided **cal** with the argument *99*, **cal** interpreted it as instruction to output the calendar for the year 99 A.D., more than 1900 years ago. When we ask for 99, we get 99.

4. Obtain the calendar for the year 1999:

>   **cal** *1999*

followed by ENTER

When we pass arguments to a utility, we must speak that utility's language. **cal** expects years in four digits. We must comply.

In the commands used so far, we entered just the name of the utility to be executed, pressed ENTER, and the shell ran it. When we enter a command followed by other information, such as **cal** *99*, we are telling the shell (1) to run the utility and (2) to pass the utility specific information that comes after the command—in this case, the number of the year we want displayed. Information passed to a utility is called an argument. Arguments provide instructions to utilities.

5. Run the **cal** utility, giving it the correct *argument* so it outputs the calendar for the current year.

Passing Multiple Arguments to *cal*

Nearly all UNIX/Linux programs accept arguments that are interpreted as instructions for the utility.

➥ 1. Examine the calendar for the year 1752 by entering the following command:

> **cal** *1752*

followed by ENTER

This command instructs the shell to run the **cal** utility and to pass **cal** the argument *1752*, which **cal** interprets as the year to display.

2. Look at September in the year 1752.

Twelve days are missing. Is the calendar broken? No, the calendar was adjusted because the old one was out of sync with how the Earth was traveling around the sun.

Adjusting the Calendar

The old Julian calendar defined the year as 365 and a quarter days long. Because the Earth did not quite make a full revolution about the sun in 365 days, our ancestors added a leap-year day every four years to keep the calendar coordinated with the trips around the sun. Unfortunately, the solar year is actually a little less than 365 and a quarter days (365.2422) long, so adding a leap-year day every four years was adding too much each time. By the 1500s, people began to notice that the shortest day of the year had moved into January, instead of December 21. In 1582, the Gregorian calendar reduced the number of leap-year days by declaring centuries to be leap years only if they are divisible by 400. The Gregorian calendar also threw out 10 days to bring the winter solstice back to December 21. In 1752, Great Britain finally adopted the Gregorian calendar. Because in the intervening 170 years the calendar had gotten even more out of sync, the British had to toss out 12 days to coordinate the calendar and solar year.

The **cal** utility, like many others, can interpret more than one argument.

3. Obtain only a month by entering:

> **cal** *9 1752*

Only the calendar for the month of September 1752 is displayed.

When two arguments are given, **cal** interprets the first as a month and the second as the year.

4. As another example, provide **cal** with the correct two arguments to see the month in which you were born.

5. Enter the following to check on the century leap-year days:

> **cal** *2 1700*
> **cal** *2 1800*
> **cal** *2 1900*
> **cal** *2 2000*
> **cal** *2 2300*
> **cal** *2 2400*
> **cal** *2 2800*

As the results show, after 1752, only centuries divisible by 400 are leap years. However, more important for your present study, you have had a lot of practice entering commands to the shell, including spaces between a utility and its first argument and between subsequent arguments.

Passing Arguments to the Spelling Utility

Many utilities accept arguments.

UNIX and Linux contain a spelling utility that can be accessed by users.

⮑   Enter:

> **look** *psycho*

This command instructs the shell to run **look** and give it the argument *psycho*. The **look** utility interprets the argument *psycho* as the first part of a word, locates all words in the dictionary file that begin with *psycho,* and then outputs the matching words.

Identifying the Components of a Shell Command

The commands issued thus far consist of a utility, placed first on the command line, followed by zero or more arguments, as follows:

> *utility*
> *utility* *argument*
> *utility* *argument* *argument*

The first token is a utility. Remaining tokens are arguments that are passed to the utility.

Examining How the Shell Executes Programs

When people first use UNIX or Linux, they sometimes get the impression that it is the shell that figures out who is logged on, the date, or the ingredients of the calendar, and all they have to do is ask the shell for such information. Actually, the shell knows nothing about these matters. When you enter the command **date** and press ENTER, you are instructing the shell to run the **date** program, usually called a *utility*.

When you log in, your shell program is started in an environment that includes code to read, a place to work, and a way to receive central processing unit (CPU) attention. An instance of a program running in its environment is called a *process*.

The shell process puts a prompt on the screen. We say what we want done by entering the name of a program to run, possibly with an argument. Then we press ENTER. The shell starts a new separate environment for executing the code of whatever utility we requested. This new environment, called a *child process*, executes whatever program we asked for when we entered the command.

Listing Processes

UNIX is a multitasking system, which means that when it is running it manages many programs at the same time. When you enter a command to execute a utility, the system allocates memory, locates the needed code, and provides CPU attention— a new *process* is under way. A process is an instance of some program code running. Any time you ask for a utility to be executed, you are requesting a child process to be started to execute the code of the utility. Processes are central to any computing environment.

1. Obtain a listing of your current processes by entering the following command:

   ps

   The output is a list of the processes currently associated with your login, along with some information about each process. For instance, the TT or TTY field is the *tty* number or port where the process is attached. The PID is the ID number of the process. Each process listed is a program you have running on the system. You probably have at least two processes running: the shell that is your command interpreter, and the **ps** utility itself. If you are in the graphical environment, there may be several others. Some systems do not list the **ps** process among the current processes, but most do. After **ps** has completed its work of figuring out what processes are running, it displays its output and terminates.

PROCESS IDENTIFICATION NUMBER	PORT WHERE USER IS LOGGED ON	CPU TIME SPENT ON PROCESS	UTILITY (CODE) THAT PROCESS IS RUNNING
PID	TTY	TIME	CMD
15937	pts/3	00:00:00	bash
18436	pts/3	00:00:00	ps

TABLE 2-1 Specifying the Output of ps

When you run a program, a new process is executed.

2. Enter the following:

> **ps**

If the process running **ps** is listed among your processes, you can see the process identification number is different each time you run the program.

After you press ENTER to indicate the end of the command line you want executed, the shell starts a new process. The shell passes the new process any arguments included after the utility name on the command line. For instance, if you enter **date** the shell locates the code for the utility and finally has the process execute it. The child process follows the code in **date**. The child process checks the system clock and formats the display output. The utility sends the results out its output "door." Initially, the output door of a utility is connected to your display screen unless, as you will see, you request that the shell connect it instead to a file or even to another utility.

Listing Systemwide Processes

The **ps** command you entered in the preceding exercise gave you the status of *your* processes. You can also display the processes running on the entire system, including those of all the users currently logged on and, system processes.

⮑ Type each of the following commands:

> **ps -aux**
> **ps -ef**

One or both commands should result in a long display of processes, probably running off the screen. You will soon see how to tame this list. The **-aux** and **-ef** are command options or flags that provide specific instructions to the utility.

Arguments that begin with a minus sign are options. Most utilities are programmed to interpret arguments that start with a minus sign as options that change the behavior of the utility.

This output of **ps** includes a list of the process status of every process currently running on the entire system, along with a plethora of information on each process. Many of these are system processes that keep all the services, such as printing and the network, alive. This information is very useful to system administrators and other people supervising the UNIX environment, especially when they are troubleshooting problems on the system. And it shows the rest of us what is going on under the hood.

The shell puts a prompt on the screen asking what we want to do. We enter a command line, which the shell interprets. The shell starts child processes to execute whatever programs we request. Then after the child process completes its task and terminates, the shell displays another prompt, and we go around again.

Self Test 1

Answer the following, and then check your answers against the information given in the chapter.

1. What utility produces a list of users currently logged on to the system?

   _____

2. When you enter the command **cal** *2004*, what are you asking the shell to do and what is the result?

   _____

3. What command lists the processes you currently have running?

   _____

4. Where a word or token is located on a command line tells the shell about that token. If we enter a command line of the following form to the shell, how does the shell interpret each token (as a utility or as an argument)?

   _____   _____   _____

5. Will the following work?

   ps-ef

   _____

6. After the shell starts a child process to execute a utility that the user requested, does the shell terminate or wait for the child process to complete its execution?

   _____

2.3 Communicating Instructions to the Shell

The shell can start new processes; can locate the code for utilities like **cal**, **who**, and **date**; and can get those instructions executed by the new process. The results generated by the program are displayed on the screen. Where does the information come from? Why is it displayed on the screen? Why isn't it placed in a file or on a neighbor's screen?

So far, you have entered the names of programs and included arguments for those arguments. New processes have been started and the programs have been executed. The shell's job is to do what you request. However, the shell does much more than start processes, pass arguments, and execute programs, if we say *please*. When we are in France, we need to speak French to order lunch. When in UNIX, we need to talk "shell" to be understood and to get work done. This next section examines how to instruct the shell to take the output from a process running a utility and connect it to a file or even another utility.

Listing Filenames

Depending on how your account is set up and whether you have used it before, you may or may not have files in your home directory. We can list the contents.

↳   Enter the following command:

     ls

     followed by ENTER.

The l<u>is</u>t utility lists the contents of the current directory's standard files. If you have some files, their names are displayed. You may not have any files yet; that will soon change.

Redirecting Output from a Utility to a File

When we tell the shell to execute the **who** utility, the code for **who** runs and outputs a listing of current users. The process running the **who** utility locates the needed information and formats the report. The default output destination for the formatted results of running the **who** utility is the user's screen. The output is *directed* to the screen, unless we redirect it elsewhere.

We can instruct the shell to *redirect* the output of a utility away from your screen to a file. Once data is in a file, it is saved, and can be modified, printed, and mailed.

Displaying Names of Files Listed in the Home Directory

Every user on the system is given a place to work and save files. This place is called the user's *home directory*. This directory, or folder, contains the names of files and subdirectories created by and owned by the user.

1. Look at your current directory contents:

    ls

    The **ls** utility lists the names of files and subdirectories created in the current directory.

2. Type the following shell command line that includes the > symbol:

    who > *users_on*

    Nothing appears on the screen except the next shell prompt. There is no confirmation or acknowledgment that your command was successful. In UNIX/Linux, silence usually means success.

    You just told the shell to create a new file and connect it to the output of the process that is running the **who** utility.

3. Confirm that the file exists by entering:

    ls

    A list of the current contents of the home directory is displayed.

    The preceding **who** command line that you entered includes three components. The shell interprets each component or token.

COMMAND	DESCRIPTION
who	Instructs the shell to start a new process to run the code for the **who** utility.
>	Instructs the shell to create a new file and redirect the output of the process to that file.
users_on	Specifies the filename that the shell assigns to the new file that receives output of **who**.

After the shell creates the new file and attaches it to the process's output, the process runs the **who** utility and writes to its output that is now connected to the new file, *users_on*. The output is said to be *redirected* away from your screen to the new file.

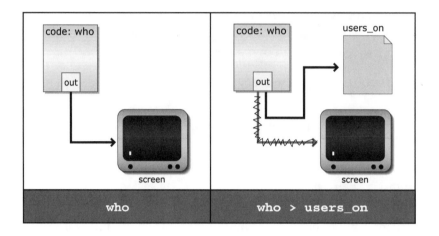

4. Create a file in your account of the calendar of the year 1752. Enter:

    cal *1752* > *lost-days*

    A child process is started, it is given the argument *1752*, and its output is connected to the new file *lost-days*. Once that "plumbing" is done, the shell tells the child process to run the **cal** utility code. To **cal**, the argument *1752* is a year. When **cal** is finished, it writes to output, which in this case is connected to the *lost-days* file.

5. Create a new file called *today* with the output of **date**:

    date > *today*

    This command instructs the shell to start a child process, create a new file named *today*, direct the output of the process to the file, and then have the process run the code for **date**.

6. Create a file called *birth* with the month of your birth as contents.

7. Confirm that the files exist by entering:

    ls

Your output should include at least the files *users_on*, *lost-days*, *today*, and *birth*. If any are missing, return to the appropriate previous step and create the files.

Examining the Contents of Files

If we store data in files, we need to be able to examine the contents of files. The UNIX system includes several utilities that describe or display the contents of files on the screen. Each utility handles the task differently.

Displaying a File One Screen at a Time

One way to examine the contents of a file is to display a screen full and then, when ready, ask for the next.

1. Enter the following command:

    more *lost-days*

    Probably only the first part of the file *lost-days* is displayed on the screen.

2. You can instruct **more** to display additional text. Press:

    SPACEBAR

    The next page of the file is displayed. Although the standard keyboard includes a PAGE DOWN key, it does not work with **more**.

3. Continue pressing SPACEBAR until you see the whole file and are returned to the shell.

    After **more** reaches the end of a file, it automatically quits, and the shell again displays a prompt. Most systems have a long file that contains information about how terminals behave. Although its content is not important at this time, the file can be used to explore how **more** works with long files.

4. Enter:

    more */etc/termcap*

    The **more** utility displays the beginning of the file named *termcap*.

5. Move through the file by pressing:

    SPACEBAR
    SPACEBAR

6. Quit **more** by pressing:

    q

    The **more** utility quits and a shell prompt is displayed.

Using Options to Count Elements in a File

In any work environment, we often need to know how many records are in a file, or how many characters are in a publication. In UNIX, a utility will count the lines, words, or characters in a file.

1. Enter the following command:

   wc *lost-days*

   This command line instructs the shell to run the **wc** utility and pass it one argument: *lost-days*. The **wc** utility interprets the argument as a file to read and examine. After counting the number of lines, words, and characters in the *lost-days* file, the word count utility outputs its results in a display similar to the following:

   ```
   35     452     1989  lost-days
   ```

   This output consists of the number of *lines* (35), *words* (452), and *characters* (1,989) in the file, followed by the name of the file that **wc** read.

2. Try another file:

   wc *birth*

Counting Only Lines

Like most UNIX utilities, the **wc** utility offers options that instruct **wc** to run in different ways.

1. For example, enter the **wc** command with an argument that is an option:

   wc -l *lost-days*   *(lowercase el)*

   The shell interprets this command as instruction to start a process and pass it two arguments, **-l**, and *lost-days*

   The **wc** utility interprets the argument **-l** as an *option* to count the lines in *lost-days*. This argument has a hyphen or minus sign in front of it. Utilities interpret arguments that start with a dash as instruction to behave in an *optional* way. The output consists of the number of lines only. The counts of total characters and words in the file are not output. We specify which optional form of the command we want by entering an argument that is an option, such as the **-l** you just used.

2. Enter:

   wc -l *users_on*
   wc -l *today*

In each of these command lines, two arguments are passed to **wc**: the **-l** option and a string of characters that the program interprets as a filename. The **-l** option instructs **wc** to output only the number of <u>l</u>ines it reads from the file. The minus sign in the argument tells **wc** that the l is an option, not a file to read as data.

3. Use **wc** to count the elements of some other files:

   > **wc** */etc/passwd*
   > **wc -l** */etc/passwd*
   > **wc** */etc/termcap*
   > **wc -l** */etc/termcap*

Creating and Listing Files in the Current Directory

In the preceding exercise, you created new files. You own them and you have access to them. The files are listed in your current or home directory.

1. To list the names of the files in your current (home) directory, type the command:

   > **ls**

   and press ENTER

   With this command line, you are asking the shell to locate and run the **ls** utility. When **ls** runs, it obtains the names of the files listed in your current directory and outputs a formatted display of those filenames. Because you did not ask the shell to redirect the output of **ls** anywhere else, it is displayed on your screen. After the **ls** utility completes its work, the program exits and notifies the shell. The shell then provides another prompt to see what you want to do next.

   Essentially, any utility's output can be redirected to a file.

2. For example, enter:

   > **ls** > *myfiles1*
   > **more** *myfiles1*
   > **ls**

   The file *myfiles* is created and contains the output of **ls**, the names of the files in the current directory.

3. As another example, enter:

   > **cal** *2003* > *2003*
   > **ls**

wc *2003*

more *2003*

The file *2003* is created with the output from **cal**.

4. Quit **more** by entering:

q

5. Enter:

ps > *myprocesses*

ls

more *myprocesses*

When a utility generates output, it is displayed on the screen, unless you tell the shell to redirect the output elsewhere. The general form of the command is **utility** > *filename*, which is instruction to redirect the output of the utility to a file.

Appending Output to the End of a File

In the previous exercises, you told the shell to connect the output of utilities to new files. We can also tell the shell to append data to the end of an existing file.

1. Try the following:

date > *thismonth*

more *thismonth*

The > redirection special character instructs the shell to connect the output of the previous utility on the command line to a file.

2. Instruct the shell to add the output of a utility to the end of the file by entering:

cal >> *thismonth*

more *thismonth*

date >> *thismonth*

more *thismonth*

Examining the file after each command line that uses a double redirect shows that the utility's output is added to the end of the file. The double redirect >> is instruction to *append* the output of the previous utility to the end of an existing file.

3. For another example, add more text to the *lost-days* file created earlier:

    cal *2002* **>>** *lost-days*
    more *lost-days*

Redirecting Output to Another Utility

When you run a utility without redirecting the output, its output is displayed on your screen. As you just demonstrated, we can redirect the output of a utility to a file using the **>** redirection special character. We can also redirect the output of a utility to another utility, without first saving it in a file.

1. Enter the following:

    ls
    ls **>** *ls.out*
    more *ls.out*

The output of **ls** comes to the screen if we do not redirect it. The **ls** **>** *ls.out* command is instruction to the shell to redirect output of **ls** to a file named *ls.out*.

2. Count the elements in the file:

    wc *ls.out*

With **wc** we can count the number of lines, words, and characters in the new *ls.out* file.

This method of counting the elements of **ls** requires several steps and the creation of a file. We can also redirect the output of **ls** directly to **wc** without creating a file.

3. Enter:

    ls **|** **wc**

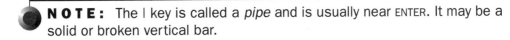

> **N O T E :** The | key is called a *pipe* and is usually near ENTER. It may be a solid or broken vertical bar.

The output of **wc** is displayed on the screen. This command line instructs the shell to start two processes, connect the output of the first process to the input of the second process, and then run **ls** in the first process and **wc** in the second.

The output of **ls** does not come to the screen, and it is not redirected to a file. It is redirected to the input of the second process, which is running the **wc** utility. Then **wc** reads its input (the output from **ls**) and counts the number of lines, words, and characters that it finds. Finally, **wc** outputs the results to your screen.

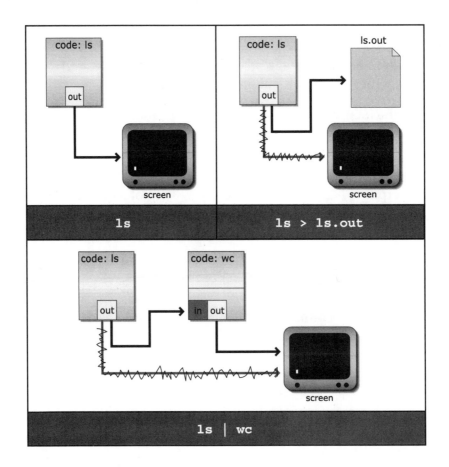

4. Count the elements in **cal's** output by entering:

   cal *1752* **|** **wc**

   The output of **cal** is redirected to **wc**, which counts the elements.

   The | is instruction to the shell to connect the output of whatever utility is on its left to the input of the utility on its right.

5. Tame output that is more than a screen long by redirecting the output to **more** by entering:

     ps -ef | more

or

     ps -aux | more

The output of **ps** is redirected to the input of **more**.

6. Examine the process list then quit **more** with:

     q

The output of **ps -ef** or **ps -aux** is a long list of all process information, which more than fills the screen. By redirecting **ps**'s output to **more**, we can control the display.

7. For a final example, enter:

     who | wc

The output of the initial utility is redirected to the input of the second utility.

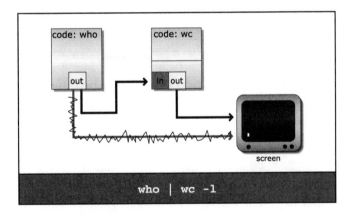

Determining the Role of Tokens on Command Lines

The shell has very clear grammar rules that we must follow when entering commands. An important rule is where we place information on the command line. Consider the placement of the utilities in the command lines you entered, such as:

who
date
who > users_on
cal 9 1752

In all of these command lines, the utility is the first word on the command line. Each word or object on a command line is also called a *token*.

The shell is programmed to read the initial token as a utility program to run or some action to take.

You have entered commands such as:

who | wc
ps -ef | more

Utilities are also located on command lines after the redirection pipes. The shell interprets the token after a pipe as the name of a utility. The shell connects the output of the previous utility to the input of the utility that follows the pipe.

The shell interprets a token following the > redirection symbol as the name for a file. All other tokens remaining are passed as arguments.

Consider the following. What must each token be?

____ ____ ____ | ____ ____ | ____ > ____

The location on the command line determines how the shell interprets each token. The first token must be a utility, and the tokens following pipes also must be utilities. The token following the redirect must be the file that receives the output from the last utility.

All other tokens, the stuff left over, must be arguments. Each argument is passed to the utility that precedes it. Hence, the shell interprets the elements as:

utility *argument argument* | **utility** *argument* | **utility** > *file*

The first utility is given two arguments. The output from the first utility is connected to the input of the second. The second utility is given one argument; its output is passed to the input of the third utility. The output from the third utility is redirected to a file.

Starting a Child Shell

When you logged on, your login shell was started and it has been interpreting your commands ever since. All systems include the code for several shells. Your current shell is probably one of the following:

SHELL	DEFAULT PROMPT	NAME
sh	$	Bourne <u>Sh</u>ell (*the original*)
bash	$	Bourne <u>A</u>gain <u>Sh</u>ell
ksh	$	<u>K</u>orn <u>Sh</u>ell
csh	%	<u>C</u> Shell
tcsh	%	<u>T</u> <u>C</u> Shell

The various shells fall into two *families*. The top three, **sh**, **bash**, and **ksh**, are the **sh** family, and the last two, **csh** and **tcsh**, are the **csh** family.

1. Start a child shell by entering:

   sh

2. List the current processes by entering:

   ps

   The child **sh** and the login shell are both running. When you started the child shell, your login shell did not terminate, but is waiting for the child shell to exit.

3. Run another command such as the following:

   date

4. Exit the child by entering:

   exit

5. Examine the processes again:

   ps

The child **sh** terminated and only the login shell remains. People often make the mistake of starting a child shell, then starting another, rather than exiting the first. Depending on your version of UNIX or Linux, some (but probably not all) of the shells are available. Linux usually has the **bash** shell but does not include **ksh** unless you install it. Other systems use **ksh** and do not have **bash**. One or both of the **csh** and **tcsh** shells are usually available.

If you try other shells, be sure to exit each before starting a new one.

Reissuing Commands

All shells except the original **sh** allow us to repeat previously entered commands. The way to request a replay of a particular command depends on which shell you are using.

Reexecuting the Very Last Command Entered

1. Type the command:

date

2. Try to reissue this command by entering:

!!

If **date** runs again, you're using the **csh** shell, a **tcsh** shell, or a **bash** shell.

3. If the **!!** did not work, enter:

date

r

If the **date** utility is executed a second time in response to the **r** command, you are using a Korn shell, **ksh**.

If neither the **!!** nor the **r** works, you are probably in an **sh** shell. You can usually start a more modern shell by entering **csh**, **tcsh**, **ksh**, or **bash**.

4. Enter:

cal *2004*

The calendar for the year 2004 is displayed.

5. Repeat the calendar display by entering:

!!

or

r

Repeating Commands with the Arrow Keys in Linux

The **!!** and **r** commands tell the appropriate shells to reexecute your last command line. On some systems we can also reexecute commands by displaying previous commands and selecting one to run again.

1. Press UP ARROW

The previous command is displayed.

2. Press ENTER

The displayed command is executed.

3. Press UP ARROW several times to return to a previous command.

4. Reexecute the command by pressing ENTER

Running Commands Again by Number and Name

The shell keeps track of commands that we issue, allowing us to access them in several ways.

 1. List the previously entered commands by entering:

> **history**

A list of the commands you have executed is displayed, with a number next to each command.

> **N O T E :** If you do not see a history list and you are in **csh** or **tch**, enter **set history** = *100* to have the shell keep track of the commands you issue, and then repeat the **history** command.

We can instruct the shell to rerun an earlier command based on its number or based on its name.

2. Enter the following:

In **csh**, **tcsh**, or **bash** enter (with no space after the **!**):

> *!d*

or in **ksh**, enter (with a space after the **r**):

> **r** *d*

The last command that begins with the letter **d** is executed.

3. As another example, enter:

> *!ca*

or

> **r** *ca*

The last command that began with *ca*, probably **cal**, is executed again.

4. Reexecute the command that displays the **history** list:

> *!h*

or

> **r** *h*

5. Identify a command on the **history** list, and use its number in place of ## in the following command (for example, if the **date** command is listed as number 27, then the command to issue would be !27 in **tcsh** and **r**, or 27 in **ksh**.):

> *!##*

or

r ##

The command of number ## is reexecuted.

We can reexecute the previous commands in three ways:

Repeat the previous command	**!!**	**r**	UP ARROW
Repeat the last command that begins with *xxx*	**!***xxx*	**r** *xxx*	
Repeat command number ##	**!**##	**r** ##	

Using Nicknames for Commands

All shells except **sh** allow you to assign to commands alternate names or aliases. Users employ aliases for commands that are hard to remember or difficult to type.

1. In the **csh** and **tcsh** shells, enter:

    alias *DIR* **ls**
    alias *now* **date**
    alias *h* **history**

2. In the **bash** and **ksh** shells, enter:

    alias *DIR***=ls**
    alias *now***=date**
    alias *h***=history**

3. Now, try each of the new aliases:

    DIR
    now
    h

    The commands **ls**, **date**, and **history** are executed because you entered their aliases. The initial commands **ls**, **date**, and **history** still work. We just told the shell of nicknames that we intend to have the same effect as the command names. They work the same.

    We can instruct the shells to list all current aliases.

4. Enter:

    alias

    You can also tell the shell to remove an alias when you no longer want it defined.

5. Enter:

   unalias *DIR*

6. Confirm that the alias is removed by entering:

   alias

The *DIR* alias is no longer listed. It was removed.

When you log out, the shell exits and takes the memory of the aliases with it.

Self Test 2

Answer the following, and then check your answers against the information given in the chapter.

1. What command tells the shell to repeat the last command?

   _____

2. What command tells the shell to create a new file named *myfile* that contains a list of the names of the files in your current directory?

   _____

3. What command tells the shell to run utilities that output just the number of files in the current directory?

   _____

4. What command tells the shell to create a new file named *friend-bday* that contains the month and year of a friend's birth?

   _____

5. What command tells the shell to add today's date and time to the end of the *friend-bday* file?

   _____

6. What command tells the **tcsh** or **csh** shells that when we enter *cl*, we want the shell to run the **clear** command?

   _____

7. How can we tell the **bash** or **ksh** shells that when we enter *cl*, we want the shell to run the **clear** command?

   _____

8. Where a token is located on a command line tells the shell a great deal about the token (utility, file, argument, or redirection). How does the shell interpret each of the following tokens on a command line?

   _____   _____   _____ | _____ > _____

9. What do each of the following commands accomplish?

    A. alias

    _____

    B. more *file1 file2*

    _____

    C. wc -l *file1 file2*

    _____

    D. !w

    _____

    E. r *12*

    _____

10. How does the shell interpret the following, and what results?

    look *psy* | **wc -w** > *psy-words*

    _____

    _____

2.4 Navigating the Filesystem

Data, letters, programs, and all other stored information in a UNIX/Linux system are contained in files. Files are grouped together in directories. By completing the previous exercises, you now have several files listed in your home directory. You created them by running utilities and redirecting output to a new file. System data and programs are also kept in files. All files are listed in directories. Your home directory is listed in one directory, which is listed in some other directory, and so forth, to the topmost directory. The whole collection of files and directories is the *filesystem*.

Determining Your Location in the Filesystem

Because UNIX can serve many users at the same time, each user is given a separate workspace or *home directory* in which to do his or her work. When users log on, each can access files in his or her own different home directory so other users don't step on each other's files.

1. To get a listing of where your home directory is located, type the command:

    pwd

    The output is something like:

    ```
    /home/cassy
    ```

    or

    ```
    /export/home/cassy
    ```

    This information is the path from the top of the filesystem to your current directory—in this case, your home directory. The topmost directory is called the *root* (and is identified as /). The output from the **pwd** utility is the path from *root* to your **p**resent **w**orking **d**irectory.

    For example, the */home/cassy* output says that the *root* directory has a subdirectory named *home*, and in the *home* directory, your home (*cassy* in this example) is listed. The last directory in the output of **pwd** is your current directory.

2. Obtain a listing of the filenames in your current (home) directory with the usual command:

    ls

The output is a listing of files that you have created. Their names are listed in your home directory, so you have access to them.

Viewing the Filesystem from the Top

The top of the UNIX filesystem is generally referred to as the *root*, or sometimes *slash*, because it is represented by the forward slash character.

1. Obtain a listing of the files and directories in the *root* directory with the following command:

    ls /

    This command tells the shell to run the **ls** utility and pass it the / argument. The **ls** utility reads the names of the files in the / directory and displays that list on the screen. The output is a listing of some of the system directories, including *dev*, *tmp*, *bin*, *usr*, and probably *home*.

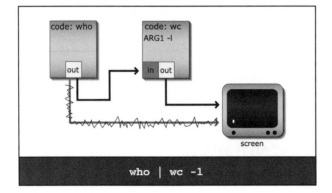

2. Check to see what your present working directory is by entering:

pwd

Your current directory is not changed, even though you generated a listing of the contents of the *root* directory. The current directory is still your home directory. The **ls** utility allows you to obtain listings of other directories without actually changing to those directories.

There is a relationship between the output of **pwd** and the output of the **ls /** command that you just entered. The output of **pwd** lists the directories from the *root* to your current directory. The first directory after the slash is probably named *home*. It is a system directory that lists users' homes. The same directory must also be listed in the *root* directory when you get a listing of its contents with the **ls /** command.

Exploring the System Directories

Although your current directory is your home directory, you can examine the contents of other directories as you examined the *root* directory's contents in the previous section.

1. Enter:

ls /etc | more

The output is a listing of the files and subdirectories listed in the *etc* directory, which is listed in the *root* or */* directory. These files are system files that control access and the way that the system functions.

2. Tell **more** to display more of the output of **ls** by pressing:

   SPACEBAR

   Among the files listed is *passwd,* which contains information about all users.

3. Quit **more** and return to the shell:

   q

4. Examine another system directory by entering:

   ls */bin*

This directory contains many of the executable programs (utilities) available on the system, such as **ls, date, cat,** and **more**.

When we provide the path to a directory as an argument to **ls**, the command lists the contents of that directory.

Creating a Directory

Users need to create new directories to store files and generally keep their houses in order.

1. Make a subdirectory called *Private* in your home directory by entering the following (in this case, use a capital *P*):

   mkdir *Private*

   The **m**a**k**e **dir**ectory command interprets its arguments as names to give to new directories.

2. Confirm that the new directory exists by entering:

   ls

   Among your files is a listing for the new directory, *Private.* Most systems list it first, not because it is a directory, but because its name begins with a capital letter.

3. Create another directory using a lowercase name:

   mkdir *kitchen*

   ls

   This time the directory is not listed first.

4. However, we can tell **ls** to identify directories by entering:

　　ls -F

In the output of **ls** with the **-F** option, directories are listed with a **/** after their names. The **-F** option to **ls** is instruction to put a slash after all directory names and also to identify other kinds of files. If you use uppercase letters for directories, they are listed at the top of the **ls** output on most systems. However, using **ls -F** also makes the directories obvious.

Changing Directories to a Subdirectory

Although you have now created a new directory, your current directory is still your home directory. You can make *Private* your current directory.

1. Change directories to *Private* by entering:

　　cd *Private*

Because *Private* is a subdirectory of your home directory, its name is listed in your current directory. Therefore, you can change directories to *Private* from your home directory by using **cd** with one argument, *Private*.

2. Confirm your location by entering:

　　pwd

3. Ask for a listing of files by entering:

　　ls

There are no regular files in your new *Private* directory. The files you created earlier are listed in your home directory, not in this subdirectory.

4. Create a new file in the *Private* directory by entering:

　　date > *secrets*

5. List the contents of the current directory (*Private*) by entering:

　　ls

The *secrets* file is listed in the current directory, *Private*.

Returning Home

At this point, your current directory is *Private*, which is a subdirectory of your home directory.

1. Return to your home directory with the following command:

　　cd

No matter where you are on the system, issuing the **cd** command with no argument brings you back to your home directory.

2. To verify that you are in your home directory, type:

pwd

ls

The listed files and output of **pwd** confirm that you are back at your home directory.

3. From your home directory, list the contents of the *Private* directory by entering:

ls *Private*

You can create directories in UNIX/Linux to organize your files. For now, create all files associated with this book in your home directory, unless told otherwise.

In Chapter 8 we will explore navigation of the filesystem in detail.

2.5 Examining and Managing Files

In UNIX/Linux, we use specific utilities to list, copy, rename, move, and remove files. This section examines how to use utilities that are essential for the management of files.

Effectively Moving through a File with more

Files contain data. Users often want to see all or part of the file, or carefully examine large files in screen-size chunks. The **more** utility, which you met briefly in a previous exercise, is an effective tool for examining the contents of files.

1. Have **more** display the first part of the very long *termcap* file by entering:

more */etc/termcap*

The top of the file is displayed on the screen.

2. Move a few screens into the file by pressing:

SPACEBAR

SPACEBAR

ENTER

ENTER

The SPACEBAR tells **more** to advance one screen; ENTER tells **more** to advance one line.

Finding Matching Text in the File

We can search the file for a specific target string of characters from within **more**.

1. While **more** is displaying a screen from the file, enter:

    /sun

    The **more** utility displays the first page of the file that contains the string *sun*.

    When we give **more** a target string of characters, **more** goes to the first page of the file containing the target string and displays that page.

2. Tell **more** to advance to the next instances of the target by pressing:

    n

    The next page that contains the target is displayed.

3. Advance through more pages that have the target by entering:

    n

    n

4. Instruct the **more** utility to move backward one screen at a time by entering:

    b

    b

    Each **b** command is instruction to move backward through the file one screen at a time.

5. Tell **more** to quit by pressing:

    q

6. Have **more** display the contents of several files by entering:

    more *users_on birth lost-days today*

7. Use the SPACEBAR to examine all files.

    The **more** utility interprets all arguments as names of files to open and display one screen at a time.

Displaying a Few Lines from a File

Sometimes users can answer a question by viewing just part of a file. Most utilities display all of a file, one utility outputs only the first few lines, and another outputs only the last lines.

1. Examine *lost-days* by entering:

    head *lost-days*

The **head** utility reads the first 10 lines of file(s) named as arguments—in this case, the file *lost-days*.

We can also pass a number as an argument to the **head** utility to specify the number of lines to read and output.

2. Enter the following:

    head *-6* */etc/passwd lost-days*

The first six lines of each file are displayed. (Several are blank lines in *lost-days*.)

On many systems, you can also view the last lines from a file or input.

3. Enter:

    tail *lost-days*
    tail *-6* */etc/passwd*
    history | **tail** *-1*   (*Number one, not the lowercase letter* el.)

The **tail** utility outputs the last 10 lines of *lost-days*, the last 6 lines of the *passwd* file, and 1 line from the output of **history**.

We can also redirect the output from **head** and from **tail** to files.

4. Create a file by entering the following:

    tail *-6* */etc/passwd* **>** *end-passwd*
    more *end-passwd*

In this **tail** command, you instructed the shell to redirect the output from **tail** to a new file named *end-passwd* instead of to the screen.

Displaying All of a File

Because the **more** utility displays files one screen at a time, we use it when we need to examine long files. Another utility displays files without interruption, which is appropriate for short files.

1. Enter the following:

    cat *lost-days*

The whole file *lost-days* is displayed, with the initial part of the file scrolling off the top of the screen.

2. Try the following:

    cat *today*

When a file is short, the **cat** utility is a quick way to display the file's contents.

Copying Files

You have thus far created several files by instructing the shell to redirect the output of utilities such as **who**, **date**, and **cal** to new files. The files you created are listed in your home directory.

We can also create new files by copying existing files.

1. List the files in your current directory:

    ls

2. To make a copy of a file, enter:

    cp *users_on users_on_2*

    The file *users_on* is copied, and the copy is given the name *users_on_2*.

3. Obtain a listing of the files in your current directory by entering:

    ls

    The new *users_on_2* file is listed among your other files.

4. Examine the contents of *users_on_2* by entering:

    more *users_on_2*

    The **cp** utility interprets its first argument as the name of an existing file and the second as the name to give a copy of the first. The file *users_on_2* is an exact copy of *users_on*. Each file is a separate entity; either one can be modified or removed without affecting the other.

5. Create a copy of *thismonth* and name it *junk* by typing the following:

    cp *thismonth junk*

6. As another example, create three other copies of files by entering:

    cp *junk junk2*
    ls
    cp *lost-days lost-2*
    ls
    cp *lost-days lost-3*

7. Confirm that the new files are created, by entering:

    ls

Copying Files to Subdirectories

At this point, you are in your home directory. From this location, you can examine the contents of the current directory and subdirectories.

1. List your files and copy one into the *Private* directory by entering:

> **ls**
>
> **cp** *users_on Private*

2. Confirm a copy is in the *Private* directory by entering:

> **ls** *Private*

If the last argument to **cp** is a directory, **cp** copies files listed as the other arguments to the directory. Because you did not specify a new name, the original name is retained for the copy.

3. Copy several files to *Private* by entering:

> **cp** *today lost-days junk Private*
>
> **ls** *Private*

In this case, you are instructing the shell to pass four arguments to the **cp** utility. **cp** interprets the last argument as a target directory, and all previous arguments as files to copy. The output of **ls** confirms that all three files were copied and given their original names in the subdirectory *Private*. After completing these exercises, your corner of the filesystem looks like Figure 2-2.

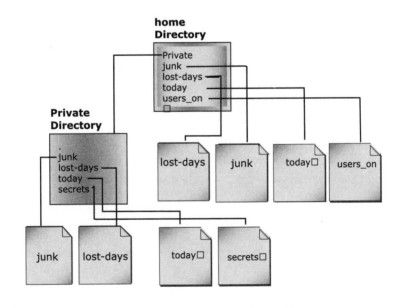

FIGURE 2-2   Copying files

Removing Files

When we decide that we no longer need a file, we can delete or **remove** it.

⤷ 1. Enter the following command to remove the *users_on_2* file:

> **ls**
> **rm** *users_on_2*

> **N O T E :** If **rm** inquires whether you really want to remove the file the **rm** utility is aliased to its inquire form. Enter and then remove the alias. Enter **unalias rm** and then repeat step 1.

2. Confirm that the file is removed:

> **ls**

The **rm** *filename* command instructs the shell to run the **rm** utility and to pass **rm** arguments, which **rm** interprets as files to remove.

Removing Files with Confirmation

There is a "silence" about UNIX/Linux systems that often disturbs people. For example, when you instruct **rm** to remove a file, all you get in response is the next shell prompt. The **rm** utility does not beep, buzz, or even send a message of acknowledgment. It silently does as requested and quits. The shell then prompts you for your next instruction.

If you would like the opportunity to confirm your request to have a file removed before **rm** actually destroys it, you must tell **rm** to prompt you.

In a previous exercise, you created a file named *junk*.

⤷ 1. Request the removal of *junk* with the command:

> **rm -i** *junk*

The **rm** command first displays a message asking whether you really want *junk* removed.

2. Tell **rm** not to remove the file by pressing:

> **n**

and press ENTER.

3. Confirm that you still have too much *junk* by entering:

> **ls**

When you enter the command **rm** **-i** *junk*, you instruct the shell to run the **rm** utility and to pass to **rm** two arguments: **-i** and *junk*. The **-i** is an argument that **rm** interprets as an option. The **-i** option tells **rm** to ask for confirmation before removing any filenames listed as other arguments. With the **-i** option, **rm** asks whether you really want to remove the *junk* file.

4. Request removal of the *junk* file again by entering:

    rm **-i** *junk*

5. This time, instruct **rm** to go ahead and discard *junk* by answering the inquiry by pressing:

    y and then press ENTER

6. Confirm that *junk* has been removed by entering:

    ls

Removing Several Files at Once

The **rm** command accepts multiple filenames as arguments.

1. Use **cp** to create a new file called *uson2*:

    cp *users_on uson2*

2. Create two more files by entering the following commands:

    date > *today3*
    ls > file-list

3. Confirm that the files are created by checking the contents of your directory:

    ls

4. Remove all three files at once by entering:

    rm *uson2 today3 file-list*

5. Confirm that the files are removed by entering:

    ls

    The **rm** command line is instruction to the shell to run the **rm** utility and to pass it three arguments, the names of three files. The **rm** utility interprets all arguments (that are not options) as files to remove.

6. Attempt to remove a nonexistent file to see the error message by entering:

    rm *xyz*

Unable to locate the file, **rm** sends an error which is displayed on your terminal.

Renaming Files

When we create a file, we give it a name. Each file's name is listed in its directory, and we use the name to identify and access the file. Filenames are not permanent. We can change them.

1. Examine the contents of your file named *lost-3* by entering:

   more *lost-3*

2. Change the name of the file *lost-3* with the following command:

   mv *lost-3 phon*

3. List the files in your current directory:

   ls

   There is no file named *lost-3* in the output of **ls**, but *phon* is present.

4. Display the contents of the new *phon* file using **more**:

   more *phon*

   It is the same file, with a new name. The **mv** command implies that the file is <u>mov</u>ed; however, it is just renamed.

Moving Files to Subdirectories

Often we create a file in one directory and then want to move it to another.

1. Confirm you are in your home directory by entering:

   pwd

2. Create two new files:

   date > *wade*

   cal > *blank*

3. Move both files to the *Private* directory by entering:

   mv *wade blank Private*

   ls *Private*

   This command passes three arguments to the **move** utility that interprets the last argument as a target directory and all other arguments as filenames. The utility <u>mov</u>es the files to the target directory.

4. Confirm that the files are no longer in the current directory by entering:

   ls

When we use the **mv** utility to change the name of a file, we enter **mv** with two arguments: the current name of the target file, and the new name that we want to assign to the file. Although the utility name implies that it <u>mo</u><u>v</u>es the file, in this instance it just changes the name of the file in the current directory. If the last argument is a directory such as **mv** *file file Dir*, then **mv** moves files to that target directory.

Deciphering Utility Error Messages

When the shell or a utility is not prepared to interpret a portion of a command we enter, it sends an error message to the screen.

1. Enter the following command, which tells the shell to run a utility that is not available:

    Copy   (Yes, with a capital **C**)

    The shell looks but cannot find the utility **Copy**. In this case, the shell sends the error message:

    ```
    command not found
    ```

2. Enter:

    cat *xyZ*

    The **cat** utility is started and passed the argument *xyZ*. Because **cat** interprets *xyZ* as a file to read, it looks for the file, but cannot locate it. **cat** sends an error message to your screen telling you that the file does not exist. The shell does not check to see whether the file exists because the shell does not interpret *xyZ* as a filename, just as an argument to pass to the utility. Once **cat** is unable to find the file, **cat** complains.

3. Instruct the shell to run **cp** and pass it three filename arguments:

    cp *users_on phon total*

    The **cp** utility informs you about its usage, namely that it can copy multiple files only if the last argument is a directory. The **cp** utility found three arguments, determined the last was not a directory, and objected.

4. Try entering:

    mv *abc def ghi*

    The **mv** utility functions in the same way.

5. Enter:

    cat *users_on xyZ > junk3*
    more *junk3*

The **cat** utility interprets its arguments as files to read. Unable to find a file named *xyZ*, **cat** complains. Because it can locate and read the *users_on* file, **cat** reads *users_on* and writes its contents to output, which was redirected to the file *junk3*.

What execution of this command line demonstrates is that output from a utility and error messages from a utility are two different things and can be handled independently. The output from **cat** is redirected to the file *junk3*, and when **cat** was executed the output was sent to the file. However, **cat** also produced an error message that the file *xyZ* could not be found. That error message was displayed on the screen, not sent to the file with the output. Each process has both an "output door" where it writes output, and an "error door" where it writes any error messages. Initially each is connected to the terminal screen, until we redirect one or both to a file or another utility.

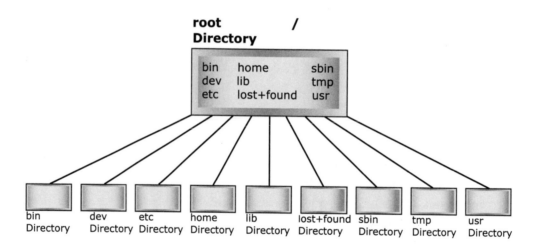

Printing a File

At this point in the chapter, you have created several files and examined them on the screen. An essential feature is printing files on paper.

The UNIX commands to send a file to a printer for printing are system-dependent. To print a file, try each of the following commands.

➡ 1. Enter:

    lp *lost-days*

or

    lpr *lost-days*

If there is silence or a confirming printer job number, the file is sent to the line printer.

The system may respond to one of these commands with an error message that the command is not found. Because this is a local setup issue, one or both of these commands may be active. In these exercises, use whichever one works.

You may get an error message about a lack of a destination printer. If so, you will need to ask a colleague or your system administrator for the name of a printer available to you.

If you need to use the printer name, type one of the following commands. The *dest* part of the argument refers to the name of the destination printer that you are selecting to print your file.

2. Type in the printer name that you obtained from your system administrator. There is no space between the option and the destination printer name:

    lp -d*dest lost-days*

or

    lpr -P*dest lost-days*

If you have several printers available, the **-P** option with **lpr** and the **-d** option with **lp** allow you to specify which printer to use.

N O T E : In these chapters, we will use the default form of the command, **lpr**. If you need to specify a printer or you use **lp**, include the appropriate **-P** or **-d** option with the correct command. To make it easier, create an alias so that when you enter **lpr**, the correct command is executed.

---

3. Try printing several files from your account, replacing *f1, f2,* and *f3* with names of three of your own files:

    lpr *f1 f2 f3*

The **lp** and **lpr** utilities manage the printer. They accept multiple filenames as command-line arguments and print all files named.

2.6 Accessing the Programmer's Manual

Mastering Linux/UNIX is a life-long process. There are literally thousands of programs that provide enormous functionality. Although the operating system is stable and user commands are seldom modified, the whole package is huge and growing every day. How does one get on top of it all, and how can one stay there? The on-line help utilities, publications, and the Internet are essential components of the professional's life-long learning aids. UNIX and Linux systems include an extensive collection of powerful utility programs, system features, application languages, and support libraries. These diverse and complex facilities are too numerous and feature-rich to remember in detail. While working, we often need to employ the exact syntax of a particular option or command format for a utility. The needed information is available from the *UNIX Programmer's Manual,* often called the *UNIX Reference Manual,* which is available online. This section examines how to access information in the manual.

The Reference Manual is an indispensable part of a functioning system. It contains readily available, detailed documentation on the uses and functions of all standard utility programs, many application programs and libraries, as well as information on UNIX system files and system programming libraries. The Reference Manual also contains supplementary information on related special files and commands for each entry. In addition, examples and error conditions are often provided.

Displaying a Manual Entry

From the shell, we can request that individual manual entries be written on the workstation screen.

➥ 1. Examine the online manual entry for the **cat** utility by entering:

    man *cat*

Every manual entry follows the same basic organization. The top line of the output includes the name of the utility, followed by a number in parentheses that refers to the section of the manual where the entry is located. Words at the left margin in all uppercase letters, such as "NAME" and "SYNOPSIS," introduce the various sections of the entry. The NAME section has a brief description of the utility.

```
CAT(1)                         FSF                        CAT(1)

NAME
      cat - concatenate files and print on the standard output

SYNOPSIS
      cat [OPTION] [FILE]...

DESCRIPTION
      Concatenate  FILE(s),  or standard input, to standard out
      put.

      -A, --show-all
             equivalent to -vET

      -b, --number-nonblank
             number nonblank output lines

      -e     equivalent to -vE

      -E, --show-ends
             display $ at end of each line

      -n, --number
:
```

2. Advance through the manual pages for the **cat** utility:

> SPACEBAR

3. Quit the **man** utility:

> q

4. Examine the manual entry for **sort**:

> **man** *sort*

Because the **more** utility is employed to display the **man** pages, all of the usual text display commands from **more** work. Enter:

SPACEBAR

SPACEBAR

ENTER

> b
>
> b

Pressing the SPACEBAR advances one screen of text at a time, pressing ENTER advances one line of text at a time, and pressing **b** scrolls back one screen of text.

Searching Through a Manual Entry

Often, manual entries are very long, and it is difficult to access the portion that contains what you want. We can search for specific words.

1. With the first part displayed, search for the word *field* by entering:

    /*field*

2. Press ENTER and the display advances to the first page that includes the word *field*.

3. Press **n** to advance to the next instance of the word *field*.

    Entries in the manual tend to follow the structure of a newspaper story: usually the most critical information comes first. By reading just the first few sections, you can examine the most important features of the utility.

4. To exit the **man** utility, enter **q**.

5. Examine the manual entries for a few of the commands you have used, such as **date**, **wc**, **more**, and **mv**. Take special note of the options available for each utility.

Searching for Manual Entries Using Keywords

On most systems, we can have the **man** utility search the online manual database for all entries containing a specific keyword. In the NAME section of each utility's manual entry is the utility's name and a brief description of what the utility accomplishes. We can have **man** search the manual pages' descriptions for keywords. Usually, the description lines are kept in a separate database for easy access.

1. Do a keyword search for the word *edit* to see which entries relate to text editors.

    man -k *edit* **| more**

    or

    apropos *edit* **| more**

2. Among the many entries listed, you will find the standard visual and stream editors: **vi**, **vim**, **sed** and **ed**.

3. Search the manual table of contents for the word *copy* by typing:

    man -k *copy* **| more**

    Each of the lines in the output contains the string *copy*, either in the title or in the brief description that follows. The keyword may be any combination of letters.

Some of the entries in the **man** **-k** output do not contain *copy* as a separate word; instead, *copy* is part of another word. When doing a keyword search, **man** **-k** searches for all instances of the string you provide as the target.

4. Do similar searches using the keywords *move, print, help,* and *file.*

2.8 Accessing Internet Resources

The Internet is a fluid assembly of more information than we can assimilate in several lifetimes. The key to success lies in being able to access what you want by narrowing your search. Unfortunately, search engines bring up a lot of chaff with the wheat. To save you trouble and get you started, we maintain, on our site, a list of other sites that we find useful. With time, new sites are developed, others go to bit heaven. Therefore, some sites on the following list may not be available or useful as you access them. To obtain our latest recommended site list, see the instructions that follow the list.

Examining Helpful Internet Sites

The following sites provide a sample of the wealth of available information.

- For recent news in the Linux world:
    http://www.linux.org/
    http://linux.com/

- For our site's list of recommended sites, some interactive web tutorials and resources for students and teachers using this book:
    http://www.muster.com

- For Linux code documentation:
    http://www.linuxdoc.org/
    http://www.tldp.com

- For recent software updates and information on how to configure the graphical user interface, GNOME:
    http://gnome.org/

Self Test 3

Answer the following, and then check your answers with the information given in this chapter.

1. What command could you enter to have the first five lines of the *letc/passwd* file placed in a new file called *password_info*?

2. What command outputs your current location in the system?

3. What is the name of the directory at the top of the filesystem?

4. How would you create a new directory named *New_dir* as a subdirectory of your home directory, and how would you verify that it is there after you create it?

5. What command would you use to copy the file *old_file* into the directory *New_dir*, which is a subdirectory of your current directory?

6. What is the result of the following command?
   more *letc/passwd*

7. What command ends the **more** command and returns you to the shell?

8. What command would you use to change the name of the file *junk* to *treasure*?

9. What command would you use to copy files *fA* and *fB* from the current directory to a subdirectory named *DirAA* ?

10. What command displays the manual entry for **man**?

11. What command would you type to search the **man** table of contents for all references to the word *file*?

Chapter Review

Use this section to review the content of this chapter and test yourself on your knowledge of the concepts.

Chapter Summary

- The shell is a process that interprets the command lines that we enter. The shell interprets the first word or token on a command line and the tokens following pipes as utilities to execute. It starts child processes to execute the utilities we request.
- Output from processes running utilities is connected to the user's screen unless we tell the shell otherwise.
- Output is redirected as follows:

**utility > ** *file*	*The output of the utility is written to the file.*
**utility	utility**	*The output of the first utility is connected to the input of the second.*
**utility >> ** *file*	*The output of the utility is appended to the end of the file.*

- All tokens or words on a command line that are not interpreted as utilities or files are seen as arguments and passed to the first utility to the left of the argument.
- The **tcsh, csh,** and **bash** shells interpret ! ! and related commands as instruction to repeat previous command lines.
- The **ksh** interprets **r** as instruction to repeat command lines.
- All shells except **sh** include an alias feature permitting users to assign nicknames for commands.
- Data, programs, and other information are kept in files. Filenames are listed in the directories. The collection of files and directories is the *filesystem,* which begins at the *root* or /. Listed in the root are directories, and each of those directories lists its files, subdirectories, and so forth.
- **mkdir** creates directories. **cd** with an argument changes to the argument directory, whereas **cd** without an argument changes to the home directory. **pwd** outputs the path from the *root* to your current location.
- Files are managed with specific utilities: **rm** to remove, **cp** to copy, and **mv** to rename or move to another directory. All interpret the **-i** as instruction to get confirmation before removing or overwriting a file.

- The shell recognizes aliases for existing commands.
- Utilities are used to examine the contents of files. **more** displays contents one screen at a time; **head** outputs the first part of a file; **tail** outputs the end of a file; **cat** displays all of a file without interruption; and **wc** counts the number of lines, words, and characters in a file and outputs the results.
- The on line manual pages accessed by the utility **man** are detailed descriptions of system utilities, files, and functionality. Each utility entry includes a description, list of available options, functionality, possible limitations and examples.
- The Internet includes many useful sites that provide information about all aspects of UNIX and Linux, the source code and teaching resources.
- Professionals consult all both sources of documentation/ help in the ongoing task of mastering the many system features and programs.

Assignment
Multiple Choice

1. In the command **ls** /tmp, the **ls** is the _____.
   - A. argument
   - B. option
   - C. utility
   - D. file
   - E. kernel
2. In the command **mv -i**, fileAA fileBB
   - A. there are three arguments
   - B. there is one option
   - C. there is one utility
   - D. If fileBB exists, it will not be overwritten without confirmation
   - E. All of the above
3. To add the output of **date** to the end of the file junk, we enter:
   - A. **junk | date**
   - B. date | junk
   - C. **date > junk**

    D. date >> *junk*

    E. junk > *date*

    F. junk >> *date*

<u>What Commands Accomplish the Following?</u>

4. Creates a file named *tmpfiles* that contains the names of the contents of the */tmp* directory.

    _____

5. Counts the number of currently running system processes.

    _____

6. Informs the **bash** shell that when you enter **see**, you want the **more** utility executed.

    _____

7. Creates a new directory named *Ballroom*.

    _____

8. Lists the contents of the *Ballroom* directory.

    _____

Project

- Create a file named *ch2* that contains a listing of the names of all files in your home directory.
- Use the various history commands to repeat the previous command, a command of a specific number, and a command that starts with a specific letter. Then tell the shell to write the output from the history command to a file named *ch2-hist* in your current directory.
- Create a directory in your home directory called *Backups*, and put copies of the following files in the *Backups* subdirectory: *users_on, lost-days, ch2*, and *ch2-hist*.
- List the commands that you employed to accomplish the previous three steps in this project.
- How many files are in the */bin* directory? What command produces the result?

COMMAND SUMMARY

**LOGGING ON
AND OFF**

exit	Terminates the current shell.
logout	Informs the shell you want to end the login session.

**WORKING WITH
DIRECTORIES**

cd *Dir*	Changes the working directory to Dir.
cd	Changes the current directory to the user's home directory.
ls	Lists the contents of the current directory.
mkdir *Dir*	Creates a directory named Dir.
pwd	Displays the full pathname of the current directory.

**SHELL COMMAND
INSTRUCTIONS**

history	Outputs a list of previously entered command lines.
!!	Reexecutes the most recent command line (csh, tcsh, and bash).
!##	Reexecutes the command number ## (csh, tcsh, and bash).
!*xxx*	Reexecutes the last command that begins with xxx (csh, tcsh, and bash).
r	Reexecutes the most recent command line (ksh).
r *##*	Reexecutes the command number ## (ksh).
r *xxx*	Reexecutes the last command that begins with xxx (ksh).
alias newname command	Tells shells to interpret newname as command (tcsh and csh).
alias *newname*=command	Tells shells to interpret newname as command (ksh).

**FILE DISPLAYING
UTILITIES**

SPACEBAR	Advance one screen.
ENTER	Advance one line.
b	Go back toward the top of the file one screen.
/xxx	Go forward to the first target (*xxx*) and display the page.

n	Go to the next target (*xxx*).
q	Quit **more**.
cat file1	Outputs file1 from beginning to end. Useful for small files.
head filename	Displays the first 10 lines of filename.
tail filename	*Displays the last 10 lines of* filename.
wc filename	Counts the lines, words, and characters in filename.
FILE MANAGEMENT UTILITIES	
cp file1 file2	Copies file1 to file2.
mv file1 file2	Renames file1 as file2.
rm filename	Deletes filename.
rm -i filename	Deletes filename, but asks the user to confirm the deletion.
DATA PRODUCING AND EXAMINING UTILITIES	
spell filename	Checks the spelling in filename.
who	Displays a list of users currently logged on.
Printing	
lp filename	Prints filename on the line printer.
lpr filename	Prints filename on the line printer.
REDIRECTION OF INPUT AND OUTPUT	
utility > filename	Sends the output of the utility to the file filename.
utility >> filename	Appends the output of the utility to the end of the file filename.
utility1 l utility2	Makes the output of utility1 the input of utility2.
man utility	Displays manual entry for the utility listed as an argument.
man -k word(**s**)	Displays all lines in the table of contents containing any word listed in word(s).

Touring Utilities and System Features

This chapter completes the tour of the major features of the system including communicating with the shell to execute processes, navigating the filesystem and employing permissions. Getting work done in UNIX/Linux generally entails asking the shell to execute utilities in specific, often complex ways. To accomplish real work, we need to give the shell exact and detailed instructions about what it should do, as well as what instructions it should pass to the needed utilities. We can issue commands to tailor or modify many aspects of UNIX and Linux to meet our particular needs. A functioning system also includes system files, directories of programs, and a system of permissions for security.

3.1 Employing Fundamental Utilities

In the previous chapter, you used several programs, or utilities, to locate system information and output it to the display. You also used utilities to remove, rename, and manipulate user files. Each utility is a tool that performs a set of very specific tasks. This section examines several new utilities. Some utilities read input from files, modify the data that they read, and send the output to your screen, to a file, or to another utility. Others provide information about the contents of a directory or information about other utilities.

Listing the Contents of the Directory

We use **ls** to output the filenames listed in the current directory. We can also instruct **ls** to provide more information by passing options as arguments.

1. List the files in the current directory with each of the following:

   ls

   ls -F

   The **ls** utility simply lists all filenames. With the **-F** option, **ls** places a forward slash at the end of the name of each directory. If you have any files that are executable, they will each have an asterisk (*) after the name.

2. List the files in the current directory, but tell **ls** to provide a long listing:

   ls -l   (minus *el*)

   The output is a list of filenames and other information, one file to a line. The important part on each line is the file's access permissions and other data about the file.

PERMISSION	LINKS	OWNER	GROUP	SIZE	DATE	TIME	NAME
drwxr-x- - -	3	cassy	staff	4096	Jan 3	14:27	Desk
-rw-rw-r- -	1	cassy	staff	62	Jan 5	08:14	cream-puff

TABLE 3-1 Fields in the Output of *ls -l*

If a filename begins with a period, **ls** is programmed to treat it as a hidden "housekeeping" file, and does not include it when you ask for a listing of the directory's filenames.

3. We can instruct **ls** to list the dot files in its output by including the appropriate option. Enter:

> ls
>
> ls -a

When we include the **-a** (**a**ll) option to **ls**, it includes in the output **a**ll files in the current directory, including the dot or hidden files. The files such as *.profile*, *.login*, *.cshrc*, and so on are files read by shells and other programs when they are started. We use them to convey instructions to our programs.

4. We can combine options to **ls**. Enter:

> ls -alF

The output is the result of all three options. It includes all files, with the long listing of information about each, and directories are marked with a slash.

Counting the Elements of a File

In Chapter 2, we used **wc** to count the number of lines, words, and characters in a file.

1. Enter the following command to examine the contents of a file created in Chapter 2:

> wc *users_on*

The output from the **wc** (**w**ord **c**ount, not water closet) utility consists of four fields:

> 2   12   102   users_on

The meaning of each field in the output of the **wc** utility is shown here:

Number of Lines	Number of Words	Number of Characters	File
2	12	102	users_on

In addition to counting the elements in files, we can instruct **wc** to count the words, lines, and characters in the output of previous utilities in a command line.

2. Redirect output to **wc** by entering:

> **date | wc**
>
> **who | wc**

The **who** utility outputs one line of information for each current user. The | is instruction to connect the output from **who** to the input of **wc**, which counts the elements. The **wc** utility then tosses the information that comes from **who** and just outputs its count totals.

3. We have used the **-l** option with **wc**. There are others. Try each of the options to **wc** we list in Table 3-2.

In each of the previous commands, we instructed the shell to pass two arguments to **wc**. The first argument included a dash such as **-c** and was interpreted as an option to output specific results. The second argument is interpreted as the name of a file to examine.

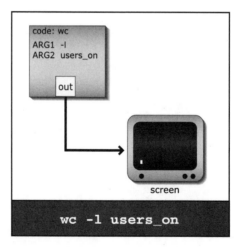

OPTION	OUTPUT
wc -l *users_on*	The count of lines only.
wc -w *users_on*	The count of words only.
wc -c *users_on*	The count of characters only.

TABLE 3-2   Options for the **wc** Command

Combining Utility Options in Arguments

The **wc** utility, like most other utilities, interprets more than one argument. Several questions arise: Can we issue multiple options? If so, must they be entered as separate arguments or can they be combined? What is the impact of the order of arguments?

↳ For example, enter the following commands:

wc -c -l *users_on*
wc -lc *users_on*
wc -cl *users_*on

Both the <u>l</u>ine count and the <u>c</u>haracter count options are passed as arguments to **wc**, and the results are displayed. Evidently it makes no difference what order the arguments are entered (**-lc** or **-cl**), nor whether the options are entered as separate arguments or combined in one argument (**-c, -l,** or **-cl**).

Sorting Lines in a File

Many files contain data concerning users or individuals. We have briefly looked at */etc/passwd* (the *password file*), which contains one line of information (a *record*) for each user. Every time a new user is added to the system, a new line is added (usually to the bottom of the file). As a result, the password file is not in a sorted order. In the following exercise, you will sort lines from the password file.

To make visual examination easier, start by creating a file consisting of the first portion of the password file.

↳ 1. Use **head** to create a file containing the first 20 lines of the password file on your system by entering:

head -20 */etc/passwd* > *mypasswd*

2. Examine the file by entering:

cat *mypasswd*

3. Output a sorted version of the file by entering:

sort *mypasswd*
cat *mypasswd*

The **sort** utility reads the file *mypasswd* into memory and rearranges the lines into a sorted order. Output is displayed on the screen. The *mypasswd* file itself is not modified; rather, its data is read, sorted, and written to your screen. We can save the sorted version in a new file.

4. Tell the shell to connect the output of **sort** to a file:

    sort *mypasswd* **>** *s-mypasswd*

    more *s-mypasswd*

The sorted version is redirected from the screen to the new file.

Employing Multiple Files with Utilities

We can also use the **sort** utility to sort multiple files.

1. Review the contents of two of your files by entering the following commands:

    cat *mypasswd*

    cat *users_on*

2. Use **sort** to sort the lines from the two files you just examined by entering:

    sort *mypasswd users_on* **|** **more**

The contents of both files are read and sorted together. The resulting output is the lines from *mypasswd* and *users_on*, merged together and sorted.

Examine the output. The **sort** utility reads both files (*mypasswd* and *users_on)* and sorts all the lines that it reads from both files. The files are not sorted individually. Neither the original *users_on nor mypasswd* file is changed.

3. Enter:

    wc *mypasswd users_on*

    more *mypasswd users_on*

Unlike **sort**, the **wc** utility operates on the files individually. It outputs the stats for each file and then produces a total.

Examining the Order Used by *sort*

Although the output from **sort** is sorted, it is not like a dictionary sort.

1. Examine the output after entering:

    sort *users_on lost-days* **|** **more**

In the **sort** order, lines beginning with numbers are output first, then lines beginning with uppercase letters, and last, lines that begin with lowercase letters. This is the same order that characters are listed in the ASCII (American Standard Code for Information Interchange) order.

2. On most systems, you can examine the ASCII order by entering this command:

    man *ascii*

When we press a key on the keyboard, we cannot send a character such as
k down the wire to the computer. We can only transmit numbers. The ASCII
table is an agreed-on set of numbers that represent all 128 characters we use.
The letter *k* is 107. The order that characters are listed in the ASCII table is
referred to as the *ASCII order*.

In ASCII order, most nonalphanumeric characters are first, then numbers,
followed by uppercase characters, more nonalphanumeric characters, and then
lowercase characters. Unless we instruct otherwise, the **sort** utility follows ASCII
order when sorting lines.

Reversing the Sorted Order

To sort a file in reverse ASCII order, we must specify an option to the utility on
the command line, instructing it to work in a particular way.

⮑ Type the following command:

    sort *users_on mypasswd* | **more**
    sort -r *users_on mypasswd* | **more**

Compare the two outputs. In the second command, you instruct the shell
to run the **sort** utility and to pass it three arguments: the **-r** option and two
arguments that **sort** interprets as filenames. The **-r** "reverse option" is one
of several options to the **sort** utility that instruct **sort** to change the way it
functions. We will examine others in Chapter 5.

Taking a Nap

Utilities perform a wide variety of functions. One of the most specialized simply
counts a prescribed number of seconds and exits.

⮑ 1. Try the following command:

    sleep *2*

There appears to be no response to the command; then, after two seconds,
the shell displays a new prompt.

2. Employ different arguments:

    sleep *8*
    sleep *4*

The sleep utility interprets its argument as the number of seconds it should
wait before exiting. As soon as it exits, the shell displays a new prompt. This
utility is very useful for exploring how the system functions and for use in scripts.

Comparing Utilities' Interpretation of Arguments

When we pass an argument to a utility, that utility's code determines how the argument is interpreted.

↳ 1. Enter:

   cal *2004*

   The **cal** utility interprets the argument *2004* as instruction to output the calendar for the year 2004.

2. Instruct the shell to redirect the output from **cal** to a file and confirm it worked:

   cal *2004* > *2004*

   ls

   Among your files is a file named *2004*.

3. Enter:

   wc *2004*

   cat *2004*

   cal *2004*

   rm *2004*

   ls

   The same argument is passed to four different utilities with four different results. The **wc** utility interprets the argument *2004* as the name of a file to read and to count the lines, words, and characters. To **cat**, *2004* is a file to read and output. To **cal**, *2004* is a calendar year to calculate and display. To **rm**, *2004* is a file to remove from the directory. The shell passes the argument. The utility interprets it.

Visiting echo Point

One utility simply reads whatever arguments we give it and writes the arguments to output.

↳ 1. We can give the same argument to **echo**:

   echo *2004*

   The argument consisting of the characters *2004* is displayed on the screen.

To **echo**, the argument *2004* is simply a string of characters that it reads and then writes to its output, which is connected to the screen unless we tell the shell to redirect it somewhere else.

2. Try several arguments:

    echo *these are five different arguments*

Five arguments are passed to **echo**, which interprets each as simply a character string to read and output. Because **echo** reads arguments and writes them to output, we will use the utility on the command line to see how arguments are processed and in shell scripts to display text on the user's screen.

Passing Arguments to Utilities

We enter command lines that consist of at least one utility and arguments. The shell passes the arguments to the utility, which interprets them.

1. Enter:

    echo *who date ls cat*

The shell interprets the command line as instruction to run **echo** and pass it four arguments consisting of strings of characters, namely *who, date, ls,* and *cat*. The command is of the form:

    util *arg arg arg arg*

To the shell, the tokens *who, date, ls,* and *cat* are not utilities to be run, because of their location on the command line. Rather, they are just arguments to pass to **echo**, which interprets them as just character strings. **echo** is programmed to read the arguments and write them to output.

2. Instruct the shell to redirect the output of **echo** to a file by entering:

    echo *A B C D > e1*
    more *e1*

This command line tells the shell to:

a. Start a child process.

b. Pass four arguments to the process.

  c. Redirect the output of the process to a new file, *e1*.

  d. Have the process execute the **echo** utility code.

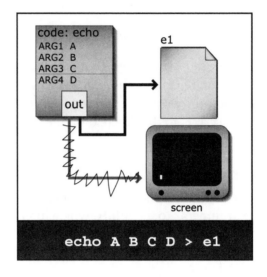

When **echo** is executed, it reads the four arguments and simply writes them to output, which the shell had redirected to the new file *e1*.

Creating Combination Files

People often place related data in several different files, such as individual chapters of a book. At times, the data that is in several files needs to be brought together.

 1. Type the following commands to create new files:

  date > *c1*
  echo *hello this is echo* > *c2*
  ls > *c3*
  ls
  ls -l *c1 c2 c3*

 The **ls** utility interprets the *c1*, *c2*, and *c3* arguments as names of files. A long listing of the information about each file is displayed.

 2. Give **cat** the same three arguments:

  cat *c1 c2 c3*

 This command line instructs the shell to run the **cat** utility and to pass it three arguments. The **cat** utility interprets each argument as the name of a file to open, read, and write to output. The **cat** utility reads each line from the first file and writes it to output (which is the screen by default). After **cat** reads and writes all the lines from the first file, it opens the next file, reads all the lines in it, and writes them to output. This process continues until **cat** reaches the end of the last file listed as an argument. The resulting output is the three files "spliced together" or con<u>cat</u>enated, hence the name for the utility.

We can also tell the shell to redirect the output of **cat** to a file.

3. Enter the following:

> **cat** *c3 c2 c1 > total*

4. Examine the *total* file by entering:

> **more** *total*

The file named *total* consists of the contents of the file *c3* followed by the contents of the file *c2* followed by the lines from *c1*. All lines read by **cat** are written to the new file *total*.

When you look at the output, *total,* there is no way to tell where one file ends and another begins.

This command line instructs the shell to start a new process, pass the process three arguments (*c3, c2,* and *c1*), and then redirect the process's output to a new file *total.* Lastly, the shell instructs the process to run the **cat** utility. Once started, **cat** interprets all of its arguments as names of files to locate, open, read, and write to output, which is connected to the file *total.*

Locating Specific Lines in a File

We often need to locate the lines in a file that contain a word or string of characters.

1. Reexamine the file *total*:

   cat *total*

2. Select lines from the file that contain a target string:

   grep *is total*

   Every line containing the character string *is* in the file *total* is selected and output.

3. Instruct **grep** to locate all lines in the file */etc/passwd* that contain the string *root* by entering:

   grep *root /etc/passwd*

   This command line asks the shell to run the **grep** utility and pass it two arguments. Many utilities, including **sort** and **rm**, interpret all arguments as files to be acted on. They sort or remove them all. Not **grep**. To the **grep** utility, the first argument is the *target string,* and all *other* arguments are files to be opened and searched. In this case, **grep** looks through the file */etc/passwd* for lines that contain the target string *root* and selects those lines that match. It outputs only the matched lines. The original file is not affected.

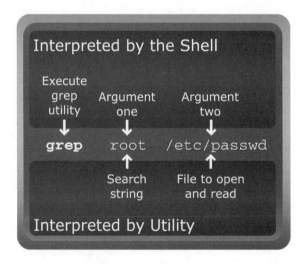

4. Look in several files for lines that contain the string *is*:

grep *is c1 c2 c3 total*

grep interprets the string *is* as the target search string and all other arguments as files to open and search. The filename and matching lines are output.

3.2 Starting Additional Linux Terminal Sessions

In the UNIX and Linux environment, we can have multiple active sessions at the same time. For example, in UNIX we can log on from several terminals connected to the same system. These different sessions all belong to the same user, but are independent of one another. In Linux, one monitor and keyboard can be used for multiple login sessions.

Once you are logged on to your UNIX or Linux machine, in graphical or terminal mode, you can access other virtual terminals.

1. Press:

   CTRL-ALT-F2

   (While holding down the CTRL key and the ALT key, press the F2 key.)

   A new logon screen appears.

2. Log on again at this prompt.

   You are given a new shell prompt.

3. Type the following:

   who

   and press ENTER.

   The **who** program lists current users, and you are listed twice. The second column of output lists the terminal port that each user is employing. You are logged on through the initial terminal and again through a virtual terminal, the one that you accessed with F2.

4. Press:

   CTRL-ALT-F3

   A new logon prompt appears again.

5. Log on again.

Exiting a Virtual Terminal

To leave a second terminal we need to terminate the shell.

1. Enter:

   exit

2. The **exit** command ends the login session in this virtual terminal; it does not log you off of others.

In Linux environments, we can press CTRL-ALT-F2, CTRL-ALT-F3, CTRL-ALT-F4, through CTRL-ALT-F7 (and sometimes CTRL-ALT-F8) to create seven (sometimes eight) independent sessions on the same computer using the same monitor. When you log on, if it is a terminal window, it is probably terminal F1. If you log on and are placed in the graphical environment, it is using virtual terminal F7 or F8.

Locating the Graphical Virtual Terminal

You can toggle back and forth between active sessions by using the CTRL-ALT-F# command, where # is 1 through 7 or 8.

1. Press:

   CTRL-ALT-F7

   If you started a graphical desktop, this is where it is usually located, although it may be at F8.

2. If you logged on into a terminal, return to it, probably by pressing:

   CTRL-ALT-F1

The multiple login sessions available through the F keys allow us to log in a second time to test multi-user features, to have both graphical and character-based sessions running, and, as you will see, to kill processes that have frozen the terminal.

3.3 Managing Input and Output

Every process that is started has three defined communication locations or "doors." One is its input, one a place to write output, and a third to write any error messages. Usually, the output of utilities is by default directed to your terminal. You have redirected output to files and to other utilities. We can also tell the shell where to connect input.

Specifying a File as Input

There are two ways to get a utility to open a file and read it. You have been using one way, passing a filename as an argument to a utility. The utility simply goes out, locates the file, and reads it.

1. For example, enter the following command:

   sort *mypasswd*

   Here the shell is instructed to run the **sort** utility and pass it one argument, *mypasswd*. To the **sort** utility, the argument *mypasswd* is interpreted as a file to open and read. **sort** reads the lines from *mypasswd*, sorts the contents, and outputs the data to its output, which by default is connected to the workstation screen.

   Because **sort** has an argument, it interprets the argument as a file and does not read from its input "door." Only when there is no filename argument does **sort** read from its input.

2. Enter:

   who | sort

   In this case, **sort** does not have an argument, so it reads from its input which the shell connected to the output of **who**.

   We can also instruct the shell to connect a file to a utility's input.

3. Enter the following:

   sort < *mypasswd*

   The results are the same as with the **sort** *mypasswd* command. A sorted version of the file *mypasswd* is displayed on the screen. The < in this command is instruction to the *shell* to open the file *mypasswd* and connect the file to the *input* of **sort**. Because no argument is given to **sort**, the **sort** utility does not open a file. The shell opens the file itself and connects the file to the input to **sort**.

4. We can also connect files to the input of other utilities. For example, type:

   cat < *mypasswd*

   In this case, we are instructing the shell to connect the file *mypasswd* to the *input* of **cat**. Because no output destination is specified, the output is connected to the monitor by default. Thus, **cat** reads the contents of the file *mypasswd* and writes it to output, connected to the workstation screen.

COMMAND	INTERPRETATION
utility **>** *filename*	Shell connects the output of the utility to *filename*.
utility **>>** *filename*	Shell connects the output of the utility to the end of the file (appends).
utility **<** *filename*	Shell connects *filename* to the input of the utility.
utility1 **|** **utility2**	Shell connects the output of **utility1** to the input of **utility2**.

TABLE 3-3 Redirection Operators

The input redirection symbol is an important feature because, as you will soon see, several utilities are not programmed to open files. We must instruct the shell to open a file and connect it to the utility's input.

The redirection operators we have discussed thus far are described in Table 3-3.

Redirecting a File to *spell*'s Input

Many UNIX systems contain a spell check program that examines files for misspelled words. On some systems, the **spell** program only reads from input. It cannot open files. We must instruct the shell to open the file and connect it to the input of the process running **spell**.

1. Examine *users_on* for misspelled words with the following command:

   spell < *users_on*

2. If you are told the command is not found, enter:

   ispell -l < *users_on*

All strings in the file that **spell** does not find in the online dictionary file are viewed as misspelled words and are displayed on the screen. In this case, the shell opens the file *users_on* and connects it to the input of **spell**. Because you did not redirect the output, it is displayed on the screen.

Determining Where Utilities Read Input

Throughout these exercises, you have often specified filenames as arguments.

Enter the following representative command:

sort *total*

The character string *total* is given to **sort** as an argument. The **sort** program interprets *total* as a file to open, read, and sort. The output is a sorted version of the lines in the file *total*.

Employing the Default Input Source

The previous exercise raises a question: If no filename argument is provided, the utility reads from its input "door." If we do not tell the shell to connect a file or the output from another utility to the input, what does the utility find when it reads from its input?

1. Enter the following command. No filename is given as an argument to read, and no utility's output is redirected to the process.

   sort

   The cursor moves to a new line. No shell prompt is displayed.

2. Enter the following lines:

   ```
   hello
   DDD
   2
   Hello
   110
   good-bye
   ```

3. Press ENTER to move the cursor to a new line, and then press ENTER again.

4. On a line by itself, press:

   CTRL-D   (Hold down the CTRL key and press the D key one time.)

   A sorted version of the lines you just entered is displayed on the screen

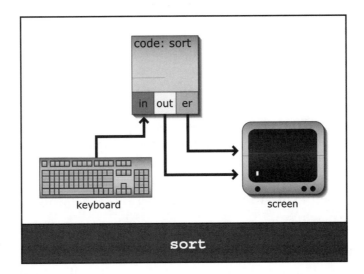

When a new process is first started, the default input is the terminal keyboard. Output and error messages are initially connected to the terminal screen.

Because no filename arguments are specified in the preceding command, the **sort** utility reads from its input, which is connected to the default input source, your keyboard. You enter lines of text and then the end-of-file command, CTRL-D. This key combination indicates to the utility that there is no more input and that the utility can do its thing and then quit. The utility **sort** reads the lines you enter, sorts them, and writes to its output. Because the output of **sort** is not redirected, it is written to your screen.

5. Start another utility without specifying input or output destination:

    cat

6. Enter several lines.

    As you type a line, it is displayed on the screen. When you press ENTER, the line is passed to **cat**, which reads the line and writes it to output, the screen. The line appears as a duplicate below the line that you entered.

7. After entering several lines, go to a new line and press:

    CTRL-D

    After **cat** terminates, the shell displays a new prompt.

8. We can specify output redirection with the default input source. Enter the following:

    sort > *sort-test*

9. Enter several lines of text.

10. When you are finished, press ENTER to put the cursor on a line by itself. Then press:

    CTRL-D

11. Examine the contents of the new file:

    more *sort-test*

You instructed the shell to connect the output of **sort** to the new file *sort-test,* but you did not specify any input for **sort**. By default, input is connected to the keyboard if it is not redirected to another source. The **sort** utility read what you entered as input and wrote its output. Because you instructed the shell to connect the output of **sort** to the new file *sort-test* when **sort** wrote its output, it went to the new file.

Creating Text Files with *cat*

You will usually create text files using an editor such as the visual editor, **vi**, which is discussed in Chapter 4. However, you can quickly create small text files without first mastering an editor, by using one of several other utilities.

⤷ 1. Type the following:

  cat > *first_file*

and press ENTER.

The cursor returns to the beginning of the next line. The shell does not display a new prompt. This command line instructs the shell to start the **cat** utility and to connect its output to the new file *first_file*. There is no request to redirect the input, so input is still connected to the default—your keyboard. You are no longer in communication with the shell; what you now type is read by the **cat** utility, which simply writes to output whatever it reads from input.

2. Type the following lines:

```
This is a line of text in the first_file.
```

3. Press ENTER and then type:

```
This is another.
```

The **cat** utility reads your input and writes it to its output, which the shell connected to a new file named *first_file*.

4. To inform the **cat** utility that you have finished adding text, press ENTER to advance to a new line and then press:

  CTRL-D

This CTRL-D (end-of-file, or EOF, character) tells **cat** there is no additional input. The **cat** utility terminates, and the shell displays another prompt.

5. From the shell, obtain a listing of your files using:

  ls

The file named *first_file* is listed.

6. Examine the contents of *first_file* by typing:

  more *first_file*

The *first_file* file consists only of the text you typed. No additional data about the file, such as the file's name or your name, is added to the file by the system. The file contains just the text you typed. The file's name is kept in the directory. The information about a file is in a system storage unit associated with your file.

7. Create another text file with another **cat** command:

  cat > *second_file*

8. Add some text, and return to the shell by pressing CTRL-D.

9. Obtain a listing of the files in your current directory with:

  ls

10. Examine the contents of *second_file* with:

> **more** *second_file*

The file consists of the lines you entered as input to **cat**.

By default, the keyboard is connected to the input of **cat**. Whatever you type is read by **cat** from your keyboard and written to output, which is connected to the file. The **cat** utility is not very complicated; it simply reads input and writes output, making no modifications. The command **cat** > *filename* instructs the shell to connect the output from **cat** to the file *filename* and to execute the **cat** utility.

Managing Input and Output with Redirection

The role and effect of file input and output redirection symbols are summarized in Table 3-4.

1. Create a new file named *file2* with the following:

> **head** *-12* */etc/passwd* > *file2*

2. Try each of the commands in Table 3-4 and confirm the data in the table.

Self Test 1

Answer the following, and then check your answers using the information within the chapter.

1. What is the effect of each of the following commands?

   A. **sort** *file1 file2*

   _____

   B. **wc** *file1 file2*

   _____

   C. **grep** *file1 file2*

   _____

   D. **who** | **sort** > *abc*

   _____

   E. **cat** *file1 file2 file3*

   _____

2. What command results in a reverse sorting of all lines in the */etc/passwd* file that contain a zero somewhere on the line?

_____

3. What would be in the file *file1* as a result of each of the following?
   A. echo *file1* **>>** *file1*
   B. cat > *file1*

_____

4. How can you access virtual terminal 3?

_____

5. What command reads its arguments and writes them to output?

_____

COMMAND	INPUT	OUTPUT	EFFECT
sort	Keyboard	Display screen	The **sort** utility receives no arguments, so it opens no file. Instead, **sort** reads from input, which is by default connected to the keyboard.
sort > *file1*	Keyboard	*file1*	Keyboard input is sorted, and output is connected to *file1*.
sort >> *file1*	Keyboard	*file1*	Keyboard input is sorted and its output is appended to the end of *file1*.
sort < *file2*	*file2*	Display screen	*file2* is opened by the shell and connected to the input of **sort**. The output is not redirected, but displayed on the screen.
sort *file1*	*file1*	Display screen	*file1* is passed as an argument to **sort**, which opens the file and reads its contents. Output connected to the screen.
sort < *file1* > *file3*	*file1*	*file3*	The shell connects *file1* to the input and *file3* to the output of **sort**. When **sort** runs, it reads from input, sorts the lines, and writes to output. The lines from the file *file1* are sorted and the output placed in *file3*.

TABLE 3-4 Passing Arguments and Opening Files

COMMAND	INPUT	OUTPUT	EFFECT
sort *file1* **>** *file4*	*file1*	file4	The shell passes *file1* as an argument to **sort** and connects the output of **sort** to the file *file4*. The **sort** utility opens *file1* and sorts the lines; the output goes to *file4*.

TABLE 3-4   Passing Arguments and Opening Files *(continued)*

3.4 Employing Special Characters in Command Lines

When we are communicating with the shell, our only tool is the keyboard. The characters available on the keyboard and words or tokens created by combining those characters constitute the entire language we can use to communicate with the shell. Many characters have special meaning to the shell, such as the redirect symbol, >. The shell interprets the > as instruction to connect the output of the previous utility to a file named right after the redirect. Likewise, the | is instruction to connect the output of one utility to the input of another utility.

This section introduces other special characters interpreted by the shell.

Replacing a Wildcard Character with Filenames

One special character to the shell is a *wildcard* character we can use when specifying filenames.

1. If you list several filenames after the **wc** utility on the command line, the **wc** utility examines all of the files. Enter this command:

   wc *total lost-days*

   The number of elements in each file is counted and output, along with the total for all files.

2. To have **wc** examine all files whose names begin with the letter *u*, enter:

   wc *u**

   The shell interprets the *u** as instruction to replace the string *u** on the command line with the names of all files in the current directory that start with the letter *u* and have zero or more additional characters following the *u* in their names. The shell then runs the **wc** utility, passing it all the arguments that it generated—the names of all files in the directory that were matched.

3. Confirm that it is the shell that is expanding (replacing the string with) the * into filenames by entering:

   echo *u**

   The shell replaces the string *u** with the filenames in the current directory that begin with the letter *u*. Those names are passed as arguments, this time to **echo**, which writes the arguments to output.

4. You can also have the shell list *all* of the files in your current directory as arguments to a command by typing:

   echo *

   The shell replaces the asterisk with the names of all the files in your directory and then executes **echo**, passing all the filenames it generated as arguments. The **echo** utility reads its arguments (the filenames) and writes them to output, which in this case is your screen.

5. Do a word count of all the elements of all the files in your directory by entering:

   wc *

   The shell replaces the * with the names of all files in the current directory and passes all the names as arguments to **wc**. The **wc** utility examines all files listed as arguments and displays output like this:

```
 8     39     190     junk
 9     29     175     mypasswd
 8     39     190     phon
 1      5      22     today
12     59     310     total
14     80     220     users_on
52    251    1107     total
```

   The output from **wc** is a list of information pertaining to all input files, followed by a total of these counts.

   N O T E : If you created a file named *total*, it is listed in alphabetical order among the other files. The *total* at the end of the **wc** output is the sum of the statistics for all files examined by the utility.

   You can also have the shell pass all filenames as arguments to the **grep** utility. The **grep** utility searches for the target string in all the files in your directory.

6. Type the following:

grep *is* *

This command line tells the shell to replace the asterisk with all the filenames listed in your current directory. The first argument passed to **grep** is a string of characters that **grep** interprets as the *target*. The remaining arguments **grep** interprets as the names of *files*. The **grep** utility then searches each line in all files listed as arguments for the target string of characters and outputs the lines that contain a match.

Accessing Shell Variables

We use variables in life all the time. We fill out forms such as:

Last name: _____

First name: _____

All of us, except Cher, have values in our memories for the last name and first name variables.

We can use specific characters to indicate which tokens in a sentence are variables. For example, consider:

I am $fname $lname. I live in $city. I was born in $birthplace.

When I read the previous line, I read:

I am John Muster. I live in Berkeley. I was born in Canton, Ohio.

To me, the value of the *fname* variable is *John*.

Everyone reads the line differently because everyone has different *values* for the variables that are identified with dollar signs. In this case, we interpret the **$** to mean, "Find the value of the variable that has the following name and replace both the dollar sign and variable name with the variable's value."

1. Ask the shell to evaluate a variable and pass its value to **echo** by entering:

echo $USER

2. If there is no *USER* variable, try:

echo $LOGNAME

The **$** character has the same special meaning to the shell. It tells the shell to "locate the variable whose name follows, and replace this string with the variable's value." In the command you just entered, *USER* is the variable that the shell evaluates, because it is preceded with a **$**. After replacing the variable and **$** with its value, your actual login name, the shell passes your name as an argument to **echo**. Then **echo** reads the argument and writes it to your screen. The important distinction here is that the shell passes your login name, not **$USER**, to **echo**. The shell interprets the variable and passes its value, not its name.

Having the shell evaluate **$USER** and replacing the variable with its value can be very useful.

3. Enter:

>   **who | grep $USER**

The shell replaces the **$USER** with your login ID and then passes that value to **grep** as its first argument. To **grep**, the first argument is its search string. The line from the output of **who** that contains your login ID is selected by **grep** and output to your screen.

4. Have the shell evaluate some other variables by entering:

>   **echo** my shell is **$SHELL** and my home is **$HOME**

The output on the screen is all the arguments, with variables replaced by their values.

In this case, the shell evaluates two variables. The resulting values are passed to **echo** as arguments. The **echo** utility reads all its arguments and writes them to output. By default, the output is connected to your monitor. The value of the first variable, *SHELL*, is the shell that is started up for you at login; the other variable, *HOME*, is where your home directory is located on the system. Your shell obtained these variables and their values when you logged on. Your colleagues have their own variable values. The shell and all other programs you run are given these variables and these values.

We can employ both a variable and the filename expansion on the same command line.

5. Enter:

>   **grep $USER ***

The shell replaces the variable *USER* with its value, the login name, which becomes argument one. The shell replaces the * with the names of all files in the current directory, which become arguments two, three, and so forth. **grep** interprets the your name as the search string and looks through all files for lines containing your login name.

6. The variable can be used to count the number of times you are logged on:

>   **who | grep $USER | wc -l**

Listing Environment Variables

The shell program that interprets your commands is started as a process when you log on. The values of several variables are given to your particular shell so that your computing environment is appropriate. We can obtain a listing of those environmental variables.

↳ From the shell, type the following:

env | more

or

printenv | more

The output is a listing of some of the variables that are currently set for your shell. Among the many lines displayed, you should find something like the following.

For C shell users:

```
USER      forbes
SHELL     /bin/csh
HOME      /users1/programmers/forbes
PATH      /usr/ucb:/bin:/usr/bin:/usr/local:/lurnix/bin:/usr/new:.
```

For **bash** and Korn shell users:

```
HOME=/usr/home/nate
LOGNAME=nate
PATH=/usr/ucb:/bin:/usr/bin:/usr/local:/lurnix/bin:/usr/new:.
SHELL=/bin/ksh      or    (/bin/bash)
```

The variables and their values are essential to a functioning shell. Your output includes variables such as the following, but with values that are appropriate for your account.

- The *user* or *USER* or *LOGNAME* variable is your account name that you entered when you logged on.
- The *shell* or *SHELL* line indicates which of several shell programs is started at login to interpret the commands that you enter: **csh** is the C shell, **sh** is the Bourne shell, **ksh** is the Korn shell, **bash** is the **bash** shell, and **tcsh** is the **tcsh** shell. They all handle basic commands in essentially the same way, and for now it makes little difference which is running.
- The *home* or *HOME* variable is the location of your workspace or home directory.

- The *path* or *PATH* variable lists the directories where the shell looks to find UNIX utilities you request.

The subject of local and environment variables is explored in some detail in Chapter 9.

Instructing the Shell Not to Interpret Special Characters

The characters *, !, |, >, and $ have special meaning to the shell. Sometimes we need to instruct the shell not to interpret special characters but to treat them as ordinary characters instead. There are several ways to tell the shell to turn off interpretation of special characters.

1. For instance, enter the following:

    echo *we can output a* * *uninterpreted*

    The output includes a literal * character.

    In response to this command, the shell does not expand the asterisk to match filenames, but passes it as a one-character argument to **echo**. It is not interpreted. The **echo** utility reads the asterisk as a one-character argument and outputs it, in this case, to your screen. When a special character is preceded by a backslash (\), the shell interprets that character as ordinary (lacking any special meaning). To put it the other way, the shell interprets the backslash character as instruction to treat whatever character follows as an ordinary character having no special meaning. Once the * is passed to **echo**, the * is just an asterisk that it outputs.

2. Enter the following:

    echo \$*HOME*

    The output is the literal string $HOME without the backslash. The $ is *not* interpreted as instruction to evaluate the *HOME* variable, because it is preceded by a backslash. The shell interprets the $ as just an ordinary dollar sign, and passes the string *$HOME* to the **echo** utility as an argument.

    In the previous commands, the arguments the shell gave to **echo** after it interpreted the * and \$ did not include the backslash. When the shell interprets *, it reads the \ as a specific instruction: Don't ascribe special meaning to the character that immediately follows. The only character that gets passed is the one character that follows the \ character. The backslash is not passed to **echo** because the shell interpreted it as instruction not to interpret the character that follows.

3. Try the following:

    echo \\$*USER* * $*USER*

The output is $*USER* * and your login name. The last $*USER* is interpreted because there is no backslash in front of the **$** telling the shell not to interpret it.

Likewise, we can use **echo** to place interpreted and not interpreted variables into a file.

4. Enter:

    echo *var1* $*USER* > *test-interp*
    echo *var2* \\$*USER* >> *test-interp*
    more *test-interp*

The shell interprets the **$** in $*USER* in the *var1* line, but does not interpret the **$** in the *var2* line. Note the second line in *test-interp* is:

`var2   $USER`

The shell does not pass the backslash to **echo**.

5. Have **grep** look for strings in the *test-interp* file:

    grep $*USER* *test-interp*

The shell interprets the variable $*USER* and passes the value of your login name to **grep** as the first argument. Then **grep** interprets the first argument (your login name) as the search string. The line with your login name is selected and output:

    grep \\$*USER* *test-interp*

This time the shell interprets the backslash as instruction *not* to interpret the very next character, the **$**, so the string $*USER* is passed to **grep** as the first argument. The **grep** utility searches for the actual string $*USER* in the file.

The same is true with the filename expansion wildcard * character.

6. Enter:

    echo *u**
    echo *u**
    wc *u**
    wc *u**

The shell interprets the *u** as instruction to replace the characters *u** with all the filenames in the current directory that start with the letter *u*. The shell then passes the names as arguments. **echo** reads the arguments and writes them to output. **wc** interprets the arguments as filenames and counts the elements of each named file.

The shell interprets $u\backslash*$ as a u and an uninterpreted *. The argument to **echo** is $u*$, which it displays. To **wc**, the $u*$ is the name of a file, a file that it cannot locate.

Not Interpreting ENTER

When you press ENTER at the end of a command line, you are signaling the end of the command. The shell interprets ENTER as a special character, one that indicates the end of the command to be executed, and starts processing. When we are entering a long command line, we often want to put part of it on a second line. However, as soon as we press ENTER, the command is executed. We need to be able to tell the shell not to interpret ENTER.

1. Enter the following command:

     **who > **

   and press ENTER

   The backslash instructs the shell not to interpret the character that immediately follows. Hence, ENTER is not interpreted. There is no end of the command. At this point, the shell has not been told to process the command line, because no real ENTER has been received. It waits for more input. In fact, what you have entered so far is not a complete command. The shell needs to redirect the output of **who** to a file, but the filename is not included.

2. Enter the filename:

     users2

   and press ENTER again.

   This time, ENTER is not preceded by a backslash. The shell interprets it as a real ENTER, signifying the end of the command line, which now happens to span two input lines. It is processed.

3. Confirm that the new file is created by entering:

     ls
     more *users2*

4. Examine the history list to see the previous command:

     history

   The **who** > *users_on* is one command even though it was entered on two lines.

When you want a command line to span more than one input line, precede the first line's ENTER with a backslash character to instruct the shell not to interpret ENTER's special meaning.

Not Interpreting Several Characters in a String

The backslash turns off interpretation for one character only, whatever single character follows.

We can turn off interpretation for more than one character.

1. Enter the following using single quotes:

> **echo '$USER * $USER'**
> **echo '$HOME $USER'**

The output is the literal string of characters entered. When inside single quotes, the * and $ are seen just as characters, so the shell does not expand the * to match filenames. The **$HOME** and **$USER** are not evaluated for the variable values. The arguments passed to **echo** are just the uninterpreted character strings.

We can instruct the shell to interpret part of a line and not interpret other parts of the line.

2. Enter the following, paying careful attention to the single quotes:

> **echo $USER '$HOME $USER' $USER**

The portion of the command line inside single quotes is not interpreted, but passed as an argument to **echo** as is. The parts of the line not in quotes are interpreted and variable values are substituted for the **$USER** variables.

When the shell encounters the first single quote, the shell turns off interpretation of all special characters. The second single quote turns interpretation back on again. Any special characters inside the single quotes are not interpreted.

Creating Multiple Token Arguments

Because we can tell the shell not to interpret special characters inside single quotes, we can tell the shell not to interpret spaces.

1. Pass several arguments to **echo** with several spaces between them:

> **echo** *AA   BB   CC   DD*

The output does not include the multiple spaces:

```
AA BB CC DD
```

The shell interprets one or more spaces as separating the tokens on the command line. The shell interprets **echo** as the utility, and passes it four distinct arguments. It does not pass the whole line of words and spaces.

When **echo** reads its argument list, it outputs the first argument, then a single space, then the next argument, a space, and so forth.

2. Use quotes to tell the shell not to interpret special characters (including spaces):

     echo '*AA   BB   CC   DD*'

A single argument is passed to **echo**. The argument consists of the line as it was entered, including spaces, namely:

     AA   BB   CC   DD

The shell does not interpret spaces as indicating different arguments, so it is all one argument. **echo** outputs the single argument, spaces and all.

Passing Complex Arguments

One of the most useful functions of modern computers is database management. The UNIX operating system provides several utilities that are used with database information. One of the most versatile is **awk**.

1. Type the following commands:

     ps -ef

     ps -ef | awk '{print $1}' | more

The **awk** utility extracts the first field from each line of the output of **ps**. The output of **awk** is displayed on the screen.

2. Change the command line to instruct **awk** to select the second field. Enter:

     ps -ef | awk '{print $2}'

This table describes the pieces of the command line:

COMMAND	INTERPRETATION
ps -ef	Instructs the shell to run the **ps** utility and pass it the argument **-ef**, which **ps** interprets as instruction to list all processes.
I	Instructs the shell to connect the output of **ps** to the input of the next utility, **awk**.
awk	Instructs the shell to run the **awk** utility.
' '	Instructs the shell not to interpret any special character between the single quotes, but to pass the enclosed characters as is to **awk** as an argument.
{print $2}	This is the contents of the quoted string that is passed to **awk**. The **awk** utility interprets this instruction as, "For every line of input, print out only the second field."

3. Have **awk** select more than one field by entering:

    ps -ef | awk '{print $2, $1, $4}'

    awk '{print $2, $1}' *lost-days*

The output is the second field, a space, and then the first field of all records (lines) in the file *lost-days*. This works because the shell does not interpret special characters such as the **$2**; rather, it passes the whole **{print $2, $1}** exactly as it is to **awk**, which interprets it as instructions.

The **awk** utility can be used to select and print specific fields, make calculations, and locate records by the value of specific fields. You will use it more extensively in Chapter 5.

Communicating with Processes

We instruct the shell to start processes. Usually the processes simply complete their tasks and then exit. We can also use control characters to send important signals to processes.

Signaling the End of File

We have used the control character CTRL-D to end input.

1. For example, enter:

    wc

2. Add a few words and then press ENTER.

3. On the new line, press:

    CTRL-D

The CTRL-D is the end-of-file (EOF) marker. When we are entering text from the keyboard to the input of a utility, we signal the end of our input by pressing CTRL-D. The **wc** utility counts the lines, words, and characters in whatever text that we enter until we press CTRL-D. The **wc** utility then displays the results and quits. Every file has a CTRL-D (EOF) character at the end to indicate where to stop reading.

Telling a Process to Quit

There are other important control characters.

1. Start **wc** again without input or arguments:

    wc

2. Enter some text.

3. Instead of the usual end-of-file character, press:

CTRL-C

The **wc** program stops, and a shell prompt is displayed. However, no output from **wc** is displayed. CTRL-C is the interrupt signal, which kills the process. The end-of-file CTRL-D says, "End of input, do whatever you do with input and then exit," but the CTRL-C says, "Stop, put toys away, process nothing more, and be gone." No output is displayed.

Which control character we use depends on the way the utility functions.

4. For example, enter:

sleep *40*

No new shell prompt is displayed. The **sleep** utility is counting 40 seconds.

5. Try to end the **sleep** process with:

CTRL-D

Because sleep is not **reading** CTRL-D the EOF has no meaning.

6. Kill the process by pressing:

CTRL-C

The interrupt signal reaches the process and it terminates.

Sending a Process to the Background

Many of the processes running on the system are not associated with a particular user, but are important elements of the operating system. These processes are running *in the background* and are invisible to most users. This section examines how users can run processes in the background.

1. Type the following command:

sleep *6*

The shell runs **sleep** and gives it the number *6* as an argument. While **sleep** is counting to *6*, the shell waits. No new prompt is presented until **sleep** is finished.

2. Enter:

sleep *60* **&**

This command line tells the shell to run the **sleep** command in the background. The ampersand (**&**) at the end tells the shell to execute the whole command line, but instead of waiting until **sleep** is finished, the shell is to return a new shell prompt so that you can continue working.

3. Obtain a list of current programs by entering:

ps

The **sleep** process is still running. When you execute this command, a number is displayed. This is the process ID number of the **ps** utility as it is executed. When the process is finished, a message is sent to the screen.

This feature allows us to run time-consuming programs in the background while we continue to work in the foreground on some other task. Obviously, with a command process that runs quickly, placing it in the background does not do much good, but there are times—such as when you are running long searches, database queries, and so forth—that it saves time and work.

Programming with Utilities

Thus far in these examples, communication with the shell has been interactive. We enter a command line; then the shell reads and processes whatever we enter from the keyboard. The shell will also read instructions that are placed in a file.

Creating a File of Commands

Until we examine the visual editor in the next chapter, we can use **cat** to read whatever we type and write it to a file.

1. Enter:

   cat > *commands-file*

2. Enter the following lines, pressing ENTER after each:

```
echo Hi $USER
date
cal
sleep 2
ps
echo Bye $USER
```

3. Conclude the input by pressing:

   ENTER

and then on a new line press:

   CTRL-D

4. Make sure the file contents are as just described:

   more *commands-file*

If there is a mistake, remove the file with **rm** *commands-file* and re-create it. There is no simple way to modify a file until you learn to use the editor.

Instructing the Shell to Read a File

We can tell the current shell to read a file and execute each line in the file.

1. If you are in a **csh** or **tcsh** shell, enter:

    source *commands-file*

2. If you are in the **ksh** or **bash** or **sh** shell, use the "dot" command by entering:

    . *commands-file*

    The commands that are the contents of the file are executed one after the other.

Both the **source** and dot (.) commands instruct the current shell to read the file named as an argument and to execute every line in the file as though we just typed it in from the keyboard. In either case we refer to it as sourcing the file.

Self Test 2

Answer the following, and then check your answers using the information within the chapter.

1. What would be the contents of *file1* if each of the following were independently executed?

    A. **grep** *file1* * > *file1*

    B. **echo** *$USER $HOME* > *file1*

    _____

2. How do each of the following commands work? What is the result?

    A. **spell** *file1*

    _____

    B. **spell** < *file1*

    _____

    C. **cat** *file1* | **spell**

    _____

    D. **grep** '*Joan Heller*' *faculty*

    _____

    E. **grep** \$USER *file1*

    _____

3. What command instructs **awk** to output just the time that each user logged on?

_____

4. What is the output of the command **echo** *$PATH*?

_____

3.5 Modifying the User Environment

One of the strengths of the UNIX operating system is its flexibility. The system allows us to customize a variety of programs to meet our individual needs. We can tailor how the shell behaves, and instruct the editor to include features. We can operate with a graphical desktop that includes color, icons, and startup programs of our own choice. Each user can tailor or modify all of these environmental features. This section explores a small part of the tailoring functionality.

Instructing the Shell Not to Overwrite Files

Thus far, we have used the > symbol to instruct the shell to connect the output of a utility to a new file. What happens when we redirect output to an existing file depends on the shell you are using and the value of a variable named *noclobber*. As users, we make the decision whether the shell should overwrite existing files or not overwrite them.

1. To make sure that the shell is functioning in its "file clobbering" mode for this demonstration, enter the following commands.
   If you are in a **csh** or **tcsh** shell, enter:
   > **unset** *noclobber*

   If you are in the **ksh** or **bash** shell, enter:
   > **set +o** *noclobber*

   The **sh** shell always overwrites files when we redirect output to an existing file. We cannot have it do otherwise.

2. Create a new file and examine its contents by entering:
   > **ls** > *test-list*
   > **cat** *test-list*

3. Instruct the shell to put the output of **date** into the same file and examine the file:

> **date** > *test-list*
> **cat** *test-list*

The original contents of the file have been *replaced* or *overwritten* by the output of **date**.

When we tell the shell to redirect the output of a utility to a file, the shell creates the file *if it does not exist*. If there is a file by that name, the current contents are removed to make room for the new output.

4. Instruct the shell not to clobber files when redirecting output:

In the **csh** or **tcsh** shells, enter:

> **set** *noclobber*

In the **ksh** or **bash** shells, enter:

> **set -o** *noclobber*

5. Attempt to redirect output from another utility to the file:

> **ls** > *test-list*

An error message is displayed.

6. To see whether shell variables such as *noclobber* are on or off, try the following:

In the **csh** or **tcsh** shell, enter:

> **set**

The list of variables currently set is displayed.

In the **ksh** or **bash** shell, enter:

> **set -o**

A list of shell operational variables is displayed.

In a **csh** or **tcsh** shell, we turn *noclobber* on with **set** and off with **unset**. In the **ksh** and **bash** shells, we turn *noclobber* on with **set -o** and off with **set +o** commands, as follows:

SHELL	TURN *noclobber* ON	TURN *noclobber* OFF
csh, tcsh	set *noclobber*	unset *noclobber*
ksh, bash	set -o *noclobber*	set +o *noclobber*

Avoiding Accidental Logout

If you accidentally enter a CTRL-D to your login shell, you may be logged out. The end-of-file character says, "No more input; exit," so the shell exits.

1. Start a child shell process by entering:

   csh

2. List your processes:

   ps

   The child **csh** is listed among the processes.

3. Issue an end-of-file signal to your shell by pressing:

   CTRL-D

4. List your processes again:

   ps

   The **csh** shell is gone. Pressing CTRL-D instructs it to exit.

5. Start another child shell by entering one of the following:

   bash

   or

   ksh

6. Identify the current processes with:

   ps

   The child shell is among those listed.

7. Instruct the child shell to terminate by giving it the end-of-file signal:

   CTRL-D

   ps

   The child shell is no longer running.

8. We can tell the shells to ignore an end-of-file character. Enter one of the following commands.

   In the **csh** or **tcsh** shells:

   set *ignoreeof*

   In the **ksh** and **bash** shells:

   set -o *ignoreeof*

9. Now press CTRL-D

You receive a message telling you to use **exit** or **logout**, not CTRL-D.

You will soon customize your account to have *ignoreeof* and *noclobber* set at all times. For now, enter each after you log on to protect yourself from accidental overwrite and accidental logout.

Changing the Prompt

Throughout this book, we have talked about the shell prompt. There are some standard shell prompts, shown in the following table. The prompt that your shell displays, like much of your user environment, can be modified.

PROMPT	SHELL
$	Bourne and Korn shells (**sh**, **bash**, and **ksh**)
%	C shells (**csh** and **tcsh**)
#	Any shell as *root*

1. Look at the current variables:

   set | more

   If the list includes a variable named *prompt*, you are interacting with a **csh** or **tcsh** shell. If the output of **set** includes a *PS1* variable, you are in a **ksh** or **bash** shell.

2. If you are using a **csh** or **tcsh** shell, type the following command:

   set *prompt*='*myname* ' (Don't omit the space)

   where *myname* is whatever you want the prompt to be.

3. If you are using the **sh**, **bash**, or **ksh** shells, type the following:

   PS1='*myname* ' (Don't omit the space)

Your prompt is now reset. This "personalized" prompt remains set until you log out. Later you will learn more about setting up your computer environment, and you will have the opportunity to customize various aspects of your workspace permanently, such as the shell prompts and the shell's behavior.

3.6 Surveying Elements of a Functioning System

We have been examining the system utilities, processes, shell interactions, and parts of the filesystem. This section lifts up the hood to addresses questions such as, where on the system are the utilities? When I log in, why do I wind up in my home directory? Why can I read some files but not others? How can we put commands in a file and run them by reading the file?

Examining the Toolboxes That Contain the Utilities

Throughout this chapter, you have been issuing commands that call for the shell to execute a utility, but we have not examined where the programs are actually located.

1. Enter the following misspelled command:

   dzatte

2. The error message displayed on the screen is something like:

   `Command Not Found`

   Where is the shell looking before it reports "Command Not Found"? I ask my five-year-old to go upstairs and get a book that is either on the desk or the nightstand. She leaves and returns with the book. It must have been on the desk or on the nightstand. Had it been on the bed with large red arrows pointing at it, she would have returned with the error message:

   `Book Not Found`

   Just like the five-year-old, the shell looks only where it's told to look.

3. Ask the shell to display the value of the *PATH* variable:

   echo $PATH

   The variable *PATH* is something like:

   `/bin:/usr/bin:/usr/local/bin:/usr/bin/x11:/usr/hosts`

   This variable consists of a series of directories separated by colons. These are the "desk" or "nightstand" places that the shell checks for a utility when you ask for one to be executed. The shell looks first in the directory listed on the left, then the next, and so on.

   The */bin* directory contains some of the utilities available on the system in the form of **bin**ary files.

4. Obtain a listing of the utilities in */bin*. (Note: The */* is important; do not omit it.)

   ls */bin* | more

   The **ls** utility outputs a list of the files in the directory */bin*. You may recognize some of these files—they are utilities you have already used, including **cat**, **rm**, and **ls**. These are some of the executable programs that you access when you type a command. As you saw when you examined your *PATH*, the */bin* directory is not the only directory that contains executable code. The list of directories (*PATH*) that your shell examines can be modified to include other directories.

Determining Where a Utility Is Located

The shell looks for utilities in the directories in the *PATH* variable and reports on their location.

⮑ Enter:

which *who*
which *xterm*
which *ls*
which *set*

If you ask for the location of a utility that you know exists, such as **set**, and the shell reports it cannot be found, that program, like **set**, is built into the shell. The shell cannot find it in the path because the code is not in a different utility file; rather, it is in the shell itself.

The search path is one of the features that make UNIX and Linux so flexible. When we want to add a new application or program, we can add it to one of the directories in the path and instantly give everyone access to it. Alternatively, we can create a new directory, put the application there, and modify the path variable for the users who should have access to the new application.

Examining the Elements of the Password File

The utilities consult many system files as they perform their jobs. When you log on, a program called **login** asks for your password and starts your shell. Your shell gets information such as *USER* and *HOME* so it can access the needed information about your account.

Your user ID number, probably your password, and other information about you reside in a file called */etc/passwd*. On a stand-alone system, the */etc/passwd* file that resides on the machine contains information about all users. If a system is a part of a network that allows users to log on from any of several machines with the same password and login information, one of the network machines contains the complete password file information, and it serves the other machines as needed. This Network Information Service is called NIS. Whenever you or any other user logs on, your entry from either the local or the NIS network *passwd* file is consulted.

⮑ 1. Examine the local password file by entering the following command (note the spelling of *pass<u>wd</u>*):

　　more */etc/passwd*

2. If it is a very long file, page through the file by pressing several times:
   SPACEBAR

3. Locate the entry for your account.

4. Press **q** to stop and return to the shell.

   If your login name is not in the output, you are probably on a network that provides the passwords.

5. To see the *passwd* information from the network server, enter:
   ypcat *passwd* | **more**

6. Locate the entry for your account.

7. Press **q** to stop and return to the shell.

   We can use **grep** to select one record from the *passwd* data.

8. Depending on whether you are on a local or network served password file, type one of the following commands:
   grep *$USER* */etc/passwd*

   or

   ypcat *passwd* | **grep** *$USER*

In these versions, you are asking the shell to evaluate the variable *USER* and pass its value to **grep** as the search target. The **grep** utility then selects the line that contains your login name.

 N O T E : If your login name record is output when you enter **grep** */etc/passwd*, you are on a locally served system, and the */etc/passwd* file should be used for password lookups throughout this text. If the **ypcat** command outputs your login name record, your system is using NIS and you should use the **ypcat** *passwd* form of commands to access password information.

The records in the */etc/passwd* file consist of seven fields separated by colons. The general format is as follows:

```
    Login    User ID       Info on user              Start-up program
      ↓        ↓               ↓                            ↓
  cassy:x:532:1000:user cassy:/home/cassy:/usr/bin/tcsh
              ↑        ↑                        ↑
          Password  Group ID              Home directory
```

The fields of the password file are described in the following table:

FIELD	INFORMATION
login	The login or name for your account.
password	Your encrypted password. (May be an *x* if the passwords are kept in a secure ***/etc/shadow*** file. May also be an *.)
uid	Your user ID, the unique number that is assigned to your account.
gid	Your group ID. Each user must be a member of at least one group. Every user who has the same number in this field as you have is in your group. You can share files with group members using permissions.
misc	Information about the user such as the user's full name. The miscellaneous field is often blank.
home	Your home directory. This is your current directory when you first log on.
Startup program	The program that is started when you log on—it is usually a shell such as the Bash shell (***/usr/bin/bash***) or the **tcsh** (***/bin/tcsh***) or the Korn shell (***/bin/ksh***), but it does not have to be a shell. It can be anything, including a data entry program or a menu for accessing your accounts at a bank.

Changing Your Password

One of the most important ways to protect the data in your account is to choose a secure but memorable password. This is not only convenient, but necessary for maintaining the security of everyone's data on the computer.

Before you begin the process of changing your password, decide on an appropriate new one. When choosing a password, there are several words you should avoid because they are easily guessed. It is unsafe to use any of the following:

- Your login name

- Any first or last name
- Your address
- A word listed in a dictionary in any language
- Obscenities
- Pop culture words

It is best to include both upper- and lowercase letters, and at least one numeral and at least one special character in addition to regular alphabetic characters.

With all these considerations, it can be difficult to create a password that we can remember and is secure. One way to formulate a memorable yet difficult-to-crack password is to use the first letters of every word in a sentence that has meaning. For example, if you enjoy the work of a particular author, your password might be:

```
MfaiMT!60
```

This looks difficult to remember. It *is* extremely difficult to crack—but for me it's easy to recall because it is the first letter of each word in the following sentence, followed by the year my daughter Cassy was born. Cassy was borne in 91.

My **f**avorite **a**uthor **i**s **M**ark **T**wain**!** and Cassy was born in 91.

or

```
{OwaiS19}
```

which stands for

{Our **w**edding **a**nniversary **i**s **S**eptember **19}**

When you have decided on a new password and are ready to change your current password, take the following steps:

1. Determine whether your system is running the Network Information Service (NIS).

   Once you have decided on a new password, type whichever of the following commands is appropriate.

2. If your system is running NIS, type:

   yppasswd

3. Otherwise, enter:

   passwd

4. You are prompted for your *current* password. To protect you, the program will not continue unless you identify yourself by correctly providing the current password.

5. Type your *current* password and press ENTER

   You are now prompted for a *new* password

6. Type your new password and press ENTER

   The program asks you to repeat the new password to make certain that you can type it correctly and can remember it.

7. Type your new password again and press ENTER.

   When the shell prompt returns with no error messages, your password has been changed. It might even confirm that all went well.

The **passwd** utility accomplishes tasks you cannot do. It actually changes a system file that you are not permitted to alter. Because you have that power when running the **passwd** utility, it grills you extensively to be sure you are legitimate and that you can remember your new password.

Forgetting Passwords

Sometimes it happens. The system administrator (*root*) cannot find your current password. It is located on the system only in the encrypted form. However, the *root* user is a 600-pound gorilla and can sit wherever she wishes, so the *root* user can *change* your password to a new one without knowing the original. See Chapter 13.

Modifying Permissions on Files

As the owner of a file, you determine who has permission to read the contents of the file or to change the contents of the file. If it is a command file, you can specify who can execute it. We can modify permissions only on files we own.

⮑ List the files in the current directory with the l̲ong option:

   ls -l

The -l option is interpreted by **ls** as instruction to provide a l̲ong listing of information about the file. The first field in the output, which consists of 10 character places, shows the permissions currently set for that file. In Chapter 9 you will explore setting file permissions in much more depth. For now, however, look at the permissions field. The very first character is a dash for files and a *d* for directories. The remaining nine characters are a mix of dashes, and **r**, **w**, and x characters that show which permissions are currently granted.

Denying and Adding Read Permission on a File

All files have a set of permissions that determine who can do what with the file.

1. To view the permissions of the *users_on* file, type the following command:

    ls -l *users_on*

2. The output resembles the following:

    ```
    -rw-rw-r--  1  cassy        453 Jul 18 11:17 users_on
    ```

    In this example, the first **rw-** indicates that *you* (the file's owner) have permission to <u>r</u>ead and <u>w</u>rite to the file. The second **rw-** indicates that other users who have been assigned to your group have **r**ead and **w**rite permissions for your file. The last three characters indicate the permission granted to all other users who are not in your group; in this case, they get <u>r</u>ead permission only.

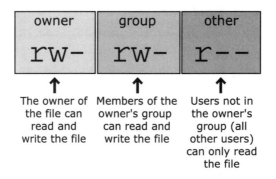

owner	group	other
rw-	rw-	r--
↑	↑	↑
The owner of the file can read and write the file	Members of the owner's group can read and write the file	Users not in the owner's group (all other users) can only read the file

If you are the owner, you can change the permissions on a file to make the file inaccessible to all users, including yourself. Because you own the file, you can still change its permissions again at any time. No user can read or copy your file if you don't grant read permission.

3. Type the following command to remove read permission from the file *users_on*:

    chmod -r *users_on*

4. Examine the permissions field for *users_on* by typing:

    ls -l

Notice that although the previous permissions were read and write for you and your group, the new permissions only include a **w**. By placing the minus in front of the **r** in the **chmod** command, you removed read permission. The **chmod** command is used to <u>ch</u>ange the <u>mod</u>e of files.

5. Verify the state of the file's permissions by trying to display the file with the following command:

    cat *users_on*

    You immediately receive an error message saying that you do not have permission to read the file. Even though you own the file, if you deny yourself read permission, you can't read the file. You still own the file, however, so you can change the permissions again.

6. Return the read permission to the file with the following command:

    chmod +r *users_on*

    ls -l *users_on*

By preceding the **r** with a **+**, you add read permission.

In Chapter 10, we will examine what each permission (**r**, **w**, and **x**) controls for files and directories, as well as how to set the permissions specifically for owner, group, and other users.

Creating a Shell Script

You can use UNIX to program in a variety of formats and languages. The UNIX operating system gives programmers a number of programming tools that either are packaged with the system or that can be added.

One of the most basic and useful program tools is the shell itself. You have been using the shell as an interactive command interpreter. It is also a powerful programming environment.

1. Type the following command to create a new file:

    cat > *new_script*

2. Type the following lines:

    ```
    echo   Your   files   are
    ls
    echo   today   is
    date
    echo   Current processes are:
    ps
    ```

3. Press ENTER to move the cursor to a new line.

4. Press CTRL-D

   At this point, the file *new_script* contains a series of shell commands.

5. Examine the file to be certain it is correct:

   cat *new_script*

   If there are errors, remove the file *new_script* and return to step 1 to create it again.

6. Try to run the script by entering its name:

   new_script

   It does not run when we enter its name. You could source it and have the current shell read the file and execute its contents as we did earlier. However, the goal is to enter the filename and have it executed.

7. Display the permissions of the file by entering:

   ls -l *new_script*

   The permissions indicate that the file is not *executable.* To run the script by simply calling its name, you must grant yourself execute permission.

8. Type the following command to make *new_script* executable:

   chmod +x *new_script*

9. To see the new permissions, enter:

   ls -l

   You now have execute permission, as well as read and write permissions for the file.

10. Execute the new script by typing its name:

    new_script

11. If you receive an error message such as:

    `Command not found`

    type the following:

    ./new_script

    This command line tells the shell exactly where to find the shell script, *new_script*, in your current directory known as "dot."

   All the commands that you typed into the file are executed, and their output is sent to the screen.

The output from **ps** indicates that a new process was started that ran the script. Your shell executed this child process to run the commands inside the script.

The steps to create and use a shell script are:

1. Create a file of shell commands.
2. Make the file executable with **chmod**.
3. Execute the file by entering the script name.

When we execute a script, the shell that is reading the script follows those instructions. It executes each line of the script as though it were a line you entered at the keyboard. All utilities in the script are executed.

In an earlier exercise, you told your current shell to read the script and execute the contents of the file with the **source** command. In this case, you issue the script name, which your current shell interprets as instruction to start a child process to read the script. Read permission is enough when you source a script. Execute permission is needed if you start a child shell to execute its contents. You will create many scripts in later chapters.

Self Test 3

Answer the following, and then check your answers at the end of the chapter.

1. When you enter the following command, what happens and why?

    cat > *dog*

    _____

2. What results from the following commands?
    A. **who** | **grep** $USER

    _____

    B. **grep** \$*HOME* *file1*

    _____

    C. **echo u*** >> *file1*

    _____

    D. echo 'u*' **>>** *file1*

_____

    E. ps

_____

    F. . *fileA*

_____

    G. set *noclobber*

_____

    H. set -o

_____

    I. chmod +x *file2*

_____

3. How can we change the prompt to be Next? in both families of shells (C shells and Korn shells)?

_____

4. What data is in each field in the *passwd* file?

_____: _____: _____: _____: _____: _____: _____

5. What command instructs the shell not to accept CTRL-D as a signal to log off?

_____

Chapter Review

Use this section to review the content of this chapter and test yourself on your knowledge of the concepts.

Chapter Summary

UNIX is a multiuser, multitasking operating system. It includes numerous utilities that can be linked together for efficiency. UNIX is a complex, powerful, and occasionally unusual operating system. In this chapter, you examined the fundamental commands and concepts:

- Utilities are essential tools for accomplishing work in Linux/UNIX.
- The **sort** utility sorts lines from input or from a filename argument. It sorts in ASCII order by default, or in reverse order if given the **-r** option as an argument.

- The **wc** utility counts lines, words, and characters, by default. It outputs only lines if given the **-l** option, words if given **-w,** and only characters if given the **-c** option. Options can be combined to output more than one count.
- The **grep** utility interprets its first argument as a target search string and all other arguments as files to examine. **grep** searches through all lines of input for the target string. If the string is on the line, the line is output; otherwise, it is ignored.
- The shell redirects input and output for processes running utilities:

|	Connects the output from the previous utility to the input of the next.
>	Connects the output of the previous utility to a file. The file's name follows the redirection character.
>>	Connects the output of the previous utility to the end of the file whose name follows; thus, the output is appended to the end of the file.
<	Connects the file whose name follows the redirection to the input of the previous utility.

- The shell interprets the **$** as specifying a variable such as **$USER** and **$HOME**. The shell replaces both the **$** and the *variable name* with its value.
- The * character is a special character to the shell which it interprets as a "wildcard" for matching filenames in the current directory. It is a wildcard such that *w** is interpreted to mean all filenames that start with a *w* followed by any number of any characters. The shell replaces the string that includes the * on the command line with all matching filenames.
- The shell interprets the \ as instruction to turn off the interpretation of the special meaning for whatever character follows.
- If special characters are between single quotes, the shell does not interpret the special meaning.
- CTRL-D is the end-of-file character (EOF), and CTRL-C is the interrupt. When a process is sent the end-of-file signal, it completes whatever processing it is programmed to do on input data and then dies. With an interrupt, the process just terminates.
- We can tell the shell to protect existing files and not overwrite them when we use the > redirect by setting *noclobber*:
  - C shell family: **set** *noclobber*
  - Bash, Korn shell family: **set -o** *noclobber*

- We can change the password using the **passwd** or **yppasswd** commands.
- Permissions determine who has read, write, and execute access to a file. The **chmod** command takes arguments such as **-r** as instruction to remove read permissions.
- When we create a file of shell commands, we can have the *current* shell execute the commands that are its contents by entering:
  - C shell family: **source** *file*
  - Bash, Korn shell family: . *file*
- We can have a child shell run the contents of a script by first changing the permissions on the script file to include execute and read permissions, then enter the filename as a utility on the command line.

Assignment

What Commands Accomplish the Following?

1. What options to **ls** accomplish the following?
   A. Lists all files, including dot files._____
   B. Provides a long listing of information about the files._____
   C. Identifies directories with a /._____

2. What command line outputs a number that is the total number of files, including dot files, listed in the current directory?

   _____

3. What command obtains information about the **ps** utility?

   _____

4. What command sorts the contents of all files in the current directory with names beginning with the letter *f*?

   _____

5. In the following commands, how does each utility interpret each of the arguments:
   A. **echo** *dogfish*_____
   B. **rm** *dogfish*_____
   C. **grep** *dogfish*_____

6. What command creates a new file called *all* consisting of the lines in the files *file1*, *file2*, and *file3*?

   _____

7. Explain what the following command lines accomplish:
   A. **grep** '*Linux is fun*' *_____
   B. **sort** > *file4*_____
   C. **grep** *$USER /etc/passwd*_____
   D. **echo** \$PATH *$PATH*_____
   E. **grep** '*1 2 3*' *f***_____
   F. **set -o EOF**_____
   Fill-in

8. What is the difference between CTRL-D and CTRL-C?

   _____

9. Assume the contents of a file are the following series of shell commands:
   date
   ps -ef
   A. If you want to source the file, what permissions are needed?

   _____

   B. If you wish to execute the script simply by calling its name, what permission is needed?

   _____

   C. Which process executes the contents when you source a script?

   _____

   D. Which process executes the contents when you execute the script by calling its name?

   _____

Project

1. Write a command line that outputs the first, second, third, and eighth fields of the output of **ps -ef**.

   _____

2. Create a script named *allproc* that outputs the first, second, third, and eighth fields of the output of **ps -ef**. How would you make it executable? How would you run it?

   _____

COMMAND SUMMARY

passwd	Changes the user's password.
ls	**Lis**ts the contents of the current directory.
ls -l	Outputs a **l**ong listing of the contents of the current directory with one file or directory per line.

FILE DISPLAYING UTILITIES

cat file1 file2	Con**cat**enates *file1* and *file2*. (Outputs *file1*, then *file2*.)
grep word filename	Searches for lines containing a particular *word* (or pattern) in *filename*.
wc filename	**c**ounts the lines, **w**ords, and characters in *filename*.

DATABASE UTILITIES

awk '{print $#}' file	Prints the #th field of *file*.

DATA PRODUCING AND EXAMINING UTILITIES

grep word filename	Searches for lines containing a particular *word* (or pattern) in *filename*.
sort filename	Displays the lines in *filename* in sorted order.
spell filename	Checks the spelling in *filename*.

REDIRECTION OF INPUT AND OUTPUT

utility **<** filename	Makes *filename* the input for **utility**.
utility **>** filename	Sends the output of **utility** to *filename*.
utility1 **|** *utility2*	Makes the output of **utility1** the input of **utility2**.

FILE PERMISSIONS

chmod -r filename	Removes permission to read *filename*.
chmod +r filename	Gives permission to read *filename*.
chmod +x filename	Grants execute permission on the file.
chmod -x filename	Removes execute permission on the file.

SHELL PROGRAMMING

set	Lists the variables that are set for your shell and their values. In C shell, lists local variables. In Korn shell, lists local and environment variables.
env	Lists environment variables.

REDIRECTION OF INPUT AND OUTPUT	
printenv	Lists environment variables.
$var	Evaluates a variable, *var*.
*	Expands to match filenames.
\	Interprets the next character as an ordinary character without special meaning.
' '	Turns off interpretation of all characters between the single quotes. They are seen as ordinary characters.
scriptname	Executes the commands in the file **scriptname**.
SETTING THE USER ENVIRONMENT	
set prompt = ' string '	In the C and **tsch** shells, makes *string* the new prompt.
PS1=' string '	In the Bourne, **bash**, or Korn shell, makes *string* the new prompt.
PROCESS MONITORING	
ps	Displays the current processes for this login session.
ADDITIONAL UTILITIES	
clear	Clears the terminal screen.
echo	Reads arguments and writes them to output.
which **utility-name**	Reports the location of *utility-name*.
ypcat	Reads network database files the way that **cat** reads local files.

Mastering the Visual Editor

S K I L L S   C H E C K

Before beginning this chapter, you should be able to:

- Access and leave the system
- Execute basic shell commands
- Redirect the output of a utility to a file
- Create a file using the **cat** utility
- Change directories and return to your home directory

O B J E C T I V E S

After completing this chapter, you will be able to use **vi** to:

- Create and access files
- Move around in a file effectively
- Add lines, words, and characters to files
- Delete characters, lines, and blocks of text
- Change characters, lines, and blocks of text
- Cut and paste lines of text
- Undo changes
- Move back and forth between the two editor modes
- Make global changes

In Linux, UNIX information and programs consist of lines of characters in files. In most respects, the computing environment is a collection of files and processes. When writing text or computer programs, we create files and modify old ones. We insert new lines, rearrange lines, change text, and make other necessary changes. Computer text editors were developed to accomplish these tasks. The UNIX/Linux **visual editor**, **vi**, usually pronounced *vee-eye*, is a powerful, fast, command-driven screen editor. We give all instructions to the editor by entering combinations of keystrokes. The **vi** visual editor is available on all systems and is an essential tool. By using the **vi** editor, we can create text as well as make specific and global changes to text—precisely and, with practice, easily.

In this chapter, you will use the visual editor to access files, move to various locations in the text, and make content editing changes within the file, such as replacing or deleting text, reading in other files, and rearranging portions of files. Copies of a document in varying stages of development can be saved to files for review and ultimately printed.

4.1 Introducing the Visual Editor

In the 1970s, people edited files on UNIX with the line editor by issuing cumbersome commands. There was no way to move the cursor to a particular word to make a correction. Instead, to correct the spelling of a word in the 14th line, you had to issue a command such as *14/s/misteak/mistake/*. A graduate student at the University of California at Berkeley, Bill Joy, wrote the visual editor, **vi**, to allow movement of the cursor to specific locations in a file for editing. **vi** is an old editing program, not a word processor. It does not support many of the features available in today's word processing programs. We have to remember commands, because there is no mouse, no pull-down menu, and no page formatting. However, the **vi** editor is present in every UNIX environment, uses few computing resources, includes many tools that make editing efficient, and once you have learned its commands, is actually quite fast.

Two major versions of the editor are widely available. Standard UNIX releases include **vi**, and Linux provides **vim**, which includes some **vim**provements. The same command, **vi**, usually accesses **vim** in Linux.

It's not easy to keep track of **vi**'s two modes—*command* mode and *append/insert* mode—nor to remember the many commands that we enter from the keyboard. Once mastered, though, **vi** is an essential tool in UNIX for three reasons:

- It is provided as part of all standard UNIX releases, so it is available everywhere.
- Once you can use the basic commands, **vi** is a fast and effective editor.
- Although **vi** uses few computing resources, it possesses advanced features not available on other editors. The visual editor is actually the editor of choice for most advanced users and programmers.

In this first section, the exercises guide you on a quick start tour of **vi**'s features. By completing the at-the-terminal steps, you will learn to use the basic editing commands and will explore the structure of **vi**. In later sections, you will employ precise ways to move around, delete, add, change, and manipulate specific text.

To get the most from this chapter, we suggest you:

1. Complete each step in the getting started tour that is the first section. Then start using **vi** with that limited set of commands to create and edit files.
2. Work through the examples and exercises in the remainder of the chapter.
3. Do not attempt to remember all the commands at first. Master a reasonable collection, and then expand your repertoire with time.
4. Return to the Command Summary at the end of this chapter and reread it often. At each review, select additional commands to employ in your editing.
5. When you want to reinforce the commands, redo the chapter. It takes much less time the second go-round, and redoing the chapter greatly increases your skills.

4.2 Working in an Existing File with vi

Files are central to the UNIX computing environment. Business letters, college theses, program code, program output, data, e-mail, and data records are all stored as files. The visual editor is used to create new files and edit existing files. Even if you create a file using another utility such as **who**, or **cat**, the visual editor can still identify the file by its name, access it, and edit it.

The visual editor, however, works differently than most other editing environments. When you start a letter with a typewriter or a PC word processor, the one thing you can do right away is type in or add text to the file. Not so with **vi**. When we start editing a file with **vi**, the one thing we *cannot* do is add text. We can move around in the file and delete words, lines, and characters. We can copy and paste text, and we can modify the editing environment. However, we cannot add text to the file without first issuing an "I want to add text" command. For that reason, it is easiest to learn to use **vi** by starting with an existing file.

Begin by creating a new practice file that you can edit throughout this chapter.

1. Log on to your user account (not as *root*).

   One of the many ways to create a file in UNIX is with the **cat** utility.

2. Start the process of creating a new file by typing:

   cat > *practice*

3. Press ENTER

4. Type in the following lines. When you make mistakes, don't try to fix them, just keep going. In later exercises, you can use **vi** to correct those errors. Be sure to include the blank lines.

   ```
   This practice file will be used
   several times in this course.

   Although I am creating this file with the cat command,
   later I will be editing it with the visual editor.

   a b c d
   2 3 4 5
   2 3 4 5
   A B C D
   E F G H

   The visual editor permits global changes,
   reading in files, cutting and pasting,
   and tailoring the environment to meet individual needs.
   There is no mouse, everything is done through commands.
   ```

5. Move the cursor to a new line by pressing:

   ENTER

6. Tell **cat** there is no more input by pressing:

   CTRL-D

   The **cat** program ends and a shell prompt is displayed.

7. Add more text to the file by entering the following command lines. Be sure to use the double redirection symbol to add the text to the file.

> **head** */etc/passwd* **>>** *practice*
>
> **cal** *1752* **>>** *practice*
>
> **wc** *practice*
>
> **more** *practice*

8. If you have not reached the end of the file, quit **more** by entering:

> q

4.3 Touring the Visual Editor

This first section takes you on a quick start tour of the editor's essential features. You will master fundamental commands and examine the structure of the editor. Following this tour, you will explore, in depth, many specific commands.

You have just used the command **cat** **>** *filename* to create a new file. The *filename* you assign to a file (such as *practice*) becomes the identification label used by UNIX to locate the file when you want to work on it.

1. To start editing your new *practice* file using the **vi**sual editor, enter the command:

> **vi** *practice*

2. Press ENTER

This command line instructs the shell to start the **vi** program and to give it one argument, *practice*, which **vi** must interpret.

Once the editor is running, it interprets the argument *practice* as the name for a file. **vi** locates the file, opens it, and displays the contents on your screen. The cursor appears at the beginning of the first line of the file. You are no longer talking to the shell. Instead, you are communicating with **vi**.

When you first access a file with **vi**, you can:

- Move around
- Delete text
- Copy and paste text
- Modify the editing environment
- Leave the editor to return to the shell

What you cannot do at this point is type text into the file.

Moving around in the File

When editing a file, we often need to move to different locations in the file to correct the spelling of a word, remove specific lines of text, or insert additional code. To accomplish edits, we must tell **vi** exactly where we want to add text, or which specific character, word, or line we want to change. The mouse does not work in **vi**. To communicate with **vi**, we move the screen cursor to the appropriate location in the text where we want to perform an editing operation.

> **NOTE:** In these first exercises, you will move around and delete text. If you suddenly are adding characters to the file, you have pressed a key that moved you to append mode. To return to command mode and continue the exercises, press the ESC key.

Moving One Character or Line at a Time

A fundamental way to move the cursor through a file is with the *direction keys*.

 1. Press the lowercase **j** one time. A letter *j* is not added to the file; instead, the cursor moves down one line.

2. If the cursor does not move, press ESC and then try again.

3. Try the following lowercase keys:

l	(*el*)
j	
h	
k	

vi interprets each of these keys as a command to move the cursor in the following ways:

h	Move the cursor *left* one character.
l	Move the cursor *right* one character.
k	Move the cursor *up* one line, staying in the same column.
j	Move the cursor *down* one line, staying in the same column.

4. Move the cursor left, down, up, and right through the text using the **h**, **j**, **k**, and **l** direction keys.

At this point, **vi** interprets your keyboard input as commands, not input text. You are in the *command mode* of the visual editor. After exploring more commands available from the command mode, we will go into *append mode*, where whatever you type is placed in the file.

Most workstations include arrow keys that also instruct the editor to move the cursor on the screen

5. Press DOWN ARROW one time:

↓

If the cursor moves down one line, the arrow keys work in **vi** on your system. When you Telnet into a location or access UNIX from a Microsoft environment, the arrow keys may not work. In that case, use the **h**, **j**, **k**, and **l** direction keys.

6. Move around the file using each of the four arrow keys.

7. Move your cursor to a blank space, whether the space is between words or is a space accidentally placed at the end of a line.

Spaces are characters.

8. With the arrows, try to move the cursor beyond the text—to the right and left, above the first line, and below the last line.

When you attempt to go beyond the existing text, the cursor does not move, and the workstation either flashes or beeps. The file is only the text, not the full screen that is displaying the file.

Moving Efficiently to a Specific Target

Thus far, you have been moving around the file character by character and line by line. There are several faster and more explicit ways to move the cursor to specific locations in a file.

An efficient way to move the cursor to a specific word in the text is with the forward search command.

1. To move the cursor forward to a textual target, enter:

    /be

    and press ENTER

    The cursor moves forward through the file to the first occurrence of the character string *be*.

    If this doesn't happen, press ESC and try again. If there is no *be* in your file, try */p* instead.

    As you type the slash character / and each letter of the target *be*, they appear in the lower-left corner of the screen. The characters are *not* entered into your file. The editor is simply displaying your forward search command as you type it.

2. Try the following:

    /me

    ENTER

    /Sep

    ENTER

    /7

    ENTER

3. Use the forward search command to locate another word, such as *text*.

After you enter a search command, press ENTER to let the editor know you have entered all of the target. The cursor moves to the target text, and you are still in command mode.

Finding Other Instances of the Target

If a string of characters appears more than once in your file, the forward search command moves the cursor to the first instance of the target string in the file after the cursor location. You can go on to other instances of the target.

1. Search for the word *the* in your *practice* file:

    /the

2. Once you've located the first occurrence of the word, locate the next occurrence by entering:

   n

3. Keep typing the <u>n</u>ext command:

   n

   n

   When the editor reaches the end of the file, it loops back to the beginning of the file and continues the search.

4. Move the cursor to the next colon by entering:

   /:

   and press ENTER

5. To move to others, press a series of <u>n</u>ext commands:

   n

We must be in command mode to search for text characters. When we enter */targetstring* and press ENTER, the cursor moves forward through the text to the next occurrence of *targetstring*. If the editor reaches the end of the file, it goes back to the beginning and searches forward until it either locates the target or returns to your previous location. To go to the next occurrence, use the **n** command without pressing ENTER.

Quitting the Editor

At this point, you are editing the file *practice* with **vi**. A single command instructs the editor to write the file back to the hard drive and quit the editor program.

1. Enter:

   :wq

   This instructs the editor to <u>w</u>rite the file and <u>q</u>uit the editor. The shell prompt is displayed.

2. Confirm you are again communicating with the shell:

   date

   ls

3. Return to editing the file by entering:

   vi *practice*

Conceptualizing the Visual Editor in Command Mode

The conceptual maps included in this chapter are designed to assist you in learning and reviewing the **vi** commands. Figure 4-1 is the conceptual map of **vi**'s command mode.

1. In Figure 4-1, locate the box marked "Shell," with the $ prompts. Notice the arrow that leads from the **who** in the shell to the box describing what the **who** command does. When **who** completes its task, you are returned to the shell.

2. Find the arrow leading down from the shell command **vi** *filename*. When you used the **vi** command earlier, you entered *practice* as the filename.

3. The conceptual map describes everyone's experience using **vi**. When we are in the shell and type the command **vi** *filename*, we are instructing the shell to start **vi** and give it one argument.

4. One of the first things **vi** does is to interpret the argument as the name of a file. Then **vi** opens the file and puts us in command mode, where we can move around and examine the file.

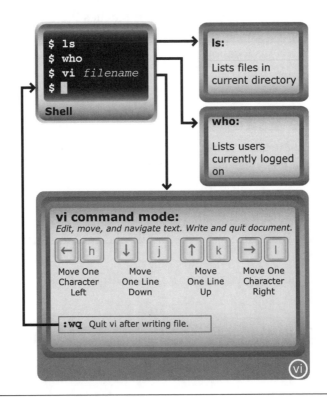

FIGURE 4-1   The command mode of **vi**

5. At this point, because we are in the command mode of **vi**, the shell is no longer interpreting the commands we type—the visual editor is. When we press a direction key, the editor moves the cursor and then waits for the next command. We can type one cursor movement command after another without ever leaving command mode.

6. Find the arrows and direction key commands in Figure 4-1. These commands do not move the editor into another mode and do not require that we press ENTER. When we issue these commands, they take effect immediately, moving the cursor around the file.

Deleting Text in Command Mode

So far, you have been in the visual editor's command mode moving around the file by issuing commands. Another important class of editing operations, available only from command mode, removes text from a file. With **vi** you can remove one or more lines, words, or characters, as well as parts of lines or whole sections of text.

Removing Whole Lines

You can easily delete one or more lines in a file with the editor.

1. Use an arrow key to move the cursor to a character near the middle of any line.

2. Type the "delete a line" command:

> **dd**

You do not press ENTER. As soon as you type the second *d* of the "delete a line" command, **vi** does what you request and **dd**eletes the line.

3. Move to another line and delete it.

When we enter **dd**, the editor deletes all of the line where the cursor is located, regardless of where the cursor happens to be on the line. We can delete blank lines, as well as text lines with the **dd** command.

4. Move the cursor to a blank line and delete it.

The **dd** command tells the editor to delete the current line. After deletion, we remain in command mode.

Deleting Individual Characters

The editor also deletes a single character from a file.

1. Move your cursor to any character, such as the *H* in the word *Hello*.

2. Delete one character by entering a lowercase:

x

The **x** (x-out) command deletes only the single character under the cursor. It is the "delete one character at a time" command.

3. Move to different locations in the file and delete individual characters.

4. Use the **x** to delete a space from the file.

Spaces between words on a line are characters just like letters or numbers. Carefully review Figure 4-2, which summarizes both navigating and deleting.

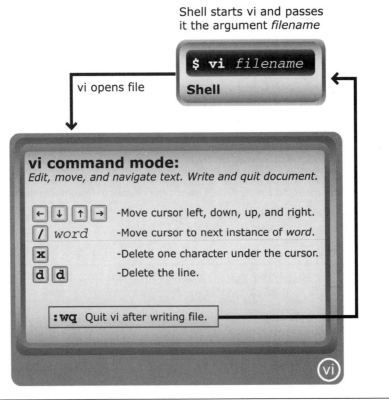

FIGURE 4-2   Navigating and deleting in **vi**

Undoing Text Changes

1. Delete a whole line of text by entering:

dd

2. To bring back the line you just removed, type:

u

The **u**ndo command goes back one change.

3. Delete a character with **x**.

4. Bring it back with:

u

After you make an alteration to the file, you can undo the change. The undo feature is quite powerful, and we will return to it after completing this tour of **vi**.

Adding Text to the File

Thus far, you have been moving around and deleting text from the file. These tasks are done from the command mode of **vi**. You have not yet added text. There are several ways to add text, including adding new text on either side of the cursor, opening a line below the cursor, opening a line above the cursor, adding text to the beginning or end of the line, and performing a whole host of text substitution operations.

However, in this tour, we will examine only two operations: how to add text after the cursor and in a line below the cursor.

Appending Text to the Right of the Cursor

You have been instructing the editor to move the cursor around the file by issuing specific commands in command mode. Pressing **dd** on the keyboard does not add *dd* as text to the file. To add text, we must tell the editor to leave command mode and go to *append* or *insert* mode.

You are presently in the command mode, where the keys are used to issue position-change and delete commands, not to enter text.

1. Move the cursor to any line on the screen, and delete the line by typing:

dd

The **dd** tells the editor to *delete one line* when you are in the **vi** command mode.

2. Enter the command mode request to undo the deletion:

u

Use the direction keys or arrows to move the cursor to the end of the first line in the file.

3. In command mode, type the following command one time:

   a

The letter *a* is not displayed on the screen; nothing appears to happen.

4. Now again type:

   dd

The letters *dd* appear on the screen and are added to the file; the line is not deleted. The **a** command tells **vi** to start adding everything you type to the file. It places the new text in the file starting on the right of the present cursor location.

At this point, **vi** no longer interprets what you type as commands, but rather as text to add (append or insert) to the file. You left command mode and are now in the editor's *append mode* or *insert mode*. What you type while in append mode is seen as text, not commands.

5. Now that you are in append mode, press:

   ENTER

The cursor moves to the beginning of a new line where you can add text.

6. Type the following into your file:

```
I am now adding more text.
Therefore, I must be in append mode.
The a command moves me into append mode.
Whatever I type is added to the file.
```

7. Examine the conceptual map in Figure 4-3. Note that the **a** command takes you out of command mode and puts you into append or insert mode. **vi** no longer interprets whatever you type as a delete or move-around command; instead **vi** reads what you type and enters it into the file starting at the right of the cursor.

Leaving Append Mode and Returning to Command Mode

In the preceding exercises, you were in command mode and issued specific commands to move the cursor around the file. In command mode, we use the keyboard to enter editing commands, such as **h, j, k, l,** and **dd.** Those keys are not text to be added; rather, they are commands to the editor. One of those commands, **a,** tells the editor to leave **vi**'s command mode and enter append mode. Once we are in append mode, the editor interprets whatever we type as text to add to the file at the cursor location.

As long as we are in append mode, every key we type continues to be appended to the text. We are not returned to command mode until we say so.

When you finish typing text, you need a way to instruct the **vi** editor to move out of append mode and back to command mode.

1. Take a look at Figure 4-3. Locate the arrow that moves you from append mode back to command mode. The command is on the arrow.

2. Enter the appropriate key:

    ESC

Nothing appears to be different on the screen.

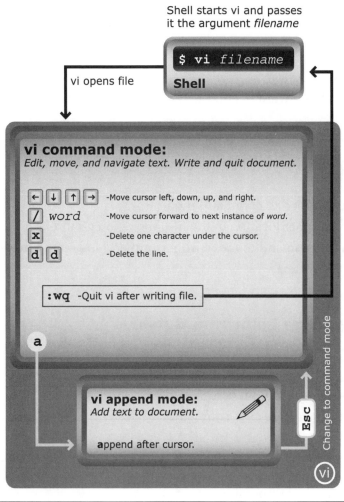

FIGURE 4-3 Adding text in **vi**

3. Enter:

   dd

   u

   A line is deleted; **dd** is now a command, not text to be added. You are again in command mode. **vi** now interprets whatever keys you enter as commands to move around in the file, delete text, and so forth. Whenever you want to quit adding text and return to command mode, press ESC.

4. To confirm that you are in command mode, press ESC a second time.

   If a beep sounds or the screen flashes, **vi** is telling you that it cannot move to command mode because you are already there.

5. Move the cursor to the end of any word on the screen by entering:

   l

   or

   → (RIGHT ARROW)

6. Tell **vi** that you want to enter text after the word, by entering:

   a

7. Add several words of text to the file.

8. When you have finished adding text, press:

   ESC

   You are returned to command mode.

9. Move to another location in the file, and again go through the cycle:

   A. Issue a command to move from command to append mode.

   B. Add some text.

   C. Return to command mode.

Opening a Line below the Cursor

We can also use the editor to add text after a line.

1. Make sure you are in command mode, and then move the cursor to a line near the middle of your screen.

2. Type the lowercase "*oh*" command:

   o

   The **o** command tells the editor to <u>o</u>pen a new blank line between the cursor line and the next line in your file.

3. Add text such as this:

```
There is more than one way to move from
command mode to append!
Each one starts adding text in a different place
with respect to the cursor.
```

4. Return to command mode by pressing:

ESC

> **N O T E :**   ESC is an essential component of the visual editor. Whenever you are in doubt about where you are in **vi**—command or append mode—press ESC. In append mode, ESC moves you to command mode. In command mode, ESC usually produces a beep or flash, indicating that you are already in command mode. In either case, after you press ESC, you are certain to be in command mode. From this point, you can decide what you want to do.

Ending an Editing Session

When we are ready to stop editing a file, we need to do two things: save changes that we made to the file, and quit the editor program.

Saving the File and Quitting the Editor

To issue commands to save the modified file and quit the editor, we must first be in command mode. Make certain you are by first pressing:

1. ESC

You have been editing a copy of your *practice* file, called a *buffer copy*. The original file is on the disk. This buffer copy is in memory where you make changes.

2. To both write the changes back to the original file and quit the editor, enter:

:wq

and press ENTER.

The file's buffer copy is <u>w</u>ritten (saved), replacing the original version, and the editor <u>q</u>uits. You are back communicating with the shell. See Figure 4-4.

3. Issue a shell command such as:

date

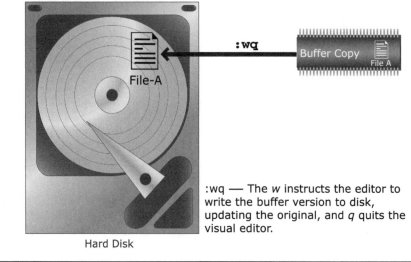

:wq — The *w* instructs the editor to write the buffer version to disk, updating the original, and *q* quits the visual editor.

Hard Disk

FIGURE 4-4 Saving a file and quitting the editor

Quitting without Saving

In this exercise, you will make changes to a file and then quit the editor without saving the changes.

1. Start editing the *practice* file by entering:

     vi *practice*

2. From command mode, delete a line of text:

     dd

3. Open a line and go into append or insert mode by entering:

     o

4. Add the following line:

     ```
     this line added to practice xxxx
     ```

5. Return to command mode:

     ESC

6. This time, attempt to quit the editor without saving the file by entering:

     :q

   The editor informs you that you have not decided the fate of the changes you made to the file:

   ```
   No write since last change.
   ```

7. Tell the editor that you want to quit without writing:

:q!

The **!** after the **q**uit command tells the editor that you know that you made changes, but that you really want to quit regardless.

8. Examine the file:

head *practice*

The line you deleted is not gone, and the line you added while editing the file is not there. The file is exactly as it was before your last editing. The **:q!** command instructs the editor to **q**uit even though there has been no write since you made a change, preserving the file as it was when you started editing it. See Figure 4-5.

Creating a New File with the Visual Editor

This last section of the tour of **vi** guides you through using the skills you have just explored to create a new file and add text.

1. Begin the editing process by entering:

vi *review*

The editor starts and a new file is opened for editing.

2. Instruct the editor that you want to go straight to the append mode to add text:

a

3. Add some text, such as your answer to the question, "What are the two modes of the visual editor, and what can be accomplished in each?"

practice

Hard Disk

:q!

:q! — Quits editor without writing to disk, the original is not updated, and the buffer is cleared.

FIGURE 4-5   Quitting the editor without saving changes

4. Write a very brief description of all the **vi** commands you can remember.

5. Inform **vi** that you want to leave append mode and return to command mode:

   ESC

6. Write the file and quit the editor:

   :wq

7. Examine the new file with:

   more *review*

And that is how we create a new file of text, commands, programs, or whatever.

- We instruct the shell to start **vi** and pass it one argument, the name we want to give to the new file.
- When the editor starts, we are in command mode.
- Using the **a** command, we tell the editor that we want to append text.
- Then, in append mode, we add text.
- When finished, we press ESC to return to command mode.
- We then enter **:wq** to write the file, quit the editor, and return to the shell.

Adding to a File

You just created a new file named *review* and added text. You can also add more text to the file.

1. Go through the steps needed to use **vi** to start editing *review*, then move the cursor to the last line in the file and add another line of text.

2. Return to command mode, write the file, and quit the editor.

Reading a File into the Editor

Often when we are editing a file, we realize that a section of code or an explanation is an existing file. How can we just read the other file into the currently edited one? Throughout this chapter, you have been editing the *practice* file.

1. Open *practice* again by entering:

   vi *practice*

2. With the down arrow, move to a line part way through the file.

   In the last exercise, you created a new file named *review,* which is listed in the current directory.

3. Read the *review* file into the current practice file by entering:

:**r** *review*

The :**r** or the :**read** command locates a file and reads its contents into the current file starting immediately after the cursor line.

Self Test 1

Examine the conceptual map in Figure 4-1, and then answer the following questions.

1. What command allows you to move the cursor one character to the left?

_____

2. What command allows you to move the cursor one line up?

_____

3. In what mode must you be to move around a file?

_____

4. In what mode must you be to issue the **dd** command?

_____

5. What command takes the cursor forward to the word *Admin*?

_____

6. What command takes the cursor forward to the next occurrence of the word *Admin*?

_____

7. What command deletes the current line of text?

_____

8. What command deletes a single character under the cursor?

_____

9. Where must you position the cursor to delete a line of text?

_____

10. What command reverses the change you made?

_____

11. What command do you type to add text to the right of the cursor?

_____

12. What command opens a line below the cursor?

_____

13. In what mode must you be to enter text into the file?

_____

14. What command tells the editor to take you back to command mode from append mode?

_____

15. What command do you type to leave **vi** without saving the changes to a file?

_____

16. What command instructs **vi** to save changes and return you to the shell?

_____

17. In what mode must you be to save the changes you made into the file and quit the editor?

_____

4.4 Quickly Moving around in a File

In the **vi** tour you just completed, you moved around the file, deleted text, and added text using just a few commands. You mastered enough of the editor to survive. Now the goal is to become proficient. The following sections of this chapter look in detail at all the components of editing. In the exercises you will move around in the file, delete, add, and change text as well as modify the editing environment.

Although you can edit files using the limited set of commands introduced thus far, the commands that populate the remainder of the chapter, once mastered, will greatly increase your speed and power.

Augmenting the Direction Keys

You have been moving through the file one character or one line at a time. You can go faster than this. The number keys (1 through 9) located at the top of your keyboard or in the keypad to the right can be used as part of the direction key commands. Try the following:

1. Begin editing the _practice_ file again by entering:

    vi _practice_

2. To have the cursor move four lines down, type:

    4

    and then immediately press either ↓ or **j** without pressing ENTER.

    By preceding the down direction key or down arrow with a **4**, you instruct **vi** to move the cursor down four lines.

3. Move around the screen using augmented direction commands such as these:

    2 ↑
    6 →
    3 ←
    4 ↓
    3 j
    2 h
    3 k
    3 l

The arrow keys and the **h**, **j**, **k**, and **l** direction keys—either alone or in conjunction with number keys—make it possible to move the cursor to any character in the file. As you will see, there are more efficient ways to move the cursor long distances.

Going to Lines Using Their Numbers

The editor keeps track of the lines in a file by numbering them, starting with line 1.

1. Request that the editor display the line numbers on the screen by entering the command:

    :set *number*

    and then press ENTER.

    The colon and ENTER are essential.

    The lines of text now have numbers displayed down the left of the screen. They are just part of the display, and are not actually added to the file.

2. Instruct the editor to turn off the numbers by entering:

    :set *nonumber*

3. The next few exercises are best accomplished while line numbers are present. Turn them back on:

    :set *number*

4. Tell the editor to go to specific lines in the file by entering:

5G

G

1G

:8   ENTER

:15   ENTER

:$ ENTER

The editor interprets a command such as **5G** as instruction to move the cursor to the fifth line. Likewise, *:8* is instruction to move the cursor to line 8. The commands **G** and **:$** are instructions to go to the last line of the file.

You have been entering some commands that start with colons such as *:8* and others that do not start with a colon such as the **G**. Some take effect immediately, whereas others wait until we press ENTER.

> **N O T E :** No **vi** command that starts with a: takes effect until you press the ENTER key. The other **vi** commands that do not start with a colon usually take effect immediately; you do not press ENTER.

Finding Target Characters in a File

You have seen how the forward search command finds the target that you specify.

1. For instance, enter:

/it

Any words in your file that are like the following are located: *with, editing, it, editor,* and *quitting.* If the target is a word or inside another word, it is located. The search command locates *target strings of characters.*

We can also use the power of the forward search command to locate a string consisting of several words.

2. Look at your file displayed on the screen and locate two words on a line such as *several times.*

3. Try a command similar to the following to search for the two words you selected:

/several times

A blank space is a character and can be included in a search string.

Searching in Both Directions

We can instruct the editor to search both forward and backward through the text to locate instances of a target word or character string. We can even change the direction of a search while we run it.

1. Place your cursor in the middle of the file, using a command such as:

   15 ↓

   or

   15 j

2. Search forward through the file for the letter *e* by entering:

   /e

   n

   n

3. Search backward through the file by entering:

   ?*e*

   The cursor goes to the previous *e*.

4. Continue the search by pressing each of the following:

   n
   n
   N
   n
   n
   N
   n

The lowercase **n** takes you to the next instance of the target in the current direction. The uppercase **N** reverses the search direction.

The slash (**/**) is used to instruct the editor to search forward for a target string; the question mark (**?**) is used to search backward. Regardless of which direction you are searching, you can move to the next occurrence of the word in the same direction using the **n** command and reverse the search direction with a capital **N**.

Ignoring Case in a Search

The search mechanism in **vi** is case-sensitive. If we ask to look for *movies,* it does not locate any instances of *Movies.* Fortunately, we can instruct the editor to ignore case.

1. In the command mode of the editor, enter:

   :set ignorecase

   Nothing appears to happen. However, you just instructed the editor to modify how it behaves.

2. Look for a word that is both capitalized and not:

   /the

   This search locates both the targets in a sentence in lowercase and the targets at the beginning of the sentence with an initial capital letter.

3. Perform a search with mixed case:

   /SeVerAl

   The search ignores case.

4. To see what environmental features are currently set, enter:

   :set

5. After examining them, press ENTER to continue.

Moving the Cursor in Word Increments

So far, you have used the **h, j, k,** and **l** keys or the arrow keys to move the cursor individual characters or lines. You can also move the cursor through the text a word at a time, either forward or backward.

Moving Forward and Backward Word by Word

1. In the file *practice,* use the */* command to position the cursor to any word in one of the first few lines of text.

2. Type the following lowercase command:

   w

   The cursor advances to the beginning of the next word. When we are in command mode, the **w** simply instructs the editor to move ahead one word.

3. Type the **w** command several more times.

   With each **w**, the cursor advances forward to the *beginning* of the next word. The visual editor can also move the cursor to the end of a word and backward to previous words.

4. Enter each of the following commands:

   w
   w
   e
   e
   b
   b

(Could this be the origin of the world wide web?) These three commands instruct the editor to move to the next <u>w</u>ord, to the <u>e</u>nd of the word, and <u>b</u>ack one word. We do not press ENTER, and the commands take effect immediately.

Moving Multiple Words

You can augment all of these cursor-moving commands to move through several words at a time.

⮑▸   Try each of the following:

3b
2e
3w
4b

Figure 4-6 summarizes these commands.

Specifying Locations on the Current Line

We can move the cursor to specific places on the current line, including the end, beginning, or any character or position on the line.

Moving to the End or Beginning of a Line

⮑▸ 1. Move the cursor to the beginning of a line that has a lot of text.

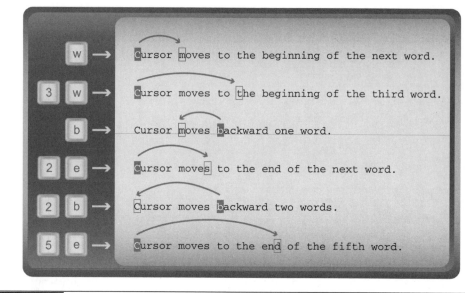

FIGURE 4-6 Moving the cursor in **vi**

2. Enter each of the following without pressing ENTER:

$

^

$

0   (zero)

The dollar sign (**$**) instructs the editor to move the cursor to the end of the current line. Both the caret (**^**) and the zero (**0**) move the cursor to the beginning of the line. The **:$** is interpreted as the last line of a file. The **$** without a colon is the end of the current line.

Moving to a Specific Textual Character or Numbered Position

We can also move the cursor to any character on the line, no matter where it is.

1. Move the cursor to the beginning of a line such as the one starting with *Each*:

   /Each

2. Select a character on the line such as the *x* in te*x*t, and use the character you chose as the *x* in the following:

   f*x*

   The cursor moves to the first *x* on the line.

3. Press ENTER or use the arrow keys until you are on another line with a lot of text.

4. Move the cursor one word by entering:

   w

5. Visually examine the line and select a character that is on the right of the cursor on the current line. Replace the *y* in the following command with the character you chose:

   f*y*

   The cursor moves to the selected character on the line.

   The editor interprets the character immediately following the **f** command as the target character. It moves the cursor to the first character that matches the target to the right of the cursor on the current line.

   We can use the **f** command from anywhere on a line.

6. Move the cursor back to the beginning of the line:

   ^

   With the **f** command, we specify the target by identifying a specific character on the line. We can also specify a location on the current line by counting a specified number of characters from the beginning.

7. Tell the editor to go to a specific character position on the line:

   5|

   The cursor moves to whatever character is the fifth character on the line.

8. Move the cursor to the 15th character on the line:

   15|

9. Move the cursor left:

   7|

   The pipe is instruction to go to a specific character position, which can be left or right of the current position. Figure 4-7 summarizes these commands.

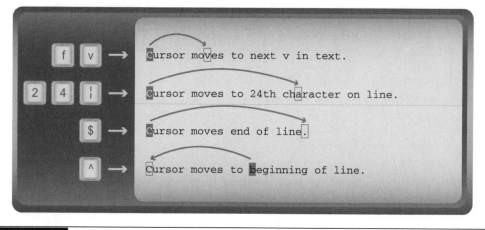

FIGURE 4-7   Moving the cursor in **vi**

Moving to Locations on the Current Screen Display

In previous exercises, you moved the cursor to lines specified by the content with */target* or the line of a particular number in the file using commands such as *30G*. The following exercise instructs the editor to move the cursor to lines that happen to be at locations on the display, such as the topmost line on the screen.

1. Enter (capital letters):

   M

   L

   H

2. Move to the end of the file:

   G

3. Try the screen location commands again:

   L

   M

   H

4. The cursor moves to whatever line is currently at the specific locations on the display. Figure 4-8 shows how the cursor moves, and Table 4-1 describes the cursor-movement commands.

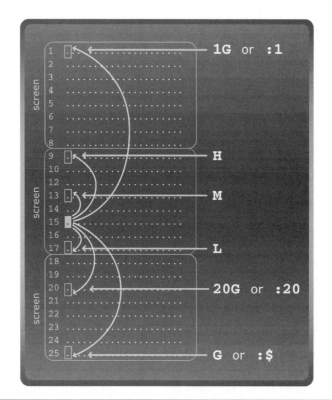

FIGURE 4-8 Moving the cursor by line address and location display

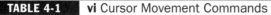

Returning to the Last Cursor Position

Often while editing, we need to move to a distant location in the file to check on some specific concern or perform an editing task, and once the task is completed, we need to return to the initial location and continue editing there.

1. Before you move the cursor, mentally note the line number where the cursor is currently located.

COMMAND	MOVEMENT
L	Positions the cursor at the lowest line displayed on the screen.
M	Positions the cursor at the line near the midpoint of the screen.
H	Positions the cursor at the highest line on the screen.

TABLE 4-1 **vi** Cursor Movement Commands

2. Reposition the cursor to some distant line that you might want to see. For example, move the cursor to the last line of the file by typing the command:

   G

3. At this location, add a line of text:

   o

4. Return to command mode:

   ESC

5. In command mode, type two *single* quotation marks (not double quotation marks):

   ' '

You just entered the secret passage. The two single quotation marks instruct the editor to return to the previous location in a file, no matter where it is, and even though you have made changes to the file at the new location.

Moving through a File One Screen at a Time

The cursor movement commands like */word* or **17G** relocate the cursor to a new character, word, or line in the file, and if that location is not currently displayed, the screen display follows along. These commands are line- and text-oriented, not display-oriented. The screen must display the current cursor location. When we move the cursor, the display comes along. We can also move the display forward or backward in the file, forcing the cursor to follow along.

1. From command mode, press:

   CTRL-F

   This time the screen moves forward to the next half-screen of text, and the cursor comes along for the ride. The commands described in the following table are used to adjust the workstation's screen display and to move forward or backward to a different block or section of text, regardless of its context. There are two commands for moving in each direction.

2. Read through these display adjustment commands.

DISPLAY ADJUSTMENT COMMAND	FUNCTION
CTRL-D	Scrolls down one-half screen of text in the file.
CTRL-U	Scrolls up one-half screen of text in the file.
CTRL-F	Displays the next screen of text in a file.
CTRL-B	Displays the previous screen of text in a file.

3. Try each of these commands several times.

The square in the center of the following illustration (over the letter *c* in *certain*) is the cursor. To move the cursor to the top-left (to the *T* in *This*), you type the uppercase command **H**. In the following illustration, the arrows connecting the cursor to the various destinations have the command key printed next to them.

The commands in this section of the chapter examine two kinds of "move around the file" functions:

- *Cursor-positioning commands* move the cursor to a particular designated position in your file. When the cursor moves, the screen display has to compensate.

- *Display-adjusting commands* move the screen display forward or backward in the file relative to the cursor's current position and display a new section of text. The cursor has to follow along.

4. Review the table in Figrue 4-9. Practice each command again several times, making sure to note the position of the cursor before and after you perform each command.

Cursor Positioning Command	Function
0 (zero)	Moves cursor to the beginning of the current line.
^	Moves cursor to the beginning of the current line.
$	Moves cursor to the end of the line.
nnG	Moves cursor to line nn, where nn is the line number.
G	Moves cursor to the beginning of the last line in your file.
-	Moves the cursor to the beginning of the prior line.
+	Positions cursor at the beginning of the next line.
nn|	Positions cursor at column nn of current line, where nn is the column number.
/abc	Moves cursor to the next occurrence of string abc in text.
L	Positions cursor at lowest line displayed on the screen.
M	Positions cursor at line near midpoint of the screen.
H	Positions cursor at highest line on the screen.
fx	Moves cursor forward on the line to next x, where x is a specified character.
n	Moves to the next pattern identified in a previously issued /word or ?word.
''	Returns cursor to the last line cursor was located on.
b	Moves the cursor to the beginning of the previous word.
w	Moves cursor to the beginning of the next word.
e	Moves cursor to the end of the current word.
h	Moves cursor left one character.
j	Moves cursor down one character.
k	Moves cursor up one character.
l	Moves cursor right one character.

FIGURE 4-9 Cursor positioning commands

4.5 Adding Text to a File

When we tell the editor that we want to start adding text, the specific command we enter determines where, relative to the cursor, the text is added to the file.

Inserting Text Before and After the Cursor

In the **vi** tour, you used the **a** command to add text to the *right* of the cursor. Another command is used to insert text to the *left* of the cursor.

   1. In command mode, move the cursor to the beginning of a word of text on the screen.

   2. Type the <u>i</u>nsert command:

       i

   3. Type the following text, and note that the existing text moves to the right as you type:

```
The difference between the
i and a commands does not seem to be very
obvious.
```

The <u>i</u>nsert command starts adding text to the left of the cursor.

   4. Return to command mode by pressing:

       ESC

Comparing the *a* and *i* Commands

Both the **a** and **i** commands instruct the editor to add text at the cursor position. The next exercise explicitly demonstrates the difference between the two commands.

   1. With the arrows, place the cursor at the beginning of a line that already has some text.

   2. Now enter the <u>a</u>ppend command:

       a

   3. Press the SPACEBAR four times to add four spaces

The first character in the line, the one that the cursor was over when you entered the **a** command, remains at the beginning of the line. The added spaces are appended to the right of the cursor location, after the first character on the line. The **a** is the **a***ppend to right of the cursor* command.

4. Press ESC to return to command mode.

5. Press ENTER to move the cursor to the beginning of the next line of the file that has some text.

6. Type the insert command:

   i

7. Again press SPACEBAR four times.
   The text is inserted at the beginning of the line. The **i** is the *insert to the left of the cursor* command.

8. Return to command mode by pressing:

   ESC

9. Move the cursor to the space between two words and try both the **a** and **i** commands.

The **a** and **i** commands move you from command mode to append mode. Every character you type after the **i** command is added as text to the file, starting to the left of the cursor. With the **a** command, text is added to the right of the cursor position.

Opening a Line above the Cursor

In addition to opening lines below the cursor with lowercase **o**, you can open a new line above the cursor.

1. Move the cursor to any location in a line of text.

2. Enter the following (capital *Oh*) command:

   O

   The **O** command is instruction to **O**pen a line above the line where the cursor resides and shift to append/insert mode.

3. Add some text, such as this:

   ```
   It is essential to be able to place
   text above the current line,
   especially when I want to enter text
   before the first line in a file.
   ```

4. Tell the editor to return to command mode by pressing:

   ESC

5. Move to the first line in your file by entering:

   1G

6. Enter the appropriate command to add some text above the first line:

   O

7. Add some text.

   As with the other commands that put you in append/insert mode, you can continue typing as many lines as you wish. You are not limited to that one line.

8. Tell **vi** to return to command mode by pressing:

   ESC

9. Save the file as it is now written and return to the shell by typing:

   :wq

Inserting Text at the Beginning of a Line

When we need to add text to the beginning or end of a line, the cursor may be located at a word in the middle of the line. Rather than overwork the arrow keys, we can issue specific text-adding commands that move the cursor directly to either end of the line and start adding text.

1. Return to editing the file *practice* by entering:

   vi *practice*

2. Move the cursor to the middle of any line of text in your file:

   5w

3. Type the uppercase command:

   I

   The cursor moves to the beginning of the line. You are now in append/insert mode, and anything you type is Inserted before the first character of the original line.

4. Add some text, such as this:

   ```
   I was in the middle of a line,
   now I am adding text to the beginning.
   ```

5. Leave append/insert mode and return to command mode by pressing:

   ESC

The **I** command instructs the editor to move the cursor to the beginning of the line and to change to append mode. Every character you type is <u>I</u>nserted as additional text until you press ESC.

Appending Text at the End of a Line

No matter where the cursor is initially located on a line, you can instruct the editor to start adding text to the end of the line.

1. In command mode, move the cursor to a line containing text, and type the uppercase command:

   A

   The cursor moves to the end of the line, and the editor is now in append mode.

2. Add some text, such as the following:

   ```
   Adding text to the end of a line
   is easy with the A command.
   ```

3. Return to command mode with ESC.

All append commands move you into append mode until ESC is pressed. The various append commands differ only in where text is added to the file, relative to the cursor. The following illustration identifies where on the line the text is added with each command.

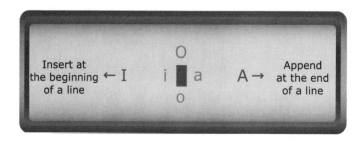

4.6 Avoiding Confusion Entering Commands to Shell and vi

So far, you have issued commands to three different command interpreters: the shell, the visual editor command mode, and the append mode. Each command interpreter acts on commands in a different way.

Giving Instructions to the Shell

To give instructions to the shell:

⮑ 1. Exit the editing session by entering:

> **:wq**

You are back communicating with the shell.

2. From the shell, type:

> **who**

A listing of users currently logged on appears on your screen. To the shell, the three characters **w**, **h**, and **o** are interpreted as "Locate and execute the utility named **who**." The **who** utility determines who is logged on and formats a report that is output, in this case, to your screen.

3. Leave the shell, and call up the editor to work on the file *practice* that you have been using in this chapter by entering:

> **vi** *practice*

You are now in the command mode of the visual editor, editing a file.

Giving the Same Instruction to the Command Mode

To give the same instruction to the command mode:

⮑ Place the cursor at the beginning of a word in the text, and type the following three characters:

> **w**
>
> **h**
>
> **o**

As you can see, the characters **w**, **h**, and **o** have a very different meaning in the visual editor command mode:

- The **w** says move to the right one word.
- The **h** says move the cursor back one space.
- The **o** says open a line below the current line and enter append mode.

You are now in the append mode of the editor.

Providing the Same Instruction for the Append Mode

⮑ 1. To complete the comparison, type the same three characters again.

This time, in append mode, the effect of typing **w**, **h**, and **o** is that three letters are added to the file.

2. Return to command mode:

   ESC

Comparing the Command Interpreters

The distinction between the two modes within the **vi** editor is a critical one. Whenever we tell the shell to start the **vi** editor, it opens the file and we are *always* placed in command mode. In this mode, **vi** understands and acts upon whatever we type as a set of specific commands. Keystrokes result in moving the cursor, deleting text, shifting into append mode, or terminating **vi** and therefore returning to the shell.

After we enter a command to go to append mode (such as **a** or **o**), the editor starts treating every character you type as input to the file. Once in append mode, the editor places virtually every character we type in the file as text and displays it on the screen. We remain in append mode until we press ESC. If we are on a UNIX system and in the append mode of **vi**, when we press an arrow key, the control characters for the arrow key are added to the file. On Linux in the append mode of the **vi** editor, **vim**, we can use the arrow keys to move the cursor around. The control characters are not added to the file.

Pressing ESC is the only way to return to command mode, regardless of which command we previously used to enter append mode. ESC is always the way back to command mode.

4.7 Deleting Text from a File

In the tour of the editor, you deleted whole lines with **dd** and single characters with **x**. Essentially, you can specify and delete any portions of a file with the commands explored in this section.

Deleting Several Objects

Like the direction keys, the various delete commands can be prefaced with a number to delete more than one object at the same time.

Deleting Multiple Lines

⤷ **1.** Move to the top of your file and issue the command:

 2dd

 The cursor line and the one following it are deleted.

 2. Undo the deletion:

 u

 3. Move to another location and issue:

 4dd

 u

 4. Go to the last line in your file:

 G

 5. Attempt to delete text with the command:

 3dd

In this case, nothing is deleted, because you are requesting **vi** to remove more lines than are available to delete.

Deleting Multiple Characters

In the tour of **vi**, you deleted individual characters using the **x** command.

⤷ Move to the beginning of a line containing text and enter:

 x
 5x

The x command is instruction to delete one character. When we put a number in front of the x, the editor deletes that number of characters.

Deleting Multiple Words

We can also instruct the editor to move one word or several words, and also to delete one or several words.

⤷ Enter:

 w
 3w
 d3w

We can tell the editor to delete multiple lines, words, or characters.

Deleting the Remainder of a Line

The visual editor does not limit us to deletion of whole lines; we can delete the rest of a line.

1. Move the cursor to the middle of a long line in the *practice* file, and type the following uppercase command:

   D

   This uppercase **D** is instruction to <u>D</u>elete the remainder of the line, starting with the character under the cursor.

2. Move to the middle of another line and delete the remainder by entering:

   D

Deleting All Text up to a Specific Character on a Line

Previously, you moved the cursor to a selected character on a line by issuing **f?**, where *?* was the character on the line that you wanted to be the new cursor location.

1. Select a line of text in your file, and place the cursor at the beginning of the line.

2. Identify a character on the line to the right of the cursor such as an *e* in a word like *the*.

3. Enter:

   f*e*

   where *e* is the target character you chose. As soon as you press the target character, the cursor moves to the first instance of the character on the line.

4. Move the cursor back to the beginning of the line by entering:

   ^

5. Now enter:

   df*e*

   Again replace the *e* with the target character you chose on the line.

   The text from the cursor to the selected character is deleted.

6. Bring the text back with <u>u</u>ndo:

   u

7. Go to another long line in the text.

8. Move right one word by entering:

    w

9. Select a character on the current line to the right of the cursor and use it in place of the *x* in the following:

    df*x*

The text from the cursor to the target character is deleted. The following table summarizes these commands:

f*x*	Move the cursor to the first character *x* on the current line to the right of the cursor.
df*x*	Delete text from the cursor to the first character *x* on the current line to the right of the cursor.

The commands used thus far are summarized in Figure 4-10. As you examine this figure, pay particular attention to the modes, which commands are executed in each mode, and how to change from one mode to another.

Deleting Lines Using Line Number Addresses

In the editor tour, you moved the cursor to specific lines. You can also enter commands such as *6G* or *51G* or *G* to move to line 6, line 51, or the end of a file. In the section on moving around in a file, you moved the cursor to specific lines using editor line commands such as *:6*, *:51*, or *:$*, which tell the editor to move the cursor to lines 6, 51, or the end of the file, respectively.

Once a line is addressed, we can take other actions.

1. Enter:

    :5d

    The fifth line is identified and deleted.

2. Undo the deletion by entering:

    u

3. Delete another line using the line address and the delete command; then undo the deletion:

    :15d

    u

There are numerous ways to delete blocks of text in a file.

Shell starts vi and passes it the argument *filename*

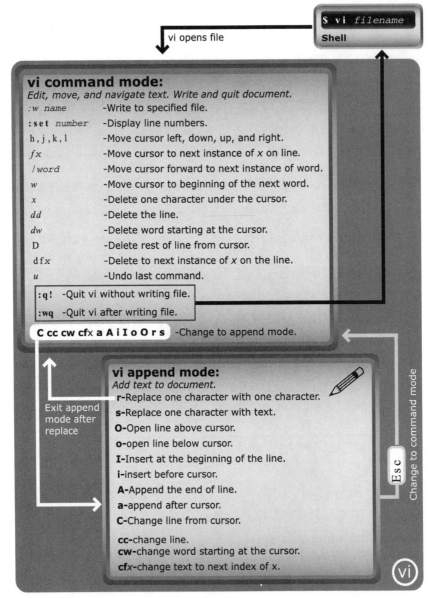

vi opens file

`$ vi filename`

Shell

vi command mode:
Edit, move, and navigate text. Write and quit document.

`:w name`	-Write to specified file.
`:set number`	-Display line numbers.
`h,j,k,l`	-Move cursor left, down, up, and right.
`fx`	-Move cursor to next instance of *x* on line.
`/word`	-Move cursor forward to next instance of word.
`w`	-Move cursor to beginning of the next word.
`x`	-Delete one character under the cursor.
`dd`	-Delete the line.
`dw`	-Delete word starting at the cursor.
`D`	-Delete rest of line from cursor.
`dfx`	-Delete to next instance of *x* on the line.
`u`	-Undo last command.

`:q!` -Quit vi without writing file.

`:wq` -Quit vi after writing file.

`C cc cw cfx a A i I o O r s` -Change to append mode.

vi append mode:
Add text to document.

r-Replace one character with one character.

s-Replace one character with text.

O-Open line above cursor.

o-open line below cursor.

I-Insert at the beginning of the line.

i-insert before cursor.

A-Append the end of line.

a-append after cursor.

C-Change line from cursor.

cc-change line.
cw-change word starting at the cursor.
cfx-change text to next index of x.

Exit append mode after replace

`Esc`

Change to command mode

FIGURE 4-10 Command summary

4. Delete the first eight lines of your file and then undo the deletion:

   1G

   8dd

   u

5. Or, regardless of the location of the cursor, you can type:

   12G

   :1,8d

   u

   This command instructs the editor to find lines 1 through 8 and delete them. The comma is used to indicate a range of lines, from the line whose number is on the left of the comma to and including the line on the right. See the graphical description of deleting text with the colons in Figure 4-11.

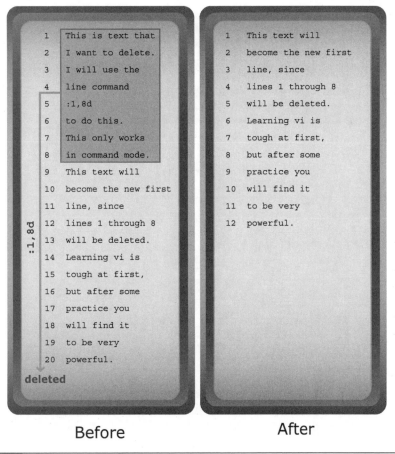

Before   After

FIGURE 4-11 Using numbers to delete text

6. Because the editor interprets the **:$** as the line at the end of the file, you can empty the file:

   :1, **$d**

7. Quickly **u**ndo the deleting of all lines:

   u

The commands that employ the line addresses, such as **:4** and **9d**, begin with a colon and require that you press ENTER to start them. Command mode instructions such as **u** or **4dd** are not preceded with a colon and occur automatically without pressing ENTER. Figure 4-12 summarizes the navigation and deletion commands that you have just used:

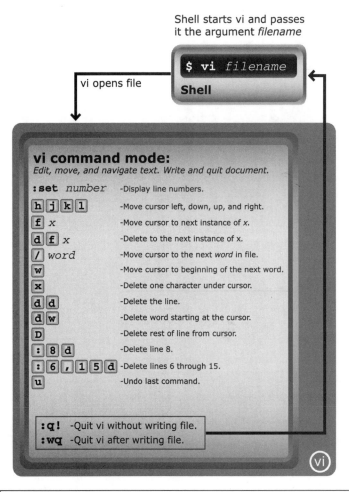

Shell starts vi and passes it the argument *filename*

vi opens file

$ vi *filename*

Shell

vi command mode:
Edit, move, and navigate text. Write and quit document.

:set *number*	-Display line numbers.
h j k l	-Move cursor left, down, up, and right.
f *x*	-Move cursor to next instance of *x*.
d f *x*	-Delete to the next instance of x.
/ *word*	-Move cursor to the next *word* in file.
w	-Move cursor to beginning of the next word.
x	-Delete one character under cursor.
d d	-Delete the line.
d w	-Delete word starting at the cursor.
D	-Delete rest of line from cursor.
: 8 d	-Delete line 8.
: 6 , 1 5 d	-Delete lines 6 through 15.
u	-Undo last command.

:q!	-Quit vi without writing file.
:wq	-Quit vi after writing file.

vi

FIGURE 4-12 Navigating and deleting text in **vi**

4.8 Undoing Editing Commands

Mistakez happen. Words are misspelled; lines are accidentally deleted; text is added that is no improvement. An essential tool for humans is the <u>u</u>ndo command, which undoes (rescinds) the most recent text-changing command. We introduced **u** in the **vi** tour and have been using it to undo deletions. The undo commands provide additional features.

Undoing the Last Editing Change

Whenever we are editing, we make additions, deletions, and substitutions. Any change can be undone.

1. Enter the following:

   dw

   u

2. Add some text and undo it:

   a

   ```
   This is new text
   ```

   ESC

   u

   When we make an editing change, we can <u>u</u>ndo it with the **u** command.

Undoing All Editing Changes on a Line

If you are on Linux or another system using **vim**, the open source **vi** from the Free Software Foundation, you can make multiple <u>u</u>ndo changes, one at a time.

1. Make multiple deletions:

   dw
   3dw
   2dd
   x

2. Undo the deletions one at a time:

   u
   u

u

u

You deleted lines, words, and a character. When you enter the first **u**, it undoes the last editing change. The next **u** undoes the previous change, and so forth. Any change or text addition can be undone. Undoing multiple changes is a feature of Linux's visual editor. In UNIX **vi**, we can undo the last change—for instance, a deletion—with **u**. The line returns. Pressing a second **u** undoes the undo, deleting the line again.

There is a second <u>U</u>ndo command that undoes any number of changes that you've made to the current line where the cursor is located, if you have not left the line.

1. Select a line of your text, and delete one word from the line:

   dw

2. Without leaving the line, move the cursor to another word, and <u>x</u> out some characters by entering:

   x

3. Move to the end of the line and add a word:

   $

   a

4. Press ESC to return to command mode.

5. Go to the beginning of a line and delete a word:

   dw

6. Without moving the cursor off the line, type the lowercase command:

   u

   One change is undone.

7. While still on the line, enter:

   U

   The line returns to its original state. All changes are reversed. The line returns to its condition before you made any changes.

8. Repeat steps 1 and 2.

9. After you make the changes, move the cursor to another line.

10. From the new location enter:

    The **U** command fails. You changed another line before entering **U**.

A summary of the undo commands is shown in the following table:

UNDO COMMAND	ACTION
u (lowercase)	**u**ndoes the effect of the last text change command given, even if you have moved from the line.
U (uppercase)	**U**ndoes the effect of all changes made to the current line, if you have not made a change on another line.

11. Save changes and quit the editor:

    :wg

4.9 Creating New Files with the Visual Editor

Thus far, you have been moving the cursor around, deleting text, and adding text to an existing file. The visual editor is also used to create new files.

Invoking the Editor and Adding Text

Starting to edit a new file is much like editing an old file, except the argument given to **vi** is the name for the new file, not one that exists.

1. Begin the process of creating a new file by typing:

   vi *scrp1*

   The screen clears, a column of tildes (~) lines up on the left of the screen, and you are placed in **vi**'s command mode. There is no text; a clean slate awaits your wisdom. But you cannot add text yet, because whenever you start the editor, you are in command mode.

2. Type the following command to go into append mode:

   a

3. Add the following lines of text:

   ```
   echo  Hello  $USER
   cal
   date
   ```

4. Tell the editor you want to stop adding text and return to the command mode:

   ESC

Adding to a Line

You just added text and returned to command mode. You can now move around the file and make changes to it.

1. While in command mode, use arrow keys to move the cursor to the beginning of the line containing the text:

   cal

2. Instruct the editor to add text at the end of the line:

   A

3. Add a space and the current year using four digits.

4. Press ESC

5. Write the file, leave the editor, and return to the shell with the usual command:

   :wq

6. Obtain a listing of the files in your directory by entering:

   ls

The new file is listed among the contents in your current directory.

The editor acts the same whether you are creating a new file or editing an old one. The command to create a new file is exactly the same command you type to edit an existing file: **vi** *filename*. In both cases, you supply the filename.

One of two things happens when you type the **vi** *filename* command:

- If the *filename* you enter already exists, **vi** makes a buffer copy of that file for you to edit.

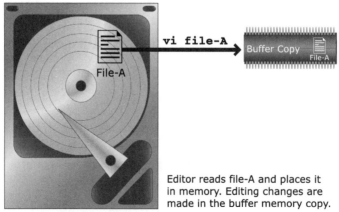

Editor reads file-A and places it in memory. Editing changes are made in the buffer memory copy.

Hard Disk

- If the *filename* you supply does not exist, the editor starts editing a memory buffer using the new *filename*.

When you enter **:wq**, the buffer is written to the disk and given *filename* as its name.

Executing a Script

You just created a file that contains several command lines. You can make the file executable and then have its contents executed.

1. Make the file you just created executable by entering:

    chmod +x *scrp1*

2. Execute the script by entering:

    scrp1

    or

    ./scrp1

All the commands in the script are executed, and the output is displayed on the screen. In Chapter 3 you created a script using **cat** to read from the keyboard and put the instructions in a file. With **cat**, we just enter text. We cannot make changes. With the editor, we can add commands to a script, make changes, and delete text.

Self Test 2

1. What command moves the cursor down three lines?

    _____

2. What command moves the cursor to the right seven characters?

    _____

3. What command locates the words *wonderful heroes*?

    _____

4. What command searches backward through the file for the string *time*?

    _____

5. What command moves the cursor to the beginning of the next word?

    _____

6. What command moves the cursor to the beginning of the current line?

_____

7. What command moves the cursor to the end of the current line?

_____

8. What command moves the cursor forward to the first instance of the character *t* on the current line?

_____

9. What command moves the cursor to the eighth character position regardless of the current cursor position?

_____

10. What command requests that the **vi** editor display the line number at the beginning of each line?

_____

11. What command takes the cursor to the beginning of the 15th line of the file?

_____

12. What command takes the cursor to the beginning of the last line of the file?

_____

13. What command do you type to leave **vi** without saving the changes to the file?

_____

14. What command positions the cursor at the lowest line displayed on the screen?

_____

15. Assume you are on a line of text, and enter */target*. The cursor then moves to the line containing the string *target*. How can you tell the editor to return to the original line?

_____

16. What command scrolls the text down one screen of text in the file?

_____

17. What command deletes the current line plus seven more?

_____

18. What happens when you are in the command mode and enter **2j3dw**?

_____

19. What command deletes the remainder of the line, starting with the character under the cursor?

_____

20. What command deletes all characters on the line, starting with the character under the cursor, up to the first character *H* on the line?

_____

21. What command do you type to add text to the left of the cursor?

_____

22. What command do you type to add text to the right of the cursor?

_____

23. What command opens a line above the cursor?

_____

24. What happens when you type in the word **open** in command mode?

_____

25. What command do you type to add text to the end of the current line?

_____

4.10 Making Text Changes

Thus far, you have added and deleted text. To edit effectively, you must be able to make character, word, and line substitutions as well.

Replacing One Character with Another

You can remove one character and replace it with a single character.

1. Start editing *practice* again with:

   vi *practice*

2. While in command mode, move the cursor to any word you want, using the forward search command:

   /word

3. Replace the first letter of this word by typing the command:

   r

4. Follow the **r** command with any *character,* such as:

   M

   The character entered after the **r** is ucsed to **r**eplace whatever character is under the cursor.

5. As another example, place the cursor on the first *o* in the word *too.*

   Type the **r** command, followed by the letter *w.*
   The first *o* in *too* is replaced by a *w, hence* the word *too* becomes *two.*

The command **r** instructs the editor to replace the character located under the cursor with the very next character that you type. The character is replaced, and you are returned immediately to command mode.

Breaking Up a Long Line

One important use of the replace character command is to break one long line into two lines. When a line is too long, we need to press ENTER somewhere in the middle to make it two lines.

1. Move the cursor to the space between two words in the middle of a long line.
2. Type the replace command (**r**) and then press ENTER.

In this command, we are replacing the space character between the two words with a newline character by pressing ENTER. As a result, the second part of the long line moves to a new line. This works because when we press ENTER, a special character that indicates a new line is added to the file.

Joining Two Lines of Text

There are times when editing that we need to join two lines together.

1. Select two short adjacent lines in your file, and position the cursor anywhere on the first line.
2. Type the uppercase command:

   J
3. The two lines are now Joined.
4. Move to another line and join it with the one that follows.

Typing Over Text Character by Character

The **r** command instructs the editor to replace the single character under the cursor with whatever single character is typed next. At times it is convenient to replace a whole string of text character by character. Using the **r** command for this would be rather cumbersome.

1. Make sure you are in command mode, and type the uppercase command:

   R
2. Start typing.

   You are now in "type-over" mode. Each letter you type replaces the single letter under the cursor as it moves down the line.

3. After you have replaced some text with the type-over command, **R**, return to command mode by pressing:

    ESC

Replacing a Single Letter with Many Characters

You have used the **r** command to replace a single character with one other character. Often an author or programmer needs to remove one character and then substitute several characters or even pages for the deleted single character.

1. With the cursor positioned over any character in the file, type the lowercase command:

    s

    The dollar sign ($) may appear on the character, or the character may just disappear.

2. Add text such as this:

    ```
    Is it true that I am now in append mode?
    I must be, text that I am entering
    is going onto the screen,
    and, I expect, into the file.
    ```

3. Press ESC to return to command mode.

4. Select another character in the text, and replace it with a different character by using the **r** command.

5. Choose another character in the file, and use the **s** command to remove it and <u>s</u>ubstitute an entire sentence for it.

Both the **r** and **s** commands add text replacing a single character in a file. Because the amount of text entered can vary in length when we use the **s** command, we must press ESC to let the editor know we are finished entering the text. This is not the case with the **r** command, because the extent of the replacement is always known—one character.

The **r** command replaces one character with a single new character and then returns you automatically to command mode. You are not left in append mode, and you do not press ESC. In contrast, the **s** command substitutes the character under the cursor with whatever text you type until you press ESC. The **s** command allows you to substitute as many characters as you wish for the one removed character. You move from command mode to append mode, and stay there until you press ESC to return to command mode. Likewise, after you enter the **R** command, the editor replaces each character that the cursor passes over with only one character, but you must press ESC to quit replacing text.

Substituting Text for One Word

It is also possible to change one word in your text into another word or into a multitude of other words.

➥ 1. Using the / command, place your cursor on a word in the middle of the file.

2. Type the change word command:

    cw

    The dollar sign ($) may appear at the end of the word, indicating the end of the text that is being replaced, or the word may be simply removed, depending on your version of the editor.

3. Add text such as this:

    ```
    XXX This is text entered
    after a cw command XXX
    ```

4. When you are finished, leave append mode by pressing:

    ESC

Typing the **cw** command tells the editor to remove one word and put you in append mode. Everything you type is entered into the file until you press ESC.

Substituting Lines

The **s** and **cw** commands allow you to substitute text for a single character and for specific words, respectively. You can also substitute entire lines in your file.

➥ 1. Place the cursor anywhere on a line.

2. To substitute new text for the line, type the following lowercase command:

    cc

    The text on the line is removed, and the cursor is at the beginning of the line. You are in append mode.

3. Add text such as this:

    ```
    And this is a new line of text!
    Well, actually two, taking the place of one.
    ```

With the change line **cc** command, whatever you type is entered into the file in place of the current line. Your replacement for the one line is not limited to only one line. You can append any number of lines at this point. The **cc** command deletes the text from the current line and moves you from command mode to append mode.

You remain in append mode, adding text.

4. Return to command mode by entering:

   ESC

Changing the Remainder of a Line

You can change text from the cursor to the end of the current line, replacing it with new text.

1. Move the cursor to the middle of a line of text.
2. Type the uppercase command:

   C

   The dollar sign appears at the end of the line, indicating the last character that is removed to make way for new text, or the remainder of the line is removed. Either way, you are in append mode.
3. Add a couple of lines of text.
4. Return to command mode:

   ESC

The **C** command puts you in append mode and lets you Change the part of the line from the cursor position to the end of the line. The characters from the left margin up to, but not including, the cursor remain unchanged. Whatever text you type until you press ESC is substituted for the remainder of the line.

Changing All Text to a Specific Character on a Line

In earlier sections, you moved the cursor to a particular character, like *e*, by entering the **f***e* command. Likewise, you deleted up to a specific character with the **df***e* command.

1. Move the cursor to the beginning of a long line.
2. Select a character on the line, such as *e*.

3. Enter:

   cf*e*

   where *e* is the character you selected on the line.
4. Enter some text. The text from the cursor to the selected character is removed, and you are in append mode entering replacement text.
5. Leave append mode and return to command mode by entering:

   ESC

The delete and substitute commands are summarized in the following table:

ACTION	CHARACTER	WORD	LINE	REMAINDER OF LINE	TEXT TO CHARACTER Y ON A LINE
Delete	**x**	**dw**	**dd**	**D**	**df***y*
Substitute	**s**	**cw**	**cc**	**C**	**cf***y*

Making Global Text Changes

The previous exercises explored how to make changes individually. We often want to make changes to every instance of a target throughout a file.

Searching for the First Occurrence of a Word

The <u>s</u>ubstitute command, a colon command, is used to exchange one regular expression for another in a file.

1. Move the cursor to a line containing the word *creating*. (If the word *creating* does not appear in the file, add it to the end of a line, and keep the cursor on that line.)
2. Change the word *creating* to *producing*, by entering:

   :s/*creating***/***producing***/**

   The first instance of the word *creating* is changed to *producing*.
   The <u>s</u>ubstitute command requires two words separated by slashes. The action performed by the **s** command is to check the line(s) for the pattern on the left (the *target pattern*) and, if it is found, substitute the expression on the right (the *replacement pattern*) for the target pattern. The previous command told **vi** to find the word *creating* on the current line and substitute the word *producing*.
   If **vi** cannot find the target pattern you specify, an error message is displayed.

Searching for All Occurrences of a String on All Lines

An extension of the **s** colon command instructs the editor to act on *all* lines in the file.

↳ 1. Add the following lines to your file:

jo 2001 2003 2002
alan 2003 2004
jo 2002 2002 2002
bob 2002 2003
margot 2002 2003 2003

2. Leave append mode:

ESC

3. To implement a change, enter the command:

:1,$ s/2002/1776/g

This command instructs the editor to check all of the addressed lines through the last. The lines are identified by two line numbers separated by a comma. The comma is instruction to look for all lines in the range from the first line to the last. This command tells **vi** to examine all lines looking for the string *2002*, and where this string is found, to substitute the pattern string *1776*. The **g** is instruction to change multiple occurrences of *2002* if more than one is on a line.

This command instructs the editor, as shown in the following table:

COMMAND	INTERPRETATION
1,$	Go from line 1 to the last line in the file (**$**)
s	Make **s**ubstitutions
2002	Replace the string *2002*...
1776	with the string *1776*...
/g	**g**lobally in the file.

The **g** at the end of the **s**ubstitute command is called a *flag*. The **g** flag, global, instructs the <u>s</u>ubstitute command to replace all occurrences of the target pattern within the addressed line(s).

Selecting Lines to Modify

You can limit the substitution to lines that have specific content. For instance, if you want to change the year but only on lines that include the string *jo*, you need to specify which lines to affect.

⤷ Enter:

*:1,$ /jo/s/2002/1776/***g**

vi changes only the lines that include the string *jo*. If there is no *jo*, the substitution does not take place.

This command instructs the editor, as shown in the following table:

COMMAND	INTERPRETATION
1,$	Go from line 1 to the last line in the file (**$**).
/*jo*/	Line target. Look for lines that have the string *jo*. Act only on lines that have at least one instance of the target.
s	Make **s**ubstitutions.
/*2002*/*1776*/	Replace the string *2002* with the string *1776*.
/**g**	**g**lobally, change all instances on each line.

4.11 Moving and Copying Text

Often when you look at your work, you realize that the task is to move or copy lines, words, or whole blocks of text from one place to another.

Copying and Pasting Text

With the **vi** editor, you can move or copy blocks of text.

⤷ 1. If you are not already editing the *practice* file, start by entering:

    vi *practice*

2. Move the cursor to a line part way down the screen.

3. Type the lowercase command:

    yy

4. Although it appears that nothing has happened, the **vi** editor has "**yy**anked" and made a copy of this line and is holding the copy in memory. The line that was copied is not deleted or otherwise affected by the **yy**ank command.

5. Move the cursor to a different location in your text, such as down a few lines.

6. Type the lowercase command:

   p

7. The line that was yanked is now put or pasted as a new line in the new location below the cursor line.

8. The yank feature is most useful for copying blocks of text. For instance, to yank seven lines of text, beginning with the cursor line, type:

   7yy

9. Move the cursor to a line where you want to put the yanked lines, such as the end of the file:

   G

10. Now **p**ut the seven yanked lines after the cursor:

    p

11. A copy of the seven yanked lines of text now appears inserted seven new lines below the current cursor location.

    At times we need to **p**ut lines above the cursor.

12. Move the cursor to the first line of the file:

    1G

13. With the cursor on the first line in the file, enter the capital letter command:

    P

    The line from memory is placed *above* the current line.

14. Yank another line into memory and use both the **p** and **P** commands to put copies of the line into the file.

Deleting and Putting Lines

The **yy**ank command makes a copy to be placed elsewhere. The yank and paste commands are the forerunners of the copy and paste commands. You can also combine any of the delete commands with **p**ut commands to accomplish cut and paste.

1. Select a line to move somewhere else in your file.

2. Position the cursor on any character on the line to be moved and type:

   dd

   The line is deleted, but is also placed in memory.

3. Move the cursor to the end of the file.

4. Put the line:

p

5. The line was "cut" and "pasted" at the end of the file.

Figure 4-13 illustrates deleting text, holding text in the buffer, and placing text.

Copying and Moving Words and Characters

We can use the yank command to yank one or more words instead of lines.

1. Move your cursor to the beginning of a word in the file.

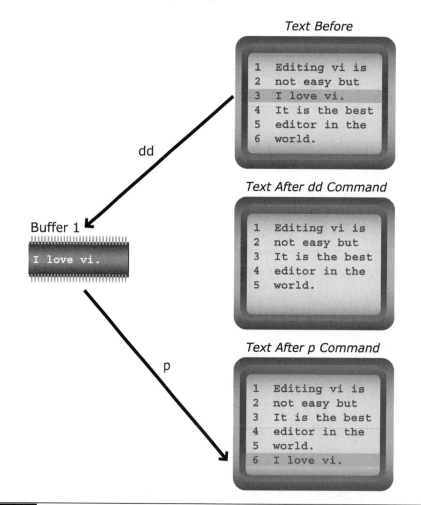

FIGURE 4-13 Deleting and placing text using a buffer

2. While in command mode, enter:

    yw

3. Move to the space between two other words in the file.

4. Enter:

    p

    The yanked word is put at the new location.

5. This time delete a word by entering:

    dw

6. Again move to the space between two words and enter:

    p

    The deleted word is placed at a new location. You can combine the lowercase **p**ut command with the **x** command to transpose characters in your text quickly.

7. Move the cursor to the first letter of any word in your text and type:

    x

8. Now type:

    p

Notice that the two characters are transposed.

When we delete a part of the text, a copy of the text is placed in memory. We can put it anywhere in the file with **p** or **P** commands.

Copying and Moving Part of a Line

Just as **df**x deletes from the cursor to the x on the current line, and **cf**x changes the text to the x, we can instruct the editor to yank a part of a line.

1. Select any character (x) to the right of the cursor on the current line and enter:

    yf$x$

    where x is the character you chose.

2. Move the cursor to the end of the line and **p**ut the yanked text:

    p

3. Move back to the beginning of the line:

    ^

4. Delete from the cursor to any character (x) on the line:

    df$x$

5. Move to the end of line 1 and **p**ut the deleted text:

   1G

   $

   p

6. Move the cursor to the middle of a line of text and enter:

   d$

   u

   d^

We can also operate on the objects "end of line" and "beginning of line."

Examining Objects and Operators

You have issued a variety of commands such as **dd**, **dw**, **yy**, **yw**, **cc**, **cw**, and so on. Examine the following table which focuses on the relationships among the commands:

OBJECT	OPERATIONS		
	Delete	Change	Yank
Whole line	**dd**	**cc**	**yy**
Rest of line	**D** or **d$**	**C** or **c$**	**y$**
To a character *x* on the line	**df**x	**cf**x	**yf**x
Word	**dw**	**cw**	**yw**
Character	**x** or **dl**	**s** or **cl**	**yl**

The operator for **d**elete is **d**, for **c**hange is **c**, and for **y**ank is **y**. When we want to operate on the whole line, we enter the operator twice: **dd**, **cc**, and **yy**. We can specify the end of the line with the $ so we can delete, change or yank the rest of a line. If the object to affect is the text between the cursor and a character *x*, we place the operator before the **f**x, as in the **df**x, **cf**x, and **yf**x commands. The object word (*w*) is affected by the operators delete (**d**w), change (**c**w), and yank (**y**w). We can move one character to the right with an **l** (*el*) command that identifies the object.

⮡ 1. Now, try each of the commands in this table one more time, keeping the operator/object model in mind.

2. With your cursor on line 1 in the file, enter the following operator-object commands:

> **d3G**
>
> **u**
>
> **d10|**
>
> **u**
>
> **d3w**
>
> **u**
>
> **d8h**
>
> **u**

Many of the commands in this chapter can be summarized in this way. Figure 4-14 lists the three operators (**d**, **c**, and **y**) in column one, many of the objects in column two, and their meaning in column three.

3. Try these objects with each of the operators.

Marking a Place in a File

It is possible with the visual editor to mark a place in a file and then later return to it or act on it. You can use marks to specify text to be deleted, moved, written, or copied.

In a file, the line number assigned to a particular line of code or text will change if lines are added or removed between that line and the beginning of the file. During editing, we often need to return to a particular line of text; but if the number has been changed, it can be difficult to find the place we want.

With the visual editor's mark command, several positions in a file may be marked. Once a line of text is marked, we can return to that line.

⮡ 1. Make certain that line numbers are displayed for the *practice* file. (If they are not, enter **:set** *nu* and press ENTER.)

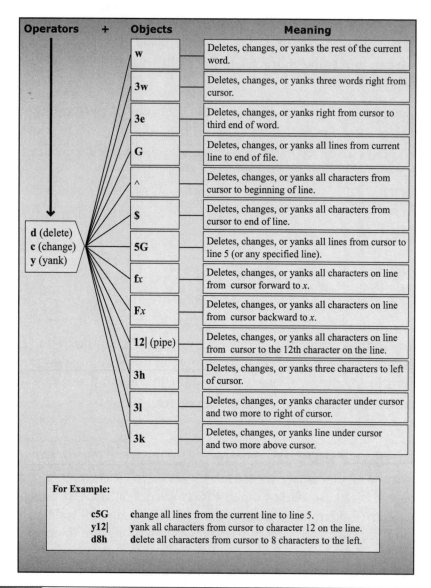

Operators	+	Objects	Meaning
d (delete) **c** (change) **y** (yank)		w	Deletes, changes, or yanks the rest of the current word.
		3w	Deletes, changes, or yanks three words right from cursor.
		3e	Deletes, changes, or yanks right from cursor to third end of word.
		G	Deletes, changes, or yanks all lines from current line to end of file.
		^	Deletes, changes, or yanks all characters from cursor to beginning of line.
		$	Deletes, changes, or yanks all characters from cursor to end of line.
		5G	Deletes, changes, or yanks all lines from cursor to line 5 (or any specified line).
		f*x*	Deletes, changes, or yanks all characters on line from cursor forward to *x*.
		F*x*	Deletes, changes, or yanks all characters on line from cursor backward to *x*.
		12| (pipe)	Deletes, changes, or yanks all characters on line from cursor to the 12th character on the line.
		3h	Deletes, changes, or yanks three characters to left of cursor.
		3l	Deletes, changes, or yanks character under cursor and two more to right of cursor.
		3k	Deletes, changes, or yanks line under cursor and two more above cursor.

For Example:

c5G	**c**hange all lines from the current line to line 5.
y12|	**y**ank all characters from cursor to character 12 on the line.
d8h	**d**elete all characters from cursor to 8 characters to the left.

FIGURE 4-14   The delete, change, and yank commands

2. Go to a line in the middle of your file, and note its line number. With the cursor to that line, enter the following command:

   m*b*

   This command **m**arks the line and assigns it the label *b*. You can replace the *b* with any letter from *a* through *z*.

3. Move the cursor to another location near the beginning of the file.

4. Remove a few lines of text at this new location.

5. To return to the line of text that you marked in step 2, type the following:

   'b

   (a single quote mark, followed by the letter used in the **m**ark command, in this case a *b* character.)

The cursor moves to the original marked location, even though its line number is clearly different because we added or deleted text earlier in the file. Marks last only for the current editing session.

Deleting Lines from the Current Position to a Marked Spot

Once a line is marked, we can manipulate all the text from the cursor position to the mark. This exercise examines how to delete all text from the current line to a marked line.

1. Place the cursor on any line of text, and mark the line:

   ma

   where *a* is any letter from *a* through *z*.

2. Now move the cursor a few lines above or below the line just marked, and enter the following:

   d'a

   All the text between your present location to and including the marked line is deleted. In this case, the operator is the **d** and the object is the text to the mark.

3. Undo the deletion by entering:

   u

Changing and Yanking from the Current Position to a Marked Line

In the previous exercise, you deleted to a marked line by putting the **d** operator in front of the '*a* marked line specification. We can use all three operators with marked objects.

1. Yank into memory all lines from the cursor to the marked line:

   y'a

2. Move to the end of the file and put the copied lines there:

   G

   p

   The lines yanked into memory from the cursor to the mark are put at the end of the file.

3. Return to the previous location with two single quotes:

   ' '

   The marked line is still available. This time use the change operator with the marked lines object.

4. Enter:

   c'a

   All lines from the cursor to the marked line are removed and the editor is in append/insert mode.

5. Add some text and return to command mode.

Deleting, Moving, or Copying Marked Blocks

You can use the **m**ark command to simplify the tasks of deleting, moving, and copying large blocks of text by marking both ends of the block.

1. Move the cursor to the first line of some text you want to delete. Mark that line by entering:

   ma

2. Next, move the cursor to the last line of text to be deleted. Mark that line by entering:

   mb

3. Now delete the marked text from *a* to *b*, with this command:

   :'a,'b d

   All text between and including the lines marked *a* and *b* is deleted. The command you just entered did the same thing as a "delete line number" command, such as *:16,32 d*. Both commands identify lines and call for action.

4. Undo the previous command, so that the deleted text reappears.

   We can use marked lines to specify lines for all colon commands: **c**opy, **m**ove, **d**elete, and **w**rite. Lines in a file can be identified by either line numbers or by marks, and all colon or line commands can be used with lines identified by either element.

5. Before continuing to the next section, practice using marks to move, delete, and write blocks of text.

Moving and Copying Blocks of Text

Marking text is a powerful way to identify lines to delete, move, or copy. We can also use line numbers. In an earlier exercise, you deleted a range of lines with commands such as **:5,10 d**, which removed lines in the range from line *5* to line *10*.

1. Move a block of text with:

   :1,5 move $

   Lines *1* through *5* are moved to the end of the file.

2. Go back to the top of the file and copy a block:

   1G

   :1,4 copy 5

   Lines *1* through *4* are copied and placed after line *5*.
   When we have line numbers on and the block is small, moving with line numbers is most effective. Larger blocks are easier with marked lines.

4.12 Writing the File and Quitting the Editor

Thus far, you have used **:wq** to write the copy of the file you edited to the disk and quit the editor. We can also write to a different file, abandon changes to the current file, and add content to the end of an existing file.

Quitting vi without Saving Changes

By now, you have scrambled your *practice* file. Before continuing, you can quit this editing session, return to the shell, and have the *practice* file remain as it was when you first called up the file at the beginning of this section.

1. From the command mode of the visual editor, type:

   :q

   Because you made changes to your file in this editing session, **vi** objects. The editor does not know whether to save or discard the changes.

2. Enter:

> **:q!**

The **!** says to the editor, "Yes, I know I made changes, but I really do want to quit." This command does not include a **write** (save), just a **quit**. It says, "Quit the editor program, but don't write the changes I have been making."

You are now back in the shell.

Saving the Original Copy and a Modified Version

Sometimes while editing, we realize that we want to keep the file as it was before we started to edit, and we want to keep the modified version as well, in a new file. (This is analogous to the "Save As" menu option in a word processor.) Keeping both versions requires the following steps.

Saving the New Version

To save both the original file and its new, modified version, we must save the present buffer copy as a new file and then quit the editor without overwriting the original file.

1. Use **vi** to edit the file *practice,* and make a few changes to it:

> **vi** *practice*

2. To save a copy of the modified version of *practice,* type the following from the **vi** command mode:

> **:w** *newpractice*

where *newpractice* is any name you want.

A message similar to the following appears on your screen at the bottom of your file:

```
"newpractice" [New file] 18 lines, 150 characters
```

You have instructed the editor to open a new file, *newpractice,* and to write to that new file the copy of the file you have been working on. Figure 4-15 compares writing a file and writing the buffer to a new file.

Protecting the Original Version

The next task is to protect the original version from being overwritten. If you entered the regular (**:wq**) command, the editor would write the new version over

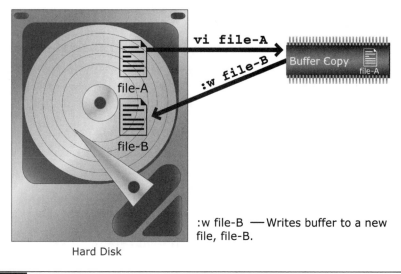

:w file-B —Writes buffer to a new
file, file-B.

Hard Disk

FIGURE 4-15 Saving the new version

the original. You would then have two copies of the new, edited version and none
of the original. The objective is to quit the **vi** editor *without* saving the changes to
the original file.

1. Enter:

    :q

    or

    :q!

    The **:q** is acceptable because you just wrote the file, even though you wrote
    it to a new filename. The **:q!** works too.

2. Enter the **ls** command to look at the latest listing of your files.

Your directory now contains a copy of your original file, *practice,* in addition
to the modified copy listed under the new filename you chose.

Writing Blocks of Text to Files

It is often useful to take portions of the file you are editing and create new files with them. To write a block of text from your current file out to a new file, you need two pieces of information:

- The line numbers for the first and last lines of the text you want to write out to a new file
- A new filename for the material to be written

1. Start editing *practice* again:

   vi *practice*

2. From **vi** command mode, type this command:

   :1,7 write *practice-2*

   or

   :1,7 w *practice-2*

   where *practice-2* is the new filename for the selected text. Both the full word **write** and the short version **w** are interpreted the same way.

   The lines specified by the line address (*1,7*) are written into *practice-2*. The text from lines 1 through 7 now exists in two places: in the file you are currently editing (*practice*), and in *practice-2*. See Figure 4-16 for a similar example.

3. Leave the editor and return to the shell.

4. Examine the new file, *practice-2*:

   more *practice-2*

   The lines are added.

5. Start editing *practice* again by entering:

   vi *practice*

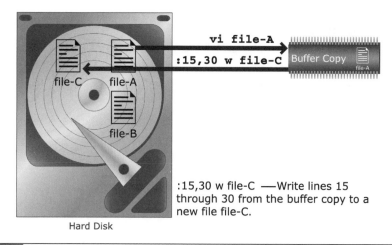

:15,30 w file-C ——Write lines 15
through 30 from the buffer copy to a
new file file-C.

Hard Disk

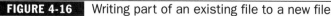

FIGURE 4-16 Writing part of an existing file to a new file

Overwriting an Existing File

You can use the <u>w</u>rite command to overwrite, or replace, an existing file.

1. Enter:

   :1,7 **write** *practice-2*

   or

   :1,7 **w** *practice-2*

2. This command is instruction to overwrite *practice-2,* a file that already exists.
   See Figure 4-17. The following command will work whether *practice-2* exists
   or not:

   :1,7 **w!** practice-2

Adding to a File

Another type of <u>w</u>rite command appends text to a file.

1. Enter a command to write lines 5 through 8 to the end of the file *practice-2*:

   :5,8 **w >>** *practice-2*

2. The lines 5 through 8 are added to the end of *practice-2.*

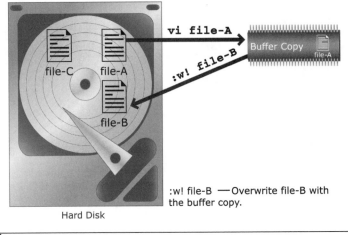

:w! file-B —Overwrite file-B with
the buffer copy.

Hard Disk

FIGURE 4-17 Overwriting an existing file

Self Test 3

1. The cursor is at the *a* in the word *Hat*. You are in command mode. What happens when you type in **rob**?

_____

2. What command joins the next line with the current line?

_____

3. The cursor is located at the first character of the word *quit*. What happens when you type in **Red** while in command mode?

_____

4. What command do you use to replace one character with all of the characters you type in until you press ESC?

_____

5. What command do you type to remove one word and add new text?

_____

6. What command do you use to replace the entire current line with whatever text you enter?

_____

7. What command deletes text from the cursor to the end of the current line and puts you in append mode?

_____

8. What command deletes text from the cursor to the first occurrence of a specified character *H* and puts you in append mode to add new text?

   _____

9. What command instructs **vi** to locate every instance of the pattern *bill* and to substitute the pattern *tom* through all the lines in the file?

   _____

10. What command puts into memory seven lines starting with the cursor line?

    _____

11. What command pastes whatever was yanked?

    _____

12. What command yanks characters on the current line from the cursor to the first instance of the character *H*?

    _____

13. What command saves a copy of the current file as a file named *practice1*?

    _____

14. What command saves lines 5 through 30 of the current file to a file named *practice2*?

    _____

15. What command writes out lines 5 through 30 into the existing file *drill*, overwriting the current contents?

    _____

16. Complete the following:

OBJECT	ACTION		
	delete	**yank**	**change**
line	**dd**	_____	_____
_____	_____	**yw**	_____
To end of line	_____	_____	**c$**
To the 12th character on the line	_____	_____	_____
_____	_____	**y8G**	_____

17. What command do you type to have line numbers displayed next to the lines of the file you are editing?

---

18. What command do you type to remove line numbers displayed next to the lines of the current editing session?

Chapter Review

Use this section to review the content of this chapter and test yourself on your knowledge of the concepts.

Chapter Summary

- The visual editor employs the standard keyboard to accomplish two tasks: first, to communicate about what the user wants done to a file (move around, delete, copy/paste), and second, to add text to the file.

- To accomplish both uses of the keyboard, two modes are employed. When the editor is started, the user is in command mode, where all keystrokes are interpreted as commands to the editor. One set of commands instructs the editor to change to append or insert mode, where the keyboard is just a keyboard for text input. In append mode, all keys are just characters, with two exceptions: First, ESC is seen as an instruction to return to command mode; second, in **vim**, the arrow keys enable the user to move through the file in append mode.

- From command mode, the user can specify where text is added relative to the cursor using specific commands: to the left (**i**), right (**a**), above (**O**), below (**o**), beginning of line (**I**), or end of line (**A**).

- Once text is in a file, it is seen as objects, such as a character, a part of a line, a line, or a series of lines. From command mode, the cursor can be moved to any object employing specific commands as listed in the "Command Summary."

- You can operate on any object by using any one of three operators: change (**c**), delete (**d**), or yank (**y**). For example, **G** moves the cursor from the current location to the last line of the file; **dG** deletes text from the current line to the last line of the file; **cG** changes all text from cursor position to the last line, allowing the user to add replacement text; and **yG** yanks the text from the cursor location to the file's last line into memory.

• The editor facilitates global changes where the user specifies a target for replacement and the replacement text.

• When the user has completed editing, the file can be written back over the original, be written to a new file, or be discarded while the original file is preserved.

Assignment

1. Assume you just entered **vi** *old-filename* and the editor started editing your *old-file*. Which of the following can you now do without leaving the current mode?

   A. Delete lines

   B. Go to line 32

   C. Yank lines 3 through 8 into memory

   D. Put the lines from memory at a location in the file

   E. Type in new text

   F. Remove a word

2. What command does each of the following?

   Moves the cursor to the end of a file? _____

   Removes the current and next three lines, placing you in append mode? _____

   Yanks the remainder of the current line into memory? _____

   Deletes from the cursor to the 23rd character on the current line? _____

   Changes from the cursor to the first *H* to the right of the cursor? _____

   Writes a file saving the changes? _____

   Moves the cursor to the end of the line? _____

   Moves the cursor to the next *H* in the file? _____

   Deletes from the cursor to the next *H* in the file? _____

   Moves the whole display forward through the file? _____

   Moves the cursor to the top line currently displayed? _____

3. This short project is to guide you in creating a small script and then modifying it.

   A. Use the visual editor to create a file called *scrp4a* that contains the following text:

   ```
   echo today is
   date
   echo this month is
   cal
   ```

   B. Save the file and make it executable.

   C. Run the script and place its output in a file named *assign-4*.

   D. Copy *scr4a* to *scr4b* and modify *scr4b* so the last two lines read:

   ```
   echo an interesting month is
   cal  9  1752
   ```

   E. Add the following lines:

   ```
   echo the number of files in the current directory is
   ls  |  wc  -w
   ```

   F. Run the script and add its output to the *assign-4* file.

COMMAND SUMMARY

STARTING THE VISUAL EDITOR FROM THE SHELL	
vi filename	Instructs shell to start **vi** and pass one argument, *filename,* which **vi** interprets as a file to open if it exists in the current directory, or to create if it does not already exist.
CURSOR-MOVING COMMANDS	
h j k l	Moves the cursor one space or line left, down, up, or right, respectively.
0 (zero)	Moves the cursor to the beginning of whatever line it is on.
^ (caret)	Like zero, it moves the cursor to the beginning of the current line.
$	Moves the cursor to the end of the line.
##G	Moves the cursor to the line specified by the number in front of the **G**. For example, **42G** moves the cursor to line 42 in the file.
G	Moves the cursor to the last line of the file.
w	Moves the cursor forward to the first letter of the next word.
e	Moves the cursor forward to the *next end* of a word. (If the cursor is in a word, the *next end* is the end of the current word. If the cursor is at the end of a word, the *next end* is the end of the next word.)
b	Moves the cursor backward to the *previous beginning* of a word. If the cursor is in a word, the *previous beginning* is the beginning of the current word.
12l	Positions the cursor at column 12 of the current line.
L	Positions the cursor at the lowest line displayed on the screen.
M	Positions the cursor at the midpoint on the screen.
H	Positions the cursor at the highest line on the screen.
' '	Two single quotes. Moves the cursor to its previous location in the file.

CURSOR-POSITIONING COMMANDS (CONTEXTUAL)	
fb	Moves the cursor forward on the line to the next *b* (or to any other specified character).
/word	Moves the cursor forward through the text to the next instance of *word*.
?word	Moves the cursor backward through the text to the prior instance of *word*.
n	Moves to the next instance of the pattern identified in a previously issued /*word* or **?***word*.
DISPLAY-ADJUSTING COMMANDS	
CTRL-D	Scrolls the cursor down a block of text in a file.
CTRL-U	Scrolls the cursor up a block of text in a file.
CTRL-F	Displays the next screenful of text in a file.
CTRL-B	Displays the previous screenful of text in a file.
SETTING DISPLAY OPTIONS	
:set number	Instructs the editor to include line numbers as part of the screen display, not as part of the file itself. The abbreviated form of **:set nu** also works.
:set nonumber	Removes line numbers from your screen. You can also use **:set nonu**.
:set ignorecase	Instructs editor to search for targets, ignoring the case of the characters.
:set	Shows you all the options you have set.
:set all	Shows you all the set options available.
TEXT-DELETING COMMANDS	
dd	Deletes the line of text on which the cursor is positioned.
#dd	Deletes # number of lines of text.
dw	Deletes one word from the text.
#dw	Deletes # number of words from the text.
x	Deletes the one character under the cursor.

#x	Deletes # number of characters from the text.
D	Deletes the rest of the line (from the cursor position on).
:#,#d	For example, **:12,37d** deletes all lines from 12 through 37, inclusive.
UNDO COMMANDS	
u	Undo. Reverses the last text-change action even if you have moved to a remote portion of the file. In Linux, additional undo commands reverse previous changes. In standard **vi** on UNIX, a second undo undoes the original undo, and restores the original change.
:redo	In Linux, cancels the undo and redoes the text change. In standard UNIX, a second **u** undoes the first, resulting in a "redo."
ADDING TEXT TO A FILE	
a	Lowercase. Inserts text starting with the space to the right of the cursor.
A	Uppercase. Starts adding text at the end of the line.
i	Lowercase. Starts adding text to the left of the cursor.
I	Uppercase. Inserts text at the beginning of the line.
o	Lowercase. Opens, or inserts a line below the cursor.
O	Uppercase. Opens a line above the cursor.
:#r filename	Reads the specified file and places it in the current file after the specified line number. For example, **:8r** *report.old* reads the file named *report.old* and places it in the current file after text line 8.
ESC	Regardless of which command is used to enter append/ insert mode, to leave append mode and return to **vi** command mode, you need to press ESC.
CHANGING TEXT IN A FILE	
cw	Changes only the one word under the cursor. (Deletes the word, and then places you in append mode to add text where the word was located.)

s	Lowercase. Substitutes for a single character.
S	Uppercase. Substitutes for an entire line.
cc	Substitutes for an entire line (same as **S**).
r	Replaces the one character under the cursor with the next character typed. Automatically returns to command mode.
R	Puts editor in type-over mode. Replaces characters under cursor with whatever is typed.
C	Uppercase. Changes the rest of the line (from the cursor position forward).
cf#	Changes text on the current line, including the target character. For example, **cf*M*** deletes all text on the current line up to and including the first *M* and puts you in append mode to add text in place of the removed text.

YANKING AND PUTTING LINES AND WORDS

yy	Copies or yanks the current line into the memory buffer. **20yy** copies the current line and the next 19 lines (a total 20 lines) into memory. The target lines remain in the file, and copies are made in memory for placement in the file with **p**.
dd	Deletes the current line, and places it in the same memory buffer used by **yy**. The target lines are removed from the file.The **p** command places the deleted lines anywhere in the file.
yw	Copies or yanks the current word into the memory buffer. **y6w** or **6ym** copies the current word and the next five (a total of six words) into memory.
dw	Deletes the current word, and places it in the same memory buffer used by **yw**. Use **p** to place words elsewhere in the file.
yf#	Yank to and include a character. For example, **yf:** copies or yanks text into memory, starting at the cursor and continuing to and including the first instance of the colon character.

p	Puts whatever lines are in memory into the file starting below the cursor line. Puts whatever words are in memory into the file to the right of the cursor.
P	Uppercase. Puts the yanked or deleted line(s) just above the cursor line. Puts the yanked or deleted word(s) to the left of the cursor.
TEXT-MOVING COMMANDS	
J	Joins the next line with the current line.
:#,#move #	Moves specified lines to a target location. :*12,35* **move** *58* moves lines 12 through 35 to after line 58. Can be abbreviated as **mo**.
:1,26 co 82	Copies lines 1 through 26 and places them after line 82. (You select the line numbers.)
GLOBAL EDITING COMMANDS	
:s /target/replacement/	Locates the first occurrence of the target character string on the current line, removes it, and replaces it with the character string replacement. Modifies only the first instance of the target on the line.
:g /target/s//replacement/	Locates the first occurrence of the target character string on all lines, removes each, and replaces them with the character string replacement. Modifies the first instance of the target on all lines.
:#,# s/target/replacement/	Makes substitutions on selected lines. For example, **:7,37 s**/*march*/*walk*/ examines lines 7 through 37, replacing the first occurrence of the target string *march* in each line with the character string *walk*. Modifies the first instance of the target on all selected lines.
:#,# s/target/replacement/g	Makes global substitutions on selected lines. **:1,$ s**/*fun*/*joyful*/**g** locates all occurrences of the target *fun* character string on line 1 through the end of the file, removes each instance, and replaces each occurrence with the character string *joyful*. Modifies all instances of the target on all selected lines.
:s /target/replacement/	Locates the next occurrence of target character string, removes it, and replaces it with the character string replacement. Modifies only the first instance of the target.

:g /target/s/replacement/	Locates the first occurrence of target character string on all lines, removes each instance, and replaces each occurrence with the character string replacement. Modifies the first instance of the target on all lines.
:#,# /target/s/replacement/	Makes substitutions on selected lines. **:7,37** /*march*/ **s**/*walk*/ locates the first occurrence of the target string *march* in lines 7 through 37, removes each instance, and replaces each occurrence with the character string *walk*. Modifies the first instance of the target on all selected lines.
:#,# /target/s/replacement/g	Makes global substitutions on selected lines. **:1,$** /*fun*/**s**/*joyful*/**g** locates all occurrences of the target *fun* character string on lines 1 through the end of the file, removes each, and replaces them with the character string *joyful*. Modifies all instances of the target on all selected lines.
READING, WRITING, AND QUITTING THE EDITOR	
:wq	Writes to the disk any changes made to a file during the current editing session, quits work on the file, and returns to the shell.
:q	Quits work on a file if no changes or additions have been made.
:q!	Quits work on a file and returns to the shell mode, but does not write changes made during the editing session.
:w *filename*	Writes the buffer (edited) version of the file to a new file.
:#,# w *newfile*	Creates a new file and copies the specified lines from the current file to the new file. For example, **:1,6 w** *newtext* creates a new file named *newtext* and copies text lines 1 to 6 from the present file into *newtext*.
:1,6 w >> *oldfile*	Appends copy of lines 1 to 6 to end of an existing file named *oldfile*.
:1,6 w! *oldfile*	Overwrites (replaces) *oldfile* with contents of lines 1 to 6.

Exploring Utilities

O B J E C T I V E S

After completing this chapter, you will be able to:

- Count the words, lines, and characters in a file
- Sort the contents of a file
- Identify and remove duplicate lines in a file
- Compare two files by identifying lines common to both
- Translate or remove characters in a file
- Search through files for a string of characters
- Select a portion of each line in a file
- Concatenate files and splice lines together
- Perform math calculations

Some of the most prominent features on the UNIX system landscape are its powerful utility programs. Specific utilities locate system information, sort lines, select specific fields, modify information, and manage files for users. Although each fundamental utility is designed to accomplish a simple task, they can be easily combined to produce results that no single utility could produce by itself. This toolbox of utilities, along with the UNIX features that facilitate using several utilities at once, provide us with a set of powerful solutions to computing problems.

In our work, we often need to collect, modify, and store data about users, results, Internet activity, finances, and so forth. We cannot reach into the machine and extract lines that relate to one user, change a field separator, and write them to a secure file. We need to use utilities to accomplish such tasks.

This chapter examines several utilities individually and in basic combinations. File data is manipulated and compared. The basic forms of robust utilities that constitute the core user tools are explored.

As you work through this chapter, always create any requested files exactly as presented, because they are used in later exercises. Carefully read each section and complete the activities. Read each summary, answer the review questions, and examine the command summary at the end of the chapter.

5.1 Examining the Contents of Files

Counting elements of files, concatenating files, and viewing files were briefly introduced in Chapters 1 and 2. In this first section, you create needed example files, then use the utilities to explore the files further.

Creating Test Files for This Chapter

The files you are about to create are essential. After you create them, you will use them for several exercises in this chapter.

➥ **1.** Use an editor to create a file named *test-file1* with the following contents:

```
abc  10
def  20
ghi  30
jkl  40
```

2. Create *test-file2* with the following contents:

```
AAA  1A  A
BBB  2B  B
CCC  2C  C
```

Counting Elements of Files with *wc*

Writers and project managers often want to know how many lines or words are in a file. Users and administrators need to determine how many files are in a directory or how many users are logged on.

1. Enter the following commands:

> **wc** *test-file1*
> **wc** *test-file1 practice*

The **wc** utility reports the number of lines, words, and characters in the contents of files. If multiple filenames are given to **wc** as arguments, **wc** reports the number of each element in each file and the *total* number of lines, words, and characters in all files together.

2. Count the elements of all files in your current directory:

> **wc** * | **more**

The shell replaces the * on the command line with the names of all files in the current directory. The shell then interprets all the filenames as arguments to pass to **wc**. The **wc** utility then interprets each argument as a file to open. **wc** counts all elements in all the files, then outputs the totals for each file, and then a grand total for all files.

The options for **wc** permit selective counts as well.

3. Enter:

```
wc -l test-file1
wc -w test-file1
wc -wc test-file1
wc -l -w test-file1
wc -wl test-file1
```

From the output of the commands you just entered, we can conclude the following:

> **SUMMARY:** **wc** employs options to count lines only (**-l**), words only (**-w**), and characters only (**-c**). The options may be employed as multiple arguments (**-w -c**) or combined as one argument (**-wc**) and the order is inconsequential; both of the arguments **-cw** and **-wc** produce the same output.

Counting Elements in Output of Previous Utilities

Using **wc** with other utilities provides useful information.

Enter the following commands:

```
who | wc
who | wc -l
ls | wc
```

In each of these command lines, the shell starts two processes, connecting the output from the first to the input of the second. This piping of output works only when the utility running in the first process generates data. The utility writes to its output, which was redirected to the input of the second process. Because **wc** is running in the second process, it counts the elements in whatever data the first utility generates.

Merging Files with cat

Previously you used **cat** to display files, especially if they were short.

➥ 1. When we provide **cat** with two arguments, both files are read:

    cat *test-file1 test-file2*

The **cat** utility interprets all of its arguments as files to open and read. Each line of the first file is read and written to output. When **cat** reads the end-of-file (EOF) character in *test-file1*, it puts that file away and then starts reading *test-file2*, which it also writes to output. No marker is placed between the files. We see the two files as concatenated on the screen.

2. To combine copies of two files into a new third file called *test-file3,* enter the following:

    cat *test-file1 test-file2* **>** *test-file3*

3. Examine the contents of *test-file3*:

    cat *test-file3*

This new file consists of the contents of the first file followed by the second.

In this command, we instruct the shell to create a new file *test-file3* and to redirect the output of **cat** to that new file. The **cat** utility is given two arguments, which it interprets as two filenames. Then **cat** reads each one and writes to output (which the shell connected to *test-file3*). Both files are read and written sequentially. The two input files are con**cat**enated into the output file.

Numbering Lines of Output

Often programmers or data managers want to include line numbers in the printout or screen display of a file, but do not wish to actually modify the file by adding the numbers.

➥ Enter the following request for **cat** to read a file:

    cat -n *test-file1*
    cat -n *practice*
    cat *practice*

Each line of output is <u>n</u>umbered in the display; the original file is not affected. If your version of **cat** does not include the **-n** option, you can number output lines using the **pr** utility.

Examining Files with *more*

The **more** utility displays long files on the terminal one page at a time. Most recent versions of the **more** utility search for strings, move forward and backward through a file, and easily shift to the visual editor.

► Access a large file by entering one of the following:

more */etc/termcap*

or

more */etc/terminfo*

One of these files should exist on your system. The contents of these files are not the primary issue at the moment—their size is. They are large enough to explore with **more**.

(These files contain instructions as to how nearly all manufacturers' terminals work, so programs that interact with terminals communicate reasonably.)

Moving Forward and Backward with *more*

► 1. Try each of the following keys:

SPACEBAR

ENTER

SPACEBAR instructs **more** to display the next page of output; ENTER is instruction to add the next single line to the display.

2. From within **more**, search for a string by entering:

/vt100

and press ENTER

Like **vi**, the **more** utility interprets the slash followed by a *target string* of characters as an instruction to search through the document for the next instance of the target string. The target string is often called a *regular expression* because it can be a complex description (expression) of a target.

The page with the target is displayed.

3. Enter the following:

b

b

Each **b** is instruction to move back one screen of text. With **more**, use the SPACEBAR to move forward through the file, and **b** to go backward.

Executing Shell Command Lines from within *more*

Sometimes when we are examining a file using **more** we need to run a utility to see the correct date, find out if a friend is logged on, and so forth. We could quit **more**, run the command at the shell, then start **more** again. Or we could have the process running **more** start a child process to run the command.

↳ 1. From within **more** enter:

   !cal

   The output from **cal** is displayed on the screen. The **more** utility interprets the bang (!) as instruction to run the remainder of the line as a command and starts a new process to accomplish that goal.

   2. Exit **more** by pressing:

   q

Shifting to the Visual Editor from within *more*

We can start examining a file with **more**, and then shift directly to the visual editor.

↳ 1. Use **more** to examine your *practice* file:

   more *practice*

   2. Tell **more** to display the second page:

   SPACEBAR

   Once you start displaying a file with **more**, you can easily shift to **vi**.

   3. From within **more**, enter:

   v

   and press ENTER

   The visual editor is executed, and you begin editing the file at whatever location was current in **more**.

   4. Make a change in the file by copying three lines:

   3yy

   p

   5. Exit the visual editor:

   :wq

   When you leave **vi**, you are not returned to the shell; rather, you exit **vi** and return to **more** wherever you left it. However, you made your changes in the file after **more** was started, so you are examining the file as it was before you made changes with **vi**.

6. Exit **more** with:

    q

7. Examine the file again:

    more *practice*

The changes you made with the editor are present in the file.

Obtaining Help

Moreover, there is much more to **more**.

↳ 1. Ask for help by entering:

    h

The following is the Help screen that **more** presents. It describes the commands examined previously plus some additional possibilities:

SPACEBAR	Displays the next screenful of text.
z	Displays the next screenful of text.
RETURN	Displays the next line of text.
q or **Q**	Exits from **more**.
b or CTRL-B	Skips backward one screenful of text.
'	Goes to the place where the previous search started.
=	Displays the current line number.
/*regular expression*	Searches file for the next *regular expression*.
!cmd or **:!cmd**	Executes **cmd** in a subshell.
v	Starts up **/usr/bin/vi**, which edits the original file starting at the current line.
CTRL-L	Redraws the screen.

The **more** utility is a powerful file-examination tool that facilitates quick and accurate viewing and editing of files.

2. Exit **more** with:

    q

The **more** utility is standard on UNIX and Linux systems and is usually used for displaying manual page entries. Systems often also have the utility **less**, and some users prefer it. The **man** pages for **less** should be available if your system supports the utility.

5.2 Selecting Portions of a File with *cut*

We often store data in lines, or *records*, with each record consisting of several columns or fields. Several utilities such as **grep** output whole line records. Other utilities such as **cut** extract columns from a file.

Creating Example Database Files

Because the next several exercises explore how the **cut** utility works on data that uses the TAB character as the field delimiter, create the next two example files with the fields separated by TABs rather than by spaces:

1. With the editor, create a new file called *names.tmp* with the following data, using TAB characters between the fields:

```
101  [Tab]  Nate   [Tab]  H.
102  [Tab]  John   [Tab]  M.
104  [Tab]  Cassy  [Tab]  T.
106  [Tab]  Mary   [Tab]  L.
107  [Tab]  Isaac  [Tab]  C.
```

2. Create a second file called *numbers.tmp* as follows, again with fields separated by TAB characters:

```
101  [Tab]  555-9136
104  [Tab]  591-1191
105  [Tab]  511-1972
106  [Tab]  317-6512
```

Selecting a Field from a File

The simplest use of the **cut** utility is to extract one field (column) from a file.

➥ 1. From the shell, enter the following command line:

    cut -f2 *names.tmp*

The **cut** utility outputs the second field of the file *names.tmp*:

```
Nate
John
Cassy
Mary
Isaac
```

2. To select the first field from the *numbers.tmp* file, enter:

    cut -f1 *numbers.tmp*

The elements of this command are as follows:

COMMAND/ARGUMENT	INTERPRETATION
cut	Instructs the shell to execute the **cut** utility.
-f	Specifies that **cut** extract field(s).
1	This argument to the **-f** option indicates which field(s) to extract. The *1* requests the first field.
numbers.tmp	Argument that tells **cut** which file(s) to read as input.

Using Options with *cut*

The **cut** utility interprets several options as instruction to manipulate the data in different ways including specifying the field delimiter, identifying a range of fields, and selecting a range of characters.

Changing the Field Separator

Although TAB characters are often used to separate fields in records of data, other characters are also used, such as the */etc/passwd* file that uses the colon.

We can instruct **cut** to use the colon as the field delimiter.

➥ 1. Enter the following:

    cut -d: -f4 */etc/passwd* | **more**

The fourth field from the */etc/passwd* file, the users' group IDs, is displayed. Fields are separated by colons in the */etc/passwd* file. The **-d:** instructs **cut** to interpret the colon as the field delimiter as it reads the input.

2. Exit **more** with:

> **q**

As another example, data fields are often separated by the space character in files such as *test-file2* created earlier. We can also instruct **cut** to use a space character as the field delimiter.

3. Enter the following with a space between the single quotes:

> **cut -d' ' -f1** *test-file2*

The first field from all the lines in *test-file2* is output.

4. As another example, enter:

> **cut -d' ' -f2** *practice*

The output is the second word from each line in the file because the spaces determine the fields. The shell interprets spaces on the command line as separators between utilities, arguments, and so on. Because the space following the **-d** is in single quotes, the shell does not interpret it. Rather, the shell passes the space as part of the **-d** argument so **cut** can use it as the field <u>d</u>elimiter.

Selecting Multiple Fields

We can output exact fields and ranges of fields with **cut**.

1. To select two specific fields, enter the following:

> **cut -d: -f1,4** */etc/passwd* | **more**

Fields 1 and 4 are extracted and output.

2. Enter the following to select a range of five fields:

> **cut -d: -f1-5** */etc/passwd* | **more**

Fields 1, 2, 3, 4, and 5 are selected and output.

3. Exit **more** with:

> **9**

Selecting Character Ranges

We can use the **cut** utility to select portions of lines based on text character position instead of fields.

Enter:

> **cut -c4-15** */etc/passwd* | **more**
> **cut -c1-3** *numbers.tmp*
> **cut -c1** *test-file1*

In the first example, characters in positions 4 through 15 are output. Starting at the left edge of the line, **cut** selects and outputs specific characters, as determined by numbered position or range.

SUMMARY: The **cut** utility is used to read a file and extract fields, ranges of fields, characters, and ranges of characters from all lines. To extract by fields, we must separate each field with a field delimiter; to use a character other than a TAB, we must specify the field separator character. Selection may be made on the basis of a list of fields or characters, or a range of those elements. Options include the following:

-flist   Displays fields denoted by list. A list consisting of **1,4** tells **cut** to display the first and fourth fields of a record, whereas **1-4** requests all four fields.

-dchar   Specifies a field-delimiting character other than TAB. Use only when requesting fields with option **-f**.

-clist   Displays characters in the positions, denoted by list, in a record (for example, the character in position **3**, or characters in the range of positions **5-10**).

5.3 Putting Lines Together with *paste*

The **cut** utility reads from files or input, selecting or cutting out specified columns or characters. The **paste** utility, of course, puts data together. This utility is useful when combining lines from various files.

1. Instruct **paste** to operate on the lines of two different files by entering:

   paste *test-file1 test-file2*

   The output is as follows:

```
abc 10  [Tab]  AAA 1A  A
def 20  [Tab]  BBB 2B  B
ghi 30  [Tab]  CCC 2C  C
jkl 40  [Tab]
```

The **paste** utility reads the first line from the first file into memory, adds a TAB character, reads in the first line from the second file, and finally outputs the line. The result is that **paste** combines corresponding lines from the two files and outputs the combined line. The second line of the first file is combined with the second line of the second file, and so on, until **paste** reaches the end of both files.

2. Redirect the output from **paste** to a new file using the original text files as data:

   > **paste** *test-file1 test-file2* **>** *test-fileout*

3. Edit the output:

   > **vi** *test-fileout*

4. From the command mode of **vi**, instruct the editor to display special characters:

   > **:set** *list*

   Between the pasted lines, the display includes a ^*I*, which is the symbol for the TAB character. The **paste** utility reads in a line from the first file, adds a TAB, then adds a line from the second file. The default output separator is the TAB character, but you will soon specify others.

5. Quit the editor and return to the shell.

   We have seen **cat** output the lines of one file *after* the other. The **paste** command, on the other hand, places the lines from each file side by side with a separator character included.

6. To focus on the difference, enter the following commands and examine their output:

   > **cat** *test-file1*
   > **cat** *test-file2*
   > **cat** *test-file1 test-file2*
   > **paste** *test-file1 test-file2*

Combining Several Files

The **paste** utility is not limited to two files.

⤷ Enter:

> **paste** *test-file1 test-file2 numbers.tmp*
> **paste** *test-file1 test-file2 test-file1*

The first line from the first file is read and placed in memory. A TAB is added to the end of the line. The first line from the second file is added, then a TAB, then the first line from the third file. The pasted line is output, and the second lines from each file are pasted, and so on.

Changing the Output Field Separator

With **paste** we can specify the character used for the delimiter in the output.

➥ 1. Have **paste** use a + character as the output separator by entering:

   paste -d+ *test-file1 test-file2 test-file1*

   The output consists of the lines from the two files pasted together with a + character between them.

   Essentially, any character can be used as the output delimiter. However, if the character has special meaning to the shell, such as the characters * $ ^ & ~ ; " ' or a space, the character must be surrounded by single quotation marks or preceded by a backslash.

2. For example, enter:

   paste -d'$' *test-file1 test-file2 names.tmp*

   A dollar sign is placed between the pasted lines in the output.

   In addition, **paste** employs other separator characters.

3. Try the following:

   paste -d'\t' *test-file1 test-file2*
   paste -d'\n' *test-file1 test-file2*
   paste -d'\\' *test-file1 test-file2 names.tmp*
   paste -d'\0' *test-file1 test-file2 names.tmp*

   paste and other utilities understand \t to be the TAB character, \n to be the newline, \\ to be the backslash, and \0 to be empty (no separator character, often called NULL).

Pasting the Lines of One File Together

The **paste** utility combines lines from two or more files when it is given multiple filename arguments. You can also instruct **paste** to combine multiple lines of one file into a single line of output.

⤷ 1. Enter the following:

   paste -s *test-file1*

The output from **paste** consists of all the lines from *test-file1* spliced together as one line using the TAB character as the separator.

2. Instruct **paste** to use a space as the separator in the output by entering:

   paste -s -d' ' *test-file1*

In this command line, the space must be in quotation marks to tell the shell not to interpret the space and instead pass it to **paste** as an argument.

> **SUMMARY:** The **paste** utility connects lines from files in numerical order. The **paste** utility can also be used with options:
> **-d***char*   Change output separator to *char*.
> **-s**   Paste lines together from a single file.

5.4 Formatting Output with the Column Utility

Data is often output in one column, leaving most of the screen blank. On Linux we can format data into multiple columns in two ways. We can put data in the first column, then after it is filled, start placing data in the second column, and so forth, or we can fill the first row across the top, then the second row, and so on.

Formatting Multiple Columns, Filling Rows First

The **column** utility, available on many systems, formats its input into multiple columns of output.

⤷ 1. Execute the following command line:

   ls */usr/bin* **>** *commands*

2. Check the contents of *commands* file:

   more *commands*

The **more** utility shows the contents of the file in just one word to a line. The data is in a single column.

3. Instruct the **column** utility to read the file and to format the contents into columns:

   column *commands* | **more**

The **column** utility reads its input and outputs the data in multiple columns, by filling the first column, then the second, and so forth.

Filling Rows before Filling Columns

We can tell **column** to work the opposite way.

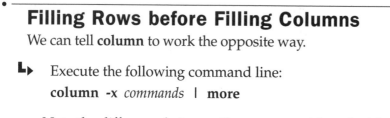 Execute the following command line:

   column -x *commands* | **more**

Note the difference between the outputs with and without the **-x** option. The **-x** option instructs **column** to fill across the first row before filling the second row. In both cases, the number of columns is determined by how many can fit in the display.

5.5 Searching for Lines Containing a Target String with *grep*

In our work, we often need to locate lines that contain words or a specific series of characters (called a *string* or *pattern*) in a file. We can search for lines containing strings in one or more files using the **grep** utility. Common uses for **grep** include quickly locating a line with someone's name in a file or identifying which of many files contains a specific string of characters.

Searching for a Target and Outputting Lines

This section explores how to search through a file for specific targets. For the examples to work properly, you need to carefully create the example file.

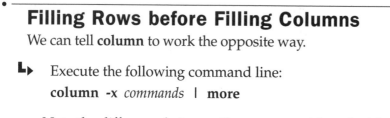 1. Use the editor to create a file named *test-g* containing the lines in Figure 5-1. In Chapter 3, we explored **grep** commands such as the following.

```
about mother
7ab
About the cat t
-2
a b
^a line
t$ 1234
ttt he
at brother
                    ←————— Leave a blank line here.
at
aBc t5t
15-23
They are at -v
Lyle Strand
                    ←————— Leave another blank line.
LyleStrand
                    ←————— Leave another blank line.
tat
a -2 b
```

FIGURE 5-1   Contents of test-g file

2. Enter the following basic **grep** command line:

   grep *ab test-g*

   All lines containing the pattern or target string *ab* in the file *test-g* are output to the screen. **grep** interprets the first argument it receives as the target to search for. The line containing the word *about* is displayed, as is the line containing the *7ab* string. Because **grep** in its basic form is case-sensitive, *About* and *aBc* are not displayed.

3. Enter:

   grep *he test-g practice* | **more**

   The first argument to **grep** is the target; all remaining arguments are files to search. All lines containing the string *he* are output.

   The line containing the word *the* is also selected, because **grep** searches for strings. When we see the string *he*, we think of the word *he*. When **grep** sees this target string, it reads it as "the letter *h* followed by the letter *e*." Because **grep** sees two characters as the target, they may be alone or part of any words such as *the, they,* and *mother*.

Rejecting Lines with the Target

The **grep** utility can also be told to output lines that do *not* contain the target string.

↳ Enter:

grep -v *ab test-g*

In this case, **grep** identifies the lines containing the target, rejects them, and then outputs all the lines from *test-g* that do *not* contain the *ab* string.

The **-v** option tells **grep** to reverse the sense of the search, to reject all target-matching lines, and to output all other lines.

Searching the Data Output by a Utility

If no files are listed as arguments, **grep** reads from input.

↳ **1.** Enter:

sort *test-g* | **grep** *at*
who | **grep** *$USER*
paste *test-file1 test-file2* | **grep** *2*

The lines of the two files are pasted together and output to **grep,** which locates lines containing the target character 2 and outputs the selected lines.

2. Enter:

grep *the*

Only one argument is given to **grep**, which interprets the argument as the search target. With no files to open, **grep** again reads from input, which is connected to the keyboard.

3. Enter:

the
input
mother

As you enter each character of each line, it is displayed on the screen. When you press ENTER , the line is given to **grep** as input. **grep** examines the line. If it finds the target anywhere on the line, **grep** writes the line to output, which in this case is your screen, producing a second copy of the line. If the line does not contain the target, **grep** does not output the line, leaving the original line that you typed all alone on the screen.

4. To tell **grep** to exit, move the cursor to a new line by pressing:

ENTER

and then pressing:

CTRL-D

Searching through Multiple Files

The power of **grep** to search multiple files for a target pattern is especially useful when we are certain that we created a file with some known contents, but we cannot recall which of several files contains the target lines.

1. Enter:

    grep *at test-g names.tmp* | **more**

    All lines containing at least one instance of the target character string *at* are output.

2. Choose a string that you believe you entered in one or more of your files. Then enter the following command line, substituting your chosen word for *string*, and your chosen filenames for *file1* and *file2*:

    grep *string file1 file2*

3. Search all files in the current directory for the word *the* by entering:

    grep *the* * | **more**

The shell replaces the * in this command line with the names of all the files listed in the current directory. The first argument passed to **grep** is the string *the*, which **grep** interprets as the target. **grep** then interprets all remaining arguments as the names of files to open and search.

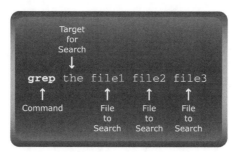

Hence, **grep** looks for the string *the* in all the files in the current directory.

The basic **grep** command line is **grep** *pattern filename(s)*, where *pattern* is the target string of characters and *filename(s)* is the name of one or more files to open and search.

Searching for Multiple-Word Targets

Often the goal is to locate a person's name or another target string that contains one or more spaces. The file *test-g* contains the string *Lyle Strand* as text in the file.

1. To locate the line in the file, enter:

   grep 'Lyle Strand' *test-g*

   The quotation marks instruct the shell not to interpret any special characters in the string *Lyle Strand*. The space between *Lyle* and *Strand* would be interpreted as delimiting two separate arguments if the shell were to interpret it. Instead, the shell passes the string *Lyle*(space)*Strand* as one argument to **grep**.

2. Try the command without the quotation marks:

   grep *Lyle Strand test-g* | **more**

   Without the quotation marks, the shell passes *Lyle* and *Strand* as separate arguments to **grep**:

ARGUMENT	*grep*'S INTERPRETATION
Lyle	The target search string.
Strand	A file to search.
test-g	A file to search.

The **grep** utility then interprets *Lyle*, the first argument, as the search string. To **grep**, all arguments after the search string are interpreted as files to search. **grep** attempts to search *Strand* and *test-g*. Unable to locate the *Strand* file, **grep** displays an error message and then outputs all lines that contain *Lyle* in the file *test-g*.

To pass a multiple-word target to **grep**, enclose the target in single quotation marks so the shell passes it as one argument.

3. As another example, enter:

   grep '*are at*' *test-g*

Because any shell special character in a target string is open to interpretation by the shell, many users simply quote the target at all times.

Ignoring Case in a Search

As seen earlier, the **grep** utility is case-sensitive when you specify the target string in a search.

↳ **1.** Try:

    grep *lyle test-g*

No matching lines are returned.

You can instruct **grep** to ignore case and match the target string, regardless of the case of the letters.

2. Enter the following command line:

    grep -i *lylE test-g*

    grep -i *He test-g*

The lines in *test-g* that contain *Lyle* and *he* are selected because **grep** interprets the **-i** option as instruction to <u>i</u>gnore case.

Outputting Only Filenames in a Search

In the **grep** commands executed thus far in this chapter, the output from **grep** consists of the actual lines in the files that contain the target string, or lines that don't contain the string if **-v** is used. You can instruct **grep** only to list the filenames where there is a match without displaying the lines.

↳ Enter the following optional form of **grep**, with the **-l** (minus el) option:

    grep -l *'04' names.tmp numbers.tmp test**

The **grep** utility interprets the **-l** option to mean to <u>l</u>ist only the filenames that contain the search string, not the matched lines, themselves.

Identifying the Line Number for Each Match

↳ To request that **grep** inform you of the location(s) in the file for each match of the target string, enter:

    grep -n *'ab' test-g*

With the **-n** option, the output of **grep** consists of the line <u>n</u>umber and the line content for each match.

Employing Special Characters with grep

Some characters are not interpreted literally but have special meaning to **grep**.

⌐▸ For example, enter the following, using single quotes to instruct the shell to not interpret the search string argument but to pass it as is to **grep**:

grep '*t.t*' *test-g*

All lines that have a *t* followed by *any single character*, followed by a *t*, are selected. The period or dot (.) is the "any single character wildcard" special character to **grep**.

Identifying the Beginning of a Line

The dot is one of many characters that **grep** interprets as having special meaning rather than as being a literal character.

⌐▸ 1. For another example, enter:

grep '*^a*' *test-g*

Every line that starts with the character *a* is selected. The line in *test-g* consisting of *^a* is *not* selected, because the *a* is not the first character on the line. The ^ (caret) is the beginning-of-line special character.

2. Tell **grep** not to interpret the special character ^ by entering:

grep '*\^a*' *test-g*

The line containing the target *^a* is selected. The \ character is inside single quotes. It is not interpreted by the shell, but passed to **grep** as part of the \^**a** argument. **grep** interprets the \ as instruction not to interpret any special powers for whatever character follows. The ^ is immediately after the \, so **grep** does not interpret the caret as having special meaning. The ^ is therefore just a ^ character, not the special character interpreted as the beginning of the line.

Selecting Lines with Patterns Located at the End of the Line

The end of a line can also be specified with a special character.

⌐▸ Enter:

grep '*t$*' *test-g*

All lines that have a *t* followed by the end of the line (designated by the **$**) are selected.

Special characters such as these are used in target strings for **grep**. A target employing special characters is called a *regular expression,* and is used by many utilities, including **awk**, **sed**, and **grep**. The **grep** utility gets its name from **g**lobal **r**egular **e**xpressions **p**rinter.

Locating Lines of Specific Length

We can use several special characters together to create a regular expression that identifies lines of a specific length.

 1. Enter:

> **grep -n '^...$'** *test-g*

Lines consisting of exactly three characters (any three) between the beginning of the line and the end of the line are selected and output with line numbers.

2. Enter:

> **grep -n '^$'** *test-g*

All blank lines, with their line numbers, are output.

The **-n** option instructs **grep** to output line numbers. The regular expression **^$** tells **grep** to find lines that have a beginning of line, followed immediately by the end of the line.

A book consisting of a front cover followed immediately by the back cover is a quick read. Regular expressions that incorporate the special characters **^.$** allow us to specify exactly the lines we want selected.

S U M M A R Y : The **grep** utility is used to search through one or more files for lines containing a target string of characters. For a single file, it outputs the selected lines. For multiple files, it outputs the filenames and located lines. Options are as follows:

grep without an option   Find pattern and output each line that contains it.

-i   Make matches ignoring upper- and lowercase.

-l   Output only a list of the names of the files that contain a specific pattern.

-v   Output all lines where the pattern is not found.

-n   Output the line **n**umber and the line content for each match.

5.6 Performing Mathematical Calculations

On most UNIX and Linux systems, a powerful calculation utility is available for computing basic arithmetic operations.

At the command line of the shell, call up the calculator:

1. Enter:

    bc

    The screen clears, you are warned not to do your taxes with **bc**, the <u>b</u>asic <u>c</u>alculator, and the cursor is on a new line. There is no prompt. The utility is waiting for input.

2. Enter:

    6 + 9

    And press ENTER

    The resulting sum of *15* is displayed.

    You instructed the shell to execute the **bc** utility. No redirection is specified, so input is connected to the keyboard and output to the screen.

3. Enter the following:

    1234 + 5678
    12 * 12
    144 / 3
    122 - 4

    The standard add (**+**), subtract (**-**), multiply (*****), and divide (**/**) operations are available.

4. Try:

    2 ^ 6

   The utility calculates 2 raised to the power of *6* or *2 * 2 * 2 * 2 * 2 * 2*. Thus, 2 raised to the 6th power is *64*.

Exiting the Basic Calculator

At this point, the **bc** utility is reading whatever we enter as instructions for making calculations.

To exit, we must issue the end-of-file character.

1. To get out of **bc** enter:

    CTRL-D

2. Start **bc** again:

> **bc**

Using Floating-Point Operations

When we divide integers with **bc**, the result is integer division.

1. Enter:

> *25 / 7*

The answer is *3* because when we divide 25 by 7, there are three whole sevens, for a total of 21, in 25, which produces a remainder of 4. The largest multiple of 7 in 25 is 3.

By default, remainders and decimals are not reported, just the integer answer. However, we can instruct **bc** to report decimal values.

2. To include decimals, enter:

> **scale=2**
> *25 / 7*

Now the output (*3.57*) has two-decimal-place accuracy, rather than integers only.

3. Modify the scale and try again:

> **scale=4**
> *25 / 7*

The output *3.5714* includes four numbers to the right of the decimal point.

4. Vary the scale by entering:

> *50 / 6*
> **scale=3**
> *50 / 6*
> **scale=6**
> *26 / 17*

In **bc**, the number of places to the right of the decimal included in the output is determined by the numeric value assigned to **scale**.

Determining the Order of Operations

1. Enter the following to **bc**:

> *8 + 2 * 5*

The result is *18* because in **bc** the multiplication operation *(2 * 5)* precedes the addition operation *(8 + 10)*.

2. Enter:

    *(8 + 2) * 5*

This time the result is *50* because the parentheses force the addition *(8 + 2)* to be completed before the multiplication. To specify the order of operation, use parentheses.

3. Enter:

    *(2 + 3) * 4 * (6 - 3)*

The addition *(2 + 3)* and the subtraction *(6 - 3)* are first because they are in the innermost parentheses. The result is *5 * 4 * 3*, or *60*.

4. Exit **bc**:

    CTRL-D

Self Test 1

1. If you are using **more** to examine a file and decide you want to look back at the previous page, what do you enter?

   _____

2. From **more**, how can you quickly start editing the current file with **vi**?

   _____

3. What command tells **cut** to output the first five characters of every line from the file *practice*?

   _____

4. What command tells **grep** to look for all lines consisting of only the letter Z followed by any four characters in a file *filename*?

   _____

5. What command instructs **grep** to look through all files in the current directory for lines containing the string *Pat Lloyd* and output just the names of the files that contain a match?

   _____

6. How do you get the answer to the following with four figures to the right of the decimal point? Add 424 to 79, divide that sum by 161, then raise that result to the 15th power.

   _____

7. What command tells a utility to search through every file in the current directory for the name *Catherine Thamzin*?

_____

8. What command results in a listing of the number of words and the number of lines in the files *practice* and *users_on*?

_____

9. What command creates a new file *chapter* consisting of the contents of the files *section1*, *section2*, *section3*, and *section4*, with all lines numbered?

_____

10. A file called *empnames* contains many employee names, with exactly one name on each line. What command outputs the names in the file in multiple columns, with columns filled before rows?

_____

5.7 Ordering the Lines of a File with *sort*

The **sort** utility sorts lines that it reads from files or its input. It sorts the lines following specific criteria, and then outputs the ordered results.

Sorting Lines in the Default Order

1. Use the editor to create the file *test-sor* with the content shown in Figure 5-2.
2. Enter the following command to have **sort** read the lines in the file, sort them, and output the results on the terminal screen:

   sort *test-sor* | **more**

   The resulting material is sorted as shown in Figure 5-3.

   The default order that **sort** uses to sorts lines varies among systems. There are two schemes. On some systems, the line *Mary* and the line *mary* are next to each other. The upper-and lowercase letters are sorted together. On other systems, all lines beginning with uppercase letters are sorted together, then later, lines starting with lowercase. If your system follows that approach, the output is like Figure 5-3 with *Mary* and *ZZ* next to each other.
3. Look carefully at your output and compare it with Figure 5-3.

   If all the lines starting with uppercase letters are together and the lines starting with lowercase letters are later in the output, all is well, so proceed to step 4.

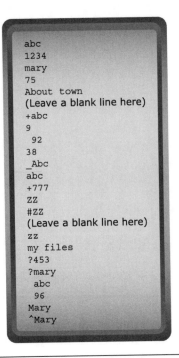

```
abc
1234
mary
75
About town
(Leave a blank line here)
+abc
9
 92
38
_Abc
abc
+777
ZZ
#ZZ
(Leave a blank line here)
zz
my files
?453
?mary
  abc
 96
Mary
^Mary
```

FIGURE 5-2   Unsorted contents of the file of **test-sor**

If your output has all lines beginning with the same letter, upper- and lowercase together (*Mary* and *mary*), complete the steps in the following note.

N O T E :   The value of the environmental variable **LC_ALL** determines the default order for sorting. If your output puts upper- and lowercase of the same letters together, you need to reset the variable.

In the **bash** or **ksh** shells enter:

    export LC_ALL="POSIX"

In the **csh** and **tcsh** shells:

    setenv LC_ALL "POSIX"

In its basic form, **sort** arranges the lines of a file in a sorted order by comparing the first character—and when needed, subsequent characters—of each line.

The criterion that **sort** follows to order the lines is the order of the ASCII character set.

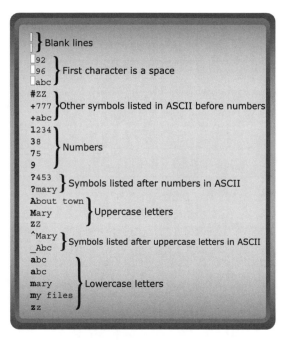

FIGURE 5-3 Sorted version of **test-sor**

4. Examine the ASCII character set by entering this command:

man *ascii*

Because computers hold only numbers in memory, there is no way to place the character *A* in memory as an *A*. Instead, every character is held in memory as a specific number, from 0 to 127. The ASCII (American Standard Code for Information Interchange) code defines all the characters we use as one of the numbers from 0 to 127.

Figure 5-4 lists all ASCII characters and the number that is assigned to each one of the characters. There are 128 characters numbered from 0 to 127.

To determine the number for a particular character, consult Figure 5-4. You must first locate the character in the body of the table and then read both the number to the left of the row that the character is in, as well as the number at the top of the column. For example, the letter *F* is in row 7 and column 0; its ASCII value is therefore 70. Likewise, the space (sp) is in row 3 of column 2; therefore, its ASCII value is 32. The + is 43, the *z* is 122, and so on.

The beginning of the ASCII character set is made up of special characters such as *newline*, then some punctuation characters, followed by numbers, more special

	0	1	2	3	4	5	6	7	8	9
0	nul	soh	stx	etx	eot	enq	ack	\a	\b	\t
1	\n	\v	lf	\r	so	si	dle	dc1	dc2	dc3
2	dc4	nak	syn	etb	can	em	sub	esc	fs	gs
3	rs	us	sp	!	"	#	$	%	&	'
4	(	)	*	+	,	-	.	/	0	1
5	2	3	4	5	6	7	8	9	:	;
6	<	=	>	?	@	A	B	C	D	E
7	F	G	H	I	J	K	L	M	N	O
8	P	Q	R	S	T	U	V	W	X	Y
9	Z	[	\	]	^	_	`	a	b	c
10	d	e	f	g	h	i	j	k	l	m
11	n	o	p	q	r	s	t	u	v	w
12	x	y	z	{	|	}	~	del		

FIGURE 5-4   ASCII numbers for characters

characters, uppercase letters, six punctuation characters, lowercase letters, and the five programming characters. This is the order that **sort** uses to sort the lines of a file, unless you provide **sort** with specific options to do otherwise.

Sorting in Dictionary Order

The **sort** utility recognizes several sorting options. One option tells **sort** to ignore punctuation and other special characters, and to use only letters, digits, and spaces in its sort.

1. Enter:

   sort -d *test-sor* | **more**

2. The dictionary-sorted output is in Figure 5-5.

The line ^*Mary* is no longer after the uppercase lines with the underscore in the sorted output. It is sorted according to where the *M* fits into the scheme, not the caret. All characters other than letters, numbers, and spaces are ignored in the sort when you use the **-d** option. The sort is based only on letters, numbers, and space characters.

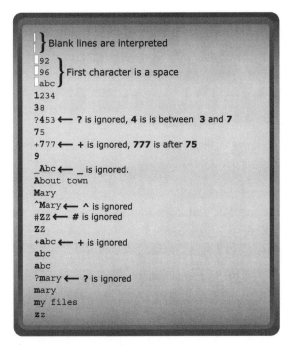

FIGURE 5-5   Output of **sort** with **-d** Option

Sorting Regardless of Capitalization

The **sort** program can be told to ignore the case (upper or lower) of the letters in its input when sorting—that is, to output the cases together.

➤   For example, enter:

sort -f *test-sor* | **more**

The output displays the lines in ASCII order, but with upper- and lowercase of the same letter folded together, as in Figure 5-6.

Sorting Based on Numerical Value

When **sort** orders the lines in sorted order, lines consisting of numbers are sorted in ASCII order, not numerical value.

➤   1. Enter:

sort *test-sor* | **more**

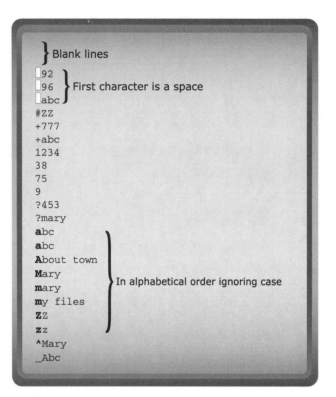

FIGURE 5-6 Output of **sort** with the *-f* Option

2. Examine the lines consisting of numbers:

   1234
   38
   75
   9

   These lines are not in ascending numerical value; rather, they are sorted in ASCII order. The initial characters on each line determine the sorting order, not the numerical value. The 1 is before the 3, which is before the 7, which is before the 9.

3. Enter:

   sort -n *test-sor* | **more**

The **-n** option instructs **sort** to make decisions about numbers based on numerical value rather than ASCII order. Your output includes all lines in the file, with the sorted numbers placed at the end of the output after the lines that start with alphabetical characters.

Reversing the Order of *sort's* Output

We can instruct **sort** to arrange the lines it sorts opposite of its normal sorting order.

↳   Enter:

sort -r *test-sor* | **more**

The lines starting with letters at the end of the alphabet are output first. Lines with numbers starting with higher digits preceed lower ones. The display is in reverse ASCII order, as shown in Figure 5-7.

Combining Options

Each of the options to **sort** is interpreted as instruction to modify the way **sort** sorts lines. We can employ more than one at a time.

↳   Enter:

sort -rfn *test-sor* | **more**

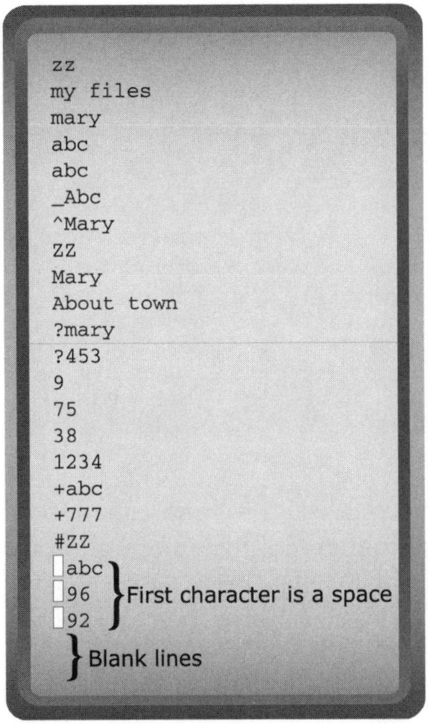

```
zz
my files
mary
abc
abc
_Abc
^Mary
zz
Mary
About town
?mary
?453
9
75
38
1234
+abc
+777
#ZZ
 abc ⎫
 96  ⎬ First character is a space
 92  ⎭

    ⎫ Blank lines
    ⎭
```

FIGURE 5-7   Output of *sort* with *-r* option

The output is the contents of *test-sor* in reverse sorted order, with uppercase folded into lowercase and with numbers sorted based on value, not ASCII order.

Sorting by Fields

The **sort** utility generally sorts lines based on the *first character* in each line. If the first characters from two lines match, the second character in each line is examined, then the third, and so on. There is an alternative: You can sort lines based on the contents of specific fields. Many files consist of lines of data that are composed of different fields separated by a character such as a colon, a space, or a TAB.

Creating a Data File

If we are to explore sorting lines by specific fields, a data file that contains lines (records), with each line composed of fields identified by a field separator, must be available.

⬐▶ Create a file named *respected* containing the following text. Each line for each individual contains five fields separated by spaces. Each field contains different information about that individual. Be sure to include the numbers as the first field.

```
000 Dyllis B. Harvey nurturer
001 Lyle C. Strand mentor
002 James V. Miller dean
003 Marjorie M. Conrad teacher
004 Orin C. Braucher farmer
005 David A. Wass professor
006 Peter M. Kindfield friend
007 Marge M. Boercker writer
```

Each line in the file provides information about one particular person. Every line, called a *record*, is divided into five information fields that pertain to the person. The following relates the data from the first record to the associated field names:

RECORD NUMBER	FIRST NAME	MIDDLE INITIAL	LAST NAME	DESCRIPTION
000	Dyllis	B.	Harvey	nurturer

A *field* is defined as a series of characters (a word, a number, a string of letters) where each field is separated from the next by some specified or default character. This character is often called the *field delimiter* or *field separator*. The default field delimiter for **sort** is the white space, either the space or TAB characters.

Sorting a Data File by Fields

Thus far you have been sorting lines starting with the initial character on the line. We can also sort based on the data in specific fields.

1. Sort the *respected* file according to last name (the fourth field) by entering:

    sort +3 *respected*

    The **+3** tells **sort** to count three field separators and then start sorting. Hence, the sort begins at the fourth field.

2. An alternative way to achieve the same result is to use the **-k** option. Enter:

    sort -k *4 respected*

In both cases, the output is sorted beginning with the fourth field.

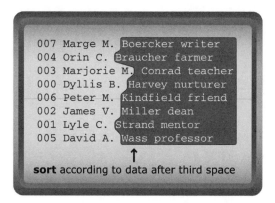

```
007 Marge M. Boercker writer
004 Orin C. Braucher farmer
003 Marjorie M. Conrad teacher
000 Dyllis B. Harvey nurturer
006 Peter M. Kindfield friend
002 James V. Miller dean
001 Lyle C. Strand mentor
005 David A. Wass professor
                ↑
sort according to data after third space
```

Sorting Starting with One Field

In the previous example, records are sorted based on the values in the fourth field, which contains the last names of the individuals. Because no two records contain the same last name, the sorting is without complication. However, because several individuals in this data have the same middle initial in the third field, it gives us the opportunity to explore how we can have **sort** decide ties.

➡ Examine how **sort** sorts by field when several records have the same value in the sorted field. Enter:

sort +2 *respected*

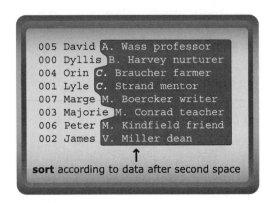

```
005 David A. Wass professor
000 Dyllis B. Harvey nurturer
004 Orin  C. Braucher farmer
001 Lyle  C. Strand mentor
007 Marge M. Boercker writer
003 Majorie M. Conrad teacher
006 Peter M. Kindfield friend
002 James V. Miller dean
```

↑
sort according to data after second space

There are two records with the middle initial *C*. The **sort** utility found both *C*s and decided the sort order by comparing the characters that follow the *C*s in the next field. *Braucher* comes before *Strand* in the ASCII order, so record 004 is output before record 001. Likewise, the three records for people with middle initials of *M* are arranged based on the contents of the text that follows, last names: *B*, *C*, and then *K*.

Limiting *sort*

It is possible to instruct **sort** to stop sorting at a given field.

➡ Tell **sort** to sort by middle initial by entering:

sort +2 -3 *respected*

The following display highlights characters that are essential in making the sort decisions:

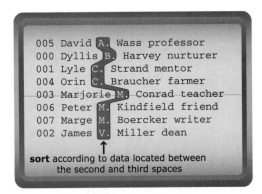

```
005 David A. Wass professor
000 Dyllis B. Harvey nurturer
001 Lyle C. Strand mentor
004 Orin C. Braucher farmer
003 Marjorie M. Conrad teacher
006 Peter M. Kindfield friend
007 Marge M. Boercker writer
002 James V. Miller dean
```
↑
sort according to data located between
the second and third spaces

In the previous command, the instruction (**+2 -3**) is to count two field separators (**+2**), start sorting, and then stop sorting at the third separator (**-3**). The net effect is to sort on field 3, the middle initial. The records that have the same value in the sort field (middle initial) are listed in an order that is decided by values in the default first field. The *Kindfield* record is output before *Boercker* because it has a lower number in the first field. Thus, the records with *M* in the third field are ordered based on the order of the default first field.

If we tell **sort** to sort lines based on some portion of the record, it breaks ties starting with the beginning of the line unless we tell it to do something else.

Including a Secondary Sort Field

Rather than defaulting to the beginning of the record when there are duplicates in the **sort** field, we can specify another field as a secondary sort, to be examined only in case of a tie in the primary sort field.

▶ Request that the third field be the primary sort field, and the second field be the secondary sort field, by entering:

sort +2 -3 +1 -2 *respected*

The output is:

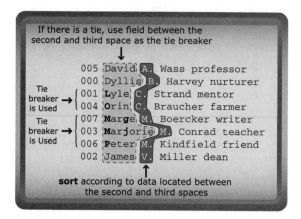

In this version, the records with the same value in the primary field (middle initial) are sorted based on the values in the secondary field, first names. For the two records with *C* in the primary field, *Lyle* is output before *Orin* because *L* precedes *O*.

Three records have a middle initial of *M*, so the first names (field 2) are consulted: *Marge* precedes *Marjorie*, which precedes *Peter*.

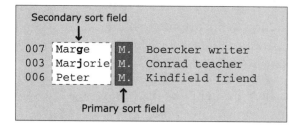

Examining the Code

Consider the command line you just entered:

sort *+2 -3 +1 -2 respected*

It is instruction to pass five arguments to **sort**:

+2	Count two field separators and start sorting each record.
-3	Stop sorting each record at the third field separator. Hence, the third field is sorted.

> **+1 -2** If the data in the third field results in two or more records with identical data, break the tie by examining the second field of those records (**+1 −2**).

Reversing a Secondary Field

On most systems, each sort field can be handled differently.

↳ Reverse the sense of the secondary sort field, while leaving the primary field as is, by entering:

sort +2 -3 +1r -2 *respected*

Figure 5-8 shows the output. Because the secondary sort is reversed, **Peter** is displayed as the first record with the middle initial of *M*.

With the **sort** utility, we can specify complex sorts based on lines or fields, and we can instruct **sort** to use another field as a secondary sort criteria. Additionally, we can specify that all sorting be based on an option such as **–r**, **–d**, or **-f**, or that just one field be sorted according to an option by including the option in the field definition, such as **+3n -4**.

Using *sort* with a Different Field Delimiter

The file */etc/passwd* contains system information about users.

↳ 1. Examine the file by entering the following:

head */etc/passwd*

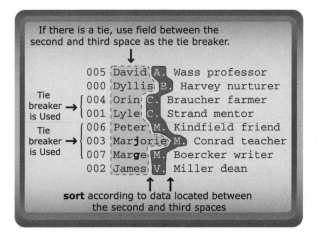

FIGURE 5-8   Reversing the secondary sort

Each line is a series of fields separated by colons:

```
cassy:RstAk9?sMZ4pQb:1991:423:child:/home/cassy:/bin/ksh
```

On some systems, the *passwd* file is quite large; on others, it is fairly small.

2. Enter:

   wc */etc/passwd*

3. Create a short file in your current directory by entering:

   head *-15* */etc/passwd* > *short-pass*

   This command instructs the shell to start a child process; connect the output of the process to a new file named *short-pass*, give the child process two arguments, *-15* and */etc/passwd*; and tell the process to execute the **head** utility. The **head** utility reads at most 15 lines from the *passwd* file and writes them to output, which is connected to *short-pass*, a new file in your directory.

4. Confirm by entering:

   wc *short-pass*
   cat *short-pass*

5. Have **sort** order the lines in the *short-pass* file by entering:

   sort *short-pass*

   In the *respected* file that you used a few sections back, the fields are separated by a space. In the */etc/passwd* and *short-pass* files, the separator character is the colon.

   The third field in each record in the password file is the user's unique identification number.

6. To see how **sort** handles the request to sort by a specific field when the file does not use white space as a field separator, enter:

   sort *+2* *short-pass*

   The results are not sorted by what we think of as the third field, because **sort** is defining fields based on spaces, not colons.

7. To request sorting by the third field with fields separated by the colon character, enter:

   sort *-t:* *+2* *short-pass*

   The records are now sorted based on the third field, user ID.

The **-t** option instructs **sort** to use a different character for the field separator. The specified character, the colon, follows the **-t** option without a space between them. The sorting in the previous command is by ASCII value, not numerical value. In an ASCII sort, the number 110 comes before 20 because sorting starts with the leftmost character on the line. Character 1 precedes 2 in the ASCII character set.

8. To sort in numerical order, include the **-n** option:

   sort -t: -n +2 *short-pass*

The records are sorted based on the numerical values in field 3.

Redirecting the Output of *sort* to a File

In the examples entered thus far, the output of **sort** is connected to your workstation screen. As is usually the case, you can redirect the output of a utility to a file.

⮡ 1. Enter:

   sort *test-sor* **>** *sorted-test-sor*

   The **sort** utility sorts the lines from the file named *test-sor,* and the output of **sort** is placed in a file named *sorted-test-sor.* This new file can be edited, manipulated, or examined by other utilities.

2. Examine the *sorted-test-sor* using **more** or **cat**.

Sorting a File and Overwriting

You may be tempted to sort a file and have its output placed back in the file.

⮡ 1. Enter the following:

   cp *short-pass sp2*
   cat *sp2*
   sort *sp2* **>** *sp2*

   One of two things occurs. Either you are told the file already exists (if *noclobber* is set), or there was no objection, the shell did as it was told, and the file *sp2* is now empty.

2. Enter:

   cat *sp2*

When we tell the shell to redirect output to an existing file, the shell empties the specified file (unless *noclobber* is set) before executing the utility. The shell empties the file before **sort** opens it to sort it. There are no lines to sort.

To solve this problem, there is an option we can give to **sort**.

3. Enter:

> **cp** *short-pass sp3*
> **sort** *sp3* **-o** *sortedsp3*

There is no shell redirection in this command line. The shell does not connect the output of **sort** to *sortedsp3*. Instead, three arguments are passed to **sort**.

ARGUMENT	INTERPRETATION
sp3	Identifies the file to read and sort.
-o	Puts the output in the file listed as the next argument.
sortedsp3	This argument to the **-o** option is interpreted as the name of the file where **sort** is to write its output.

Because **sort** reads input first and writes last, we can tell it to read and write the same file without a problem.

4. Enter:

> **sort** *sp3* **-o** *sp3*
> **cat** *sp3*

The file is now sorted because **sort** read the file, sorted the lines, and after sorting overwrote the unsorted file with its sorted output.

Although **sort** is a powerful and flexible utility, it sorts only lines. Once it reads in the lines and sorts them, it outputs the whole lines, not just selected portions. The **cut** and **awk** utilities can be used to overcome this limitation.

> **S U M M A R Y :** The **sort** utility takes all lines it receives as input and rearranges them into a variety of orders, based on the following options:
> **sort** (without option)   Sort following the ASCII order.
> **-r**   Reverse the sorted order.
> **-d**   Output based only on letters, numbers, and space characters.
> **-f**   Sort with uppercase and lowercase of the same letter sorted together (folded); if there is a tie, uppercase is first.
> **+***n*   Sort by a specific field, where *n* is the number of field separators that **sort** is to count before beginning the sort.
> **-***n*   Stop sorting at the *n*th field separator, where *n* is a number.
> **-k** *n*   Sort lines based on the values in the *n*th field.
> **-n**   Sort by numerical value rather than ASCII order.
> **-t***x*   Use the character *x* as the field delimiter, which can be any character.
> **-o** *arg*   Put output in a file named *arg*.

Examining the *man* Pages for *sort*

Now that you have explored the **sort** utility and several of its options, review the manual pages for these and other **sort** options available on your system.

1. Enter:

   man *sort*

2. When you are ready, quit **man** by entering:

   q

As you have seen in the several forays into the manual pages, a wealth of information is available concerning each utility. We suggest that you look up each utility in the man pages after you work through the exercises in this chapter.

5.8 Identifying and Removing Duplicate Lines

Often, when we sort a file containing information such as an index or word list, the resulting output includes lines containing duplicate data. The **uniq** utility reads the input and compares each line with the line that precedes it. If the two lines are identical, action is taken.

⤷ **1.** Create a test file called *test-u* consisting of the following:

```
aa
bbb
ccc
aaa
aaa
aaa
bbb
bbb
eee
fff
aaa
```

2. To examine how **uniq** works, enter the following command line:

    uniq *test-u*

Examine the output:

```
aa
bbb
ccc
aaa
bbb
eee
fff
aaa
```

The **uniq** utility reads a line, then reads a second. If the second line is just like the first, **uniq** discards that line. All duplicate lines that are *not* adjacent to each other remain. Duplicates that are on adjacent lines are reduced to just one copy.

Removing All Duplicate Lines

Because the **uniq** utility compares only *adjacent* lines, duplicate lines must be next to each other in the input if we expect **uniq** to remove the duplicate. One way to be certain that all duplicates are adjacent is to sort the file first.

1. Examine *test-u*, create a sorted version, and examine it:

>   **cat** *test-u*
>   **sort** *test-u* **>** *sor-test-u*
>   **cat** *sor-test-u*

2. Now run **uniq** on the sorted file:

>   **uniq** *sor-test-u*

   The **uniq** utility reads each line from the file, removes duplicate adjacent lines, and displays the results.

   The sorted file has all duplicate lines grouped together. The **uniq** utility removes all but one of each set of duplicates.

   Sorting and using **uniq** can be accomplished in one step.

3. Enter the following:

>   **sort** *test-u* **|** **uniq**

One copy of all lines is output. There are really two kinds of lines in the sorted file. Some lines are unique, some have adjacent lines that are duplicates. The **uniq** utility without an option outputs the unique lines and one copy of the lines that have duplicates.

In this case, after the lines from *test-u* are sorted, the output of **sort** is connected directly to the input of **uniq**, which removes all but one copy of lines that have duplicates and sends the output to your screen.

Identifying the Lines That Have No Duplicates

In *test-u*, there are some unique lines and some lines with duplicates. The duplicates are not all adjacent.

1. Sort the file:

>   **sort** *test-u* **-o** *test-u*
>   **cat** *test-u*

   The file is sorted and overwritten with the sorted version.

2. Use **uniq**:

> **uniq** *test-u*

We get one of every line, even if originally there were several.

The lines that are unique (have no duplicates) in the file can be selected as well.

3. Enter the command:

> **uniq -u** *test-u*

With the **-u** option, **uniq** examines the contents of the file and outputs only the lines that have no adjacent duplicates. If lines are duplicates, all are discarded. The lines that are truly <u>u</u>nique in the input are the only ones selected.

Identifying the Duplicated Lines

Lines that do have duplicates can be selected and output by **uniq**.

1. Enter the command:

> **uniq -d** *test-u*

With the **-d** option, **uniq** ignores all lines that are unique and outputs one copy of a line if it has <u>d</u>uplicates.

The **uniq** utility with the **-d** option outputs a single copy of each duplicate line, no matter how often it is repeated in the sorted file.

2. Instruct **uniq** to count the number of times each line is in the input:

> **uniq -c** *test-u*

Each line is output with the <u>c</u>ount of that line on its left, indicating how many times that line is in the sorted file.

SUMMARY: Unless an option is specified, the **uniq** utility compares adjacent lines in its input, discarding a line if it is a duplicate of the preceding line. If the input is sorted, the resulting output consists of one copy of all unique lines and one copy of all duplicate lines. Options are as follows:

-u Output only the unique lines, discard all of the duplicates.

-d Output only a single copy of the lines that are duplicated; discard the duplicates and all unique lines.

-c Output a single copy of each line with a number to its left indicating the number of times that line is in the input.

5.9 Comparing the Contents of Files with *comm*

Each line in any two files can be fit into one of three categories:

- Lines uniquely in the first file
- Lines uniquely in the second file
- Lines that are in both files

   The **comm** utility compares two files, line by line, and identifies in which of the three categories each line belongs. Is it a line found only in the first file, only in the second file, or a line that is in both files?

Creating an Example File

To examine how the **comm** utility compares data, you need to create two files of specific content. In the United States, some states are located on the coast of an ocean; others are not. Some states are in the western part of the United States, and some are not. Some states are *both* in the West *and* on the coast.

1. Use the <u>vi</u>sual editor to create a file called *west* with the following contents:

   ```
   California
   Washington
   Oregon
   Nevada
   Utah
   ```

2. While still editing the file *west*, make sure you are in command mode and enter:

   :set *list*

   This is instruction to **vi** to display special characters, including the end-of-line characters.

   A dollar sign appears at the end of each line.

3. If any spaces exist at the end of lines, or if any state name is not spelled correctly or is in the wrong case, correct it.

4. Write the file and quit the editor.

5. Create a second file named *coast*, with the following contents:

   ```
   Florida
   Washington
   Maine
   ```

```
Oregon
California
Georgia
```

6. Check to be sure the data is correct with:

    :set *list*

7. Write and quit the editor.

8. For **comm** to work properly, the files need to be sorted. Enter these commands:

    sort *west* > *sor-west*

    sort *coast* > *sor-coast*

Grouping Unique and Common Lines

Consider the following illustration, which represents the lines in the two sorted files. Notice that some lines (states) are unique to each file, and some lines are in both files.

There are three groups of lines:

- Lines found in *sor-west* but not in *sor-coast* (western states not on the coast)
- Lines found in *sor-coast* but not in *sor-west* (coastal states not in the West)
- Lines found in both files (western states and on the coast)

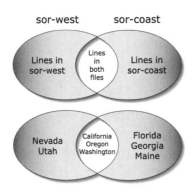

Identifying Unique and Common Lines

We can look at the data and determine which states are uniquely in each file and which are in both. The **comm** utility accomplishes the same thing.

1. To identify the common and unique lines in the two sorted files, enter:

> **comm** *sor-west sor-coast* > *west-coast*

This command instructs **comm** to compare the two files listed as arguments. The output from **comm** is redirected to a new file, *west-coast*.

2. Call up the file *west-coast* with the editor:

> **vi** *west-coast*

The output of **comm** is three columns of data:

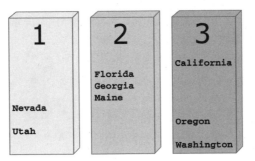

The three columns are as follows:

- The first column contains those lines that are uniquely in the *first* file: *Nevada* and *Utah*.
- The second column contains those lines that are uniquely in the *second* file: *Florida, Georgia,* and *Maine*.
- The third column contains those lines that are in *both* files: *California, Oregon,* and *Washington*.

While editing this output file, again ask the editor to display special characters.

3. From command mode, enter:

> **:set** *list*

The display shows the content with special characters identified. A few of the output lines are included in the next illustration:

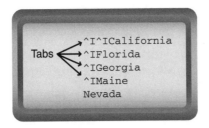

The special character ^I is the editor's way of displaying the TAB character. When **comm** reads *California* as the first line in the first file and then also finds it in the second file, **comm** outputs two TABs and then the line *California*. The two TABs put the line in the third column of output. The line *Florida* is found in the second file only, so **comm** precedes it with only one TAB to put it in the second column of output. *Nevada* is only in the first file, so **comm** outputs no TABs before the line. All lines uniquely in the first file, group 1, are against the left margin. All lines in the second file only, group 2, are in the middle because one TAB was output in front of each line. All lines in common, group 3, are on the right because two TABs are output in front of each line that is found in both files.

4. Quit the editor and return to the shell.

Selecting Unique or Common Lines

The three columns of output are related to the three kinds of lines:

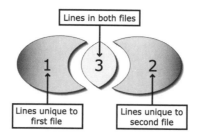

Column 1, group 1, includes the unique lines from the first file; column 2, group 2, includes lines uniquely in the second file; column 3, group 3, includes the lines common to both files.

With options, we can select lines common to both files or just those that are unique to one or the other file.

1. Enter:

> **comm** *-3 sor-west sor-coast*

This command instructs **comm** to discard group 3, the lines in common in both files. The output is group 1, which consists of the lines unique to the first file, and group 2, which consists of the lines uniquely in the second file (groups 1 and 2). Those lines found in both files (group 3) are suppressed.

To list only those lines common to both files—that is, to select group 3—we must leave out groups 1 and 2.

2. Enter this command:

   comm *-12 sor-west sor-coast*

   With the *-12* flag, **comm** suppresses printing of groups 1 and 2, the lines unique to each file. Only those states in the West that are also on a coast are listed—the lines in both files.

3. Likewise, a listing of western states that are not on the coast can be attained by entering:

   comm *-23 sor-west sor-coast*

   This flag is an instruction to suppress groups 2, lines unique to the second file, and 3, lines common to both. It outputs only group 1, lines uniquely in the first file.

4. To see how **comm** works, have **comm** compare the original unsorted files, *west* and *coast*:

   comm *west coast*

The output is not correct. Several states that are in common are listed in the output as uniquely in both files. This is a practical impossibility. How did this occur? The **comm** utility compares the files line by line. When **comm** reads the line *California* in the first (unsorted) file and later finds *Florida* as the first line in the second file, **comm** concludes that there can be no *California* in the second file. The logic is this: **comm** assumes that since *Florida* is on the first line of the second file, there can be no other line that starts with a letter before *F* in that file. The input files to **comm** must be sorted first because the **comm** utility was written based on this assumption.

S U M M A R Y : The **comm** utility compares the contents of two files, line by line. It reports a table indicating the lines unique to each file, and the lines common to both. Because **comm** works only with one line at a time, input must be sorted. Options are as follows:

-1 Suppress output of lines uniquely in the first file.
-2 Suppress output of lines uniquely in the second file.
-3 Suppress output of lines that are common to both files.
-12 Options can be combined. This combination is instruction to suppress lines unique to each file so that only lines common to both are output.

5.10 Examining Differences between Files

The **diff** utility indicates how two files are **diff**erent. It reports the lines that are not the same, the location of these lines in their respective files, and what lines you need to add, change, or delete to convert one file to the other.

1. Create a file called *alpha1* containing the following lines:

```
Mary
Robert
Pat
Nancy
```

2. Create a second file, *alpha2*, containing these lines:

```
Mary
Robert P
Pat L
Nancy
Ivan
```

3. Find the differences between *alpha1* and *alpha2* by entering:

   diff *alpha1 alpha2*

   The following output is displayed:

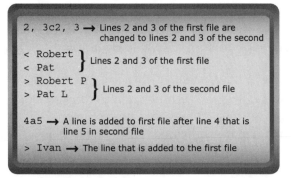

```
2, 3c2, 3 → Lines 2 and 3 of the first file are
              changed to lines 2 and 3 of the second

< Robert  }
< Pat       Lines 2 and 3 of the first file

> Robert P }
> Pat L      Lines 2 and 3 of the second file


4a5 → A line is added to first file after line 4 that is
      line 5 in second file

> Ivan → The line that is added to the first file
```

This output contains two kinds of lines. Lines such as *Robert* indicate that the line *Robert* is in the first file, but not in the second. Likewise, *Robert P* is in the second file, not the first. A line that includes numbers and letters (2, 3c2, 3) indicates the location of the differing lines in their respective files and what needs to be done to convert the first file into the second.

In contrast to **diff**, the **comm** utility just lists the lines unique to each file and in common to both.

For more information concerning **diff**, consult the output of **man**.

> **S U M M A R Y :** The **diff** utility compares two files and indicates what must be done to the first file to make it match the second. Lines unique to each file are marked. Lines in common are ignored.

5.11 Translating Characters with *tr*

The **tr** utility reads input and either deletes target characters or translates each target character into a specified replacement character. The output is a <u>tr</u>anslated version of the input.

Translating Specified Characters to Other

The **tr** utility accepts two and only two arguments.

1. For example, enter:

   who

   who | tr *t* Z

   The output from the second command line contains no *t* characters. They are translated to Zs. The output of the **who** utility is connected to the input of **tr**. The **tr** utility searches through every character in the input looking for the specified target character (*t*) and then replaces every instance of *t* with Z.

The output of **tr** remains connected to the screen. Two arguments are given to **tr**. The **tr** utility interprets its first argument as a target character to locate. The second argument is the character used to replace the target. Hence, every *t* that **tr** finds in input is replaced with a Z. See Figure 5-9.

2. To have a translation made of the contents of the *test-sor* file, enter the following command:

> **tr** *a* Z < *test-sor*

This command line includes the redirection symbol, which tells the shell to open the file *test-sor* and connect it to the input of **tr**. The utility **tr** is not programmed to open files. In this command line, **tr** is given two arguments: the letter *a* (target) and the letter Z (replacement). The **tr** utility locates each instance of the letter *a* and replaces the instance with Z. The output from **tr** is displayed on the screen. The original file is not altered. See Figure 5-10.

The **tr** utility also translates several target characters at the same time.

3. Try this command:

> **tr** *'Ma7' '|&s'* < *test-sor*

The two arguments are in single quotation marks to instruct the shell to pass each argument to **tr** without interpreting any special characters. The < instructs the shell to connect the file *test-sor* to **tr**'s input. The **tr** utility reads from input and makes translations. The translated version of the file is output, in this case, to the screen. The arguments are interpreted by **tr** as target and replacement

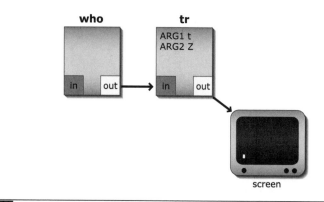

FIGURE 5-9   Passing arguments to **tr**

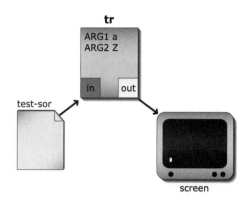

tr

ARG1 a
ARG2 Z

in | out

test-sor

screen

FIGURE 5-10 Redirecting input to a file

characters. All instances of the letter *M* are replaced with a pipe (|). Every *a* is replaced with an *&*, and each *7* character becomes a small *s*.

The *Ma7* characters constitute the target characters or *array*, and the | *&s* are the elements of the replacement array:

M	becomes		
a	becomes	*&*
7	becomes	*s*

Translating a Range of Characters

With the **tr** utility, you can also translate a range of characters such as *0–5* or *A–M*.

⮡ For example, enter the command:

tr *'a-z' 'A-Z' < test-sor*

Older systems require brackets around ranges, so we have to enter:

tr *'[a-z]' '[A-Z]' < test sor*

The output, sent to the terminal screen by default, is in uppercase:

This command instructs the **tr** utility to read from *test-sor* and translate all lowercase alphabetical characters *a* through *z* into uppercase *A* through *Z*.

Deleting Specified Characters

In addition to making translations, **tr** also deletes identified characters.

⇨ To delete specific characters from *test-sor*, enter:

    tr -d *'cbmZ4o'* < *test-sor*

Two arguments are given to the process running **tr**: **-d** and *cbmZ4o*. The file *test-sor* is connected to the input of **tr**. Every instance of each character in the file that matches a character in the second argument is removed.

Employing the *tr* Utility to Change Case

The **tr** utility is a useful tool for managing data.

⇨ 1. Enter the following:

        ls | tr *'a-z'* *'A-Z'*

The output of **tr** displayed on your screen is an all-uppercase listing of the output of **ls**, which makes those of us who used mainframes or DOS feel all warm and fuzzy.

2. Have **tr** change the case of a file by entering:

> **tr** *'a-z' 'A-Z' < practice*
>
> **tr** *'A-Z' 'a-z' < practice*

There are many programs that ask for all input data to be uppercase so there is no case confusion. **tr** to the rescue.

Changing the Field Separator

Sometimes we want the data from a file to be presented with a different field separator.

⮡ 1. Enter:

> **head** *-30 /etc/passwd* | **tr** *':' ' '*

The **tr** utility replaces each colon (:) with a space and outputs the modified version of the file.

We can replace every space with another character using **tr**.

2. Enter:

> **tr** *' ' '+' < practice*

Two arguments are passed to **tr**: a space and a plus. Your *practice* file is read, every space is replaced with a plus, and the modified version is output to the screen.

Outputting One Word to a Line

Files often have many words to a line. Because many utilities operate on whole lines (**sort**, **uniq**), they do not produce meaningful results unless the input data is one word to a line.

⮡ 1. Edit practice:

> **vi** *practice*

Use your arrow keys to place the cursor on the space between the first and second words.

2. Replace the space with a new line by entering:

> **r**
>
> ENTER

The first word remains on the old line. The rest of the text goes to the next line.

3. Replace the next space with an ENTER.

You could continue replacing spaces with new lines until the file was one word to a line. There must be an easier way.

4. Leave **vi** without saving the file:

> :q!

5. Enter:

> **tr** ' ' '\n' < *practice*

The **tr** utility interprets the \n as the newline character. In this case, we are telling **tr** to replace each space in the file with a new line, so every word is output on a line by itself.

 SUMMARY: The **tr** utility translates specific characters into other specific characters and translates ranges of characters into other ranges. It also deletes listed characters. If two arguments are given, the characters in the first argument are translated into the characters listed in the second argument, with one-to-one mapping. One option of **tr** is discussed:
-d *argument* Instructs **tr** to delete all instances of each specified character in the argument that follows.

Self Test 2

1. What command tells **sort** to sort the file *junk1* and put the sorted version in *junk1*, replacing the unsorted version?

2. A file named *employees* consists of information about employees. Each line is a record for one employee consisting of several fields separated by the % character: lastname, firstname, department, and employeeID, in that order, such as:

```
Kirby%Mike%Management%2176
McKinney%Charles%Administration%3265
```

What command tells **sort** to output the data such that everyone in each department is listed together, alphabetically by last name? Because some employees have the same last name, use the first name as a tiebreaker.

3. Using the **man** pages, determine what options accomplish the following:

    A. Tells **sort** to check to see whether a file is already sorted, and if so, not to sort it.

    B. Tells **bc** to invoke the math library so you can determine sine, cosine, and so on.

    C. Tells **grep** to output only the number of matches in a file, not the actual matched lines.

4. What command instructs **tr** to delete all ! , . ? " & $; * . and () characters from the file *practice*?

    _____

5. What command line instructs **tr** to output a sorted version of the results of **who** in all uppercase?

    _____

6. A file named *awards* consists of lines with only employee ID numbers and last names for employees. Every time an employee gets a commendation letter from a client, another entry is made in the file. What command outputs the employee names and ID numbers and the number of commendations?

    _____

7. What command results in a sorting of the file *people*, ignoring case and ignoring punctuation at the beginning of the line?

    _____

8. What command sorts the file */etc/passwd* using the fourth field, group ID, as the primary sort, and the third field, user ID, as the secondary sort?

    _____

9. Consider two files. The first file, *students*, is a sorted list of the names of all students enrolled in the school. The second file, *paid*, is a sorted list of the names of students who have paid their tuition. What command lists those students from the first file who have *not* paid their tuition?

    _____

10. What command displays the output of **who** in all capital letters?

    _____

5.12 Listing Names of Files and Directories

The **ls** utility outputs file and directory names listed in the parent directory. You have used it several times to determine the contents of a directory.

1. Enter the following:

> ls
>
> ls -a
>
> ls -l   (Not a "one" but an "*el*")
>
> ls -F

With no option, **ls** outputs the names of files and directories listed in the current directory, unless their names begin with a period (dot files).

To see all files including the dot files, the **-a** option is used. These *hidden* or *dot* files are the files read by your shell and other programs when they are first executed. They contain instructions that either the user or the system administrator placed there to tailor how the system works. Do not modify a dot file unless you are certain what you are doing and only if you have first created a backup copy of the file.

The **-l** option is an instruction to locate all information about each file and include it in the output. The option **-F** is instruction to put a slash in the display after the name of any directory.

The **ls** utility outputs the names either in one column or with names in several columns.

2. Enter:

> ls -C
>
> ls -1   (the numeral *one*)
>
> ls -Ca

The **-C** option is an instruction to output names in as many columns as the length of the names permits (longer filenames, fewer columns). The **-1** option is an instruction to output filenames one name to a line, all names in the first column.

When you run **ls** and have its output sent to your screen, the multicolumn output is probably the default. Consider what happens when the output from **ls** is redirected to another utility.

3. Enter:

   ls | more
   ls -1 | more   (the numeral *one*)
   ls -C | more

   The default output setting when **ls** is connected to **more** is to output one filename per column. The same result occurs when we instruct **ls** to output filenames in a single column using the **-1** option. However, if we insist on multicolumn output with the **-C** option, then **ls** obliges.

   Redirect the output of **ls** to **wc**.

4. Enter:

   ls | wc

   The number of lines and number of words are equal. The **ls** output must be one word to a line when it is connected to **wc**.

5. Confirm by entering:

   ls -C | wc
   ls -1 | wc

   When **ls** outputs to the screen, it is programmed to output in multicolumn format. When its output is connected to another utility, **ls** creates a display of one filename to a line. We can instruct **ls** to output whichever way we want with the **-C** and **-1** options.

6. A quick look at the manual reveals that **ls** comes with many options:

   man *ls*

   The **ls** utility is a powerful, useful tool that provides us with many features and options for listing information about files and directories.

5.13 Editing from the Command Line with the Stream Editor

When you begin editing a file using the visual editor, the file is read into an *editing* or *buffer space* in memory. The whole file is read into memory, and you proceed to make changes anywhere in the file you want to work. Available memory determines the maximum size limit of the file when you are editing using **vi**.

Another way to edit a file would be to read in just one line, make changes, write the line, and read in another. With such an approach, we can edit very large files, because only one line at a time is in working memory. An editor that reads in individual lines works on *streams* of data and is known as the <u>s</u>tream <u>ed</u>itor, **sed**.

Creating a Sample File

To examine stream editing, we need a file of specific content.

↳ Use the visual editor to create a file called *caffeine* with the following contents:

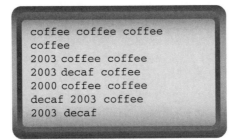

```
coffee coffee coffee
coffee
2003 coffee coffee
2003 decaf coffee
2000 coffee coffee
decaf 2003 coffee
2003 decaf
```

Changing Target Words

Suppose your caffeine addiction has changed flavors, and you want to replace the word *coffee* with the word *chocolate* at every instance where *coffee* occurs in a copy of the file *caffeine*. Without calling up **vi**, you can create a version with the substitutions.

↳ Enter the following command:

sed '**s**/*coffee*/*chocolate*/' *caffeine*

The most common error is leaving out the last **/** before the last quote. All three slashes are required.

The output comes to the screen; the file itself is not altered. The results show that the first instance of *coffee* is changed to *chocolate* on each line. A <u>s</u>ubstitution was made. The **sed** utility read and modified every line that had *coffee*, but not all instances on each line.

Examining the Code

The following illustration and table describe the components of this **sed** command.

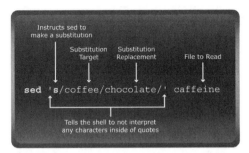

COMMAND	INTERPRETATION
s	Instructs **sed** to make a **s**ubstitution.
/coffee/	Identifies the string coffee as the target to be searched for on each line. It is the target string to be replaced.
/chocolate/	Specifies the replacement string. In cases where there is more than one instance of the target word on a line, only the first is affected.

In summary, the file *caffeine* is not altered. Each line of the file is read into memory, modified, and output by **sed**. Not every instance of *coffee* is replaced in the output.

Changing All Instances of the Target

The previous **sed** command modifies only the first instance of the target word on each line it reads as input. You can instruct **sed** to change all instances of a target occurring on each line.

1. Enter the following **sed** command including the **g**lobal request:

    sed '**s**/*coffee*/*chocolate*/**g**' *caffeine*

Each line of the file *caffeine* is read, and each instance of the target string is replaced. The resulting lines are displayed on the screen. The **g** after the replacement string instructs **sed** to **g**lobally affect each line; making substitutions for all instances of the target encountered on the line, not just the first.

2. Enter:

    sed '**s**/*root*/*ROOT*/**g**' *short-pass* | **more**

Each instance of the target string *root* is changed to *ROOT*.

Selecting Lines and Then Making Replacements

The previous commands instructed **sed** to modify text on any lines of the input. You can also request that **sed** act only on lines that meet specified criteria.

↳ Enter the following:

sed '/2003/s/coffee/chocolate/g' *caffeine*

The */2003/* in front of the substitution specification is the line target. It instructs **sed** to select lines only if they have the string *2003* somewhere on the line. If a line matches and is selected, then look for the substitution target *coffee*. If *coffee* is located on that line, **sed** substitutes *chocolate* for *coffee*. Lines are selected for processing only if the line target string matches; a substitution takes place on the line only if the substitution target is matched. The line with *2000* did not match *2003*, so the string *coffee* is not replaced. Although the last line does match with its *2003*, there is no *coffee* to replace. This command is illustrated in Figure 5-11.

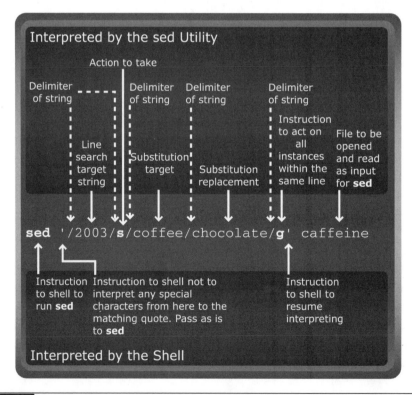

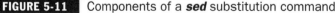

FIGURE 5-11 Components of a *sed* substitution command

Making a Substitution for the Line Search Target

In the previous example, a target was specified for locating lines, and then a different target for a text substitution was provided. The line target can be used as the substitution target, as well.

⮑ 1. Enter the following, which does not specify a substitution target:

> **sed** **'/2003/s//2010/g'** *caffeine*

Lines are selected if they have the line target string present: *2003*. The line target string *2003* is replaced with the string *2010*. In this command, no substitution target is specified; the two slashes after the **s** have no target between them. When no substitution target is specified, the line selection target is used for substitution. Lines are selected if they contain the line search target string, and then that string is replaced.

2. Enter:

> **sed** **'/decaf/s//DECAF/'** *caffeine*

Lines that have the string *decaf* are selected, then the first instance of *decaf* on the line is replaced with *DECAF*.

Deleting Lines

The **sed** editor will do much more than make substitutions.

⮑ Enter:

sed **'/dec/d'** *caffeine*

In this case, every line that has *dec* anywhere on the line is deleted.

Using Regular Expressions with *sed*

The regular expressions examined with **grep** have the same meanings to **sed**.

⮑ 1. Enter:

> **sed** **'/^2/s/coffee/chocolate/g'** *caffeine*

All lines that start with a 2 are selected for operation. If the selected line has the string *coffee*, it is replaced with *chocolate*, **g**lobally.

2. Enter:

> **sed '/^c/d'** *caffeine*

All lines beginning with *c* are targeted and deleted.

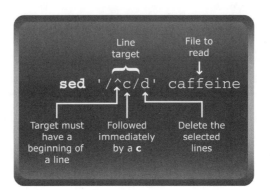

3. Enter:

> **sed '/^$/d'** *test-sor*
> **cat** *test-sor*

The target specification is, "Beginning of the line followed by the end of the line." For a line to be selected, no text can be between the beginning and end of the line. Thus, all the blank lines are selected and deleted.

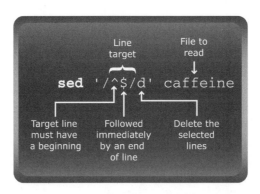

SUMMARY: The **sed** utility takes an input line, makes whatever editing changes are requested, and then outputs that line. It is a **s**tream **ed**itor that uses editing commands and regular expressions.

5.14 Manipulating Data with *awk*

The output of **who** consists of one line for each user who is logged on to the system. Each line, called a *record*, consists of several fields of information about the user. Likewise, data is often stored in files with individual lines (records) containing multiple fields. The **awk** utility is designed to locate particular records and fields in a database, modify them, perform computations, and then output selected portions of the data. The **awk** utility is particularly useful for information retrieval, data manipulation, and report writing.

The name of the **awk** utility is derived from the last names of the Bell Labs programmers who wrote it and many other parts of UNIX: <u>A</u>ho, <u>W</u>einberger, and <u>K</u>ernighan.

 For this section of the chapter, create a file called *food* and enter the following text:

```
milk   dairy  2.00
hamburger  meat  2.75
cheese  dairy  1.50
```

The *food* file consists of three records. Each record contains three fields: name of product, kind of product, and the price. In a record, each data field is separated from the next by a space, which is the default field delimiter for **awk**.

Selecting Lines and Printing Fields

The **awk** utility does its work by selecting records based on the presence of a specified pattern and then performing a prescribed action on the selected record.

 1. Enter the command:

> **awk '**/*dairy*/ **{print $3}'** *food*

The output consists of just the third field (*price*) from the first and third records. This command line instructs **awk** to select each record in the *food* file that contains the character string *dairy*, and then to perform the action of printing the third field (price) from each of the selected records. In this example, the pattern used to select the lines is not in the field (3) that is output. You can use one field for selection and then output entirely different fields.

The components of the command line are as follows:

COMMAND/ARGUMENT	INTERPRETATION
awk	Instructs the shell to execute the **awk** utility.
' '	Instructs the shell not to interpret special characters inside the quoted string, but rather to pass the enclosed characters as an argument to the **awk** utility.
/dairy/	Instructs **awk** to select lines that have the string *dairy* anywhere on the line. Lines that contain this pattern are selected for whatever action is specified in the { } section.
{print $3}	Instructs **awk** to take action on selected lines—namely to output, or **print**, the third field, *$3*. The action, identified by curly braces, is performed on all the lines that have *dairy* in them. The **print** statement is one of **awk**'s many possible actions.
food	This argument tells **awk** which file to read for input.

Multiple fields can be output.

2. Enter:

   awk '/*dairy*/ {**print** $3, $1}' *food*

The third field (a space) and then the first field are output for lines that contain the target string *dairy*.

Changing the Field Delimiter

In the file *food*, the fields in each record are delimited by spaces. Often data files use other characters as field separators. For example, login information is kept in the */etc/passwd* file, where fields are delimited with colons.

➭ 1. Have the system display your password record by entering the following:

   grep *$USER* */etc/passwd*

   If you are on a stand-alone system, the password file is on your system; otherwise, it is on a network server. If you do not get an output line consisting of several fields separated by colons, you are probably on a network server. You will need to issue commands like the following.

2. Request a display from the network server by entering:

   ypcat *passwd* | grep *$USER*

   The line in *passwd* containing your login ID is selected and output.

   We can instruct **awk** to use the colon as the field separator.

3. Enter the following:

   awk -F: '{print $1, $3, $4, $5}' */etc/passwd* | more

4. After you have examined a screenful of data, quit **more** by entering:

   q

The output consists of just the first, third, fourth, and fifth fields of all records in the password file.

The fields are separated by colons in the input; **awk** is instructed to use the colon as the field delimiter because the command line included the argument **-F** followed by a colon. However, **awk** displays its *output* using its default output field separator, a single space.

Selecting Records Based on the Value in a Field

The **awk** utility will also select records when a specific field's value matches a target.

➭ Enter:

awk -F: '$1 == "*root*" {print $1, $3}' */etc/passwd*

awk examines the file */etc/passwd* selecting records that have the value *root* in the first field, then **awk** outputs the first and third fields of the selected records. This command is detailed in Figure 5-12.

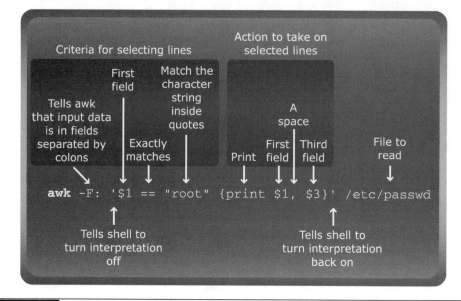

FIGURE 5-12 Using the *awk* utility

S U M M A R Y : The **awk** utility locates records that are stored in rows and columns (records and fields) in files (databases). It modifies records, performs computations, and outputs selected fields. One option is examined:

-F*char* Changes field delimiter to *char*.

5.15 Sending Output to a File and to Another Utility

When you construct a command line, the output of a utility can be sent to only one of three places: the default terminal, a file, or another utility. When we use redirection, output from a utility is redirected to just one place. It cannot be sent to both another utility *and* a file. There are times when we want to have the output of a utility sent to a file for later examination, and at the same time have the output redirected to another utility or the screen. Because the shell cannot send output to two places, another utility was created to accomplish this goal.

↳ 1. Count the files of your home directory by entering:

   ls | wc -l

   The number of files in the current directory is output. In this command line, the output of **ls** is passed to **wc**, which counts the number of words. The output of **wc** is displayed on the screen.

2. Enter the following:

   ls | tee *current-files* **| wc -w**

   The output of **wc**, the number of files in the current directory, is displayed on the screen.

3. Examine the contents of your new file, *current-files,* by entering:

   more *current-files*

   The file *current-files* contains the output of the **ls** utility.

   The **tee** utility reads from input (the output of **ls**) and then writes each line to output, which is connected to **wc**. In addition, **tee** writes a copy of each line to memory. After reaching the end of input, **tee** writes the buffer copy of all lines to a new file. Then, **tee** interprets its argument (*current-files*) as the name to give the new file that contains a copy of all lines processed. In this case, a copy of all the lines that **tee** read from input is also written to the file *current-files.*

4. We can use the screen as the output of **tee**:

   cal *2003* **| tee** *yr2003*

The **cal** utility is given *2003* as an argument. The **tee** utility is given *yr2003* as an argument. To **cal**, *2003* is a year. So, **cal** outputs the calendar for the year *2003.*

The **tee** utility reads from input (the output of **cal**) and writes to its output, which is connected to the screen and also writes each line to memory (the buffer). To **tee**, the *yr2003* argument is instruction to write the buffer copies of all lines read to a new file called *yr2003*. See Figure 5-13.

S U M M A R Y : Like a plumber's tee that sends water in two directions, the **tee** utility sends what it reads from its input in two directions: to a file named as an argument and to standard output. Standard output is connected by default to the workstation screen or it can be redirected to another utility, or even to another file. The **tee** utility does not modify the data in any way.

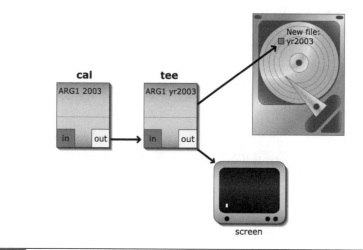

FIGURE 5-13 Examining redirection with *tee*

5.16 Using *file* to Determine the Type of a File

On UNIX systems, there are many different kinds of files: text files, executable binary files, database files, e-mail messages, graphic files, archives, directories, font files, and so on.

We can check what sort of file the *letclpasswd* is.

1. Enter.

   file */etc/passwd*

   The output reports that */etc/passwd* is an ASCII text file.

   ```
   /etc/passwd: ASCII text
   ```

   It is just a file containing text.

2. Now request information about some other files:

   file */usr/bin/passwd*
   file */bin/ls*

   The programs **ls** and **passwd** are binary. They are executables that run when we enter **ls** or **passwd** at a command line.

   ```
   /bin/ls: ELF 32-bit LSB executable, .....
   ```

   The **file** utility reports on one or several files listed as arguments.

3. Enter:

   file *new_script* */tmp Private /dev/fd0*

The output lists all four objects and what type of file each one is: a script, a directory, another directory, and the floppy, which is a device that accepts input in blocks, not individual characters. When in doubt as to what something is, use **file** to determine its type.

5.17 Modifying Timestamps on Files

Whenever a file is created, the system keeps track of the creation time. Whenever it is modified, that time is recorded as well. These *timestamps* allow us to determine which copy of a file such as a program is the most recent. Managers of complex projects use file timestamps to coordinate components of the projects. Additionally, we can create empty files to use the timestamps for record keeping.

1. List your current files with a long listing of information:

   ls -l

   The output is something like:

   ```
   -rw-r--r--   1 sk      users      260 Aug 15 16:20 lost-days
   ```

   The sixth through eighth fields are the date and time at the moment of the file's creation. This date/time information associated with each file makes up the file modification timestamps. Probably several files have not been touched in several days.

2. Use **vi** to edit an old file such as the following:

   vi *lost-days*

3. Make a change and then write or quit the file.

4. Examine the timestamp on the file that you modified:

   ls -l *lost-days*

   The timestamp is changed to reflect when you modified the file.

Creating Empty Files for Their Timestamps

When we modify a file, we alter its timestamp. When we create a file, it gets its initial timestamp. We can quickly create empty files to get timestamps.

1. Enter the following command:

   touch *newfile1A newfile2B2.*

2. Get a long listing of these files:

ls -l *new**

The **touch** utility created new files that have the current timestamps and have a size of zero. Some programs create empty timestamp files using **touch** whenever the program is being executed. In this way, we can keep track of when the program is executed.

Updating the Modification Time of a File

Check a long listing of your files.

1. Enter:

ls -l *users_on*

You can change the modification time without actually changing the file.

2. Enter:

touch *users_on*

3. Get a long listing of *users_on* again.

ls -l *users_on*

The output lists a new modification time, namely when you **touch**ed it. Note that only the modification time is updated. Administrators often have programs touch a file to update the timestamp whenever they are executed. The timestamp then reports the last time it was executed.

5.18 Employing Multiple Utilities to Achieve Broader Goals

Each UNIX/Linux utility accomplishes only one task, usually a simple one. The **sort** utility sorts lines, period. If we want to sort the words in a file, we must first modify a copy of the file so that only one word is on each line. Then when **sort** sorts the lines, it is sorting the words. The **ls** utility displays the names of files listed in a directory, not a count of the files. To count the files in a directory, we must run **ls** and then redirect the output to **wc**. To achieve more complex goals, we must employ one utility to do its thing, accomplishing part of the task, then pass the output to other utilities that work on the output of the first utility and complete the goal.

Counting Directories

There is no utility that outputs the number of subdirectories listed in a directory. The **ls** utility can identify directories, but does not provide a count.

1. Make sure you are in your home directory where you created subdirectories in Chapter 3, and list its contents:

   cd
   ls -F | more

   The **-F** option instructs **ls** to put a slash after each directory name in its output. When **ls** sends its output to another utility such as **more** or **grep**, **ls** puts one filename on each line of output.

   We can pass the output of **ls** to **grep** and tell **grep** to look for lines containing a specific target.

2. Enter:

   ls -F | grep /

   The output of **ls** is redirected to **grep**, which looks for lines that include a slash somewhere on the line. Matched lines (the directories) are output.

3. Count the number of directories:

   ls -F | grep / | wc -l

   The number of subdirectories listed in the current directory is output.

   Create an alias.

4. In the **ksh** or **bash** shells:

   alias *numdir*='ls -F | grep / | wc -l'

   In the **csh** or **tcsh** shells:

   alias *numdir* 'ls -F | grep / | wc -l'

5. Try the alias:

   numdir

   numdir is aliased to the full **ls grep wc** command line. When we issue the command *numdir*, its alias is executed and the number of directories in the current directory is output.

6. Change directories to / and try it, then return home:

   cd /
   numdir
   cd

Listing All Words Used in a File

A text file consists of several words to the line, the same word in different lines, sometimes capitalized, sometimes lowercase. In the tour, you created a file named *practice* that contains many words.

1. Display the file *practice* in all lowercase letters:

    tr '*A-Z*' '*a-z*' < *practice* | **more**

    The shell connects the file *practice* to the input of **tr** and gives **tr** two arguments, *A-Z* and *a-z*, which **tr** interprets as instruction to locate all uppercase letters and replace each with its lowercase equivalent.

2. Replace spaces with newline characters:

    tr '**A-Z**' '*a-z*' < *practice* | **tr** ' ' '\n' | **more**

    In this command line, the output of a process running **tr** is redirected to a second process also running the code for **tr**. The second **tr** is given the arguments a *space* and a \n, which **tr** interprets as instruction to locate each space in the file and replace it with a newline character. Words on a line are separated by spaces. When a space is removed and a newline character is inserted as a replacement, the next word is moved to the new line. Each word is now on a line by itself.

3. Sort the output:

    tr '*A-Z*' '**a-z**' < *practice* | **tr** ' ' '\n' | **sort** | **more**

The output from **sort** is a list of all words in the file *practice* in alphabetical order. Punctuation is still included, blank lines are output, and duplicates are listed. In the next chapter, a script is created to accomplish this task more thoroughly.

Self Test 3

1. How would you output only the first two fields of *letc/passwd* using **awk**?

   _____

2. What **sed** command outputs all lines of a file named *ohio*, quitting at the line containing "Otterbein College"?

   _____

3. What command line instructs **sed** to replace all instances of the string "UCB" with the string "University of California" on all lines where "UCB" is at the beginning of the line in the file *alma_mater*?

   _____

4. What command instructs **awk** to output the home directory, user login name, and user ID for the first 20 users in the *passwd* file?

_____

5. What single command line accomplishes the following? The output of **who** is passed to a utility that both writes to its output, which is connected to **sort**, and at the same time, writes a copy of its input to a new file named *who.out*. The output from **sort** is passed to a utility that both writes to its output, connected to the input of a process running **wc**, and writes to a new file, *sort.out*. Finally, the **wc** utility outputs the number of lines, words, and characters in the sorted **who** to the screen.

_____

6. Imagine you found a file named *README* in a directory and tried to read the file using a text editor, but the editor couldn't properly display the contents. Instead, what you got was a bunch of weird characters. To view the contents of the file properly, you need to find out what sort of file it is. What command will tell you what type of file *README* is?

_____

Chapter Review

Use this section to review the content of this chapter and test yourself on your knowledge of the concepts.

Chapter Summary

- Utility programs in Linux/UNIX form a core group of powerful data manipulating and mining tools that are essential to system administration, project record keeping, and system/network programming.
- The **wc** utility counts lines, words, and characters in its input or in files, and outputs any one or more of the counts (**-l -w -c**). If given multiple filename arguments, **wc** outputs the totals for each file and a grand total of each element for all files read.
- **cat** reads from input or files and writes to output. It interprets all arguments as files to open and read unless the argument is an option identified with a - character. With the **-n** option, **cat** outputs the line number at the beginning of each line.

- The **more** utility displays files or the output of previous utilities on the screen, one page at a time. The user can search for target text, advance forward and backward through a file, and slide into the visual editor from **more.**

- Using **cut**, we can extract one or more fields (**-f**) or characters on lines (**-c**) from input or files. The default field separator is a TAB, but we can declare the separator to be any character by using **-d**.

- The **column** utility takes input that is one word to a line and outputs the data several columns to a line. It can fill the first row, across columns, or fill the first column, then the second and so forth if you specify the option **-x**.

- The **paste** utility reads corresponding lines from two or more files and outputs them as one line placing a default TAB character between the sections contributed by different files. If a file consists of many lines, one word to a line, **paste** will splice all the lines together (if you specify the option **-s**), forming one line instead of many.

- The utility that searches input or files for lines containing a target string is **grep,** one of the most used programs on the system. **grep** will locate lines containing a target of specific characters, or select all lines that do not contain the target string. Additionally, **grep** can ignore case (**-i**), list filenames that contain the target (**-l**), and output line numbers for selected lines (**-n**). Regular expressions can be used to describe targets as containing a number of characters, characters located at one end of the line, and so forth.

- The **bc** utility is a basic calculator that performs math calculations. We input problems from the keyboard. The utility then solves the problems and outputs the results.

- We can **sort** lines of files or input, in ASCII order unless we specify dictionary (**-d**), reverse (**-r**), or numerical (**-n**) order, or unless we specify that **sort** ignore case (**-f**) capitalization. **sort** also sorts lines based on the value in specified fields, both with a primary and secondary sort. Fields are described by default as separated by white space, but if we use the option **-t**, we can specify any character to be the field delimiter.

- The **uniq** utility in standard operations reads files and input, deleting all duplicate adjacent lines. It also outputs a count (**-c**) of the number of identical adjacent lines that were in the input, or outputs only the lines that had duplicates (**-d**) or were unique in the input (**-u**).

- Files are compared with **comm**, which outputs three columns of output, lines unique in file one, lines unique in file two, and lines in common for both files.

Additionally, **comm** will output lines uniquely in file one (**-23**), or uniquely in file two (**-13**), or only the lines in common (**-12**).

- The **diff** utility examines two files and reports how they are different as well as how one file must modified to make it like the other.
- The **tr** utility reads input and makes character-by-character translations. It takes two arguments: the list of target characters and the list of replacement characters. Additionally, with a **-d** argument, **tr** deletes all characters listed in a second argument.
- **ls** outputs the names of files and directories listed in the current directory, or in any directory provided as an argument to **ls**. It outputs all files including the dot files (**-a**), a long listing of information about files (**-l**), single column format (**-1**), or multiple column format (**-C**), and identifies whether files are executable or directories and so forth (**-F**).
- The stream editor, **sed**, reads lines from input and makes changes based on contextual information, the first instance on a line, or all instances (**g**). **sed** makes substitutions and deletions, and employs regular expressions.
- The **awk** utility is a powerful manipulator of data that resides in rows and columns. It will select specified data based on values in a field, and output only those portions of records selected.
- With **file** we can determine the nature of files and directories.
- The **touch** utility creates empty files and modifies the timestamp on existing files.
- Each utility performs a limited set of operations, but does whatever it does very well. When we employ several utilities together in a command line that pipes results from one utility to another, we can manipulate the data to reach much more complex goals than can be accomplished with single utilities.

Assignment

1. Compare the output from the following:

   wc *fileAA*

   wc -c -w -l *file AA*

   wc -wlc *file AA*

2. What command tells **more** to display the next screenful of text? _____

3. What do the following accomplish?

   cut -d: f1,4,6 */etc/passwd*

> **paste -d'\\'** *names.tmp numbers.tmp*
>
> **grep -i** *bill* *
>
> **grep '^j...k$'** *datafile*
>
> **sort -f +2 -3** *datafile*
>
> **man** *man*
>
> **uniq -c** *datafile*
>
> **ls -Fal**
>
> **sed '/operations/s/UNIX/Linux/g'** *history-file*

Project

Complete each of the following. Write the commands used on the printed output for each task.

A. Create a file called *log-home* that contains just the login names and home directories, sorted by login names for all users who have accounts on your system.

B. Make a copy of the *log-home* file called *cap-log-home* that is in all uppercase letters.

C. Use the **file** utility to create a file called *contents-etc* that contains a list of all objects listed in the */etc* directory and includes information about what each file or directory is.

D. Use **sed** to create a file called *me-passwd* that contains a copy of the */etc/passwd* file with your login name changed to your real name.

E. What is the total number of lines of text in all your files in your home directory?

F. Print out a copy of *caffeine* with the following change made by **sed**: If the line has *decaf* anywhere on the line, change *2003* to *2010*.

COMMAND SUMMARY

awk *pattern* {*action*} *filename*	Performs the action on all records in filename that contain pattern.
cat *file1* *file2* **>** *file3*	Creates a new *file3* with the contents of *file1* and *file2*.
comm *file1* *file2*	Compares *file1* to *file2* and shows the lines common and unique in each of two files.
cut *option* *filename*	Outputs selected fields from *filename*.
diff *file1* *file2*	Shows lines that are different in each file and how to modify the first file to match the second.
grep *regular-expression* *filename*	Outputs all lines in filename that contain the *regular expression*.
paste *file1* *file2*	Combines line 1 from *file1* with line 1 from *file2*, and so on.
sed *command* *filename*	Executes specified *sed* editing command(s) on *filename*.
sort *filename*	Sorts the contents of the file *filename*.
tee *filename*	Reads from input and then writes both to output and to a file *filename*.
tr *string1* *string2* **<** *filename*	Reads input and translates each character string1 characters into *string2* characters.
uniq *filename*	Removes duplicate adjacent lines from *filename*.
wc *filename*	Counts words, lines, and characters in *filename*.

Using Utilities to Accomplish Complex Tasks

O B J E C T I V E S

After completing this chapter, you will be able to:

- Combine basic utilities to accomplish complex tasks
- Create shell scripts that use utilities to output formatted, relational data from more than one file
- Create a script that filters and modifies data
- Construct scripts incrementally
- Identify errors in scripts and repair them

E very day, users around the world employ powerful UNIX/Linux utilities
to accomplish complex tasks. At the shell prompt, we enter commands that
use one or several utilities in combination to read data, to identify particular
portions to output, and to alter, sort, or delete information. This chapter
investigates how to create several powerful shell scripts that employ multiple
utilities to accomplish complex data manipulation and retrieval tasks. Putting
utilities together in scripts to accomplish specific goals is a fundamental, useful,
and exceedingly important set of abilities. System administrators, programmers,
and users employ short scripts to accomplish tasks that require complex
command lines. By doing so, they increase efficiency, save time, and eliminate
typing errors.

6.1 Creating and Executing a Script to List User Information

Often when we need to collect basic information, we enter a series of commands.
By placing the commands together in a script file, we can repeat the series by just
entering the script's name, avoiding errors and saving time.

Creating the Script

This first exercise guides you through creating a script to obtain specific
information about your login session.

➦ 1. Use the visual editor to create a file named *mydata*:

    vi *mydata*

2. Add the following content to the file:

    echo *'id output:'*
    id
    echo
    echo *'my entry in output from who is:'*
    who | **grep** *$USER*
    echo
    echo *'the present directory is:'*
    pwd
    echo

```
echo 'current system name is:'
hostname
echo
echo 'my current processes are:'
ps
echo 'the shell search path is:'
echo $PATH
```

3. To write the file and return to the shell, enter:

   ESC

   :wq

Executing the Script

The file contains a series of shell commands. We have two ways to get the commands in the file executed. We can instruct the current shell to read (*source*) the file and execute all the commands, or we can make the script file executable, enter its name, and start a child shell to read the script file and execute the commands.

1. At the shell, make *mydata* executable and run it:

   chmod +x *mydata*

   mydata **|** *more*

   The output from all the command lines in the script is displayed on the screen.

> **N O T E :**   When you enter ***mydata***, the commands in the script should be executed. However, if you get an error message such as "mydata not found," the shell is not looking in the current directory for ***mydata***. You can inform the shell that ***mydata*** is in the current directory and that you want it executed by entering **./mydata**. You can also add the current directory to the list of directories that your shell searches by entering one of the following: In a **bash** or **ksh** shell add a colon and a dot to the **PATH** by entering: ***PATH=$PATH:***. In a **tcsh** or **csh** shell: **set** *path=($path .)*

2. Tell the shell to redirect the output of *mydata* to a file:

   mydata **>** *me_A*

or

    ./mydata > *me_A*

3. Examine the file:

    more *me_A*

The contents of the file consist of data generated by the programs in **mydata**, namely information about your present login session. Every time you run the script, the shell executes each command in the script, one after the other. The output from the script goes to your screen unless you redirect it to a file or utility.

6.2 Listing Directories and Files Separately

The **ls** utility outputs the names of the files and directories that are listed in the current directory in alphabetical order. Nearly every file you have created thus far has been listed in the directory you are "in" when you log on, your home directory.

The output of **ls** does not list all the directory names together and then the filenames together. Rather, the output is filenames and directory names mixed together, sorted by name, date, or size. We can write a script to produce a listing of all directory names together in alphabetical order followed by all filenames, also in order.

Identifying Directories

Before creating a script that displays directories and files independently, you need to create specific directories as follows.

1. Make sure you are in your home directory, and then create three new directories:

    cd

    mkdir *Resumes Papers Recommendations*

Because **mkdir** interprets all arguments as names to assign to new directories. **mkdir** can make multiple directories at one time

2. Confirm that the new directories exist in your current directory:

    ls -F | more

Because you included the **-F** option for **ls**, the directories listed in your current directory are displayed with a slash at the end of the name. Because the output of **ls** is passed to a utility, **more**, the output of **ls** is one filename to a line.

The **ls** utility is passed one argument, **-F**, which **ls** interprets as an instruction to identify the nature of the objects in the directory, and in particular, to identify directories by attaching a **/** (slash) character to the directory names in the output.

Selecting Only Directories or Files

By passing the output from **ls** to other utilities, we can select the directories and determine how they are listed in the output.

1. Select only those lines that contain directory names from the output of **ls**:

   ls -F | grep /

   The output of **ls** that is passed to **grep** contains one filename on each line. The **grep** utility is given one argument, the **/**, which **grep** interprets as the target search string. Only those lines containing a slash match the target and are output by **grep**, namely the directory names. Filenames do not have a trailing **/**, so they are not selected.

2. If you are on a Linux system, request that the output be put into columns by entering:

   ls -F | grep / | column

   Many systems include the utility **column**, which formats output into columns. However, some do not. If you do not have access to **column**, just use the command line as it was in step 1, leaving out the **| column** portion that is added in step 2.

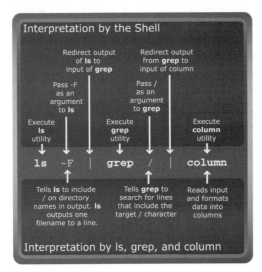

The **grep** utility outputs lines that have directory names. The output of **grep** is redirected to the utility **column**, which formats the data into as many columns as is practical to display.

The shell starts three child processes to execute this command line. The output (*o*) of the first process running **ls** is redirected to the input (*i*) of the second process running **grep**. The output of the second process is redirected to the input of the third process running **column**. The output of the third process is not redirected, so it remains connected to the screen.

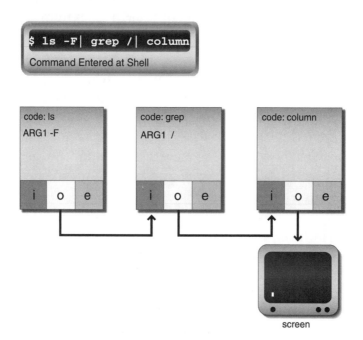

We can reverse the way **grep** works.

3. Tell **grep** to reject directories and select only files by entering:

    ls -F | grep -v / | column

In this command line, **grep** is given two arguments. The slash is interpreted by **grep** as the target string. **grep** identifies lines that meet the search criteria of having a slash somewhere on the line, namely the directory names. The **-v** option is instruction to reject those matching lines, and to output all the lines that do not match. Because filenames lack the slash, they are the output of **grep**.

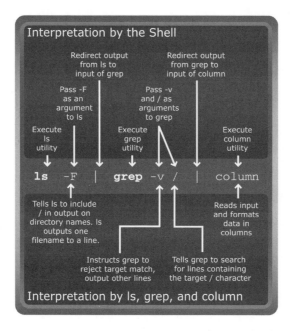

Creating a Script

A long command such as the one you just entered can be included in a script file and employed easily.

1. Use the editor to create a script named *lsdf* (**lis**t **d**irectories and **f**iles), and then enter the following contents:

    echo
    echo
    date
    echo
    echo *'Directories are:'*
    ls -F | grep / | column
    echo
    echo *'Files are:'*
    ls -F | grep -v / | column
    echo

2. Make the file executable and run it:

    chmod +x *lsdf*
    lsdf | more

The names of directories are listed first, then the files. They are not mixed in one alphabetical listing, the way **ls** operates.

This script uses **echo** to output empty lines as well as the "Directories are:" or "Files are:" information. The real work is done by **ls**, **grep**, and **column** in the two lines that output either just directories or just files.

With this script, you can easily obtain a listing of the directories and files listed in the current directory.

Adding Comments to Scripts

A project is not completed until the paperwork is done. The script works, so now it's time to document it.

1. Add the following to the top of the **lsdf** script:

```
#   This script outputs the names of directories and files
#   listed in the current directory.
```

2. Run the script again.

There is no difference in the way the script behaves because the shell interprets the # (pound sign) as instruction to ignore the rest of the line. We often use # simply to add comments about our scripts. Using # to identify comments can be tricky. We cannot use them inside a long command line, for instance. It is best to place comments at the beginning or end of a script.

3. Add your name and the date and then complete a brief explanation of how the script works. Make certain that a pound sign (#) is at the beginning of each line.

```
#   Name      Date
#   The script uses ls to . . .
```

6.3 Identifying Changes Made to Files in a Directory

When we work on projects or need to keep data secure, it is helpful to determine what changes have occurred to the files and subdirectories listed in a directory. Have any new files been added? Are any of the permissions changed? Have files been renamed?

Creating a Sample Directory's Content

In an earlier exercise, you created a directory named *Resumes.* This section's exercise uses that directory to examine how to monitor changes in a directory.

First, you will create a series of files in the *Resumes* directory, and then you will make a file that contains a "snapshot" of information about the files in the target directory. After creating the snapshot file, you will make changes to the directory's contents, and then make another snapshot file. You will then use various utilities to identify the differences between the information in the two snapshot files.

1. Make *Resumes* your current directory and confirm your location:

    cd *Resumes*

    pwd

2. While in *Resumes,* create several files by entering:

    date > *today*

    cal > *month*

    who > *logged.on*

    id > *mylogin*

    head -5 */etc/passwd* > *short-passA*

    cp *month month.bak*

3. Confirm you created all six files with:

    ls -l

Resumes is your current directory.

4. Return to your home directory and confirm your location:

    cd

    pwd

Collecting Data about Files in a Directory

The next step is to create a file or snapshot in your home directory that contains data about all files listed in the *Resumes* subdirectory.

1. From your home directory, enter:

    ls -l *Resumes*

A long listing of information about the files listed in the *Resumes* directory is displayed. When **ls** is given a directory name as an argument, it reports on the files listed in that directory.

2. Redirect the output of **ls** to a snapshot file:

> **ls -l** *Resumes* | **sort** > *file.info1*

3. Examine the contents of *file.info1* with:

> **more** *file.info1*

The *file.info1* file contains a sorted list of lines containing information about each file listed in the directory *Resumes*. Each file's permissions, date modified, owner, and so on are included. It is a snapshot of the current status of all files in the *Resumes* directory.

Modifying the Directory's Contents

The next task is to make changes to files listed in the *Resumes* directory so that later we can identify the changes.

1. Change back to the *Resumes* directory:

> **cd** *Resumes*
> **pwd**
> **ls**

2. Modify aspects of the files by entering:

> **chmod -w** *today*
> **mv** *month month2*
> **date** > *new.date*
> **who** >> *month.bak*
> **ls -l**

The directory now has one added file, one file with a new name, one file with altered permissions, and one file with added content.

3. Return to your home directory and confirm your location:

> **cd**
> **pwd**

Comparing Current File Information with the Original

The contents of the *Resumes* directory have been modified.

1. Create a second file containing information about the files listed in *Resumes*:

> **ls -l** *Resumes* | **sort** > *file.info2*

The files *file.info1* and *file.info2* are the two files in your home directory that are snapshots of the contents of *Resumes.* They contain information about each of the files listed in the *Resumes* directory before and after you made changes.

2. Have **comm** identify the differences in the two snapshot files:

    comm *file.info1 file.info2*

The output from **comm** is a series of lines that are in three columns. Some lines begin against the left edge of the screen. Some lines begin after one TAB, and the remainder after two TABs. The two snapshot files contain information about the contents of the directory *Resumes* at two different times. **comm** outputs three columns of output: lines uniquely in the first file, lines uniquely in the second, and lines in common.

- Lines uniquely in *file1*
- -rw-rw-r-- 1 user 29 Sep 15 01:09 today
- -rw-rw-r-- 1 user 130 Sep 15 01:09 month

- Lines uniquely in *file2*
- -r--r--r-- 1 user 29 Sep 15 01:09 today
- -rw-rw-r-- 1 user 29 Sep 15 01:12 new.date
- -rw-rw-r-- 1 user 130 Sep 15 01:09 month2

- Lines in both *files*
- -rw-rw-r-- 1 user 103 Sep 15 01:09 mylogin
- -rw-rw-r-- 1 user 156 Sep 15 01:09 short-passA

The output indicates which lines are not changed (in the third bullet), and what each file looked like originally if it was modified in some way or deleted (bullet one). The output also describes each new file (bullet two).

3. Have **diff** identify the differences in the snapshots:

    diff *file.info1 file.info2*

Although the output from **diff** does not include the lines that are the same in both files, the "arrows" at the beginning of lines such as the following clearly show what is different between the files:

```
< -rw-rw-r--    1 user    user         29 Sep 15 01:09 today
---
> -r--r--r--    1 user    user         29 Sep 15 01:09 today
```

Users employ both the **comm** and **diff** utilities to determine what is in common among files and what changes have been made to data—in this case, the contents of a directory.

The snapshot files are created in your home directory rather than in *Resumes,* so the contents of the snapshots will not be seen in the output of **comm** or **diff**.

6.4 Creating a Complex Word Analysis Script

By employing several utilities connected together using pipes (a *pipeline*) in a script, we can accomplish tasks that are much more complex than any single utility could accomplish.

This pipeline feature of UNIX is very useful and is central to manipulating data effectively with UNIX utilities. As Peter said while running the Pickled Pepper utility, "primitive programs prove positively powerful when properly piped." Shell scripts vary in complexity, from simple pipelines of commands to very intricate structures involving code that makes decisions, runs loops, and manipulates data in complex ways.

Regardless of how extensive a program is after it is completed, accomplished users and programmers start out by writing a simple, basic script that accomplishes a limited task. After the initial version of the script works, the programmer includes additional code to increase its power. One advantage is that if a problem arises, it must be related to the new code. Then more functionality is added, and the script is tested and debugged. This cycle continues until all features are added. By first making a small program work, then adding features incrementally, the programmer can more easily control the development of the script and more quickly detect errors. To try to write all of a program at once and then locate the errors is a novice approach that leads to frustration and failure.

The last section of this chapter guides you through an incremental development of a complex script. The script is useful, but more important is exploring how to write scripts effectively.

Planning How to Determine the Number of Unique Words in a File

It is sometimes instructive when examining our writing to know what different words we are using in a file. This exercise guides you through the creation of a complex script that reads a file and outputs a list of unique words that are in the file, the number of times each word is used, and the total number of unique words employed.

The **uniq** utility removes duplicate *adjacent* lines from its input. It outputs both the unique lines and single copies of any lines that were duplicates and adjacent. If the same words are in a different order on two adjacent lines, **uniq** will not delete one of the lines, because the two lines are not identical. The **uniq** utility deletes a line only if it is adjacent to another identical line.

If each line contains only one word, the lines must be sorted for **uniq** to remove duplicate adjacent lines (words). In text files, punctuation characters often are attached to some of the words. Because *friend* is not the same as *friend?* (with a question mark), all punctuation must be removed. The goal of this script is to prepare data from a file so that **uniq** can work properly: Punctuation and blank lines must be removed; differences in case for the same word must be reconciled; and the words must be one word to a line in a sorted order.

Creating a Long Text File

This first section guides you to create a file of moderate length containing text that a later script will analyze.

⤷ 1. Create a file of some length by entering:

    cat *practice west-coast.names practice* **>** *manywords*

    2. Edit the file *manywords* and add a 10 line paragraph of any text containing real words:

    vi *manywords*

    3. Write and quit the *manywords* file:

    :wq

Removing Punctuation

A first step in massaging the file's contents is to create a version that removes punctuation.

⤷ 1. Use the editor to create a new script file named *wordsUsed1*:

    vi *wordsUsed1*

2. Enter the following line in the file *wordsUsed1*:

   tr -d '?."!:,();' < *manywords*

3. Write the file and quit the editor:

   :wq

4. Make the script executable and run the script:

   chmod +x *wordsUsed1*

   wordsUsed1 | **more**

   The output from *wordsUsed1* is the contents of *manywords* with the standard punctuation characters removed. Other characters like $ and % are not removed. The specific characters listed in the argument following the **-d** are the characters removed by **tr**. See Figure 6-1.

Examining the Code

The components of the **tr** command line are as follows:

COMPONENT	DESCRIPTION
tr	Instructs the shell to execute the **tr** utility.
-d ' '	Passes **tr** two arguments: **-d** and the characters inside the single quotes. The **tr** utility interprets the **-d** as instruction to delete all characters listed as the second argument. The single quotes tell the shell to pass the punctuation characters uninterpreted to **tr** as the second argument.
?.":,();	Specifies the contents of the second argument. Hence, **tr** searches for the literal ? . " ! :,( ); characters in the input and deletes those characters.
< *manywords*	Instructs the shell to open the file *manywords* and connect it to the input of **tr**. The **tr** utility only reads from its input. It does not interpret an argument as a filename. We must have the shell connect the file to **tr**'s input.

Making All Characters Lowercase

Once the punctuation characters are removed from the data, there is still the matter of capital letters. Some words are capitalized and others are not. At this point, *the* and *The* are seen as two different words. To remove duplicates properly, we must ensure that the case of each instance of the same word, as well

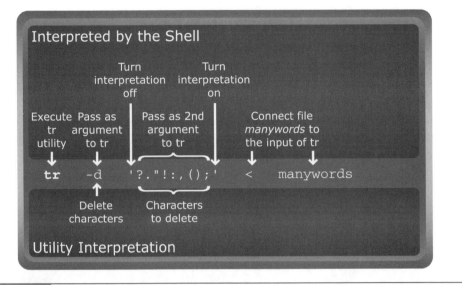

FIGURE 6-1   Shell and utility interpretations

as characters, matches. A simple solution is to just make the whole file lower- or uppercase.

1. Make a copy of *wordsUsed1* named *wordsUsed2*:

    cp *wordsUsed1 wordsUsed2*

2. Use **vi** to edit the file *wordsUsed2*, and add a backslash to the end of the first line:

    tr -d *'?."!:,();'* < *manywords* \

3. Then add a second line to the script:

    | **tr** *'A-Z' 'a-z'*

4. Run the script and examine its output:

    wordsUsed2 | **more**

    The output is a copy of the data from the file *manywords* with all characters in lowercase. See Figure 6-2.

If your script ran and produced the appropriate output, you entered the code correctly. If your script ran correctly in the previous version, but produced an error this time, the problem is in the code you just entered. Check it carefully and fix it, then run the script again. Make sure the backslash is the last character of line 1.

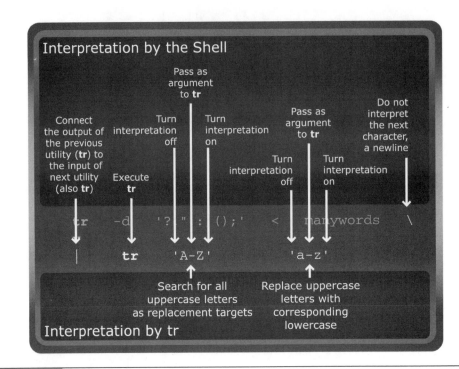

FIGURE 6-2   Shell and *tr* interpretations

Examining the Code

The components of the added text are as follows:

COMPONENT	INTERPRETATION
\	Instructs the shell not to interpret the special meaning of the next character, which is a newline. Without a newline character, the shell is not told to process a complete line. Therefore, the shell keeps reading from the next line in the file as though both lines were actually one. The shell sees multiple lines as one line of input.
|	Instructs the shell to connect the output of the previous process, which is running **tr**, to the input of the following process, also running **tr**.
tr	Executes the second **tr** utility.
' '	Instructs the shell not to interpret the enclosed characters as having significance to the shell. The text between the quotes is passed, verbatim, to **tr** as an argument.

COMPONENT	INTERPRETATION
A-Z	A-Z is the contents of the first quoted argument passed to **tr**. The **tr** utility interprets A-Z as instruction to search for all uppercase letters A through Z as targets for replacement.
a-z	This a-z is the contents of the second argument passed to **tr**. The utility interprets this argument as a range of replacement characters. All uppercase letters are replaced with their matching lowercase letters.

Putting Each Word on a Line

The output of the script has many words on each line. We want to remove duplicate words, not duplicate lines, but **uniq** works only on lines. To remove duplicate words with **uniq**, we must modify the data so that each word is on a line by itself. To accomplish this task, we need to use the code for a newline character in the *ASCII character set*.

1. Examine the ASCII characters and their associated codes by entering:

   man *ascii*

   The character with *012* beside it is the newline character. This character separates lines in a file so that terminals and printers are able to display individual lines. The alternate name for newline is **\n**, which is often used.

2. Copy *wordsUsed2* to *wordsUsed3*:

   cp *wordsUsed2 wordsUsed3*

   This procedure is recommended. Create the basic script, copy it, make additions and changes, run it, copy, change, run…until it is finished. If a line is modified from the previous version, the change is described following the # at the end of the script. Don't include the # or comments.

3. Use the editor to modify the script *wordsUsed3* to include the following lines:

   tr -d '?."!:,();' < *manywords* \
   | **tr** 'A-Z' 'a-z' \
   | **tr** ' ' '\n'
   # *A backslash is added at the end of the second line in this script.*
   # *The last line is new, a space is the first quoted argument.*

   Spaces are used both to separate arguments and as the contents of the first quoted argument. They must be carefully entered.

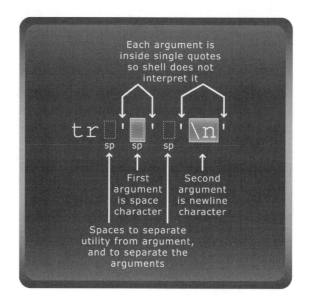

4. After completing the changes, run the script *wordsUsed3*:

wordsUsed3 **| more**

The output is one word to a line because each space is translated into a new line.

Examining the Code

The additions to the script are as follows:

COMMAND	INTERPRETATION
\	Instructs the shell not to interpret the newline character at the end of the second line in the script.
|	Tells the shell to connect the output of the previous process running **tr** to the input of the next process, also running **tr**.
tr	Instructs the shell to execute the **tr** utility, which locates target characters and replaces them with other replacement characters.
' '	Instructs the shell to pass **tr** a first argument consisting of one space. The **tr** utility interprets this first argument to be the character to locate and replace with the character listed in the second argument.

COMMAND	INTERPRETATION
'\n'	Instructs the shell to pass to **tr** a second argument, **\n**. The **tr** utility interprets this second argument as the replacement character. The *n* is the ASCII character for the newline. The **tr** utility locates each target character (space), and replaces it with the newline character everywhere in the file. The resulting output of **tr** consists of every word from the input file on a new line. The ASCII specification *012* is equivalent to the **\n** and can be used as well.
#	Instructs the shell not to interpret the remainder of the line.

Each word is output on a line by itself. If there were places in the file with two spaces next to each other, both are changed to newlines. So there are probably blank lines in the output as well.

Locating Errors

If you have made at least one error and had to repair it, you are one step ahead. It is useful to introduce an error to see how the shell or the utility responds.

➥ 1. Go back into the script and make an error in the line you just added (remove a space, delete the backslash, or whatever).

2. Run the script again.

Because you know where the error is, it is easy to fix. Keep following this set of instructions to grow the script, one section at a time. When you make an error, debugging is much easier.

Replacing Tabs with Newlines

The previous version of the file, *wordsUsed3,* changes all spaces to newlines, resulting in most of the text being output one word to a line. However, if you have any TAB characters in the file, they remain.

We can replace the TAB characters with newline characters, too.

➥ 1. Copy *wordsUsed3* to *wordsUsed4.*

2. Modify the last line of *wordsUsed4* to search for both space and tab characters by adding a TAB to the first argument and another new line to the second argument:

    | tr ' \t' '\n\n'

3. Run the script again and examine the results:

    wordUsed4 | **more**

The script's last line instructs **tr** to locate spaces and replace them with newlines, and to locate TAB characters (**\t**) and replacing them with newlines, also.

Removing Blank Lines

The output of *wordsUsed4* includes whatever blank lines were in the input file and any that were added when double spaces became two new lines. We can remove the blank lines.

1. Copy *wordsUsed4* to *wordsUsed5*.

2. With **vi**, include the **sed** utility in *wordsUsed5* by modifying the script to read as follows:

   tr -d '?."!:,();' < *manywords* \
   | **tr** 'A-Z' 'a-z' \
   | **tr** ' \t' '\n\n' \
   | **sed** '/^$/d'
   # *A backslash is added to the end of line 3*
   # *The fourth line is added*

3. Run the script again:

   wordsUsed5 | **more**

4. Blank lines are removed from the output data.

Examining the Code

One line consisting of the following is added to *wordsUsed5*:

COMMAND/ ARGUMENT	INTERPRETATION
\	The \ is placed at the end of each of the previous three lines. Each backslash instructs the shell to not interpret the newline that follows. As a result, the shell interprets all four lines of the file as *one* command line.
|	Connects the output of **tr** to **sed**.
sed	Executes the **sed** utility.
' '	Instructs the shell to pass the enclosed string to **sed** as an argument without interpreting any special characters.
/^$/d	The argument passed to **sed**, which **sed** interprets to mean "locate lines that consist of a beginning ^ and ending $ with no text in between (blank lines), and then delete (**d**) those lines."

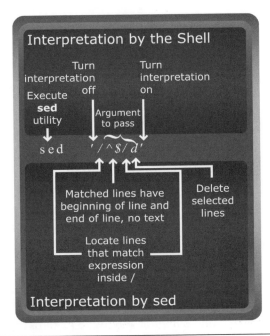

A View from the shell

Sorting the Lines

At this point, the output of *wordsUsed5* consists of all the words in the file, in their original order, in lowercase, without punctuation, and without blank lines. The word *the* is in several places in the file.

For **uniq** to remove duplicate lines, they must be adjacent. It's time to sort.

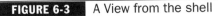 1. Copy *wordsUsed5* to *wordsUsed6*.

   2. Modify the *wordsUsed6* script as follows:

   tr -d '?."!:,();' < *manywords* \
   | **tr** 'A-Z' 'a-z' \

```
   | tr ' \t' '\n\n' \
   | sed '/^$/d' \
   | sort
   # A backslash is added to the end of line 4
   # Line 5 is new
```

3. Run the script to confirm the effect of the sorting:

   wordsUsed6 | **more**

Because the output is sorted, all lines containing the same word are on adjacent lines.

Examining the Code

The added commands are as follows:

COMMAND	DESCRIPTION
\	Instructs the shell to not interpret the newline that follows.
|	Connects the output of **sed** to the input of the next utility, **sort**.
sort	Runs the **sort** utility, which sorts all lines it receives from **sed**. Because every word is on a line by itself, the output is a sorted list of words from the file, one word to a line. If the file contains 10 instances of the word *the*, they are listed on sequential lines.

Removing Duplicates

At last, the data is ready for **uniq** to toss out the duplicates.

1. Copy the script file *wordsUsed6* to *wordsUsed7*.

2. Modify the *wordsUsed7* script as follows:

```
   tr -d '?."!:,();' < manywords \
   | tr 'A-Z' 'a-z' \
   | tr ' \t' '\n\n' \
   | sed '/^$/d' \
   | sort | uniq -c        # This line is modified
```

3. After writing the file and quitting the editor, run the script by entering:

   wordsUsed7 | **more**

All duplicate lines are removed in the output.

Examining the Code

The addition to the script is:

COMMAND	INTERPRETATION
|	Connect the output of **sort** to the input of **uniq**.
uniq -c	Run the **uniq** utility, passing it the **-c** option. **uniq** outputs all unique lines, only one copy of duplicate adjacent lines, and the number of duplicates for each line it encountered. Multiple lines containing the same word are reduced to just one line containing that word with the number of times that line was present in the input. The output consists of a list of all the words that are in the file with the number of instances of the word.

Listing Most-Used Words First

The output from **uniq** consists of a listing of all words in the *manywords* file and the number of times each was in the file, such as:

```
12   a
2    about
4    at
2    bill
1    box
6    can
2    charlie
```

It is probably more useful to output the words based on their frequency, with most-used word listed first.

1. Copy *wordsUsed7* to *wordsUsed8*.

2. Modify *wordsUsed8* to include a final **sort**:

    tr -d '?."!:,();' < *manywords* \
    | **tr** '*A-Z*' '*a-z*' \
    | **tr** ' \t' '\n\n' \
    | **sed** '/^$/d' \
    | **sort** | **uniq -c** \
    | **sort -rn**
    # *A backslash is added to the end of line 5, and line 6 is new*

3. Run *wordsUsed8*:

    wordsUsed8 | **more**

The script now outputs the words with the highest number of occurrences at the top of the list. This time, the output of **uniq** is piped to another **sort**, which sorts the lines based on the number that is at the beginning of each line. To follow numerical sort rather than ASCII, we include the **-n** argument. **sort** normally outputs the lowest numbers first. To see the most commonly used words on the top of the list, we reverse the sort order with the **-r** option.

Writing to Both a File and the Next Utility

The resulting unique lines (words) are displayed on the screen. The last addition to the *wordsUsed* script sends the output of **uniq** to a file and also to **wc** to count the total number of lines (unique words) employed.

1. Copy *wordsUsed8* to *wordsUsed*.

2. Modify the file so it looks like this:

    tr -d *'?."!:,();'* < *manywords* \
    | **tr** *'A-Z' 'a-z'* \
    | **tr** *' \t' '\n\n'* \
    | **sed** *'/^$/d'* \
    | **sort** | **uniq -c** \
    | **sort -rn** \
    | **tee** *words.out* | **wc -l**
    # *The backslash is added to the end of line 6, and line 7 is new.*

3. Run the script:

    wordsUsed

    The screen displays the total number of lines in the output of **sort**, which is the number of different words in the file.

4. Examine the contents of the new file, *words.out*, which is in your current directory:

    more *words.out*

The file *words.out* contains a list of all unique words and the number of times each is in the file *manywords*.

Examining the Code

The addition to the script is:

COMMAND	INTERPRETATION
\	Do not interpret newline.
|	Connect the output of **uniq** to the input of the next utility, **tee**.
tee	Run the **tee** utility, which reads from its input and then writes to output and saves a copy in memory, to be written to a file when it has read all input.
words.out	Argument passed to **tee**, which uses it as the name for the file that **tee** creates. A copy of all the input that **tee** receives is written to this file as well as to output.
|	Connect the output of the previous utility, **tee**, to the input of the next utility, **wc**.
wc	Run the **wc** utility.
-l	Instruct **wc** to count and display only the number of lines, ignoring the number of words and characters. Because each word in the input is on a line by itself, the output from **wc** is the number of different words employed in the file.

Reviewing the Completed Script

There is no utility in UNIX that lists the unique words used in a file. By piping several utilities together, we can list the unique words, how many times each is used, and the total number of words.

In summary, the program accomplishes the following:

COMMAND	INTERPRETATION
tr -d '?."!:,();' **<** *manywords* \	Removes punctuation.
| **tr** 'A-Z' 'a-z' \	Makes all characters lowercase.
| **tr** ' \t' '\n\n' \	Replaces spaces with newlines and TABs with newlines.
| **sed** '/^$/d' \	Removes blank lines.
| **sort** | **uniq -c** \	Sorts the data and removes duplicate lines, outputs a count of number of each line in input.
| **sort -rn** \	Sorts by number of times each word is in the file.
| **tee** *words.out* | **wc -l**	**tee** reads from input and writes to output and to the *words.out* file. Output from the **tee** utility goes to **wc**, which counts the number of lines (which are words, in this case).

The diagram in Figure 6-4 identifies how the data is passed and transformed by the script's utilities. The arguments passed to each utility are labeled ARGS.

The process you just completed is important. You wrote a short script, made it work, added more code to make it more functional, debugged it, added more code, debugged, and continued repeating the process until all functionality was successfully added. This approach results in fewer errors, and makes fixing the errors that are made much easier, because you know that the problem must be somehow related to what was just added.

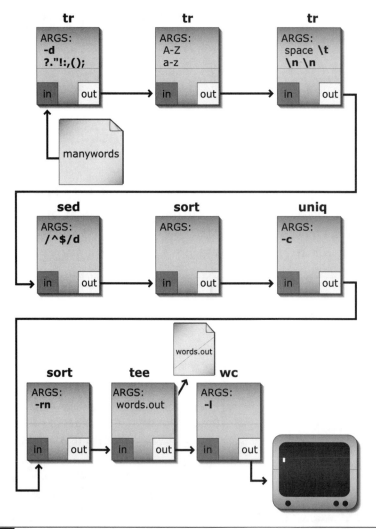

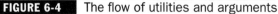

FIGURE 6-4 The flow of utilities and arguments

Self Test 1

Answer the following questions. Check your answers using the information within this chapter.

1. Examine the following script, *n-on*:

   **who | sort **
   ** | awk '{print $1}' **
   ** | uniq | wc -l**

   What will be in the output of *n-on*?

   _____

2. Where will output of the *n-on* script be sent?

   _____

3. How does the shell interpret each of the following in *n-on*?

   A. who

   _____

   **B. **

   _____

   C. '{print $1}'

   _____

   D. | uniq

   _____

   E. wc

   _____

   F. –l

   _____

4. When the shell reads the *n-on* script, how many command lines does it find?

   _____

Chapter Review

Use this section to review the content of this chapter and test yourself on your knowledge of the concepts.

Chapter Summary

- We can put complex command lines in scripts, make then executable, then execute the scripts whenever they are needed.
- When we enter the name of a script to the shell, the shell searches for the utility in the directories listed in its **PATH** or *path* variable. If the current directory (.) is not listed in the path, we must either specify the local directory using *./scriptname* or by changing the value of the path to include the current directory.
- Individual utilities perform a specific task well. By piping data from one utility to another, we can accomplish much more complex tasks.
- Script writing is best accomplished by first creating a short script of limited functionality, then adding features one at a time. Programmers carefully plan the sequence of increased functionality or complexity when they are creating code to make sure each modification is of reasonable size and complexity, so errors can be quickly located.

Assignment

<u>Fill-in</u>.

1. What option instructs **ls** to output a slash after each directory's name in output?

   _____

2. What command instructs the shell to add execute permission to the *p.scri* file?

   _____

3. Explain what results from the following commands, and what each piece of the command line accomplishes.

   A. **ls -F / | grep -v / | column**

   _____

   B. **tr ' ' '\n'** < *textfile*

   _____

4. What is the reason several lines in scripts have a \ character at the end of the line?

   _____

Projects

1. Make a copy of the *wordsUsed* script and name it *w-Used-p*, then modify it so that:

   A. When you run the script, your file *practice* is examined.

   B. Words are output in uppercase.

   C. A copy of the data is saved in a file named *sor.out* when it is one word to a line, and is sorted, but is not yet made unique.

   _____

2.

   A. Use the **man** pages to find the option to **ls** that outputs your files with an asterisk (*) after all files you made executable, and which option lists files in the order of the creation date.

   B. Create a file called *myfilesA* that contains a long listing of all the files in your home directory, sorted by date, with directories and executable files identified by **ls**.

   C. Create another file called *myscripts* that outputs just the names of your scripts, in the order that you created them.

   D. Write a script that outputs the number of users with entries in the */etc/passwd* file.

   _____

COMMAND SUMMARY

SCRIPT WRITING COMMANDS	
#	Instructs the shell not to interpret the remainder of the current line. This command is used to add comments to a script. It cannot be used inside a pipeline.
\	Instructs the shell not to interpret any special powers to whatever character follows. If placed as the very last character on a line, it tells the shell to not interpret ENTER so the next line of input is interpreted as a continuation of the first command line.

Creating and Changing Directories

O B J E C T I V E S

After completing this chapter, you will be able to:

- Create directories
- Change to a directory
- Use the complete pathname for a file
- Identify the role of inodes, data blocks, and directories when managing files
- Specify the path to a file relative to a user's home directory
- Use parent and current directories in path specifications
- List a file in more than one directory
- Move whole directories and their contents
- Remove directories

In this chapter, we explore creating and using new directories, called *subdirectories,* which are listed in your home directory. Files can be created and accessed within these subdirectories. Your home directory is one of many directories in a complex *directory structure* or *filesystem* that stores files belonging to all users, the system administrator, and the system itself. Because files are stored in different directories depending on the system and user, a successful computer professional must be able to change quickly from one directory to another, even if the target directory is in some remote part of the filesystem. This chapter examines the underlying structures that the UNIX/Linux engineers built into the filesystem and how we use them to access other directories and their files efficiently.

The filesystem allows us to create files and directories in a hierarchy. For example, a letter to a client named Greg Forbes on July 2, 2004, can be a file named *g.forbes7.2. 2004* that is listed in a directory named *Clients.* The *Clients* directory can be listed in another directory, *Correspondence,* which is listed in your home directory. Such an arrangement is essential for locating information quickly on the system. If you are an experienced DOS/Windows user, the directory structure examined in this chapter will be familiar, because the DOS filesystem was developed to be similar to the UNIX filesystem. The workstation screen is a small porthole through which we look into our collection of files. When a carefully designed hierarchical file system is in place, we can access the needed information with minimal effort using the commands examined in this chapter.

7.1 Employing Directories to Create Order

Managing files in directories requires a set of important, fundamental skills because nearly everything on the system is a file, and all files are accessed through directories. In the tour of the UNIX/Linux system in Chapter 2, you created new directories and then used them. This chapter examines those skills in much more detail, and investigates how the filesystem really works.

A collection of information stored electronically on the hard drive of a system is a *file.* The data stored in files can be accessed, modified, copied, and removed. In the same sense, a library's shelves contain books of information stored on paper. Those books can be accessed, copied, removed, and even modified. In a library, the cards in the card catalog or records in the online catalog provide users with information about the books and their location in the stacks. Similarly, in UNIX/Linux, there is an "index card" or *inode* that contains all the information available about each file, including the location of the actual file on the disk.

Files are not actually "in" directories. Files are in *data blocks* on the hard drive. The only things in a directory are the names and the inode numbers (index cards) for each of its files.

Reexamining the Home Directory

Nearly everything you have created thus far has been listed in the one directory that you access when you log on: your *home directory*.

1. Log on now to your account. As you have experienced before, you are automatically placed in your home directory.

2. Enter:

   pwd

   The path from *root* to your home directory is displayed.

   You are given the same place to work each time you log in, because the path to this directory is the sixth field in the record for your account in the */etc/passwd* file.

3. Enter:

   grep *$USER* */etc/passwd*

   or

   ypcat *passwd* | **grep** *$USER*

   The sixth field is the path to your home directory. At login, whatever directory is the contents of the sixth field in the */etc/passwd* file becomes your current directory after you log in.

4. List your current files:

   ls

   The files you created in previous exercises are probably listed in your home directory.

5. Create a new file by entering:

   who > *f-name*

The new file *f-name* contains the login names and other information concerning users currently logged on to the system. You do not specify where the new file is to be located. As a default, the file is created and listed in your current directory, which at the moment is your home directory.

6. Ask for a listing of the filenames in your current directory. Enter:

   ls

The names of the files you have created appear on the screen. If you have only a few files, this listing is brief. However, if you have many files, this listing fills up the screen and is difficult to read. By using a well-thought-out directory structure, you can store related files together in different directories and then have shorter listings in each directory.

All filenames you include in a command refer to files listed in your current directory, unless you specify otherwise. The following illustration shows the relationship between your home directory and some of the files probably listed in your home directory.

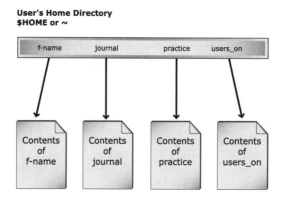

Because specific files are needed in the exercises that follow in this chapter, do the following:

7. If your home directory does not have files named *practice, users_on, respected,* and *f-name,* create them now using your favorite editor. Append a few lines of any content to each file.

8. Create a file named *journal* by entering the following:

   date > *journal*

Examining How Files Are Listed in Directories

People often think of UNIX directories as holding files much like physical file cabinets contain files. Although this "folder" metaphor is commonly used, it is unfortunately inaccurate and misleading. A directory does not actually contain files. The **ls** command reads the names of the files listed in the current directory and then outputs those names. The total contents of a directory can also be shown.

⌐ 1. To see the actual contents of your current directory, enter:

> **ls -i**

The output is similar to the following:

```
21188  f-name
51234  journal
44333  names.tmp
66554  numbers.tmp
87666  ordered_1
42233  phon
33773  practice
55666  prtest
77665  test_file
91919  users_on
```

Your output includes very different numbers on the left of your filenames. However, the contents of your directory are structured the same: just filenames and a number associated with each file.

For each of its files, the directory contains only the name of that file and a number that leads to the *inode* for that file. The inode contains all the information about that file and has the addresses of the data blocks on the hard drive where the file is actually located. The **-i** option to **ls** is instruction to include the inodes in its output.

Inodes are small pieces of memory created on the hard disk when it was formatted. Each inode simply stores information about the file (the owner, permissions, date created, date modified, size, and more). The inode also has a list of the addresses of the blocks on the disk where the data that comprise the file is actually located. A directory contains only a filename

and its index number (inode number) for each of its files and directories—
nothing else.

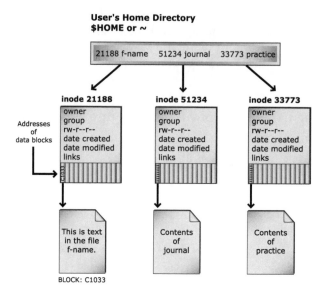

Each user's home directory is just a file containing the name and inode
number of each file that the user created for this directory. The inode
contains the remainder of the information about the file and the addresses
needed to locate the data.

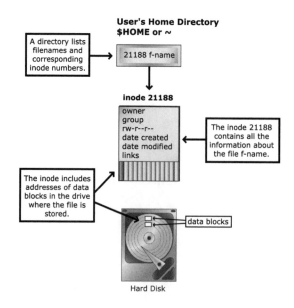

The inode for a file contains all the information about the file and has room for the addresses of up to 13 data blocks on the hard drive. The first 10 data blocks addressed from the inode contain actual file data. If a file is too large to fit into the 10 blocks, additional blocks are allocated. However, their addresses are not placed in the inode; rather, they are placed in a data block with its address placed in the 11th slot in the inode. For large files, the addresses of the blocks on the drive that hold the data are in the inode or in a data block that the inode can access.

This chapter examines not only how to move around in the filesystem, but also how the inodes are the essential components that makes it possible to list files in directories. We have found in the last 20 years of UNIX and Linux education that people who think about the filesystem by including the role of directories, inodes, and data blocks are better able to solve problems and conceptualize more advanced topics such as permissions, links, and so on. Hence, we developed this chapter as a careful investigation of the entire directory structure.

2. Add another file to see what is added to the directory:

    who > *users_test*

3. Examine the contents of your current directory:

    ls -i | more

The new filename, *users_test*, and its index (inode) number are added to the current directory.

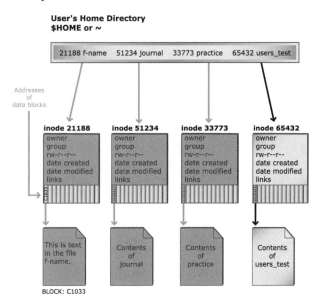

Whenever a file is created, its name and its inode number are entered into the directory's contents.

Creating Directories

Usually when we create or make directories, they are listed in the current directory.

⮑ 1. Create a new *Projects* directory by entering:

mkdir *Projects*

The command **mkdir** accomplishes but one task: It **ma**k**es** a **dir**ectory. The new directory is listed in whatever directory we are "in" when we create the new one. Each new directory we create, often called a *subdirectory*, can list additional files and other directories.

2. Obtain a listing of the contents of the current directory by entering:

ls | more

The new directory, *Projects*, is probably among the first listings if you used an uppercase *P* when you created it. If you give directories names that begin with uppercase letters and you name files in lowercase, directories are listed first when **ls** is run.

> **N O T E :** In this book, user-created directories are usually given names with the initial letter capitalized so they are listed first by **ls**. UNIX and Linux, however, do not require capital letters in directory names.

Obtaining Information about a Directory or Its Contents

We often run **ls** to determine the contents of the current directory. If we run **cd** to change directories to the new directory and then run **ls**, we see a list of the new directory's contents. We can also list the contents of a subdirectory without leaving the current directory.

⮑ 1. Enter:

ls *Projects*

The *Projects* directory is read, and because there are no filenames listed in it nothing is displayed on the screen. To list the contents of a subdirectory without leaving the parent directory, enter the **ls** command with the name of the subdirectory as an argument.

2. Obtain a long listing of the content of *Projects*:

   ls -l *Projects*

The files, permissions, owners, and so on, of the files listed in *Projects* are displayed.

3. Obtain information about the contents of the current directory by entering:

   ls -l

This time the permissions and such of the files in the current directory, including *Projects*, are displayed.

4. Obtain a complete listing of the current directory's contents, including inode numbers, by entering:

   ls -i

Projects has an inode that is unique to it. All information about the *Projects* directory—including the directory's permissions, owner, and so forth—is kept in the inode.

The following illustration depicts your home directory. The graphic for your home directory is bordered in bold. The one for the new *Projects* subdirectory is not bold, to indicate that although you created a new directory, your home directory is still your current directory, the one in which you are working.

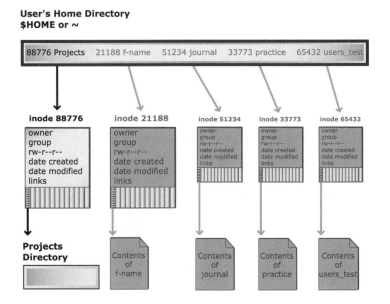

5. Enter:

pwd

You remain in your home directory.

Changing Directories

We inform the shell when we want to change to a different directory; that is, make it the current directory.

⤷ Change your current directory to the newly created *Projects* directory by entering:

cd *Projects*

The **cd** or <u>c</u>hange <u>d</u>irectory command instructs the shell to locate the directory listed as an argument (*Projects*) and to make it the current directory. The following illustration indicates that your current directory is no longer your home directory. The subdirectory *Projects* is now your current directory and is shown outlined in bold.

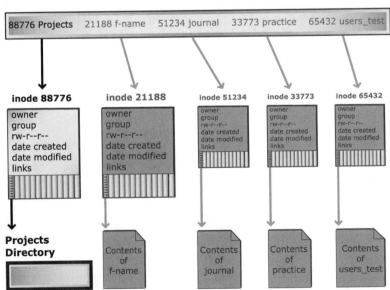

Examining the Path to Your Current Directory

Regardless of your location in the filesystem, you can always identify your current directory.

↳   You are in *Projects*. Confirm your location by entering:

pwd

The output is the absolute *path* from the top of the file system (***root*** or ***/***) to your current directory. It is something like:

```
/home/cassy/Projects
```

The topmost directory, called ***root***, or the ***root***, is symbolized by the first forward slash (*/*) in the pathname. All other directories from ***root*** to the current directory are separated by slashes. The *path* is a list of directory names separated by the */* (slash) character. In this example, the last directory in the output of **pwd** is *Projects*. The one to its left is the parent directory of *Projects*, which in this case is your home directory. To the left of your home directory is its parent directory and so on to ***root***. The **pwd** command outputs the names of the directories starting at the ***root*** that must be accessed to go from the ***root*** to your current directory. It is the full or absolute pathname of your current or working directory.

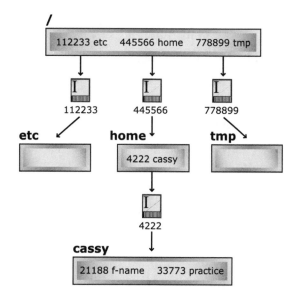

Listing the Contents of the Current Directory

On several occasions, you have obtained displays of the names of files listed in whatever directory was your current directory at the time.

 List the contents of the directory that is now your current directory (*Projects*), with the usual command:

ls

Nothing is listed. You have no ordinary files in the new *Projects* directory. The files that appeared when you last entered **ls** still exist, but they are not in this directory. The **ls** command displays only the names of the files listed in your *current* directory. You changed your current directory to be *Projects*, leaving your home directory by typing the **cd** *Projects* command.

Creating Files within a Subdirectory

The current directory is *Projects* and it contains no regular files when created. We can create new files in a directory.

 1. With *Projects* as your current directory, create a new file named *testing*. Enter:

    vi *testing*

2. Add a few lines of text to the new file.

3. Write the file and return to the shell.

    :wq

4. With **vi**, create another new file named *practice*, and add the following:

    `This is a file `*`practice`*` located in the `*`Projects`*` directory.`

5. After you have created the two new files, list the filenames in the *Projects* directory by entering:

    ls

The files *practice* and *testing* are listed.

6. As usual, the contents of the directory include filenames and inode numbers:

    ls -i

The following illustration shows the relationship between your home directory and its files. The files you just created in the *Projects* subdirectory are included.

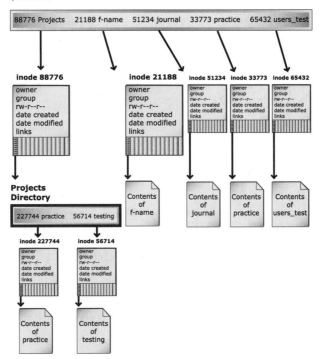

Returning to Your Home Directory

You used the command **cd** *subdirectory* (in this case, **cd** *Projects*) to change the current directory from your home directory to the *Projects* directory.

1. To make your home directory your current directory again, enter:

   cd

2. Confirm that you are now back at your home directory by entering:

   pwd

   The output of **pwd** is the same as when *Projects* was the current directory, except that your home directory is now the last directory listed, and *Projects* is not listed at all.

3. Confirm your location by listing the names of the files in your current directory by entering:

   ls

   The directory *Projects* appears, along with your other files, including a file named *practice.* Your home directory is again your current directory.

No matter where in the filesystem we are currently working, the **cd** command, without any directory name as an argument, returns us safely to our home directory. In the *Wizard of Oz*, Dorothy could go home from anywhere at any time by clicking her heels together and saying, "There's no place like home," three times. The **cd** command (**c**ommand **d**orothy) takes us to our home directory in Linux and UNIX.

4. Examine the contents of the file *practice* with:

   cat *practice*

This file *practice* is not the one you created when you were in the *Projects* directory, but the one created in an earlier chapter in your home directory.

NOTE: Files can have identical names only if the files are listed in different directories.

Distinguishing between Files and Directories

In this book, directory names have an uppercase first letter to distinguish them from ordinary filenames. The **ls** utility provides another way to identify directories.

 1. From the shell, type the command:

   ls -F | more

Examine the output of **ls** with the **-F** option. Directory names are displayed with a slash appended to the end, as in *Projects/*. The slash character is not a filename extension, but just a character that **ls** adds to the output to indicate the nature of the **F**ile.

Filenames displayed with an asterisk (*) at the end are *executable* files, such as the scripts you created in previous chapters. The **ls** command interprets the **-F** option as instruction to display all **F**iles (including directory names), identifying directories with a slash, executables with an asterisk, and so on.

Because the output of **ls** is redirected to another utility, it puts one filename to a line, unless we instruct it to put several names in a line.

2. Enter:

   ls -C -F | more

The **-C** option to **ls** instructs **ls** to make several **C**olumns in the output instead of one.

Obtaining Information about a Directory or Its Contents

We often want a list of the contents of a directory. At other times, we need information about the directory itself.

↳ 1. Obtain a long listing of the content of *Projects*:

   ls -l *Projects*

   The files, permissions, owners, and so on of the files listed in *Projects* are displayed.

2. Obtain information about the <u>d</u>irectory *Projects*, not its contents, by entering:

   ls -ld *Projects*

   This time the permissions and so on of the directory *Projects* itself are displayed, not information about the files listed in *Projects.*

   Without the **-d** option, the **ls** command returns a listing of information about the contents of the target directory. When passed the **-d** option, **ls** provides information about the directory itself.

Listing Directory Content Recursively

The **ls** utility lists files in the current directory. We can list both the current directory files and the contents of subdirectories.

↳ Enter:

   ls -R -C | more

   All files listed in the current directory are output. The names of the directories listed in the current directory are also displayed, as are the files listed in each subdirectory. The **-R** option to **ls** is instruction to descend through each subdirectory in the directory tree, listing information about all directories. Because this is a <u>R</u>ecursive examination, the **-R** option is used.

7.2 Managing Files in Directories

To impose order on the chaos of an untamed home directory, we create subdirectories and list files in them.

Moving a File into a Subdirectory

What really happens when we move a file from one directory to another?

1. List all files that start with an *f* and their inodes in the current directory:

   ls -i *f**

   The output includes a listing of the *f-name* file. The name and inode are listed.

2. Record the inode for *f-name*: _____

3. Move the file to the *Projects* directory with:

   mv *f-name* *Projects/*

4. List the files in your home directory:

   ls

   The file *f-name* is no longer listed.

5. List the contents of the *Projects* directory:

   ls -i *Projects*

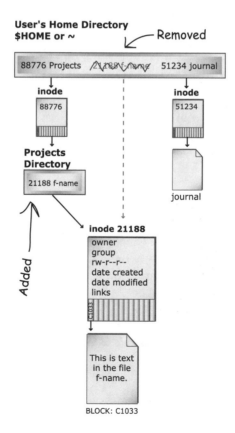

Your files *practice, testing,* and *f-name* are listed. The listing for the file *f-name*, including its inode number, was moved to the *Projects* directory. The inode for *f-name* as it is listed in *Projects* is the same inode that was listed for *f-name* in the home directory before it was moved.

When you issue the command **mv** *file directory*, the system cannot move the electronic file into the subdirectory, because directories do not contain files. Instead, the name and the inode number (which provides information about the file including the data block addresses) are erased from the current directory and are written in the subdirectory. The new directory now lists the file's name and the same inode number. When we **mo̲ve** the listing for a file from one directory to another directory we are moving the file.

Copying Files into Subdirectories

Copying a file and putting the copy in a subdirectory is somewhat like moving a file.

1. Create a new file in your current (home) directory:

   cd
   cal > *month*
   ls -i

2. Copy *month* to the *Projects* directory and examine it by entering:

   cp *month Projects/*
   ls -i *Projects*
   cd *Projects*
   cat *month*
   cd

   The copied file does *not* have the same inode number as the original. When we copy a file, a second electronic version is created. The copy has its own inode, permissions, and data blocks that contain the new file's actual content. Each file now has a life of its own.

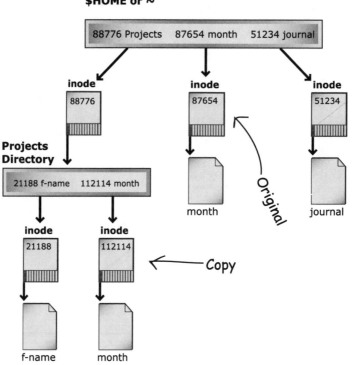

The syntax of the commands you just used to **mo**ve or **co**py files from the current directory to a subdirectory is as follows:

mv *filename subdirectoryname*   (The listing is moved, but the inode is the same.)

cp *filename subdirectoryname*   (A second file is created with a new unique inode.)

SUMMARY   If a **cp** or an **mv** command is given one or more filename arguments followed by a last argument that is a directory, the files are moved or copied into the directory, with the files retaining their original names. In fact, it is the listing for a file that is moved. If a copy is created, a new listing is written in the target directory. If a file is moved, it retains its inode number. If a file is copied, the copy is given its own new, unique inode.

Accessing a File in a Subdirectory

You are in your home directory. Listed in this home directory is the subdirectory *Projects.* You moved the listing of *month* from your home directory to *Projects.*

1. Without leaving home, you can access *month*:

> **more** *Projects/month*
>
> **pwd**

The file *month,* listed in *Projects,* is displayed. You do not change directories, but reach into a subdirectory and access the file.

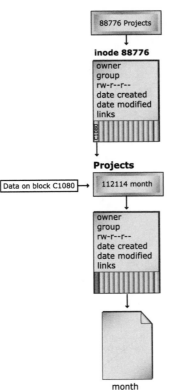

User's Home Directory
$HOME or ~

88776 Projects

inode 88776

owner
group
rw-r--r--
date created
date modified
links

C1080

Projects

Data on block C1080 → 112114 month

owner
group
rw-r--r--
date created
date modified
links

month

This command is really a significant set of instructions:

A) Look in the current directory for a subdirectory named *Projects* and identify its inode number.

B) Locate the inode that has the correct number.

C) Check on permissions.

D) If permitted to access the directory, get the directory's address from the inode.

E) Open the directory *Projects*.

F) Look in *Projects* for a file named *month*.

G) Identify the inode associated with *month*.

H) Examine permissions from *month*'s inode, and if permitted to read the file, get from the inode the data block addresses of the data blocks that hold the file.

I) Read the file from the data blocks.

You have been following this format for some time when you entered commands like **more** */etc/passwd*.

Avoiding Mistakes When Moving Files into Directories

When you are moving a file into a subdirectory, what happens if you misspell the directory name?

1. In your current (home) directory, create a new file *trouble*:

    date > *trouble*
    more *trouble*
    ls -i *t**

2. Record the inode for *trouble*. _____

3. In the next command, you attempt to move *trouble* into the *Projects* directory, but misspell *Projects* as *ProjectZ*.

    mv *trouble ProjectZ*

4. Get a listing of the files in the *Projects* directory:

    ls *Projects*

    The file *trouble* is not there.

5. List the files in the current directory:

    ls -F

    The file *trouble* is missing; it was moved, but to where? A new listing named *ProjectZ* is in the current directory. It is not a directory.

6. Examine the file *ProjectZ*:

>   **more** *ProjectZ*
>
>   **ls -i** *ProjectZ*

When you issued the command **mv** *trouble ProjectZ*, there was no directory *ProjectZ*, so the file *trouble* was renamed to *ProjectZ*. It is the same file with the same inode, but we changed the name that is listed in the directory.

If the **mv** utility is given two arguments, it changes the name of an existing file (argument one) to a new name (argument two), unless the second argument is a directory. If the second argument is a directory, the name and inode number listing for the file (argument one) is moved into that directory. In this example, there is no directory named *ProjectZ*. The **mv** utility simply changes the name of *trouble* to a new filename, *ProjectZ*.

7. Change the name of the file back to *trouble*:

>   **mv** *ProjectZ trouble*

8. To avoid this problem, enter the **mv** command with a slash after the directory name:

>   **mv** *trouble ProjectZ/*

This slash informs **mv** that you want the listing for file *trouble* to be moved into a *directory* named *ProjectZ*. This time, the shell cannot find a directory named *ProjectZ*, so on most systems it displays an error message. With the **/** at the end of the last argument, **mv** interprets the argument as a directory name. When it cannot find a directory of that name, it cries foul. Without the **/** at the end of *ProjectZ*, there is no insistence that *ProjectZ* be a directory. The argument does not match a directory name and so is seen as simply the new name for the file in a rename request.

Changing Filenames When Moving Files

In the commands you've used so far in this chapter, the files kept their original names in the new directory listings. You can also change the name of a file as you move it.

1. Create a file and move its listing into a subdirectory, with a new filename, by entering the following:

>   **touch** *junkness*
>
>   **ls -i** *j**

2. Record the inode number of the file *junkness* _____

> **mv** *junkness Projects/treasure*
> **ls** -i *Projects*
> **ls** *junkness*

The file that was *junkness* in the current directory is now no longer listed in the current directory but it is listed in the *Projects* directory under a new name, *treasure*. It retains the same inode. It is the same file. One directory's junk is another directory's treasure.

The syntax for the command to move a file listing from the current directory to a new directory and also change its filename is **mv** *filename subdirectory/newfilename*.

The **mv** command really does mean <u>mov</u>e, but it moves the *listing* for a file or directory to another directory. It does not move the file's contents. The file or directory remains on the drive in the data blocks where it always was. The file does not move; its listing moves from one directory to another.

Removing Files from Subdirectories

You have just used the **mv** command to move the listing of a file from the current directory into a subdirectory without changing directories. You can remove (delete) files from a subdirectory in essentially the same way.

➥ **1.** Try this series of commands to remove the files *treasure* and *month* from the *Projects* directory:

> **ls** *Projects*
> **rm** *Projects/treasure*
> **ls** *Projects*

2. The file *treasure* is removed.

> **cd** *Projects*
> **ls**

In fact, the inode is consulted to identify the data blocks used by the file; then, the entry for the file is removed from the *Projects* directory. The data blocks listed in the inode that the file used are then released so that others can use them.

Creating Subdirectories within Subdirectories

Earlier in this chapter, you created the *Projects* directory as a subdirectory of your home directory. You can also create a subdirectory to be listed in the *Projects* directory.

1. Check to see that the *Projects* directory is still your current directory by entering:

   pwd

2. Create a new subdirectory to be listed in *Projects*:

   mkdir *Code*
   ls -i

   The new directory is created and listed with its own inode in the current directory.

3. Leave the *Projects* directory, and change to your new *Code* directory:

   cd *Code*

4. Make sure the *Code* directory is your current directory with:

   pwd

   This time the output of **pwd** consists of the path to your home directory, followed by */Projects/Code*. The new subdirectory, *Code,* is listed in the *Projects* directory. The *Projects* directory is listed in your home directory, and your home directory is listed in some other directory, and so on, to the topmost directory, */ (root)*.

5. Use an editor to create a file named *report3* in your current directory (*Code*) that contains the following:

   This is report 3 created in the Code directory.

6. Write the file and quit the editor:

   :wq

7. List the files in the current directory by typing:

   ls
   pwd

   You now have the file named *report3* listed in the *Code* directory, which is listed in the *Projects* directory, which is listed in your home directory.

At this point, your directory structure should look like the following illustration:

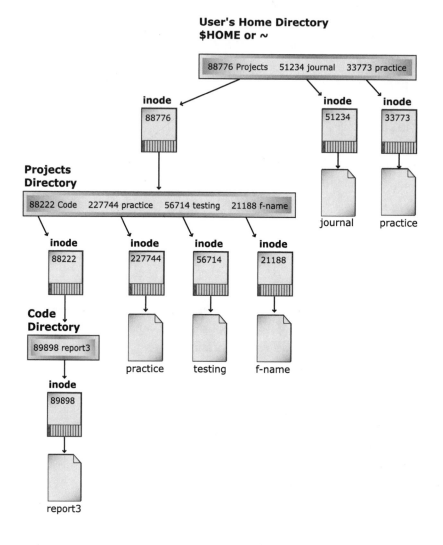

Moving through the Filesystem

You are in the *Code* directory.

1. Change your current directory back to your home directory with:

> **pwd**
> **cd**
> **pwd**

2. List the files and directories in your home directory with:

> **ls -F**

A complete listing of all the files and directories located in your home directory is displayed.

3. Enter the following commands to move through the path to the *Code* directory and view the *report3* file:

> **pwd**
> **cd** *Projects*
> **ls**
> **pwd**
> **cd** *Code*
> **pwd**
> **ls**
> **cat** *report3*

At each step, you confirmed your location, listed files, and changed to a subdirectory.

In the next section, we will examine how to access files and directories more efficiently.

Self Test 1

1. What is the command to create a directory named *Proposals*?

_____

2. What command changes your current directory to the *Proposals* directory?

_____

3. What command changes your current directory back to the home directory?

_____

4. What shell command can you enter to identify your current directory?

_____

5. What **ls** command option tells **ls** to distinguish files from directories in its output?

_____

6. Your home directory is your current directory, and you enter the command **cd** *Projects*. You then create a file named *confused*. What directory will list the *confused* file?

_____

7. How is it possible to have two files with the same filename in your account?

_____

8. Assume your home directory is your current directory. What command will move a file named *florence* to a directory named *Proposals*, which is a subdirectory of the home directory?

_____

9. Assume you want to move the file *ideas* from the current directory to a subdirectory named *Work*, and you enter the following command:

    mv *ideas* *work*

When you examine the *Work* directory, the file is not listed there. Where is it?

_____

10. In the current directory, what command would list the files of a subdirectory named *Cows* and distinguish between files and directories?

_____

7.3 Using Pathnames to Manage Files in Directories

In the previous section, you moved through the directory system by entering a series of **cd** commands, such as **cd** *Projects* and then **cd** *Code*. Each **cd** command changed one directory. This section introduces an explicit way to reach distant directories using a single complex argument.

Accessing a Subdirectory

1. Make your home directory your current directory:

    cd

2. Change your current directory from your home to the *Code* directory in a single step, by typing the following command. (A common error is to enter spaces between the directory names and the **/** character. The full path is one argument, with no spaces.)

>   **cd** *Projects/Code*

3. Check the path to your current directory by entering:

    pwd

    Your current directory is now *Code*.

The command **cd** *Projects/Code* is instruction to change your current directory to a subdirectory (*Projects*) and then move on to its subdirectory (*Code*).

The *Projects/Code* argument is a list of directories that describes where a directory or file is listed. *Projects/Code* is a pathname. In this case, *Projects* is listed in the current directory, and *Code* is listed in *Projects*. This path instruction tells the shell to look in the current directory for a listing of *Projects*, then to look in *Projects* for a listing for *Code*, and finally to make *Code* the current directory.

The shell keeps track of your current directory. A filename or directory name in a command line refers to a file or directory listed in the current directory. *Pathnames* are the mechanism used to tell the shell what path to follow to access a file or directory that is *not* listed in the current directory.

Using Pathnames with Utilities

Pathnames can also be used as arguments to utilities. After the previous exercise, your *Code* directory is now your current directory.

1. Enter:

    ls

    A few sections back, you created a file in the *Code* directory called *report3*.

2. Change directories to your home directory by typing:

    cd
    pwd

    To get to the desired *report3* file that is listed in the *Code* directory, you could change directories to your *Code* directory and then edit the file. Or, you could use a more efficient pathname.

3. Use **vi** to edit the *report3* file listed in your *Code* directory without changing your current directory from your home directory. Enter:

    vi *Projects/Code/report3*

    The argument passed to **vi** is the pathname from your current directory to the file *report3*. The file is *report3*, listed in *Code*, which is listed in *Projects*, which is listed in the current directory. This is a *relative pathname* because it shows the path to the file relative to the current location.

4. Use the editor to make some changes or additions to *report3*:

   vi *report3*

5. Leave the file, return to the shell and confirm the current location:

   :wq

   pwd

Although you accessed a file at the end of the relative path, you did not change directories. You remain where you started.

Examining How the Relative Path Is Employed

The following illustration examines how the directories, inodes, and the file are related when we use the argument *Projects/Code/report3*:

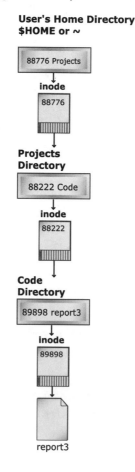

The following steps are completed when the argument *Projects/Code/report3* is employed:

A) Look in the current directory for a *Projects* listing.

B) Identify the inode number associated with *Projects*.

C) Locate the appropriate inode on the hard drive.

D) Open *Projects'* inode, check permissions, and if permitted, obtain the address of the data block that holds the contents of the *Projects* directory.

E) Open the data block holding the contents of *Projects*.

F) Locate an entry in *Projects* for the directory *Code*.

G) Identify the inode number associated with the *Code* directory listed in *Projects*.

H) Locate the *Code* directory's inode on the hard drive.

I) Open the inode and determine where on the drive the block is located that holds the data for the *Code* directory.

J) Open the *Code* directory data block.

K) Look through *Code* for an entry for *report3*.

L) Identify the inode number for the inode for *report3*.

M) Locate *report3*'s inode on the drive.

N) Open *report3*'s inode, check permissions, and identify the address of the block on the drive where the file's contents are located.

O) At long last, open the correct data block, and read the file into a buffer for **vi** to edit.

Comparing a Relative Path with the Default Path

When we access a file by specifying its relative path, we remain in the current directory. This exercise examines what happens if we are editing a file at a distant location and write its contents out in a new file.

➥ **1.** Confirm your present location:

> **pwd**

Your current directory is still your home directory. Even though you worked on the file listed in a different directory, you did not change your current directory from your home directory to that directory. When you wrote the file with the **:wq** command, it was written to its original directory, not to your current directory. However, what happens when you write to a new file from **vi**?

2. Again use **vi** to access *report3*:

   vi *Projects/Code/report3*

3. Make another change in the file.

4. From the command mode of **vi**, write the file as a new file, and then quit the editor with:

   :w *report3-new*

   :q

5. List the files whose name begins with the letter *r* in your current directory and in *Code*:

   ls *r**

   ls *Project/Code/r**

From **vi**, a new file is written to the *current* directory, unless you specify a path to some other directory.

6. Once again, edit *report3*:

   vi *Projects/Code/report3*

7. This time specify where to write a copy using a pathname. Enter:

   :w *Projects/r3*

8. Exit **vi**:

   :q

9. List the files in *Projects*:

   ls *Projects*

The file *r3* that you created from within the editor is listed in *Projects*, and *report3-new* is listed in the current directory.

N O T E : The *relative* pathname of a file combines both a directory path to the directory where the file is listed and the file's name, all separated by slashes. The path to a file starting at **root** is the *absolute* path. We can work with any UNIX utility on any file, regardless of its location, by using the file's pathname.

Copying Files into Other Directories Using Paths

Pathnames are particularly useful with the **cp** and **mv** commands. You can copy or move files from one directory to another. In this exercise, you copy the file *journal* to the *Code* directory and give it a new name.

↳ 1. Make sure your home directory is your current directory:

   cd

2. Type the following command (leaving no spaces between the names and the / characters):

   cp *journal Projects/Code/journal2*

   The relationship among directories, files, and inodes for the previous command is summarized in the following illustration:

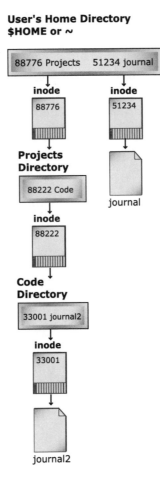

With the **cp** *journal Projects/Code/journal2* command, you are giving **cp** two arguments that tell the **cp** utility to use the appropriate inodes to:

a) Locate the file *journal* that is listed in the current directory.

b) Open the *Projects* directory to obtain information on the location of the *Code* directory.

c) Open the *Code* directory.

d) Make a copy of *journal* (from the current directory), and list the copy in the *Code* directory, giving the new copy the name *journal2*.

3. List the journal file and associated inodes with:

>   **ls -i** *journal*

4. Change from your home directory to the *Code* directory by entering:

>   **cd** *Projects/Code*

5. Confirm that *journal* was properly copied and listed in its new directory as *journal2*:

>   **ls -i**

Because *journal2* was created as a copy of another file, a duplicate electronic copy of the file is made. The new directory listing includes a new inode number that contains information needed to locate this new copy. Both the original and the copy can be edited independently.

6. Examine the file with:

>   **cat** *journal2*

It has the same file contents.

7. Finally, return home and create another directory named *Docum*:

>   **cd**
>   **mkdir** *Docum*

8. Without changing to the *Docum* directory, create a new file:

>   **touch** *Docum/readme*
>   **ls** *Docum*

Any command that takes a filename or directory name as an argument can be given an explicit pathname argument like this one.

The filesystem now looks like that depicted in the following illustration:

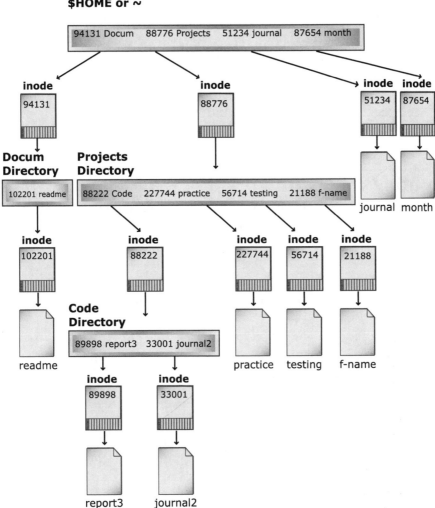

SUMMARY The general form of the **cp** command used earlier is as follows:

cp *filename Directory1/Directory2/newfilename*

where *filename* is a file in the current directory; *Directory1* is listed in the current directory; *Directory2* is listed in *Directory1*; and *newfilename* is the new name given to the copy of *filename* when it is listed in its new home, *Directory2*. You don't need to include the *newfilename* in the command. Omitting the *newfilename* results in the copy of the file having the same name as the original file. Duplicate names are acceptable because the second file is in a different directory.

Creating a Subdirectory Using a Pathname

Thus far, you have only created subdirectories, listing them in whatever was the current directory. You can also create subdirectories for remote directories.

1. Make certain you are in your home directory by typing:

   cd

2. Without leaving home, make one more directory by entering:

   mkdir *Projects/Corresp*

3. Find the names of the files and directories listed in the subdirectory, *Projects*, by entering:

   ls -F *Projects*

   The new directory *Corresp* that you created while in your home directory is now listed in the *Projects* directory.

4. Change to the new directory *Corresp* and confirm your location by entering:

   cd *Projects/Corresp*
   pwd

5. Create a file named *replies* in the *Corresp* directory, and add a few lines of text to the file:

   vi *replies*

6. Save the file and return to the shell.

7. Leave the *Corresp* directory and return to your home directory with:

   cd

Your directory hierarchy now matches the structure shown in the following illustration:

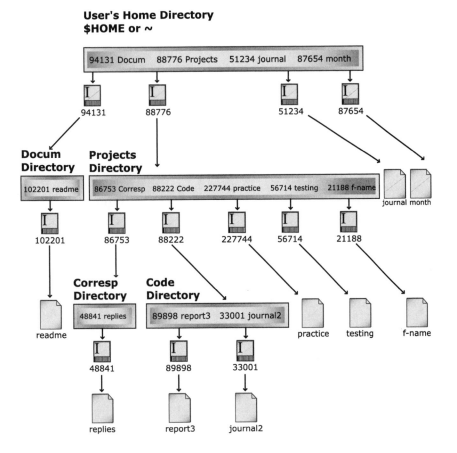

8. Make sure you are in your home directory by typing:

   pwd

You can change directories to subdirectories located below the current directory, and you can change from a subdirectory back to your home directory. You have not yet, however, changed from one subdirectory to another subdirectory located on a different branch of a directory tree (from *Code* to *Docum,* for instance). The special characters introduced in the next section allow for changes of this kind.

Using Parent Directory Names

There are very efficient ways to move around the filesystem. The techniques in this section are useful when you are unsure of where you are within the directory hierarchy and when you want to accomplish more complicated goals.

1. Change to the subdirectory *Code* by entering:

   cd *Projects*/Code

2. Obtain a listing of all files in your current directory by including the **-a** option with the listing command, as follows:

   ls -a

   Your listing looks something like this:

   .   ..   *journal2   report3*

   You are in the *Code* directory, and the files *journal2* and *report3* have appeared before. Dot (.) and dot-dot (..) are also listed.

3. Use the following to figure out what kind of file the dot is:

   file .

   In this case, the **file** utility examines whatever argument you give it and reports what kind of object it is. You receive a message indicating:

   ```
   .: is a directory
   ```

4. Now examine the dot-dot (..) file by typing:

   file ..

   The output tells you that the .. file, too, is a directory.

5. Confirm that your current directory is the *Code* directory:

   pwd

6. Display the inodes with all the files and directories listed in the current directory:

   ls -ai

7. Change to the dot (.) directory by typing the command:

   cd .

8. Determine the path to the dot directory by typing:

   pwd

The output of **pwd** is the path from the *root* to the current directory. It shows that your current directory is again *Code*. But *Code* was also your current directory before you typed the **cd .** command.

9. Obtain a listing of the contents of the dot directory:

   ls .

   The files listed in the current directory are displayed.

   The single dot is the "name" for your current directory used in the listing. The dot is how your current directory accesses itself. Every directory refers to itself as the **.** directory. It's the personal pronoun of Cyberville.

10. Determine the path to your current directory by typing:

    pwd

11. Change your current directory to the dot-dot directory by typing:

    cd ..

12. Confirm your present location with:

    pwd

You are now in the *Projects* directory. *Projects* is the parent directory of the *Code* directory where you were located before. The command **cd ..** changed your current directory from *Code* to the *Projects* directory, *Code*'s parent.

Examining the Inodes of Current and Parent Directories

In a directory, the **..** (dot-dot) is the listing for its parent directory. The parent directory is the directory located one level above your current directory and is the directory that lists the current directory's name and inode.

1. Examine the inodes for the files and directories listed in the *Projects* directory:

   ls -aiF

   The output lists the inodes for *Projects* (the **.** directory), the subdirectory *Code,* and various files.

2. Compare the results with the inodes listed in the *Code* directory:

   ls -ai *Code*

The *Code* directory is accessed through its inode.

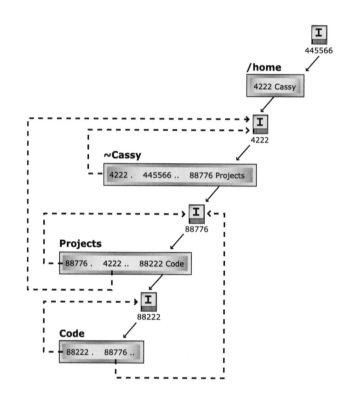

In *Code*, the inode for the dot directory has the same inode number that the parent directory, *Projects*, lists next to its subdirectory, *Code*. In the *Projects* direcory, the *Code* directory has the same inode that dot has in *Code*.

My daughter refers to herself as "Me" (.), and I refer to her as "Cassy." We both address the same person.

3. Now move up two directories with:

    pwd
    cd ../..
    pwd

At any directory level, when you type **cd ..**, you change directories to the (parent) directory; hence, typing **../..** moves to the grandparent.

4. Change directories to your home:

    cd

5. Confirm your location:

    pwd

6. Move to your home's parent and confirm:

   cd ..

   pwd

   You are probably in a directory named *home* or a subdirectory of it. The *home* directory is no one's *home*, but lists many users' homes. (Should it have been called *city* or *homes*?)

7. Go to the parent of *home*:

   cd ..

   pwd

   When we create a directory, it is listed in the current directory unless we specify otherwise. Return to your home and create a new directory.

8. Enter:

   cd

   mkdir *Skye*

9. List the contents of the current directory by entering:

   ls -iF

   The directory *Skye* and its inode are listed.

   A fair question at this point is to ask about the contents of the new directory as soon as it is created.

10. To answer the question, enter:

    ls -ai *Skye*

When a directory is created, it gets two listings: itself (the . directory) and its parent (the .. directory). When we create directories, they are part of the filesystem because the parent knows the newly created subdirectory's inode, and the subdirectory knows its parent's inode. They can locate each other.

SUMMARY It is possible to change directories in both directions within the filesystem. The command **cd** *subdirectory* changes from a directory to the *subdirectory*. The directory name must be specified, because several directories may be listed in one parent directory. The **cd ..** command changes from a subdirectory to its one and only parent directory. The dot-dot can be used because each directory has only one parent directory. The dot specifies the current directory. The **/** placed at the beginning of a path is instruction to start the path at **root**.

Copying Multiple Files to Subdirectories

Thus far, you have used the **cp** and **mv** utilities in several ways. You changed the names of files and copied files within the same directory. You have also used these utilities to move or copy a single file into a subdirectory, as with the **mv** *practice Projects/* command. This section examines how to use **mv** and **cp** to move and copy multiple files into other directories.

Both <u>mo</u>ve and <u>cop</u>y commands have been used thus far with two arguments, such as **cp** *file1 newfile1* or **mv** *file1 DIR1/file1A*.

1. Make sure you are in your home directory, and try entering a **cp** command with these three filenames as arguments:

    cd
    cp *practice journal f-name*

    The **cp** utility displays a usage error message telling you only two arguments are acceptable, unless the last one is a directory.

    Commands with more than two filename arguments, such as **cp** *file1 file2 file3*, are ambiguous. Should the new *file3* contain both of the other files? Or is *file1* copied and given two names? Because no clear meaning is attached, an error message is displayed.

2. Commands such as the following, however, *do* make sense. Enter:

    cp *practice journal Docum/*
    ls *Docum*

    Although three arguments are given to **cp**, the last argument is a directory, not a file. The meaning is clear: Copy both files (listed as the first two arguments) into the destination subdirectory (listed as the last argument).

    Both the **cp** and **mv** utilities accept more than two arguments, providing the last argument is the destination directory.

3. Create a new directory called *Archives* by entering:

    mkdir *Archives*

4. Copy several of your files into the *Archive* directory by entering:

    cp *users_on practice journal l* Archives/*
    ls *Archives*

The shell replaces the *l** on the command line with all filenames beginning with an *l* that are listed in the current directory. The shell then passes all the filename arguments and the last argument *Archives* to **cp**. To **cp** the intention is clear. It copies all files listed as arguments to the directory *Archives*.

Moving Multiple Files

Likewise, you can use **mv** to move multiple files into a directory. Both **mv** and **cp** can affect many files as long as the last argument is a directory.

↳ 1. While you are in your home directory, create several new files by entering:

    touch *cassy dimitri owen danny monika*
    ls -i

2. Move all five files to your *Docum* directory by entering:

    mv *cassy dimitri owen danny monika Docum/*
    ls -i

Because *Docum* is a directory that exists, and it is the last argument in the command line, all argument filenames and inode listings are moved into that directory. They are no longer listed in the current directory.

3. Confirm that the listings have been moved. Enter:

    ls - i *Docum/*

Moving Files into a Parent Directory

We have moved files from the current directory to a subdirectory and to more distant directories. We can also move them to the parent directory.

↳ 1. Change directories to the *Code* directory, a subdirectory of *Projects*, which is in turn a subdirectory of your home directory, by entering:

    cd
    cd *Projects/Code*

2. Confirm your current directory:

    pwd

3. Examine the listing for *report3*:

    ls -ai *report3*

4. Record the inode number for *report3*: _____

5. Move the listing for the file from the *Code* directory into its parent, the *Projects* directory, by entering:

    mv *report3* **..**

The last argument is a directory, namely the parent directory, so it is acceptable.

The **mv** utility moves the listing for the file *report3* from the current directory into the parent (..) directory. Because the *Projects* directory is the parent of *Code*, you have just moved the name and inode number for the file *report3* from *Code* into *Projects*.

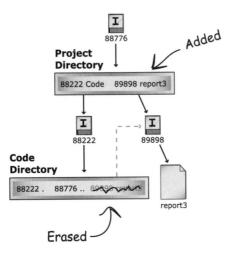

6. Return to the *Projects* directory:

   cd ..
   pwd

7. Confirm that the listing for *report3* was moved into *Projects*:

   ls -i

   The listing for *report3* is now in *Projects*. It is the same file; it has the same inode. A file is not affected when we move it. All we do is change the listing for the file from one directory to another.

8. Move *report3* back to *Code*:

   mv *report3 Code*

9. Create three files, and then move them to your parent directory:

   touch *megan daniel betty*
   ls -i
   mv *megan daniel betty* ..
   ls -i

   The directory .. is listed in the current directory. Because the last argument in the command line is a directory, namely the .. parent directory, all three files are moved into the specified directory.

10. Change to your parent directory, and confirm that the listings have been moved with:

> **cd ..**
> **ls**
> **ls -i**

The file listings of names and inodes are moved from the current directory to its parent.

Examining the Full Path from Root to Directories and Files

Thus far we have mostly explored accessing directories using the relative path between the current directory and the object. We can also specify a directory's location with the full path from the top of the filesystem.

1. From your home directory, identify the path from the *root* (*/*) to your current directory:

> **cd**
> **pwd**

The full path starts at *root*; the */* directory, and then lists all directories to your current directory. It is something like:

`/home/cassy`

or

`/user/class/fall/student01`

The files in your current directory are easily listed or accessed.

2. Enter:

> **ls**
> **cat** *practice*

We can access the same file using its full path and name.

In the following command, replace */home/cassy* with the path to your home directory from the previous **pwd** command:

> **cat** */home/cassy/practice*

This instruction says to start at *root* (*/*), find home, in home find *cassy*, and in *cassy* find *practice*. The fact that one of those directories is your current directory is irrelevant.

3. Go to **/tmp** and create a directory using your login name:

   cd /tmp

   mkdir $USER

4. Change to your new directory:

   cd $USER

5. Make a subdirectory in your current directory, make that subdirectory your current directory, and then confirm your location:

   mkdir *Mydir*

   cd *Mydir*

   pwd

   If all is well, you are in */tmp/yourlogin/Mydir.*

6. While in the *Mydir* directory, create a file:

   date > *myfile*

   ls

   cat *myfile*

   pwd

7. Now return home:

   cd

8. From your home directory, access the file you just created using its explicit full path:

   more /tmp/$USER/*Mydir***/***myfile*

   (*Use either $USER* or your actual login name.)

   The full path starting at *root* identifies any file explicitly.

   Because no two objects can have the same name in a directory, the path starting at the *root* uniquely identifies all files. If two objects have the same name, they must be in different directories so that the full pathnames must be different. Because the pathname for every file describes a particular file uniquely and absolutely, the full pathname to a file is called its *absolute pathname.*

Explicitly Calling Your Home Directory

In shells other than **sh**, we can identify the home directory in relative pathnames.

1. Change directories to **/tmp** and confirm:

cd */tmp*
pwd

2. Your present working directory is */tmp*.

3. Without changing directories, obtain a listing of the files in your home directory by typing the following command:

ls ~

The filenames listed in your home directory are displayed as the output of **ls**. This works because the C shell and all shells developed after it define the tilde (~) as the path to the user's home directory.

4. Examine your current directory path:

pwd

Your current directory is still */tmp*. The shell interprets ~ as the path to the user's home directory. Hence, you are given a listing of the files in your home directory, while remaining elsewhere.

5. Use the tilde to access a file that is in your home directory without changing directories. Enter:

more *~/practice*

This is instruction to examine your home directory, look there for a file *practice*, and display it.

6. Go directly to the *Code* directory by entering:

cd *~/Projects/Code*
pwd

The argument *~/Projects/Code* is instruction to examine your home directory for a directory named *Projects*, follow the inode to the *Projects* directory, look in *Projects* for the directory called *Code*, and make *Code* your current directory.

7. To see how the shell interprets the tilde, enter:

echo ~

The shell replaces the tilde with its value: the path to your home directory.

8. Try:

echo *~/Projects*

The shell replaces the ~ with the absolute path to your home directory, then adds */Projects* to that path. The result is the absolute path to the *Projects* directory.

9. Enter the following:

> **echo** *~/..*
> **echo** *~/Projects/Code*
> **echo** *~/ABCDE*
> **echo** *my home is ~*

The shell replaces the tilde in any command line with its value, the absolute path from root to the user's home directory.

Including Other Users' Logins in Directory Paths

In the previous exercise, you used the tilde (~) to indicate your home directory. It can also be used to specify *any user's* home directory. On UNIX/Linux systems, the system administrator or *superuser* is the user ***root***, and ***root*** has a home directory, as specified in the */etc/passwd* file.

1. Examine the ***root*** entry in the password file by entering:

> **grep** *root /etc/passwd*

2. You'll see a display much like the following:

```
root:wAbLLbMiF+xBI:0:1:Operator:/root:/bin/ksh
```

The fields of this line are separated by colons. The sixth field is the home directory of ***root***, usually */root* on Linux or */* on UNIX.

3. Request a listing of the path to the home directory for ***root*** by entering the following command. Do not put a slash or a space between the ~ and the user ID ***root***.

> **echo** *~root*

The path to the home directory of the user ***root*** is displayed.

4. Obtain a listing of the contents of the home directory of another user on the system by entering the following command, where *otherlogin* is the login ID of a user on your system:

> **echo** *~otherlogin*
> **ls** *~otherlogin*

The contents of the home directory of the user whose name you specified are displayed if you have appropriate permission. If you do not have permission to access another user's account, you can use the same approach on your own account.

5. Substitute your login name for *mylogin* in the following command line:

   ls *~mylogin*

6. Return to your home directory and confirm the locations:

   cd
   pwd
   ls

SUMMARY Modern shells interpret the tilde used alone as the path to your home directory. Paths to files listed in a user's home directory may be specified starting with the tilde. The tilde attached to the login name of any actual user is interpreted to be the path to *that* user's home directory.

For the tilde to work, the shell must determine where the home directory for your colleague, *otherlogin,* is located.

7. Request a display of the */etc/passwd* record for the login you are using for *otherlogin.* Enter:

   grep *otherlogin* */etc/passwd*

   or

   ypcat passwd | **grep** *otherlogin*

   When you use the tilde, the shell consults the */etc/passwd* file data to locate the path to the user's home directory. The next-to-last field in */etc/passwd* is the home directory for *otherlogin.* The key is the fact that the shell interprets the tilde as a special character with a specific meaning. Enter:

   echo *~*
   echo *~root*

   The home directory information from the ***passwd*** file is displayed.

   The shell interprets a tilde used alone as the home directory of the user; it interprets the tilde attached to a user login name as the path to that user's home directory.

   People often attempt to use the tilde to change directories to a directory that is an ordinary directory, not a user's home directory.

8. For example, attempt to go to the */tmp* directory with the following command:

   cd *~tmp*

The error message indicates there is no user on the system named *tmp*. Although there *is* a **tmp** directory, there is no user *tmp*; hence, there is no *home* directory for a user *tmp*.

9. Confirm that you are still at home:

   pwd

Returning to the Previous Directory

Many shells allow us to change directories and then return to our previous location, no matter where that is. The **bash** and **ksh** shells maintain the previous directory path as the value of a variable. The **tcsh** shell maintains a list of previous directories in a list that can be accessed.

Going Back to the Last Current Directory Using *bash* and *ksh*

These shells keep the path to the current directory and the previous directory in variables:

1. If you are not using a Bash or Korn shell, start one for this exercise:

   bash

   or

   ksh

2. Make sure your present location is your home directory:

   pwd
   echo $PWD

3. Change directories and confirm the new location:

   cd /tmp/$USER
   echo $PWD
   pwd

4. Enter the following:

   echo $OLDPWD
   cd $OLDPWD
   echo $PWD
   pwd

   The value of the variable *PWD* is the path to the current directory, and the variable *OLDPWD* is the path to the previous current directory. The

OLDPWD variable can be used as an argument to **cd** to return to the previous directory.

5. An alternative way of specifying the previous directory on many **bash** and **ksh** shells is with a dash argument:

    cd */tmp*
    pwd
    cd -
    pwd

6. If you started a child **bash** or **ksh**, return to your login shell with:

    exit

Returning to Previous Directories Using the *tcsh*

The **tcsh** shell does not use a variable, but rather a *list* of previously visited directories. As users we must instruct the shell to add a directory to the list.

1. If you are not communicating with a **tcsh**, and it is available on your system, start one now:

    tcsh

2. Make sure you are at your home directory:

    cd

3. Enter:

    pushd */tmp*
    pwd
    pushd */etc*
    pwd

    You changed directories to */tmp* and added that directory to the directory list. Then you changed directories to */etc* and added that directory to the list. We can go back to directories on the list, in the order of most recent first.

4. Enter:

    popd
    pwd

    You are now in the */etc* directory, the one on the top of the list.

5. Enter:

    popd
    pwd

With each **popd**, you go to the directory currently on the top of the list of directories that you added to the list.

Summarizing Methods for Accessing Files in Directories

In the previous sections, you examined several ways to specify a file's location. The following bulleted list reviews the available methods and includes a series of integrative commands to enter and compare.

1. Make sure you are in your home directory by entering:

   cd

   We can specify a file to access in four basic ways:

   - **Current directory:** Locate a file in the current directory by using its name.

2. For example enter:

   wc *practice*

   This is enough information to uniquely identify a file if the file's name is listed in the current directory. If we have a shell script located in the current directory and the shell does not include the current directory in its search *PATH* for locating utilities, we need to enter commands like *./scrA*, which specify the current directory with a dot.

   - **Relative path starting in the current directory:** Specify the path to a file starting with the name of a directory that is listed in the current directory.

3. Reach through two directories to a file with:

   wc *Projects/Code/report3*

   This is an instruction to look in the current directory for a listing for *Projects*; open the directory *Projects*, and then locate the requested subdirectory, open it, and so on. A path to a file beginning at the current directory is a *relative path*; it will be different depending on your current location.

   Among the directories listed in your current directory is the parent or .. directory. Paths starting with the parent are actually starting in the current directory because the parent is listed here as the .. directory.

4. For instance enter:

   ls *../*

   The *../* looks in the current directory for the parent directory, opens it, looks for its parent directory, then opens it and lists its contents.

   - **Start at root:** Specify the absolute path from *root* to a file. The absolute path is the same for a file, regardless of your current directory.

5. Create a new file in a distant directory with

   touch */tmp/$USER/newname*
   ls -l */tmp/$USER/newname*

   This is an instruction to examine the **root** directory for the requested subdirectory, *tmp*, open it, and so on. Every file has a unique absolute pathname.

   - **Start at a home directory:** Specify a path beginning at your home or any other user's home directory. The path to a file starting at home is the same regardless of your current directory.

6. For instance, enter:

   wc *~/practice*

   It makes no difference what directory is your current directory if you start the path at your home

7. Likewise, it makes no difference where you are located when you start the path at another user's home. Enter:

   wc *~otherlogin/*practice

where *otherlogin* is some other user. This argument is instruction to look up the home directory for the user *otherlogin* in the */etc/passwd* file and then to use the path to that home directory in the command, plus whatever additional path is specified.

7.4 Accessing Files in Remote Directories Using All Methods

Because the **cd** command allows you to move around a UNIX filesystem, at any moment, your current directory could be any directory you have permission to access anywhere on the system. Likewise, you can reach from wherever you are to any other directory to access a file. When you want to access a file that is not located in your current directory, you must specify a path to the file: either an absolute path from **root** or a relative path from your current directory, or the relative path from a user's home directory.

The following exercises explore more examples that integrate the various ways to provide a path to a file.

Specifying the Path Starting in the Current Directory

The most common way we specify a file or directory is to simply use its name in a command as an argument. A filename that includes no relative path defaults to the current directory. The path ./ is the default.

1. To access a file or directory that is listed in the current directory, we have been specifying its name. Enter:

   cd

   wc -l *practice users_on*

2. Of course, the same result is obtained when we specify the current directory:

   wc -l *./practice ./users_on*

   To access a file or directory listed in a directory that is listed in the current directory, we specify the directory, then a slash, then the target file or directory.

3. Make sure you are in your home directory, and then create a new file in the *Projects* directory called *actions* by entering:

   cd

   ls *Projects*

   vi *Projects/actions*

   Add text that is a brief description of how to access files at a distance.

4. Write the file and quit the editor:

   :wq

5. Obtain a listing of the files in the current directory with:

   ls

   The file *actions* is not listed in the current directory.

6. List the contents of the *Projects* directory:

   ls *Projects*

   The new file is listed in *Projects*.

   Because a subdirectory is a directory listed in the current directory, we can access a subdirectory by specifying its name.

   A common mistake is to use a slash in front of the name of a directory or file. For instance, if we want to go to a subdirectory *Projects* and we enter **cd** */Projects*, the slash is instruction to start at **root** and look there for the directory *Projects*. The requested directory is not found in **root**, and an error message is presented. The other common error is to use a backslash rather than a slash, for some "unknown" reason.

7. Change to the *Projects* directory:

   cd *Projects*

8. Obtain a word count of the *users_on* file, which is listed in your parent directory. Enter:

   wc *../users_on*

   Because the *..* directory is listed in the current *Projects* directory, it can be used as the starting point for the path to a file in one of its subdirectories.

9. Enter:

   pwd

   The output indicates that you remain in the *Projects* directory.

10. Access the *readme* file, located in *Docum*, which is in your parent directory:

    wc *../Docum/readme*

    This command is instruction to look in the current directory for a dot-dot directory (your parent), then to look in *..* for the directory *Docum*, and then to look in *Docum* for a file named *readme*.

11. Enter **cd** to return to your home directory.

12. The same procedure is available for specifying subdirectories of directories listed in the current directory, such as:

    ls *Projects/Code*
    wc *Projects/Code/journal2*

13. Return home:

    cd

Specifying the Absolute Path to a Directory

Within any directory, all files and/or directories must have unique names. Except for *I* (*root*), all files and directories must be listed in another (parent) directory. The result of these two conditions is that every file on the system has a unique pathname from *I* (*root*).

1. Identify the absolute path to your present directory:

   pwd

2. The output of **pwd** is something like this:

   `/home/cassy`

3. Change to the *Code* directory:

   cd *Projects/Code*

4. Obtain the absolute path:

   pwd

5. Ask for a display of the file *journal2* located in the current directory by entering:

   cat *path-to-this-directory/journal2*

6. Using the *cassy* example from earlier, you would enter:

   cat */home/cassy/Projects/Code/journal2*

7. Change directories to */tmp*, confirm your location, and reissue the previous **cat** command line:

   cd /tmp

   pwd

   In a **tcsh**, **bash**, or **csh** shell, enter:

   !cat

   In a **ksh** shell enter:

   r cat

   Even though you are in a completely different directory, the absolute path to the file journal identifies the correct file.

   Every file has a unique, absolute pathname. It always starts at *root* (*/*) and includes the appropriate subdirectories. For example, the file *passwd* located in the *etc* directory has an absolute pathname of */etc/passwd*.

Specifying Paths Starting at the Home Directories

The path specification can start at any user's home directory and proceed from there.

1. Change to the */tmp* directory by entering:

   cd */tmp*

   pwd

2. Without changing directories, get a listing of the files in your *Code* directory by entering:

   ls *~/Projects/Code*

   echo *~/Projects/Code*

   This command line is instruction to:

   A) Access the user's home directory.

   B) Locate a listing for *Projects*.

C) Use the inode to access *Projects*.

D) Locate a listing for *Code* in *Projects*.

E) Read from *Code* to determine the names of all files listed there.

The starting point is the path to the home directory for the user who issued the command.

Accessing Directories Using All Methods

The activities in this section utilize the various methods of path specification you have explored in this chapter in more complex ways. It is suggested that you examine each instruction and try to accomplish the goal before reading our solution that follows.

1. Make sure you are in your home directory, and then obtain a display of the names of the files listed in the *tmp* directory, which is listed in *root*:

   cd
   ls */tmp*

2. List the files in the directory in *tmp* that has your login name:

   ls */tmp/$USER*

3. Confirm that you are still in your home directory:

   pwd

4. Copy your file *practice* to the */tmp/$USER/* directory, and give the file a new name, *practice2*:

   cp *practice* */tmp/$USER/practice2*

5. Without changing directories, obtain a listing of the files in */tmp/$USER*:

   ls */tmp/$USER*

6. Change directories to */tmp/$USER*, confirm your location, and obtain a listing of files:

   cd */tmp/$USER*
   pwd
   ls

7. Copy the file, *practice2* (which you just created here) back to the *Code* directory, which is in *Projects* in your home directory, and obtain a listing of the files in *Code*:

   cp *practice2* *~/Projects/Code*
   ls *~/Projects/Code*

8. Change directories to *root* and confirm your location:

   cd /

   pwd

9. Without changing directories, copy the file *report3*—which is listed in *Code*, in *Projects*, in your home directory—to the *Docum* directory, which is also listed in your home directory:

   cp *~/Projects/Code/report3 ~/Docum*

   This instruction is to start at your home, locate *Projects* and then *Code*, and then find *report3*. Finally, copy *report3* to *Docum*, which is also listed in your home directory.

10. Make *Projects* the current directory, and create a file named *greeting* containing the word *hello*, but list it in *Projects'* parent directory. Confirm.

    cd *~/Projects*

    echo *hello* > *../greeting*

    ls *..*

11. Copy the file back from the parent to your current directory:

    cp *../greeting* .

    The parent directory is specified with .. (dot-dot), and the destination directory is the current directory, dot.

12. Copy all files listed in your parent directory into the *Docum* directory:

    cp *../* ~/Docum/*

    ls *~/Docum/*

    Without an argument to the contrary, the **cp** utility copies files only. Therefore, it issues error messages that directories are present and not being copied.

13. Run **wc** on the file *users_on* listed in your home directory, and put the output in a file named *num_users_on* listed in your directory in */tmp*:

    wc *~/users_on* > */tmp/$USER/num_users_on*

14. Create a file named *friend-listing* in your *Projects* directory, containing the filenames listed in the home directory of a friend:

    ls *~login-of-friend* > *~/Projects/friend-listing*

15. Make *Projects* your current directory and confirm that the file was created:

    cd *~/Projects*

    pwd

    ls

    more *friend-listing*

Self Test 2

1. What command takes you back to the previous directory if you are using a
   bash or **ksh** shell? _____

   If using a **tcsh** shell? _____

2. What directory can a user be in to access a file using commands with
   arguments such as:

   A. more */etc/passwd*

   B. more *~/Study/diary*

   C. more *../Desk/journal*

   D. more *Desk/journal*

3. At this point, we have specified directories using a variety of instructions.
   In the following table, a **cd** command, including its argument, is on the left.
   Fill in the result of entering the specified **cd** command on the right.

Command	Result
cd ..	Change to parent directory.
cd ../bill	
cd ~	
cd ~/bill	
cd ~bill	
cd ~bill/bill	
cd /bill	
cd bill	

   SUGGESTION: To solve the following problems, start by drawing
   a sketch of the directory tree information presented.

4. Assume your current directory is not known. What command changes your
   current directory to a directory named *Education*, which is listed in a directory
   named *Proposals*, which is listed in your home directory?

5. From your home directory, what command do you enter to edit a file *mikekirby* that is listed in the *Proposals* directory?

_____

6. From any directory, how can you create a directory *Rejected*, listed in the *Proposals* directory in your home directory?

_____

7. Regardless of your current directory, how would you copy a file *selquist* from your home directory into *Education*, which is a subdirectory of the *Proposals* directory that is listed in your home directory?

_____

8. What command changes directories to the parent directory?

_____

9. What command changes to the *Marilyn* directory listed in your home directory?

_____

10. Assume that the directories *Programs* and *Letters* have the same parent directory and that you are currently in the *Programs* directory. How do you change your current directory from *Programs* to *Letters*?

_____

11. How would you move the file *report7* in the current directory to the parent directory?

_____

12. How can you copy all files from the current directory to the parent?

_____

13. Given that you are located in your home directory, what are three different ways you can create a directory named *Junkyard* in a subdirectory called *Location* that is in your home directory?

_____

14. You are in your home directory, using the **vi** editor to edit a file called *client-list* that is under *Proposals/Contracts/*. You end the session. Which directory are you in now?

_____

15. What command do you issue to use the **vi** editor to edit the file *cats* in the home directory of the user named *Chris*?

_____

16. What command will copy a file called *rhino* to a subdirectory *Africa* and rename the file *elephant*?

_____

17. What command would move the file *vans* from the subdirectory *Transportation* in the home directory of the user named *pjaddessi* to the */tmp* directory, renaming the file *cars*?

_____

7.5 Managing Files from More Than One Directory

Whenever you create a file, the filename and inode number are listed in a directory, namely, its parent. A listing for a file in a directory is a *link* to the file. In these exercises, you have accessed each file from the parent directory either by specifying the file's name, or by including the parent directory in the pathname to the file. If a directory just links us to our files, can we list or link a file to multiple directories? For example, can we put the name and inode number for a file in several directories, allowing us to access the file from any one of the directories? Of course.

Whenever we need to see the current permissions and other information about files, we enter the **ls** command with a **-l** option.

⮕ Obtain a long listing of the files in your home directory by typing the following:

cd

ls -l | more

The **ls** -long listing has the following components:

```
total 13
drwxrwxrwx 4 cassy staff  4096  Nov 13 17:04 Projects
-rw-rw-rw- 1 cassy staff  1452 Sep 7  11:58 journal
-rw------- 1 cassy staff  1064 Sep 2  21:14 practice
-rw-rw-rw- 1 cassy staff  6100 Oct 12 11:32 users_on
```

The first piece of information seen here (`total 13`) indicates the total number of data blocks used by everything in the current directory. In this case, 13 blocks are used. Each of the lines that follow contains fields of information for one file or directory.

In a long listing entry, or *record,* the information for each file or directory is divided into seven fields. In the example just discussed, the first record's fields are as follows.

Permissions Field	drwxrwxrwx
No. of Links	4
File's Owner	cassy
File's Group	staff
Size in Bytes	544
Date of Last Modification	Nov 13 17:04
Directory or Filename	Projects

Although most of the fields are fairly self-explanatory, the number in the second field, links, is not so obvious.

The second field in each record is a number that indicates the number of directories where the object is listed. You created the *Projects* directory in your current directory. There probably are four directories that have entries that refer to the *Projects* directory: *Projects*'s parent directory lists *Projects*; the *Projects* directory lists itself as the . directory; and the two subdirectories of *Projects* each have a listing for its parent, *Projects*, as the .. directory.

Files generally have a *1* in this field, indicating that they are listed in their current directory only. If a file is listed in two directories, it is *linked* to both directories and has a *2* in this field, and so on.

Listing a File in a Second Directory

When we create a file, it is listed in its directory. We can also have it listed in other directories, allowing us to access it from there.

Make sure you are in your home directory.

1. Enter:

   cd

2. Use the **vi**sual editor to create a file named *testing-links*:

   vi *testing-links*

3. Add the following text:

   This file is listed in my home directory.

4. Write and quit the editor:

   :wq

5. Confirm that the name and inode for *testing-links* is listed in the current directory, your home directory, by entering:

      pwd

      ls -i *testing-links*

6. Record the inode number of *testing-links*: _____

7. Change directories to the *Archives* subdirectory, and get a listing of its files:

      cd *Archive*s

      ls

At this point, the file *testing-links* is not listed in *Archives.*

8. List the files in your parent directory:

      ls ..

The output indicates that *testing-links* is listed in the parent directory, your home directory.

9. Instruct the shell to also list the *testing-links* file in the current directory, but use the name *testing2*:

      ln *../testing-links testing2*

The file is being listed in or **lin**ked to a second directory. There are two arguments to the **ln** command: the target file and the name that the file is to have in its new listing in the current directory. In this example, the file is given a different name in the second directory. It could be the same name, if you wish.

10. Obtain a display of the files now listed in your current directory:

      ls -i

The *testing-links* file listed in the home directory is also listed in this directory with a new name, *testing2*. The file *testing2* is listed with the same inode number associated with *testing-links* in the parent directory. It is the same file, just listed in two directories, with different names but connected to the same inode.

11. Access the file *testing2*:

      vi *testing2*

12. Add the following line:

      And now listed in Archives, too.

13. Write the file and quit the editor with:

      :wq

14. Return to your home directory:

      cd

15. Examine the *testing-links* file from your home directory:

> **more** *testing-links*

The line you added when you accessed the file from the *Archives* directory is in the file. It is the same file listed or linked to two directories. The following illustration describes the linked file:

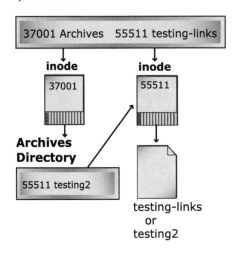

User's Home Directory
$HOME or ~

37001 Archives   55511 testing-links

inode   **inode**
37001   55511

Archives
Directory
55511 testing2

testing-links
or
testing2

16. Examine the original and linked files using **ls**:

> **ls -li** *testing-links*
> **ls -li** *Archives/testing2*

They are equivalent listings. Both access the same inode, and both report that the file is linked to two directories with the 2 in the links column of the long listing output.

17. Use the **file** utility to explore the files:

> **file** *testing-links*
> **file** *Archives/testing2*

There is no hint that one was the original, and the other was linked later.

Both listings, testing-links and testing2, are associated with the same inode number—they are the same file. There is only one file with one inode; however, it is listed or linked to two directories and can be accessed from either.

Removing Linked Files

Every file's "index card," the inode, keeps track of the number of directories that list it. Each instance of a file listed in a directory is one link.

1. Obtain a long listing of the file in the current directory with:

   ls -l *testing-links*

   In the listing, the field to the right of the permissions is the number of links or the *link-count*. The file *testing-links* has two links: the current directory and the *Archives* directory.

2. Remove the file *testing-links* from the current directory by entering:

   rm *testing-links*
   ls

   Although it was originally created in this directory, the file is now removed and not listed in this directory anymore.

3. Does that mean it is also removed from the *Archives* directory? Enter:

   ls -l *Archives*

4. The link count is back to 1. The file is now listed only in *Archives*.

   more *Archives/testing2*

When you remove a file, you remove its listing in the specified directory. If after the removal the number of links remaining is one or more, the file is kept on the hard drive in its data block(s). Only when it is no longer listed in any directory (that is, when the link count goes to zero) is the file actually removed (that is, the data blocks' addresses are made available for new use).

Linking a File to a Directory Using the Original Name

You do not have to link files by giving the new link a new name.

Link another file with:

ln *users_on Archives*
ls -i *users_on*
ls -i *Archives/users_on*
ls -l *users_on*

If **ln** is given a directory as its target (second) argument, the file is listed in the target directory using the same name of the original listing. The link count in the output of **ls -l** reflects that the file is listed in two directories.

Linking Multiple Files

The **ln** utility will link several files at a time.

1. Change to your home directory and issue:

    ln *megan daniel betty Archives*

2. List your current files with link count and inodes:

    ls -il *megan daniel betty*

3. List the files in the *Archive* directory:

    ls -il *Archives*

All the files listed as arguments to **ln** preceding the target directory (*Archives*) are now listed in the *Archives* directory as well as the current directory. They have the same inodes in the listings in both directories.

> **SUMMARY** We can link a file to multiple directories using the **ln** command. The first argument is the current filename; the last argument is the new directory where the file is to be listed. A file is removed from any linked directory with the **rm** command. When it is removed from the last directory that lists it, the file is actually removed. Only files can be hard-linked in this way.

Linking Files with Symbolic Links

The links you created in the previous exercises listed the actual inodes for a file in two directories. Links created in this way are called *hard links* because the inode is hard-coded into the various directories that list the file. As will be examined later, hard links do not work for some files, and only the super user (*root*) can create hard links for directories.

An alternative method for linking an existing file to another directory does not list the linked file's inode in the second directory.

1. Make sure you are in your *Projects* directory:

    cd *~/Projects*

    pwd

2. Create a link to the *journal* file from *Projects* by entering:

    ln -s *~/journal*

3. Examine the inodes of the two files:

    ls -i *journal*

    ls -i *~/journal*

    They do not have the same inode number.

4. Confirm that both links actually access the one file with:

    echo '*In Projects File*' >> *journal*

    cat *~/ journal*

    When you add text to the file listed in *Projects,* and then read the same file listed in your home directory, the added text appears because you are writing to and reading from one file.

    When we use the **-s** option to **ln** a small file is created in the current directory that contains the information needed to locate the linked file wherever it is actually listed. This type of link is called a *symbolic* link.

5. Examine the long listing of the symbolic link with:

    ls -l *journal*

6. The output looks like this:

    ```
    lrwxrwxrwx  1 cassy    users     6 Oct 24 16:47 journal
    --/home/cassy/journal
    ```

    The initial character is not a **d** for directory, not a - for file, but an **l** for symbolic link. The arrow in the following illustration indicates that the filename *journal* in the current directory is a link to the file *journal* in *cassy*'s home directory listed in *home,* listed in /. This is clearly a different creature.

The link is a small file in the current directory containing a pointer to the inode of the real file wherever it is located.

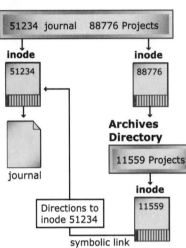

User's Home Directory
$HOME or ~

7. Ask for a description of *journal* listed in the current directory:
   file *journal*
8. The output from **file** is:
   ```
   journal: symbolic link to /home/cassy/journal
   ```

Both of these commands report that *journal* is not a regular file the way hard links are. Rather, *journal* is a symbolic link in the current directory with its own inode.

Removing a Symbolic Link

Removing the link is like removing a file.

1. Enter:
   rm *journal*
2. Confirm that the *journal* listing was removed.
   ls
   The entry for *journal* (the symbolic link) is removed from the current directory.

Removing a File That Has a Symbolic Link

In the last exercise, you removed the link to a file. What happens if you remove a file that has a symbolic link pointing to it?

1. Enter:

   date > ~/realfile
   ln -s ~/realfile rf
   ls -l rf
   cat rf

   The entry *rf* in the current directory is a symbolic link to the real file named *realfile* listed in the home directory.

2. Remove *realfile*, the original file, from the home directory:

   rm ~/realfile

3. Examine the effect on the symbolic (soft) link in the current directory:

   ls -l rf
   cat rf

   The real file is removed, so the pointer (symbolic link) points to nothing. It is a broken link. The symbolic link is not equivalent to the file it links.

Linking Directories

On some systems, the super user *root* can use a **-d** option to the **ln** utility and create hard links to directories in other directories. Ordinary users cannot create directory hard links. Ordinary users can, however, create symbolic links to directories.

1. You are presently in the *Projects* directory:

   pwd

   One of the directories listed in your home is the directory *Docum*.

2. Link the *Docum* directory to your current directory with:

   ln -s ~/Docum

3. List the contents of the current directory:

   ls -F

   The *Docum* directory is listed as a subdirectory of your current directory; however, note that it has an @ following it instead of a /, denoting that it's a symbolic, or *soft*, link.

4. List the contents of *Docum*:

   ls *Docum*

   The filenames listed in *Docum* are displayed.

5. Change directories to *Docum* and confirm your location:

   cd *Docum*

   pwd

6. Create a file:

   touch *filefromProjects*

7. Change to your home directory and list its files:

   cd

   ls

   The *Docum* directory is listed in your home directory.

8. List the contents of the *Docum* directory:

   ls *Docum*

   The file you created when you accessed the *Docum* directory from *Projects* is listed.

9. List the contents of *Projects*:

   ls *Projects*

   The *Archives* directory is listed in *Projects,* too.

10. Confirm that the contents of both *Docum* directories listings are the same:

    ls -i *Docum*

    ls -i *Projects/Docum*

    You can now access the *Docum* directory from your home or from *Projects*.

Assessing System Directories

Users often link system directories for easy access.

1. Link the */tmp* directory to your home:

   cd

   ln -s */tmp* *tmp*

2. List the contents of your current directory:

   ls -l | more

   The *tmp* directory is now listed in your home.

3. List the contents of your *tmp* and of */tmp*:

ls *~/tmp*
ls */tmp*

You now have the */tmp* directory listed as *tmp* in your home directory.

SUMMARY Hard links are used to make equivalent links to a file from two or more directories. If the original file is removed, the listing in the second directory still accesses the file. Symbolic or soft links are used to link directories or files to another directory. A symbolic link is a pointer in a small file in another directory that points to the inode of the original file. The original file and the symbolic link have their own unique inodes. When the original file or directory is removed or moved to a different location, the symbolic link points to nothing and is broken.

Examining the Reason for Symbolic Links

When a hard drive is formatted in preparation for installing the system, the administrator has the option of dividing the drive in smaller pieces, called *partitions*. Usually several unique sections or partitions are created. Each partition holds part of the UNIX/Linux directory tree.

1. To see what partitions are employed on your system, enter:

   mount

2. The hard drive partitions and where they are mounted are listed.

   The information displayed is like:

   ```
   /dev/hda2     on      /
   /dev/hda3     on      /home
   /dev/hda5     on      /tmp
   /dev/hda6     on      /usr/bin
   ```

   One partition is labeled **/** and holds the core of the hierarchical directory tree. Some systems have only the **/** filesystem, rather than multiple partitions.

If there are additional partitions, they are attached or mounted onto the **/** filesystem, giving the user a complete directory tree to use. Often, **/** and */home* and */usr/bin* and */tmp* are on separate partitions and are "connected to the main filesystem" or mounted when the system starts up.

Most of each partition on the hard drive is formatted into small pieces of memory called data blocks, often 1,024 bytes in size. Data blocks hold the actual data that we call files. In addition to the data blocks in a partition on a drive, space is set aside in each partition for the inodes that manage the files in that partition. Each partition, holding one filesystem, has a set of *unique* inode numbers for that partition. And that's the problem. If a system has */home* as a specifically separate partition and */tmp* as another, there could be a file in each partition having the same inode. Inodes are unique only within a single partition filesystem, but can have duplicates in another partition. Because inode 12345 refers to one file in the */tmp* filesystem partition and refers to a different file in */home*, creating a hard link in */home* to the file that has inode 12345 does not link it to the file in */tmp*, but links it to the file of that number in the */home* filesystem.

A *symbolic link* is a small file in a directory on one filesystem partition that points to the correct file system and then the correct inode for the linked file. We can use hard links only for files within the same filesystem. Symbolic links are used to link directories and files in the same or different filesystems.

Lastly, inodes are the key to UNIX/Linux filesystem mastery. What is a file? Is it just the data, or is a "file" also its characteristics, permissions, owner, creation date, group, size, and so forth? If we want to think of the file as embodying all of its characteristics, not just the data in the data blocks, then *the inode is the file.* The inode contains the whole of a file, including its descriptive characteristics and the addresses of the blocks where the file data reside. The network is the computer; the inode is the file.

7.6 Moving and Removing Directories and Their Contents

You have used the **mv** command to move files into directories and to rename files within a directory. As we have seen, a directory is just a file that contains the names of other directories and files, with their associated inode numbers. Many file management operations are performed by modifying the contents of a directory. For instance, to change the name of a file is to change its entry in its parent directory.

To create a new directory is to create an entry in one directory that includes the new directory name and its inode number so that the shell can change directories to or access the new directory.

Because directories are just files, it seems reasonable that we can change the name of a directory and move it in the same way we move and change names of other files. We can. Read on, Macduff.

Changing a Directory's Name

Directories are named initially by the owner when they are created. The name can be changed.

1. Make sure you are in your home directory and that the *Projects* directory is listed:

   cd

   ls -F

2. Identify the inode for the *Projects* directory:

   ls -id *Projects*

3. Record *Projects'* inode number: _____

4. Change the name of the *Projects* directory by entering:

   mv *Projects Old-projects*

5. Obtain a listing of the contents of your current directory:

   ls -F

   There is no *Projects* directory listed in your home directory anymore. However, *Old-projects* is listed.

6. Examine the contents of *Old-projects*:

   ls -F *Old-projects*

   The contents are not changed; only the name of the directory is different.

   There is one place the directory is named: the entry in your home directory. That entry was modified to read *Old-projects* instead of *Projects*.

7. Examine the inode number for *Old-projects*:

   ls -id *Old-projects*

You changed the name for the *Projects* directory in the current directory, but the new name is attached to the same inode number. The entry points to the same directory, just using a new name.

User's Home Directory
$HOME or ~

88776 Old-projects Projects

inode 88776

owner
group
rw-r--r--
date created
date modified
links

Old-projects

8. Change the name of *Old-projects* back to *Projects*:

   mv *Old-projects Projects*
   ls -id *Projects*

   The two directories use the same inode.

Moving a Directory

Every user directory is listed in a parent directory. You can move a directory to a different location in the hierarchical file structure, that is, list it in a different parent directory.

1. Obtain a listing of the files and directories in the current (home) directory:

   cd
   ls -F

   The directories *Projects* and *Archives* are both listed.

2. Note the inodes referenced by *Projects* and *Archives*:

   ls -id *Projects*
   ls -id *Archives*

3. Enter the inode for *Projects*: _____

Enter the inode for *Archives*: _____

4. Move the listing for the *Projects* directory from your current directory to the *Archives* directory:

> **mv** *Projects Archives*
>
> **ls**
>
> **ls** *Archives*

Projects is no longer listed in the current directory, but is listed in the *Archives* directory. The following illustration depicts the directory structure before and after the move.

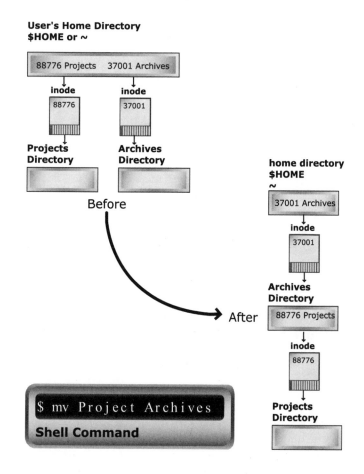

Your current directory, which is the parent directory of its subdirectories, contains the subdirectories' names and inode numbers. You can change the directory where a directory is listed. If you change the listing, you "move" the directory. Inodes remain the same for each directory.

5. Examine the contents of *Projects,* now listed in *Archives*:

   ls *Archives/Projects*

   When a directory is moved, its contents are undisturbed. Moving a directory is just moving the listing for the directory from one parent directory to another. It does not affect the "child" contents of the moved directory. The two parent directories are affected. One directory loses the listing for the moved directory, the other directory gains a listing. The directory that is moved has a new parent directory in its listing. Moving a directory does not affect the moved directory's subdirectories.

6. Revisit the inodes:

   ls -ai *Archives*
   ls -ai *Archives/Projects*

   The *Projects* directory in *Archives* has the same inode number as . in *Projects*. Yes, *Projects* sees itself as the same inode that the parent (*Archives*) sees as *Projects*. Even though the directory is moved, it keeps its inode number.

   In *Projects*, the **..** directory has the same inode number as the . listing in *Archives*. *Projects* sees *Archives* as its parent.

7. Move the *Archives* directory back to your home directory by entering:

   mv *Archives/*Projects ~
   ls -ai *Archives*
   ls -ai *Projects*

   The listing for *Projects* is moved from *Archives* to your home directory. Both now see your home directory as their parent.

Removing an Empty Directory

In UNIX/Linux, we remove directories using specific commands, just as we remove files.

> **CAUTION:** Always use remove commands with great care, because often it is difficult if not impossible to recover lost items. Make sure you are in the appropriate directory for each of these activities.

Two commands are available for removing a directory. The first command removes an empty directory—a directory with no files listed in it.

⤷ 1. Make sure you are in your home directory with:

   cd

   pwd

2. List the files and directories in your home directory with:

   ls -F

3. Create a new directory by typing:

   mkdir *Dirempty*

   ls -F

   ls -id *Dirempty*

4. Check to see whether any files are in the *Dirempty* directory by typing:

   ls *Dirempty*

5. Remove the empty directory *Dirempty* by typing the command:

   rmdir *Dirempty*

6. Confirm that the *Dirempty* directory has gone to Dirheaven by typing:

   ls -F

7. Attempt to remove the *Archives* directory even though it contains files:

   rmdir *Archives*

The error message indicates that the *Archives* directory is not empty, and **rmdir** does not remove directories that list other files or directories. Leave it as is.

Removing a Directory and Its Files

You have seen how the **rmdir** command removes only empty directories. With an alternate command, you can remove directories that are either empty or that contain listings of files.

   We will next attempt to remove a directory that has contents.

⤷ 1. Change to the *Projects* directory:

   cd *~/Projects*

2. Double-check that you are in the proper directory and that *Code* is listed:

   pwd ; ls

3. Attempt to remove the *Code* directory. Type:

   rmdir *Code*

4. The directory cannot be removed with **rmdir** because it contains files. You receive an error message:

```
rmdir: Code: Directory not empty
```

5. To remove the *Code* directory *and* its files, type:

rm -r *Code*

The **-r** option of the command instructs **rm** to recursively remove files. The utility starts by removing files from the directory, then enters a subdirectory and removes its files, then removes the empty subdirectory, and so on, recursively down through the target directory's subdirectories.

6. Confirm that *Code* has been removed by typing:

ls -F

Not only is the *Code* directory removed, but so are all the files listed in the directory and any subdirectories you might have created in *Code*.

 CAUTION: The **rm -r** command has significant impact and should be used very carefully. Double-check that the directory you are removing doesn't contain any subdirectories that you may need. Move anything you want to keep to another directory before you use the **rm -r** command.

7. To demonstrate the power of **rm -r**, carefully enter the following commands to create a series of directories:

mkdir *DIR10*
touch *DIR10/skye*
mkdir *DIR10/DIR20*
mkdir *DIR10/DIR21*
mkdir *DIR10/DIR20/DIR30*
date > *DIR10/DIR20/today*
cp * *DIR10/DIR20/DIR30*

The structure just created is described in the following illustration:

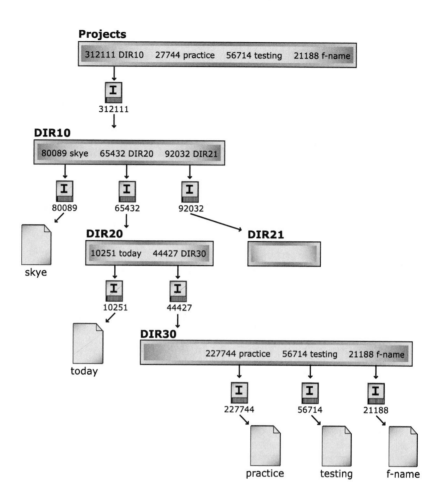

8. Check with the following:

    ls

    ls *DIR10*

    ls *DIR10/DIR20*

    ls *DIR10/DIR20/DIR30*

    ls -R *DIR10*

    pwd

9. Now attempt to remove the directory tree with:

    rmdir *DIR10*

    ls

    rm *DIR10*

ls
rm -r *DIR10*
ls

The **rm -r** directory command removes all files and directories starting with the target directory and recursively descending through all subdirectories.

Self Test 3

1. What command would you enter to move the file *eakins*, which is in your current directory, so it's listed in your home directory?

2. What is the difference between the commands **rmdir** and **rm -r**?

3. Assume you are in the *Projects* directory, which has the subdirectories *Old-projects* and *New-projects*. What is the command to move the *Bookproject* directory from *New-projects* to *Old-projects*?

4. You are in your home directory, where there is a file named *users_on*. What command will list the file in both your home directory and in the subdirectory *Projects*?

Chapter Review

Use this section to review the content of this chapter and test yourself on your knowledge of the concepts.

Chapter Summary

- The hard drive is formatted into very many blocks of a given size, such as 1,024 bytes, that hold data.
- Files reside in one or more data blocks on the hard drive.
- For every file, there is one and only one inode, a small piece of memory on the hard drive that contains all the information concerning its file. Such

information includes owner, permissions, creation and modification dates, number of links, owner, group, size, and the addresses of the data blocks that contain the file (or in the case of very large files, data blocks that contain addresses of the data blocks for the rest of the file).

- A directory is a special kind of file with very specific contents, namely the names of files and directories, each with its associated inode number.

- The directory consists only of filenames and their inode numbers. The inodes contain all the information about a file, and the data blocks on the drive contain the file itself.

- When we log in, our current directory is our home directory, as specified in the *passwd* file.

- We can make directories be listed in the current directory with the **mkdir** *dirname* command.

- We change our current directory to another directory using the **cd** *targetdir* command where:

  - A character string name lacking any special characters is a directory listed in the current directory.

  - A directory following an initial **/** is listed in the **/** or **root** directory at the top of the filesystem..

  - The tilde (~) is interpreted as the user's home directory.

  - The ~*loginname* is interpreted as the home directory of the user *loginname*.

  - The name **..** (*dot-dot*) is interpreted as the parent directory .

  - We can employ a mixture of specifications such as:

    cd ~/.. (Go to my home and then its parent.)

    cd ~*bkoettel/Study1* (Go to *bkoettel*'s home directory and then to a subdirectory named *Study1*.)

- Files or directories and their files are moved from one directory to another with the **mv** *name newname* command.

- Empty directories are removed with the **rmdir** *dirname* command.

- A directory and its contents, including files and subdirectories, are removed with the **rm -r** *dirname* command.

Assignment

1. What **ls** command results in a listing of the contents of the current directory, including all files with names that start with a dot, as well as the permissions and so forth for each file?

   A. **ls -a**

   B. **ls -l**

   C. **ls -ai**

   D. **ls -al**

   E. **ls -il**

   F. **ls -rl**

   G. None of above

2. What command removes the directory *XXX* and all of its contents, including its subdirectories and their contents?

3. Which of the following creates a new directory?

   A. **touch** *Dir-A*

   B. **mkdir** *~/jobs*

   C. **mkdir** *~/jobs/*

   D. **mv** *Dir-A Dir-B*

   E. **mkdir** *addessi*

   F. **cat** *DIR-C > DIR-D*

4. What do each of the following accomplish?

   A. **cd** *~/Work*

   B. **cp** */tmp/manywords* .

   C. **cd** *~/..*

   D. **grep** *bash* **/etc/passwd** *> ~/bash.pw*

   E. **mv** *~/Stuff ~/Old* (Both directories exist.)

   F. **cp** *Dir-A/* Dir-B/* (Both directories exist.)

5. For the following command to be successful, what must each one of the four arguments to **cp** be?

   cp *one two three four*

   one_____   two_____   three_____   four_____

Project

    A. Create a directory named *BACKUPS* and copy at least 10 of your most important files to that directory.

    B. Create a file named *mywork* that contains a listing of all files in your home directory and all its subdirectories. Have **ls** identify directories and executable files, and list inode numbers for each file.

    C. On a printout of the *mywork* file, use the inode numbers to identify the parent/child relationships between your home and at least three subdirectories.

    D. Create a directory called *Assignments* and link the files you have created for assignments to that directory. Print out a long listing of the contents of *Assignments*.

    E. Link several files to the */tmp/$USER* directory, which is probably in a different filesystem. Print out a long listing of the contents of your directory in */tmp*.

COMMAND SUMMARY

cd *pathname*	Changes to the directory specified by pathname.
pwd	Displays the full pathname of your current directory.
mv *filename path/newfilename*	Moves the listing for the file named filename into the directory specified by path and renames the file newfilename if it is specified.
mv *directoryname path/ new_directoryname*	Moves the listing for the directory named directoryname into the directory specified by path and renames the moved directory new_directoryname if it is specified.
cp *filename path/newfilename*	Puts a copy of filename into the directory specified by path and names the copy newfilename if it is specified.
ls *-a*	Displays a list of files and subdirectories in your current directory, including files with names beginning with a period/dot.
ls *-F*	Displays the names of files in your current directory and places a / after directory names. Executable files are displayed with an asterisk (*).
ls *-ld*	Outputs a long listing of information about the directory itself, not its contents.
ls *-l*	Lists filenames and their associated inodes in the current directory.
ln *file directory*	Creates a listing of a file in another directory. The ln without an argument creates a hard link; the inode is the same in both locations. It is one file listed in two directories. Files in different filesystems cannot be hard-linked.
ln *-s file directory*	Creates a soft link, or listing of a file or directory in a second directory. A soft link can list directories and files in a different filesystem in a second directory.
mkdir *directory*	Creates a new directory called directory.
rmdir *directory*	Removes directory, but only if it contains no files or subdirectories.
rm -r *directory*	Removes directory, as well as everything it contains.

Specifying Instructions to the Shell

The various shells interpret our commands to accomplish tasks we specify. When the shell produces a prompt on the terminal screen, it is asking us what we want to do next. We type in a response requesting that some program(s) accomplish a task. If our request exactly follows the shell's grammar rules, the shell does as we ask and starts whatever program(s) we request. After the programs complete their work, the shell pops back up and asks what's next.

We have to "talk shell language" when we issue commands if we want to be understood. The shell interprets the grammar (*syntax*) of command lines in very specific ways, and of course, it does what we *say*, not what we intend. When we properly make requests, communicating our intentions exactly, the shell does as we intend, and we get work done.

This chapter examines how we can ask for and get exactly what we want. To make sense out of communicating with the shell, we will carefully examine how the shell interprets the commands and special characters we issue.

But our goal is more than syntax mastery. Execution of a program is a complex event in any computing environment. Fortunately, in Linux and UNIX we can explore how the shell interprets our commands, how child processes are started, how the correct code is executed, and how to troubleshoot errors. If we know how the shell functions, we can more effectively make requests.

The fundamental components of a UNIX or Linux computing system are hardware, files, and processes. The hardware—consisting of the central processing unit (CPU), storage devices, working memory, connecting bus, keyboard, terminal, and cables—could be used to run any one of several computing systems. When the hardware is running UNIX/Linux, the core program, called the *kernel,* schedules the CPU's work on the processes in the queue, allocates primary memory, and handles the input/output of terminals, disk drives, and other peripherals. The kernel program virtually defines UNIX and Linux. (This complex, extensive program has consumed an enormous number of programming hours. There is, however, no truth to the rumor that programmers who spend their time removing the rough edges from the kernel are called Kernel Sanders.)

This chapter's exercises begin with a detailed examination of how the shell interprets a command line to determine how many processes to start; how to redirect input, output, and error messages; how to pass arguments; and how to execute the code. The second section explores how the shell expands portions of command lines by interpreting filename wildcards, variables, and other special characters. The last section examines how the shell and child processes interact in the execution of complex command lines.

8.1 Examining Shell Command-Line Execution

When you are logged on to UNIX, you do not communicate directly with the kernel. Rather, you tell the shell what you want, and the shell translates your requests into the proper kernel *calls*, which instruct the kernel to do the work. When you request that the shell run a utility, the shell asks the kernel to start a new process, redirects input and output, passes arguments to the process, and locates the compiled utility program code in a file on the filesystem on the hard disk. The shell then instructs the process to run the appropriate code.

The login shell, just another utility, is started when you log on and exits when you log out. We often start other shells and exit them as needed. The shell's job is to interpret our instructions. The shell is the interface between us, other utilities, the filesystem, and the kernel. Each shell process executes code that resides in a file in a system directory. The shell process gets CPU time, follows instructions in the code file, sends output and error messages to your terminal, and generally behaves like any other utility.

One of the shell's primary functions is to read each command line you issue, examine the components of the command line, interpret those pieces according to its rules of grammar (syntax), and then to do what you request.

Interacting with the Shell

Obviously, the basic way we communicate with the shell is to enter a command line from the keyboard that requests execution of utilities. When we examine the events carefully, even a simple command communicates a lot of information from our heads to the shell and ultimately to the kernel. A continuous cycle takes place.

1. At the shell prompt, enter:

   echo *HELLO*
   ls

   First, you typed the individual characters *e c h o   H E L L O* and then pressed ENTER. The shell executed a new process, passed it the string of characters *HELLO* as an argument, and told the new process to execute the code for **echo**. The shell did not send a new prompt to your screen until after the process running **echo** completed its work. Then at the new prompt, you entered an *l* followed by an *s* and then another ENTER. The shell went through the steps needed to execute **ls**, and the output from **ls** appeared on the screen.

Every time we ask for a utility to run, we are instructing the shell to start a child process to execute the code that is the utility.

2. Compare the PIDs for the **ps** utilities in the following:

> **ps**
>
> **ps**

The output should include both your shell and the **ps** with their process identification numbers. Each time we run a new **ps**, it is a new process.

> **NOTE:** If the output of **ps** does not include the **ps** itself, enter the following to determine your current port:
> **tty**
> The last part of the output following **/dev/**, such as **pts06** or **console**, is your terminal number. Use your terminal number and enter a command like one of the following:
> **ps -t console**
> or
> **ps -t tty03**
> or
> **ps -t pts06**
> The output should now include the **ps**.

3. When we enter commands, we are not always successful. Enter:

> **wc -z** *users_on*

The same cycle of events takes place, but when **wc** starts, it does not recognize the option **-z** and after sending an error message to your screen, it terminates. A new shell prompt appears.

Examining Communication with the Shell

A lot happens between your entry of a command line and the execution of the utility. The shell must interpret each aspect of the command line. If we look carefully at what happens, many questions present themselves. This first section raises some questions concerning how the shell works. These and other questions are examined in the next few sections.

⮑ 1. Enter the command:

ls

The shell interprets these two characters as a request to execute the **ls** utility. Why not interpret the command as instruction to read the contents of a file named **ls**? Or to move the cursor to a <u>l</u>ower <u>s</u>ection? Or to evaluate a variable named **ls**?

The shell interprets **ls** as a utility to execute. To do so, the shell must first locate the code. Reasonable questions are, Where is the utility code located? How does the shell find it?

The **ls** utility locates the names of the files in your current directory and then formats a listing as output. The output comes to your screen. More reasonable questions are, Why my screen and not to a file? Why doesn't the output appear on someone else's display?

2. Enter the command:

ls -l

The output is a <u>l</u>ong listing of the files in the current directory. We could ask whether **ls -l** is a different utility than **ls**, or if it is the same code acting in some optional manner.

3. Make a mistake, leaving out the space between the utility and its option, as you enter the following command line:

sort-r *users_on*

We get an error message indicating that the command **sort-r** is not found. But we know the **sort** command does exist. Why the complaint?

4. Enter:

sleep 5

This command raises questions such as: Why does the shell wait until after the **sleep** is finished to present a new prompt? How does it know when **sleep** has concluded its work?

To explore the implications of this set of questions and related issues, we will carefully examine a series of familiar commands.

Parsing Basic Command Lines

The shell proceeds through a series of specific steps after we issue commands. When the shell receives a line of input from a user or file, the shell first decides whether the user intends the input line to be a command by itself or a part of a multiline command. The shell determines the number of processes to start, starts the child processes, passes arguments, redirects input and output, and finally tells the child processes what utility code to execute.

Identifying Complete Commands

When we type a command line, as soon as we press ENTER, the program that is controlling the terminal moves the cursor to the next line, and passes the line that we typed to the shell for interpretation.

↳ 1. Enter the following on two input lines:

> **who**
> **| sort**

If we try to put a command on two input lines, the shell interprets the first line as a complete command and executes it, if it can, and then attempts to interpret the second line as a separate command. In this case, the shell complains bitterly about the second line not starting with a utility. The shell is programmed to interpret ENTER as signaling the end of a complete command that it should start interpreting.

Carefully examine how the shell responds to the following. To make it clear when to press ENTER, we explicitly specify it in this exercise.

2. Type the following commands, and note the backslash that preceeds ENTER:

> **ls** \ENTER
> **-l** ENTER
> **history** ENTER

A long listing is displayed as though you entered the **ls -l** command on one line. The history output shows that even though the command **ls -l** was entered on two input lines, the shell interpreted them as one command line with one number. The shell interprets \ as instruction *not* to interpret the special meaning of the single character that immediately follows. You pressed ENTER immediately after the backslash, so the shell does not interpret the ENTER. Because the shell does not find an ENTER indicating that it has a complete command, the shell displays a secondary prompt, which tells us that the shell expects more input. We provide additional input on the next line. When the shell encounters an ENTER that it can interpret, after the **-l**, the shell processes the two input lines as one command line.

3. As a more complex example, type in the following and press ENTER at the end of every line, each preceded by a \, except in the last instance:

> **who** \
> **| tr** \
> **-d** \
> *12345* \
> **| sed 5q**

The shell interprets the five lines of input as one command line because we told it not to interpret the first four end-of-line (ENTER) characters. The shell interprets only the fifth to mean, "at last, the end of the command."

4. Examine the history:

> **history**

Although we had many input lines, they are all part of one command line. When the shell receives a line that lacks the needed end-of-line character, it displays its secondary prompt and waits for additional input.

Identifying Command-Line Tokens

When we enter commands such as **ls -l**, we usually include several words or *tokens* on the command line. The shell interprets some tokens as utilities, others as arguments, others as filenames. How does the shell identify a string of characters as being a token in the first place? If a command line consists of one word or token, it is easy. ENTER identifies the end of the command and therefore certainly identifies the end of the single token.

The shell uses white space to identify the words or tokens of a command line.

1. Enter:

> *grepthepractice*

The error message that appears is instructive. To the shell, this is a single token line, and the first token is always the program to run. Therefore, the shell complains that the utility *grepthepractice* command is not found.

2. Enter:

> **grep** *the practice*

The spaces tell the shell how to divide the line into tokens.

3. Enter the following, including the several spaces between the tokens:

   ls   -l
   who | grep $USER
   history

   Both command lines run as though we included only one space between the tokens. The shell interprets one *or more* spaces as separating the tokens on the command line. "One space, two space, red space, blue space," it makes no difference. One or many more spaces indicate where one token ends and another starts.

   We are not limited to spaces when we want to specify multiple tokens.

4. Enter the following without spaces:

   who | wc>*filewho*

   Even though there are no spaces around the | and > redirection characters, the shell still identifies the **who**, **wc**, and *filewho* as separate tokens on the command lines. The shell interprets >, <, and | as special characters that control input and output for the utilities and files that are adjacent. The shell recognizes them as instructions, not part of filenames, so spaces are not needed. We usually include spaces in command lines around each token or redirection to make it easier for humans to read the code.

5. Enter:

   echo $USER$USER$USER

   The shell recognizes the **$** as starting a new variable, even though no spaces delimit them.

   After we enter a command line, the shell must identify the tokens we entered.

Identifying Utilities to Execute When Output Is Redirected

One of the first steps the shell must accomplish when it interprets a command line is to determine how many child processes to start. To determine the number of processes, the shell must first identify which tokens on the command line are the utilities to be executed because each one is executed in a child process.

Interpreting the Initial Word on a Command Line

Whatever string of characters we provide first on the line is interpreted by the shell as instruction or a utility to execute.

➥ 1. Enter the following at the prompt:

   abcde *fghij*

   The shell responds that the utility *abcde* is not found. The string *abcde* is the first token on the command line, so from the shell's perspective, it must be an instruction or a utility. When the shell is unable to locate *abcde* in the system directories that it searches for utilities, the shell reports the "cannot find" error message.

2. Try:

   users_on **sort**

   While we clearly intend the file *users_on* to be sorted, the shell draws no such conclusion. The first token must be a program or an instruction.

   Because C shell family variables are set using a different syntax than shells in the Bourne family (**sh**, **bash**, or **ksh**), the following works only in a Bourne family shell.

3. If you are using a C shell, start *one* of the following **sh** family shells:

   bash

   or

   ksh

   or

   sh

4. In an **sh** family shell, create a variable by entering:

   a=date
   echo $*a*

   This almost looks like we are violating the "first token is a program or instruction" rule.

   Try the following, which includes spaces around the equal sign:

   b = hello

   The error message indicates that the command *b* is not found. The shell interprets the first token as the instruction. The space following the *b* makes it the first token.

5. Remove the spaces around the equal sign:

   b=hello
   echo $*b*

   Without the spaces, the first token includes the equal sign; thus, the shell interprets the first token as an instruction to create a variable. With spaces, there is no = in the first token. For that reason, variables are created in the **sh** family of shells with no spaces around the equal signs.

6. Evaluate the value of the variable:

   echo $a

   When **$a** is entered as an argument to **echo**, the value *date* is displayed on the screen.

7. Enter:

   $a

   Interpretation of the command consisting of only the variable displays the current date and time. You just entered two command lines that included the variable *$a*. In the first command, **echo $a**, the shell interprets the $a variable, and replaces the $a with its value on the command line. The value, *date*, is the second token and is passed as an argument to **echo**, which reads it and outputs it to the screen.

   In the second command line consisting of only $a, the variable $a is replaced by its value, *date*, which is the first token on the line. The shell interprets the, *date*, as the utility to execute.

Unless it is a shell built-in instruction like creating a variable, the first token is seen as a utility to execute.

Interpreting the Token Following a Pipe Redirection Symbol

The initial token on a line is the first utility. Many times, you have redirected (piped) output from one utility to another.

1. Enter the following command lines:

   who | wc
   who > *wc*
   ls -l *wc*
   more *wc*

   In the first command line, **wc** is placed after the pipe. The shell interprets **wc** as a utility to be executed and connects the output from **who** to the input of **wc**. The second command line includes *wc* after the > redirect. In this case, the shell does not interpret *wc* as a utility; rather, it is seen as the name to give a new file. The output of **who** is written to the new file *wc* when the *wc* follows a redirect. The new file is created. When the **wc** is the first token, it is seen as a utility. It is not the name **wc** that tells the shell to execute a utility, it is the location of **wc** on the command line that makes the difference. The first three rules of real estate apply: *location, location, location.*

2. As a further example, enter:

      ls | *abcde*

The shell attempts to execute the utility following the pipe: *abcde.* Again the shell complains that the utility does not exist.

A word or token placed immediately after a pipe or at the beginning of a command line is interpreted by the shell as a utility to be executed. There are also other locations that indicate that a token is a utility.

Identifying Utilities in Pipelines

Every command line issued thus far has consisted of either one utility (**ls**), or if there were more than one, the output from the first is connected to the input of the second and so forth (**who** | **wc**). Each set of one or more utilities that handles data independently is called a *pipeline* because the data flows from a utility to output, and possibly another utility. Usually there is one pipeline on each command line, but as you will soon see, there can be more.

Interpreting Tokens Following Semicolons

We can have the shell independently run one pipeline after another on a single command line without redirecting output from one to another.

1. Enter the following:

      ls; cd */tmp*; **ls; cd; history**

The shell runs the **ls** utility and then, after the **ls** is completed, the command to change the directory to */tmp* is executed. After changing directories to */tmp*, a new **ls** is run. After **ls** produces a list of files in the current directory, */tmp*, a final **cd** brings you home. Examination of the history shows that there is no output redirection. Each segment separated by semicolons is an independent pipeline. Each could be run on a command line by itself. They are run one after another as though you entered them sequentially at the prompt.

2. Enter the following:

      cal *1752* > *yr1752* ; **sleep** *3* ; **ls** | **wc -l** ; **wc** *yr1752*

The semicolons separate the four pipelines that comprise the one input line. When the first is finished, the second is executed, and so forth. This one command line consists of several independent pipelines that are executed one after another.

3. Enter:

listz ; date
sleep 2 ; date
zzzz ; sleep 2 ; listz ; date ; ls | wc ; sleep 3

As soon as execution of the pipeline to the left of the semicolon is completed, execution of the pipeline to the right is started, whether the first is successful or not. The shell interprets the semicolon as making no restriction on success or failure of the previous command or pipeline.

When we have several pipelines to run, we often separate them with semicolons.

4. Enter:

pwd ; cd .. ; pwd ; cd .. pwd ; cd .. ; pwd ; cd ; pwd

The output on the screen is the output from **pwd** as you move up the parent directories in the absolute path toward *root*. The screen just displays the output of **pwd**, not the commands. By entering all the pipelines at one time on a single command line at the beginning, we ensure that they are executed sequentially.

The first token after a semicolon begins a new pipeline, so it must be a utility.

Interpreting Tokens Following Logical AND Conditional Execution

Although it is useful to string commands together, it's even more useful to be able to execute a command or pipeline, and then, if it is successful, run another. Likewise, only if the first fails, then execute another utility or pipeline.

We can tell the shell to run or not run a pipeline based on the success or failure of the preceding pipeline.

1. Have the shell run the following:

daxx && echo *HI*

An error message that the command *daxx* is not found is displayed. The **echo *HI*** following the **&&** is not executed.

2. Enter:

wc -z *practice* && echo *HI*

In this command line, the shell runs the pipeline on the left of the **&&** (namely **wc -z** *practice*). The utility **wc** complains that:

wc: invalid option -- z

The shell does not execute the pipeline that follows the double ampersands (**echo** *HI*).

3. Explore the following alternatives:

> **wc -l** *practice* **&& echo** *hello*
> **date && xxxxx**

The **wc** on the left of **&&** runs successfully, so the shell executes the **echo** *hello* command that follows. In the last command line, the first pipeline, **date**, is successful. There is a **date** utility, and once it is run, the shell tries to run the **xxxxx** command and complains:

xxxxx: command not found

The shell interprets **&&** as instruction to run the pipeline that follows only if the preceding pipeline executes successfully.

This conditional execution is very handy when we want to run a utility, and then after it has run successfully, run another.

4. Enter:

> **ls -R** ~ **>** *~/allmyfiles* **&& wc** *~/allmyfiles* **&& more** *~/allmyfiles*

Only after **ls** successfully completes creating the *allmyfiles* file is the **wc** utility executed. After it is successful, **more** examines the file.

A token following **&&** is interpreted as a utility.

Interpreting Tokens Following Logical OR Conditional Execution

We can also require conditional execution based on failure of the previous pipeline.

➥ Enter:

> **xxxx || echo** *HI*
> **date || echo** *HI*

An error message is delivered that **xxxx** is not found, but this time the **echo** command *is* executed. The **date** utility runs successfully, but the **echo** is not executed. If the part of the command line to the left of the double pipes is successful, the command after the **||** is *not* executed. The shell interprets the **||** as instruction to execute the pipeline following the **||** only if the preceding pipeline on the command line fails. If the command to the left of the double pipes is successful, the pipeline on the right is not executed.

The token following a | | must be a utility.

Conditional Execution Summary

The following is a listing of execution summaries.

Conditional Execution Using &&   If the preceding pipeline is successful, execute the pipeline that follows.

Likewise, if the preceding command is not successful, do not execute the command that follows.

Conditional Execution Using || If the preceding command is not successful, execute the command that follows.

Likewise, if the preceding command is successful, do not execute the command that follows.

Conditional Execution Using ;   When the previous command is completed, whether successfully or not, execute the command that follows.

The impact of these conditional execution special characters is that the first token after a | | or && or a ; begins a new command or pipeline; hence, it must be a utility.

Interpreting Tokens in Command Substitution

We tell the shell that a token or string of characters is a variable by placing a $ in front of the variable name string.

 1. Enter:

   echo *I am* **$USER** *with a home directory at* **$HOME**

   Because variables are clearly identified, they can be placed anywhere on the command line. Utilities are placed in command lines at the beginning, following a pipe, or after one of the conditional execution symbols. Often it is useful to execute a utility in another location on a command line.

 2. Enter the following commands and compare the results (the quote mark is the *back quote*, usually the shift of the same key as the tilde (~) in the upper-left of the keyboard):

   echo *today is* **date**
   echo *today is* **`date`**

The resulting output of the second command line includes the output of the **date** utility, not the word *date*. If your output is *today is date* after issuing both commands, you probably used regular quotes, not back quotes.

The shell first has the **date** utility executed and then replaces `` `date` `` on the command line with the output of **date**. The **echo** utility received seven arguments: *today is Fri April 23 14:31 2004*. **echo** sends all seven arguments to output, which is connected to the terminal. This is an example of shell *command substitution*. The shell interprets the back quote character as instruction to have whatever pipeline is inside the back quotes executed first. The shell then replaces the back quotes and the pipeline that they enclose with the output they generated.

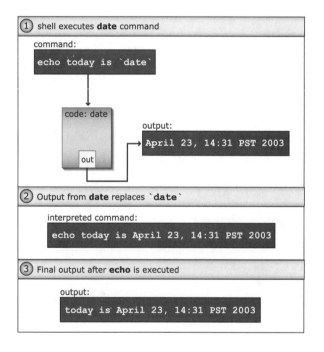

In addition to the back quotes, there is another syntax that instructs some shells to do command substitution.

3. Enter:

> **echo** *today is* **$(date)**

The shell first executes the command line inside the **$( )** and then removes the **$( )** and its enclosed command from the command line, replacing them with the output.

4. Create the following file:

   touch *names*

5. List the files in the current directory:

   ls

6. Create a file named *some-files*, and include in it a line of text listing the names of four files in the current directory. For example, your *some-files* file might have this line:

   first-file   names   lost-days   west

7. After creating *some-files*, enter:

   ls -l `` `cat `` *some-files*` ``

   ls -l $(cat *some-files***)**

The shell first executes the **cat** *some-files* command and then removes the command **cat** *some-files* from the command line. In its place, the shell puts the output that the command generated. This command substitution creates an executable command line of:

```
ls -l first-file names lost-days west
```

The four filenames and **-l** are passed as arguments to **ls**, which creates a long listing of information about the four files:

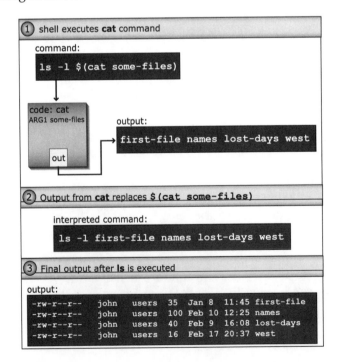

8. Have the shell use command substitution by entering:

>   **wc `cat** *some-files*`
>   **wc $(cat** *some-files*)

The lines, words, and characters are counted in all four files whose names are in the file *some-files*. The shell interprets the back quotes as instruction to execute the enclosed command and replace the back-quoted string in the command line with its output.

9. Try the following commands:

>   **echo** *My current directory is* `**pwd**`
>   **echo** *My current directory is* **$(pwd)**
>   **echo** *there are* `**who | wc -l**` *users_on*
>   **echo** *there are* **$(who | wc -l)** *users_on*

The internal command or pipeline is executed first. The shell takes the generated output, and removes the back quotes and the enclosed command, replacing the command with its output.

10. Include a utility that does not exist in a command substitution:

>   **echo** *today is* `**aabbzz**`
>   **echo** *today is* **$(aabbzz)**

The shell complains that *aabbzz* does not exist.

The command substitution feature of modern shells allows us to include the output of a command anywhere in a command line. We are not limited to just first token, after pipe, and so forth.

In a command line, the first token after a back quote or after **$(** must be a utility because it starts the command or pipeline that is substituted.

Starting a Shell That Is More Communicative

Command substitution and variables are two of the many actions the shell performs when interpreting the command lines we enter. We can start a shell that tells us what it is doing as it goes along, which makes it easier to examine under the hood.

1. Enter one of the following:

>   **bash -x**

>   or

>   **tcsh -x**

>   or

>   **ksh -x**

A new shell prompt is displayed.

2. Ask the shell to interpret variables by entering:

echo *I am* **$USER** *at* **$HOME**

The output resembles the following:

```
+ echo I am noahkindfield at /home/noahkindfield
I am noahkindfield at /home/noahkindfield
```

The shell receives the command line. It interpreted the variables, replacing them with their values. The shell then outputs a plus sign followed by the command line with variables replaced with their values. The shell displays this first line that begins with the **+** character. It tells us what interpretation of the command line the shell accomplished. The last line is the output produced by running the interpreted command line. The **-x** option tells the shell to explain how it is interpreting a command line, before executing it.

3. Examine how the shell does command substitution:

echo Today is `` `date` ``
echo Today is **$(date)**

The first plus line is just **+ date**. The shell runs **date**, and then takes the output and places it in the command line, removing the `` `date` `` or **$(date)** and displays it as the second plus line of output The fully interpreted **echo** command line is then executed with the output of **date** as part of its arguments.

4. With the **-x** shell in operation, try:

echo *My current directory is* `` `pwd` ``
echo *My current directory is* **$(pwd)**
echo *there are* `` `who | wc -l` `` *users on*
echo *there are* **$(who | wc -l)** *users on*

Each step of the shell's execution of the command lines is displayed with **+** lines, and the final output is displayed without.

5. Whenever you want to exit the explain shell, just enter:

exit

Identifying Utilities on the Command Line

Examine the following schematic of a command line. Each blank line represents a token. What is each one (utility, file, argument)?

_____ | _____ && _____;_____`_____ | _____` || _____

If a token is first on the command line, what is it? After a pipe? Following a semicolon? After a double ampersand? A double pipe?

In this example, every token must be a utility:

<u>utility</u> | <u>utility</u> **&&** <u>utility</u> ; <u>utility</u> `<u>utility</u> | <u>utility</u>` || <u>utility</u>

In summary, utilities are:

- The first command or token in a command line.
- The token that follows a pipe (the utility to receive input).
- The token that follows **&&** (the utility to run if the previous pipeline is successful).
- The token that follows a semicolon (the utility to run after the pipeline to the left of the semicolon is complete).
- The token that follows | | (the utility to run if the previous pipeline is *not* successful).
- The token that follows a back quote (`` ` ``), which is the first utility to run in the command substitution pipeline. Its output replaces the back-quoted section of the command line.
- The token following **$(** which is another form of the command substitution syntax.

Starting Processes to Run Utilities

Thus far, in this exploration we have examined how the shell receives a command line consisting of one or more pipelines; identifies the tokens using spaces, redirection, and other special characters; and then identifies which tokens are utilities. The shell then starts child processes that will ultimately run all utilities. If the command pipeline contains three utilities, the shell must start three child processes.

↳ Examine your current processes by entering:

ps | sort | uniq

The output includes the shell(s), probably the **ps**, and a process running each of the other utilities, **sort** and **uniq**. The shell starts a child process for each utility on the pipeline that the shell is interpreting.

The shell you are using is an active process, running in the foreground. The kernel has assigned it a process identification number (PID), so it gets CPU attention when its turn comes up. The shell maintains variables and their values in memory; the code to run was located and is being executed. The input to the shell process is connected to your keyboard. Error messages and output from the shell come to your screen. The resources allocated to a running process are called a *process space* or a *process image.* The following illustration depicts your shell process:

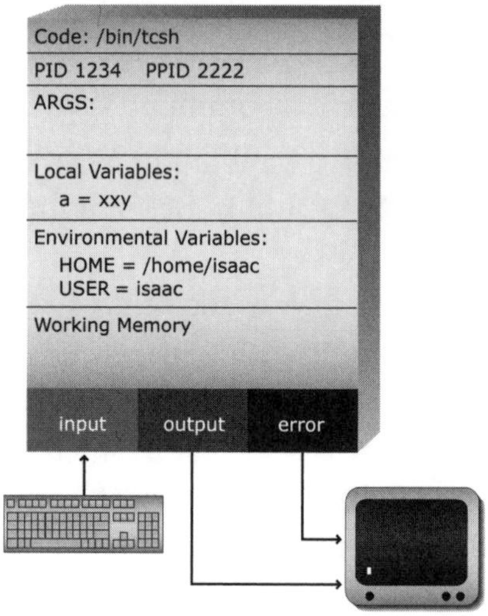

When you issue a command to run a utility, such as **ls**, the shell interprets the command line and then starts a child process that will ultimately execute the utility **ls**, which is no simple task.

The first thing the shell does is request that the kernel make an *almost* exact copy of its own process space. The copy of the process space includes the environmental variables, such as your user ID, your search path, and your home directory. Environmental variables are passed to child processes from the parent. Each time the shell starts a child process, it issues a kernel *call* that starts a child process (known as a *fork*).

Initial Input, Output, and Error Connections

The new (child) process space is a *copy* of the shell. Hence, the input, output, and error are connected to your keyboard and screen, as they are for your shell process.

1. Enter a command line that calls for no redirection:

   wc

2. Enter a few lines of text, such as:

   1 2 3 4
   second line
   third

3. Tell **wc** you are through with the end-of-file character by pressing:

CTRL-D

The shell determines that one child process is needed. When the child process is started, it inherits from the shell the keyboard for input and the screen for output and error. There is no redirection, and there are no arguments to pass. The shell tells the process to execute the code for **wc**. The process executes the **wc** code, which tells it to read from input, which is still connected to the keyboard. Any lines of text you type are read and the elements are counted. After you press CTRL-D, the end-of-file marker, the **wc** process writes its results to output, which is still connected to your screen because we made no request to redirect it.

Because the child process inherits the shell's input, output, and error destinations, when the process later runs, you receive its output, not your neighbor and not a file, unless you choose to redirect the output. No matter how many processes you start after you log in, they are your login shell's child processes. They have you listed as the user, and your terminal for output, because your shell has that information. When child processes are created, they inherit variable information and input/output error connections from the parent.

At this point, the process is still just a process, and is not yet running the code for the utility. The child process is not told the new code to execute until all redirection and argument passing "plumbing" is completed.

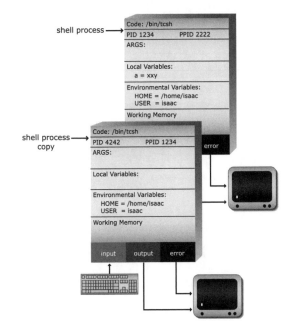

Redirecting Input and Output

At this point, we have examined how the shell identifies tokens, counts utilities, and starts the right number of child processes so that later each one will execute one of the utilities. Once the child processes are initially started, the shell modifies each as directed by the command line. Input and output are redirected, arguments are passed, and after all that plumbing is completed, the process is told what utility code to execute. We have redirected the output of utilities many times in previous exercises. This section examines what actually happens when the shell interprets redirection.

Redirecting Output to a File

The following exercises look at how the shell identifies files.

1. Enter:

    ls

    The shell identifies the token and determines that there is one utility; hence, one child process is started that inherits the shell's input/output connections: input to keyboard, output to screen, and error to screen. The command line specifies no redirection. The process runs the **ls** code and writes the names of files to its output, which is connected to the terminal.

2. Tell the shell to redirect the output:

    ls > *ls-files*

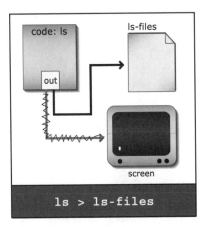

The shell's job is to interpret the command line. In this case, there is redirection instruction: the redirect symbol and a token that follows it, namely,

> *ls-files*. The shell interprets the > as instruction to redirect the output for the new process away from the workstation screen and to attach it to the file named after the >, in this case *ls-files*. With the plumbing done, the process is told to run the **ls** utility. When the process has completed its tasks, it writes the listing to its output, as it always does; however, because the shell previously connected the output of the process to the file, the results are written in the file.

Redirecting Output to an Existing File

When we redirect the output of a utility to a *filename,* the shell creates the new file. What happens when the file we specify already exists depends on the shell you are using and how the *noclobber* variable is set.

1. Make sure *noclobber* is *off*, so the shell will clobber (overwrite) existing files when redirecting output.

2. In the C family shell, enter:

   unset *noclobber*

   In the **ksh** or **bash** shell, enter:

   set +o *noclobber*

   When you redirect the output of a utility to an existing file, the Bourne shell (**sh**) interprets your command as instruction to overwrite the existing file, and you have no way to tell the **sh** shell otherwise. The **ksh**, **bash**, **csh**, and **tcsh** shells overwrite the existing file if the shell option *noclobber* is turned off.

3. Enter the following:

   head -10 /etc/passwd > *testing*
   more *testing*
   cal > *testing*
   more *testing*

   In each case, the shell starts a child process, redirects the output as specified, then later tells the process to execute a utility's code. If the file exists when the shell is redirecting output, the shell deletes the contents of the file and attaches the empty file to the output of the utility.

   When you enter commands such as **sort** *file*, the **sort** utility reads the contents of *file* and outputs a sorted version. The original file itself is not sorted.

   Often, we need to sort a file and want the file itself sorted, not just a copy. There is a temptation to redirect the output back to the original file. This exercise demonstrates why that approach does not work.

4. Make a copy of your old file *practice,* and then sort the copy using redirection, as follows:

> **cp** *practice pract-2*
> **more** *pract-2*
> **sort** *pract-2 > pract-2*

5. Now examine the contents of *pract-2*:

> **more** *pract-2*

The shell first completes the interpretation of a command line, does all output redirection, and *then* executes the utility. In the **sort** command you just entered, the *> pract-2* is instruction to redirect the output of **sort** to an existing file. The shell empties the existing file before it attaches the output of the process to the file. The process is given the argument *pract-2*. With the plumbing completed, the process is told to run the **sort** code. The process, which we can now call **sort**, interprets the argument *pract-2* as a file to read. When **sort** opens the file, it finds it is empty, making sorting quite easy. Be careful. Many an important file has been lost by accidentally overwriting it with output.

Protecting Existing Files

When we set the *noclobber* variable on, we are instructing the shells not to overwrite files by redirecting the output from a utility.

⮡ 1. Set the *noclobber* variable *on* by entering one of the following commands:

> In the C family of shells:
>
> **set** *noclobber*
>
> In a **ksh** or **bash** shell:
>
> **set -o** *noclobber*

At this point, the shell is told not to overwrite using redirection. What choice does it have when we later instruct the shell to redirect to a file?

2. Enter:

> **who** *> testing*

The shell complains that the file exists and processes no further.

Escaping *noclobber* in the Shell

There may be times when you actually do want the shell to overwrite a file while you have the *noclobber* variable set *on*. You can specifically instruct the shell to overwrite a file even though you set *noclobber*.

⤷ 1. Instruct the shell to overwrite using the output of a utility.

> C shell family:
>
> **date >!** *testing*
>
> **ksh** or **bash** shell:
>
> **date >|** *testing*

2. Confirm that the file was overwritten:

> **more** *testing*

By placing the exclamation point (!) after the output redirect symbol (>) in the command, you instructed a C shell to overwrite the file, if it exists. In the **bash** and **ksh** shells, the pipe following the redirect is instruction to overwrite even if **noclobber** is set.

Adding to an Existing File

With *noclobber* set, you cannot redirect the output of a utility to an existing file, but you can still *append* the output to the end of an existing file.

⤷ Enter:

> **cal >>** *testing*
>
> **more** *testing*

The output of **cal** is added to the end of the *testing* file. The double redirect instructs the shell to open the file, and rather than remove the contents, set it up so the output of the previous utility is connected to the *end* of the current file.

Avoiding Accidental Removal of Files with Other Utilities

The *noclobber* feature is an instruction to the shell, not to other utilities.

⤷ 1. Make sure there is no alias for **cp**, and copy a file onto *testing*:

> **unalias cp**
>
> **cp** *practice testing*

2. Examine the contents of *testing* now:

> **more** *testing*

Even when *noclobber* is turned on, you can still accidentally destroy files by using a utility that creates files such as **cp** or **mv.** If you copy or move an existing file and use the name of another existing file as the second argument, the utility overwrites the file. Because the shell is not redirecting output, *noclobber* has no effect.

3. Enter:

   cp -i *practice testing*

   You are prompted to confirm your choice to rename (and thus overwrite) *testing*. Do not overwrite the *testing* file. Enter:

   n

   To protect yourself from accidental removal of files with the **cp** and **mv** utilities, employ the inquire option (**-i**), to the utilities. People often establish aliases for these commands.

Employing Default Input

If a utility needs input to sort or count, we usually supply a filename argument or redirect something to the input of the process. What really takes place when we do not specify input?

1. Enter:

   wc > *junk-wc*

   The shell starts one process, connects the output to a new file named *junk-wc*, and then tells the process to execute the **wc** code. No file is listed as an argument, so **wc** does not open a file for data. Lacking a file to read, **wc** is programmed to read from input. In this command line, we make no request to redirect the output from a previous utility or file to input, so when **wc** reads from input, it finds the keyboard that is inherited from the shell. Whatever you type is the input.

2. Add some text, then provide the end-of-file character, CTRL-D.

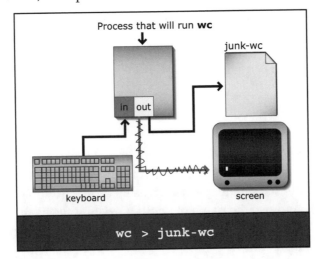

3. Enter:

   grep *the*

   The cursor is placed on a new line.

4. Enter the following:

```
hello
Is grep looking for the target string?
Yes
the is the target
```

5. Conclude by pressing CTRL-D.

In the command line, only one argument is passed to **grep**. Because **grep** always interprets its first argument as the target search string, **grep** knows what to look for: *the.*

However, no files to search are provided as additional arguments, so **grep** reads from input, which is still connected to the keyboard because it has not been redirected elsewhere.

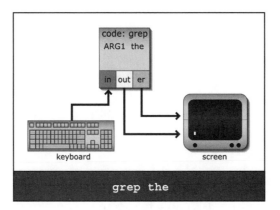

Redirecting Output to Another Utility

You have also, in previous exercises, told the shell to redirect output of a utility to the input of another utility.

⮑ Enter:

who | **grep** *yourlogin* | **wc -l** > *n-on*

This command line tells the shell to start three child processes and to connect the output from the first child process to the input of the second.

Then the shell is to connect the output from the second to the input of the third, and the output of the third to the file *n-on*.

After arguments are passed to the processes, the shell ultimately tells each process what utility code to execute. The **who** utility creates a list of logged-on users and writes to its output. The first process's output is connected to the input of the second process, running **grep**. This **grep** process selects all lines it reads from input that include your login and writes them to output, which is connected to the input of the third process, running **wc**. After **wc** counts the number of lines that it reads from its input (the output of **grep**), **wc** writes its results to its output, which is redirected to the file *n-on*.

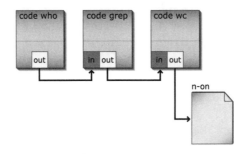

All of that is possible because the shell starts child processes that are copies of its own process space or resources, then redirects the default output and input. After the shell starts a child process and completes whatever plumbing the user requests, the shell, at last, tells the process to execute the appropriate code.

Redirecting Error Messages

When the shell or a utility is unable to execute a command, an error message is issued. Unless you redirect it, error output is displayed on your workstation screen.

↳ Enter:

ls *xxxxA practice*
wc *xxxxA practice*

The shell starts the child process, passes arguments, and then instructs the process to execute the correct code. When the child process cannot locate a file named *xxxxA*, the child process sends an error message out its error door (*standard error*), which is connected to the monitor screen.

These error messages can be redirected from your screen into a file. The various shells work differently in this regard, as shown next.

Redirecting Error in *bash*, Korn, and Bourne Shells

We can redirect standard error of child processes away from the screen to a new file in **sh** family shells.

1. Make sure you are in a shell that is in the **sh** family.
2. Run a command that generates an error:

   ls -l *practice xxxxA*

   The file *xxxxA* does not exist.
3. Redirect the error message to a file named *myerrors* by entering the following command:

   ls -l *practice xxxxA* **2>** *myerrors*

   With the **2>** *myerrors* added to the command line, no error message is displayed, even though you do not have an *xxxxA* file and the process running **ls** generates an error.
4. Examine the contents of the file named *myerrors*:

   more *myerrors*

   The error message was redirected to the file.
5. Redirect output and error messages to different locations:

   ls -l *practice xxxxA* **>** *lsoutput* **2>** *lserror*
   more *lsoutput*
   more *lserror*

   To the **bash, ksh,** and **sh** shells, **1>** or **>** is instruction to redirect output to a file, whereas **2>** is interpreted as the redirection instruction for the error messages from the process.

   If we really want to get rid of error messages, we can redirect the process's error to a system file that quietly consumes whatever we redirect there.
6. Enter:

   ls -l *practice xxxxA* **>** *lsoutput* **2>** */dev/null*
   cat */dev/null*

   Although you redirected the error from **ls** to */dev/null*, there is nothing in the file. */dev/null* accepts whatever we redirect there, but does not record it. The information is not available after it is redirected to */dev/null*.

Redirecting Both Error and Output Together

You can redirect standard error and output into the same file in **sh** family shells.

1. To redirect *both* standard error and standard output to the same file, enter the following command:

   ls -l *practice xxxxA* **>** *outerr* **2>&1**

2. Examine the result by entering:

   more *outerr*

The file contains both the long listing of the *practice* file and the error message that *xxxxA* is not found. The **2>&1** is instruction to connect the error (**2**) to the same place the output (**1**) is connected.

Redirecting Error in the C Shell Family

The C shells do not support redirecting the error independent of output. We can only redirect both error and output away from the terminal.

1. In a **csh** or **tcsh**, enter:

   ls -l *practice xxxxA*
   ls -l *practice xxxxA* **>&** *outerr2*

   In the C shell, the **&** after the redirection symbol tells the shell to route the error, along with the output, to the named file.

2. We can also route the error with the output to the next utility:

   ls -l *practice xxxxA* **| wc**
   ls -l *practice xxxxA* **|& wc**

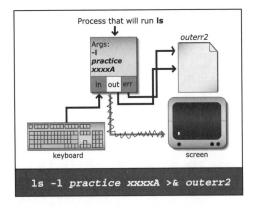

Passing Arguments to Processes

Another task performed by the shell in interpreting your commands is to pass arguments to the utility being run. In an earlier exercise, you entered **ls-l** and received a message that the command was not found.

L▸   Examine the following command line:

ls -l *practice*

When you enter this command, including the space between the **ls** and the **-l**, the output is a long listing of the file *practice*. As you have experienced, the shell uses the space as one of the ways to identify the pieces of a command line. The **ls** is the first token on the command line, so from the shell's view, it must be a utility. The **-l** is the second token. The string of characters *practice* is the third. These second and third tokens are the two arguments—strings of characters that have no special meaning to the shell. They are not the first token, and they do not follow a redirection symbol. Thus, they cannot be utilities. They do not follow >, so the shell does not see them as files to use in redirection. The shell is programmed to pass all leftover strings to the preceding utility as arguments for the utility to interpret. To **ls**, the **-l** argument has special meaning; it is instruction to produce a long listing.

The **ls** utility interprets any arguments not preceded by a minus sign, such as *practice*, as the names of files. The result of this command, then, is production and output of a long listing of information about the file *practice*.

Any tokens left over on a command line when the shell has completed its interpretation are passed as arguments to the associated utility. Each utility interprets its arguments in its own way.

Using Options as Arguments

The shell also interprets command options as arguments. We often specify more than one option to a utility on a single command line, each preceded by a minus sign, each as a separate argument.

L▸ 1. Enter the following multiple-argument command line:

ls -a -l

The shell passes two arguments to the utility. Each argument is an option that tells the **ls** utility to modify its output: provide a <u>l</u>ong listing of <u>a</u>ll the files in the current directory.

2. We can also specify two or more option flags on the command line as one argument:

ls -alF

Only one argument, **-alF**, is passed to the utility; however, the utility interprets the one argument as containing three options: **-a**, **-l**, and **-F**.

3. As another example, enter:

    sort -rd *practice*

Two options are passed as one argument.

Comparing the Shell's View of Options with the Utility's View

Options have meaning to the utility; from the shell's view, however, the options are just arguments to be passed to the utility.

⮥ Examine the following utilities and their arguments. Enter them if you wish:

    ls -l

    wc -l

    pr -l *15 practice*

In all three instances, the shell passes the same argument, but it is interpreted very differently by the three utilities. To **ls**, the **-l** means produce a long listing. To **wc**, the **-l** is instruction just to output the count of lines in the input. To **pr**, the **-l** is instruction to make the page length equal to whatever argument follows.

Expanding Tokens on the Command Line

When the shell is interpreting the command line, there are several special characters that instruct it to expand the line. For instance, the wildcard character, *****, tells the shell to include (at that location in the command line) all filenames. Variables are interpreted. The shell completes expansions and modifies the lines as appropriate.

⮥ 1. If you are not communicating with a shell in the **-x** mode, start one now:

    ksh -x

or

    bash -x

or one of the others.

2. Enter the following:

    ls -l *u**

    who | grep $USER

The shell first expands the *u** to all filenames that match, then places those names on the command line. Each is then interpreted as an argument and passed to **ls**.

The shell interprets the *$USER* variable and replaces the variable name with its value. Your login name then becomes an argument that is passed to **grep**. The **grep** utility interprets the string of characters that it reads as argument *1* to be the search string. All lines matching your login are output.

3. Enter:

   who | awk '{print $1}'

   The shell does not interpret the *$1* in this command line, but passes it as part of the argument to **awk**. The first single quote instructs the shell to turn off interpretation of all special characters, so the string {**print $1**} is not interpreted; rather, it is passed as a literal argument to **awk**.

Following this overview of command-line interpretation, the next section looks in detail at expansions.

Locating the Code to Execute

After you enter a command requesting that one or more utilities be run, the shell starts processes, interprets the redirection, and completes argument passing. With the plumbing done, the shell must locate the code for the requested utilities. The C shell variable *path* and the **sh** shell family variable *PATH* contain a list of directories that the respective shells search to locate the code for each requested utility.

1. List the value of your search *path* variable by entering:

   In the C shell:

   echo $path

   In the **sh** family:

   echo $PATH

   The list of directories displayed shows the places that the shell checks for the utilities you include in any command line. Notice that one of the directories in your path is */bin*.

2. List the contents of */bin*:

   ls -F /bin

   The directory is full of the executables we know and love.

3. Obtain a long listing of the code file for the **ls** utility. Enter:

   ls -l /bin/ls

The output is similar to the following:

```
-rwxr-xr-x 1 root   65536 Jun 23 2003 /bin/ls
```

This file contains the executable program **ls**. It is the compiled version of the program, which includes a lot of machine-readable control characters that will disrupt a workstation dramatically if you try to display the file using ordinary file-reading utilities.

4. Examine the character strings in the file by entering:

strings */bin/ls*

A list of disjointed words and phrases is displayed. The **strings** utility ignores all machine code and outputs only the *strings* of ASCII characters that it finds. The displayed output from **strings** consists of the error messages and other character strings included in the binary file of **ls**.

Specifying the File Containing the Code

To run a utility, you can provide the shell with the path to the utility code file, rather than have the shell check the path to find the code.

1. Enter:

*/bin/*ls -l

When you provide the absolute path to a utility, the shell does not have to use the search path to locate the utility.

2. Locate several programs:

which *ls*
which *xterm*
which *date*

Starting Code Execution

After the shell locates the program by searching the path, it gives the process the absolute path to the utility that it is to execute and tells the process to execute the code. While execution takes place, the shell waits for the process to complete before presenting a new prompt, unless we executed the command line in the background.

Examining the Exit Code after a Utility Is Executed

Just before a process exits, it tells its parent how things went.

⤷ 1. Enter:

> **date**
> **echo $?**
> **wc -zz** *users_on*
> **echo $?**

The **date** utility ran successfully; it reported a zero as its exit code. The shell interprets the variable **?** as the exit code of the last process. There is no option to **wc** named **-z**, so **wc** exits and tells the shell that things did not go well. Exit codes other than zero are error codes.

2. Try:

> **grep** *xxxx* */etc/passwd*
> **echo $?**

There is no output from **grep**. There is no error message, either. But **grep** reported an error exit code to the shell as it exited (*1*).

3. In contrast, try:

> **grep** *aa* */etc/xxxx*
> **echo $?**

There is no file named *xxxx* in the */etc* directory. However, the exit error code is different (*2*), conveying a different message. If **grep** finds the appropriate file, but does not locate any matching lines, it issues an exit code of *1*. An exit code of *2* conveys the message that the file could not be located.

Every time a process completes its execution and exits, it informs its parent that it was successful with an exit code of *0* or unsuccessful with an exit code of other than zero. No additional information is passed to the parent process, just the exit code. Much like when parents ask a young person coming home from a date how the night went, the reply is only, "Fine," or, "Terrible." Don't look for more.

Identifying the Function of Command-Line Tokens

The shell is programmed to ascribe the role of each command-line token or word *based on its location* in the command line.

Consider the following schematic of a command line. Each blank line represents a token. What role must each token have?

_____ _____ | _____ ; _____ _____ ` \_\_\_\_\_ \_\_\_\_\_ `

The various tokens have specific roles:

- The first token on a command line must be a utility to execute.

- The token that follows a pipe, semicolon, or back quote must be another utility.
- Any tokens left must be arguments to the foregoing utility.

Thus, the roles for each token in this example must be

utility *argument* | **utility** ; **utility** *argument* `**utility** *argument*`

This schematic represents a command line such as:

ls -l | **wc -l; grep** *alec* `**cat** *somefiles*`

Yes, the **cat** must be a utility and *somefiles* an argument. The back-quoted command line **cat** *somefiles* is executed first, and its output replaces the back-quoted command on the command line. The command line then looks like:

s -l | **wc -l; grep** alec first-file names lost-days west

Each token in the output of the command substitution is an argument passed to **grep**.

Here's another example. Each token plays a specific role in the following command line:

_____ _____ | _____ $_____ > _____ ; _____ > _____

The tokens following the > must be files, and a variable is evaluated. Once evaluated, the variable's value is passed to the previous utility as an argument.

Using the Model to Interpret Command Lines

We issue commands to the shells. We want work to be done. By considering how the shell interprets commands, we can formulate our request more effectively and make sense of complex structures.

Completing Plumbing before Execution

The key is the fact that the shell does the redirection and passing of arguments (plumbing) before telling the child process to execute the code.

1. Make sure *noclobber* is off:

   In **bash** or **ksh**:

   set +o *noclobber*

   In **tsch** or **csh**:

   unset *noclobber*

2. Enter:

   ls *j**

The files in the current directory with names starting with a *j* are listed.

3. Enter the following complete with error:

>   **wc -z** *users_on* **>** junk-wc1
>   **ls** *j**

The utility complains that the option **-z** is not a valid option and it exits. However, the new file *junk-wc1* is created but empty. The shell starts a child process, passes arguments, and handles redirection. It creates the file and connects the new file to the output of the child process. With the plumbing completed, the shell tells the process to execute the code for **wc**, which complains about the **-z** option and exits. The shell created the file before it told the process to execute the code.

4. Enter:

>   **daxxx >** *junk-wc2*
>   **ls** *j**

Plumbing is completed first. The file is created and connected to the child process's output. Then, when trying to execute the code, the shell cannot find the utility **daxxx** and the child process ends.

5. Turn *noclobber* back on:

>   In **bash** or **ksh**:
>
>   **set -o** *noclobber*
>   In **tsch** or **csh**:
>
>   **set** *noclobber*

6. Enter:

>   **daxxxx >** *junk-wc2*

The shell starts to handle output redirection, determines that the file *junk-wc2* exists and that *noclobber* is set, so it issues the error message. The shell makes no mention of the fact that the utility **daxxxx** cannot be found because it did not get that far in processing the line. The shell started a child process and then ran into trouble trying to complete the plumbing. Because the file already exists, the shell complains and exits without even trying to locate the **daxxxx** utility.

7. Try:

>   **daxxxx >>** *junk-wc2*

The redirection plumbing is successful because we can add to an existing file even when *noclobber* is set. After completing the plumbing, the shell cannot locate the utility and quits, issuing the appropriate error message.

8. Finally, try:

   daxxxx > *junk-wc3*

   The shell creates a new file, and plumbing is successful. The command is not found, so the error message is displayed.

9. Fix the utility name so it is legal by entering:

   date > *junk-wc3*

   Now the shell complains that the file exists. It was created in the previous step when the shell could not find the utility.

Instructing a Utility to Read Input

We tell the shell to redirect input and output for processes, but we should ask, does the child read from input just because it is there?

1. Output only five lines of a file:

   head **-4** *coast*

2. Sort all lines in a file:

   sort *coast*

   The child process is given an argument. To **sort**, the argument is a file to read and sort.

3. Read a two files and sort the lines:

   sort *west coast*

   Two arguments, two files.

4. Provide no arguments to **sort**, and it reads from input:

   head **-5** *west* | **sort**

   The output from the process running **head** is connected to the input of the process running **sort**. Because **sort** has no filenames to open, it reads from input, the output of *head*.

5. Connect the output of one utility to **sort**'s input and also pass it an argument:

   head **-5** *west* | **sort** *coast*

   The output is the sorted version of *coast* with each line present only one time. The output of **head** is not read, so the lines from *west* are sorted nor included in the output. Because **sort** has an argument, it opens that file and sorts it and does not read from input. The fact that the shell connected the output of **head** to **sort** is not noticed because **sort** does not read from input when it has an argument filename.

Of course, we can tell **sort** to read from input as well as the file argument.

6. Enter the following, which includes a second argument for **sort**:

 head -5 *west* | **sort** - *coast*

The output includes all lines from both files. When utilities such as **sort** receive a *dash* as an independent argument, they interpret the dash as instruction to *read from input*. In this example, **sort** reads from input (the output of **head**) and reads the file.

Providing Ambiguous Redirection

This example is best examined in a **tcsh** or **csh** shell.

1. If you are not interacting with a **tcsh** or **csh**, start one for this example.

2. Consider the following command before pressing ENTER:

 who > *who-junk1* | **sort** -r

We are telling the shell to start two child processes and to connect the output from the first process to a new file, *who-junk1*. We are also asking to connect the output of the first process to the input of the second. How can the output be redirected to two places?

3. Press ENTER and see how the shell responds.

The **csh** family agrees that the command is ambiguous and quits.

4. Try the command again in a **ksh** or **bash** shell.

These shells ignore the second redirection request and simply connect the output of **who** to the file. It doesn't really do as we want; it doesn't complain either.

Changing How the Shell Executes a Command

In the analysis of command-line interpretation covered thus far, the shell waited for child processes to complete execution before it presented a new prompt. Executing child processes in this way is called execution in the foreground. We can also have the shell start a process, immediately display a new prompt, and then execute another command line, while the first continues to run *in the background*. We can also temporarily interrupt execution by putting a process "on hold."

Running a Command Line in the Background

When we enter a command line, the shell interprets it, executes needed utilities, and *waits* until the utilities complete their work. We can ask the shell to interpret, execute, and *not* wait, but instead to present a new prompt for continued interaction.

⮑ 1. Enter the following command:

    sleep 5

sleep counts to *5*, and then it exits. The shell's wait is over, so it presents a new prompt.

2. Put **sleep** in the background by entering:

    sleep 200 &

When you enter this **sleep** command line with the **&**, the shell immediately presents a new prompt. You can enter a new request. A command consisting of utilities, arguments, and redirection terminated by ENTER is called a *job*. With the **&**, the whole *job* is placed in the *background*. The CPU still works on the job. The shell does not wait for the **sleep** to finish, but instead displays a prompt immediately.

3. List your current processes:

    ps

The child process running **sleep** is among the processes. It will continue until it counts to *200* and exits, a little more than three minutes later. This is much like watching a movie on the VCR, then while it is running, we change channels to catch the news. The VCR continues to run in the background until it is finished and rewinds.

Suspending a Job

The **csh**, **tcsh**, **bash**, and **ksh** shells allow us to *suspend* a job in midstream and return to it later.

⮑ 1. Start editing a file:

    vi *practice*

2. Add a line of text to the *practice* file.

3. Return to the command mode of **vi** by pressing:

    ESC

and then press:

    CTRL-Z

The shell presents a prompt, and the **vi** display is no longer active.

4. Enter:

    ps

The **vi** job is still in the list of processes. It is suspended, not killed.

The output shows that **vi** is still a process on your process list; however, it is not active. It gets no CPU attention, but it is not destroyed, either.

> **N O T E :** If pressing CTRL-Z does not suspend the job in your shell, enter **stty -a** and in the output locate **susp= (***value***)**. Whatever is listed as the value should be used in this exercise instead of CTRL-Z.

5. Bring the job back into the foreground by entering:

   fg

6. Put the file away and quit the editor:

   :wq

We can suspend the processing of a foreground job and return momentarily to the shell by pressing CTRL-Z. To bring the job back into the foreground, we enter **fg**. We start a video on the VCR. At some point, we press the stop button and change channels. We don't rewind, eject, or put the tape back on the shelf. We just mark our place and stop processing. Later we return and press the Play button to proceed.

Identifying Multiple Processes in One Pipeline

Being able to suspend a job allows us to examine aspects of how the shell works. Processes are started as part of the shell's interpretation of a command line.

1. Enter the following:

   sleep *100* **&**

   ps -l

   The **sleep** job is listed as a process that is currently alive. It is running in the background.

2. Enter the following:

   sort | **grep** *aaa* | **tee** *bb* | **wc**

   Four processes are started. Because this command line does not specify an input source for **sort**, it reads whatever you enter at the keyboard as input data.

3. Enter the following text:

   baaa
   abab
   aaaahhh

The job is in the foreground. We are giving input to **sort**, not to the shell.

4. Suspend the **sort grep tee wc** job by pressing:

   CTRL-Z

   The whole job is suspended and another shell prompt is displayed.

5. Request a list of processes currently running, with:

   ps -l

   All four of the processes that you requested in the last command—**sort, grep, tee**, and **wc**—are still running. They were not told to exit. The job was suspended, the processes got no CPU attention, they were not terminated, they still exist. The output of **ps** shows that each utility included on the command line is a child process and that all have the same parent, your shell. They have the same number in the **PPID** field that your shell has in the **PID** field. The output from **ps** lists the status of the suspended jobs as *T* for <u>T</u>raced. The suspended job (**sort grep tee wc**) still exists, but is not running.

6. Bring the job back to the foreground by entering:

   fg

7. With the job in the foreground, enter another line:

   This is all.

8. Inform **sort** that you are finished by pressing:

   CTRL-D

   The output from the job consists of the lines entered before and after the job was suspended.

When we ask for a utility to be executed, the shell starts a child process to run the code. If we don't say otherwise, it is executed in the foreground. The shell waits until the child exits before interacting with us. We can also put the job in the background, where it continues execution, even though at the same time we interact with the shell in the foreground to do other tasks. If a job is in the foreground, we can suspend it by pressing CTRL-Z, and the shell displays another prompt. If a job is suspended, no work is done on the processes that constitute the job, but the job is not destroyed either. It just sits until we ask for it to return to the foreground with **fg**.

Self Test 1

1. What is a token? How does the shell decide where one token ends and another begins?

_____

2. The file *list* contains the names of several of the files listed in your home directory. What is the result of running the following?

   **wc `cat** *list*`

_____

3. If a user enters the following with *noclobber* set off, what is the error message? Assume the file *junk1* exists and the utility **datxxx** does not exist. What impact does issuing this command have?

   datxxx *junk1* > *junk1*

_____

4. How can you overwrite a file if *noclobber* is set in the C shell? In the Korn shell?

_____

5. How does a shell interpret each of the following tokens?

   _____ _____ < _____ | | _____ > _____ ; _____ | _____

_____

6. When a user issues the following distinct commands, what happens and why? Assume *noclobber* is not set and all files exist.

   A. CTRL-Z
   B. *PATH=$PATH:~/mybin*
   C. **echo $?**
   D. **wc** *filexx* > *filexx*
   E. **cp -i** *fileCC fileDD*

_____

7. If *noclobber* is set *on*, both files exist, and the following is issued, what happens?

   mv *fileAA fileBB*

_____

8. How many processes does the shell start when a user issues the following?

   grep *'Helen Chellin' phone friends* | **tr** *'a-z' 'A-Z'* > *ghc*

_____

8.2 Shell Command-Line Expansion

The previous section examined how the shell walks through interpreting command lines that we issue. Simple commands work as described. When we issue more complex lines, the shell must expand tokens to their meanings. In the previous sections, you explored how the shell interprets command lines, matches filenames, and executes processes to run the requested utilities. Several aspects of command lines are given to the shell in a sort of shorthand notation. In earlier exercises, we requested the number of lines, words, and characters in all files in the current directory by entering **wc** * at the prompt. The shell expands the wildcard * to match all filenames. Variables, command substitutions, filenames, and special character expansions are part of the shell's features.

Using Shell Characters to Expand Filenames

You can create filenames that contain common base names with number or letter extensions. Then, by entering shell commands that contain special characters, you can match and select the filenames in groups. As the shell examines each command line you enter, it looks for the special characters. Some characters are interpreted as wildcard characters and used for matching unspecified characters of a filename. Other characters are used to select a range of characters for matching with filenames. This feature is often referred to as filename *expansion* or filename *matching*, because you can select many filenames while entering only one name with special characters embedded.

Matching Filenames Using Wildcard Characters

We often name files using a scheme that creates a relationship among the files. Using wildcard characters, we can list groups of filenames that have similar characteristics.

➥ 1. Create a new directory and make it the current directory with:

> **mkdir** *NewBook*
> **cd** *NewBook*

2. Create a series of empty files with the following commands:

> **touch** *chap chapter2 chapter5 summaries*
> **touch** *chapter chapter3 chapter5A chapter57 chapter62*
> **touch** *chapter1 chapter4 index chapterA chapterR chapter2-5*
> **ls**

The **touch** command creates empty files.

This is another place where interacting with a shell using the **-x** option is very useful.

3. If you are not interacting with a verbose shell, enter:

    ksh -x

   or

    bash -x

   or whatever shell you want, with an **-x** option.

4. Obtain a long listing for selected files:

    ls -l *chap**

   This command contains the asterisk (*) wildcard character, which matches any number of any character. The first **+** line shows that the shell matches the string *chap** with names of files in the current directory. It replaces *chap** on the command line with all the filenames that begin with the characters *chap* followed by zero or more additional characters of any kind. Thus, the files named *chap*, *chap62*, and so on are selected. The matched filename strings are passed to **ls** as arguments. The **ls** utility then produces its long listing about those files listed as arguments.

   The shell does filename expansion and replacement because of the * that is present. It has nothing to do with the utility involved.

5. For example enter:

    echo *chap files are: chap**

   The shell interprets the *chap** and replaces it with the list of filenames that start with *chap*. Those names are passed to **echo**, which reads the arguments and writes them to output. It is as though you entered the command line including all the filename arguments at the keyboard.

   The shell matches the * with any number of any characters. We can also tell the shell to match just one character.

6. Enter the following command:

    ls *chapter*?

   This time, neither *chapter* nor *chapter5A* is selected, because the ? character matches any one character. There must be one and only one character, but it can be anything.

   The * and ? are two of the special characters interpreted by the shell.

   As the shell interprets the command line, it does not open files. It just matches the filenames with the string of regular and special characters you enter, and then passes this list of matching filenames as arguments to whatever utility precedes the arguments on the command line.

7. To explore how the shell interprets the command line, enter:

wc *chap**

The shell interprets the filename expansion * and replaces the *chap** with all filenames that match. The names are passed to **wc** as arguments, so **wc** outputs a count of the elements in each file, in this case zeros, because the files are empty.

8. Try:

wc *

The elements of all files in the current directory are counted.

Selecting Filenames within a Range

We can also have the shell match filenames that include letters or numbers that fall within a specified range.

1. Enter:

ls *chapter*[2-7]

The square brackets tell the shell to match any filename that has the letters *chapter* followed by one and only one number in the range 2-7. In this case, the files *chapter2, chapter3, chapter4,* and *chapter5* are selected, but neither *chapter1* nor *chapter5A* is included in the output. The number *1* is not included in the specified range, and the filename *chapter5A* has a character after the number, which is not specified in the requested range. The file *chapter2-5* does not match, because the shell interprets the [2-5] on the command line as instruction to match one character in the range of *2* through *5*, not the three-character string *2-5*.

2. To include *chapter5A* in the match, change the command to:

ls *chapter*[2-7]*

This command tells the shell to expand the filename *chapter* to include one character from the list of numbers 2, 3, 4, 5, 6, 7, and then zero or more of any other characters.

You can select filenames that contain more than one specified range of characters.

3. Try this command:

ls *chapter*[0-9][0-9]

The selected filenames now include *chapter57* and *chapter62*, because they are the only filenames that start with *chapter* followed by one digit and then followed by another digit.

The characters listed in the brackets need not be a range. A list of acceptable values works, too.

4. Enter:

   echo *chapter[R3A1]*

   The output is *chapter1, chapter3, chapterA,* and *chapterR.*

Using the Curly Brace Expansion Characters to Specify Filenames

The curly brace characters, { and }, are also used by the **bash** shell and modern **ksh** shells for matching and creating multiple filenames from one pattern.

1. Enter the following:

   echo *chapter{1,3,5A}*

   The output is files named *chapter1, chapter3,* and *chapter5A.* When used for matching existing filenames, the curly brace matches all strings separated with commas listed inside.

2. Use the curly braces to attempt to select all files in a range:

   echo chapter{1-7}

   The curly braces match existing filenames if each match is specified in the braces, but will not expand ranges.

   However, the curly braces can be used to expand a range for *creating* files or directories.

3. Create five new files by entering:

   touch *ABC{1,2,3,4,16}*
   ls *AB**

   The shell creates new files with the name *ABC* as the base name, and then adds each of the strings separated by commas in the curly braces. Hence, new files are created with names *ABC1, ABC2, ABC3, ABC4,* and *ABC16.*

   You may wish to make multiple directories that all begin with the same name.

4. Enter:

   mkdir *Newprojects-{one,two,three}*

5. Now examine the results:

   ls

The shell created three new directories with the same base: *Newprojects-one*, *Newprojects-two*, and *Newprojects-three*.

In the command you just entered, the curly braces around the strings *one*, *two*, and *three* tell the shell to use each portion to create a new file or directory name.

Creating and Using Local Variables

Throughout the previous chapters, we have been employing variables to hold information. We created variables, changed their values, and evaluated them.

This section takes a careful look at variables of two different kinds. If a shell keeps a variable private and does not give the information to child processes, it is a *local* variable. If the shell does pass a variable and its value to its child processes, the variable is an *environmental* variable.

Examining How Both Families of Shells Work

For the following exercises, we suggest you complete the tasks first in a shell in the C family and then in a shell in the **sh** family by choosing one of the following approaches:

- Employ two windows on the graphical interface, one with a **csh** or **tcsh** shell running, and one with either a **bash** or **ksh** shell.
- Or, use virtual terminals accessible through the F keys to have one terminal running a **csh** or **tcsh** shell, and one terminal running either a **bash** or **ksh** shell.
- Or, operate in one shell, start a child of the other type and explore how it works. When finished, exit the child and return to the original shell.

Evaluating Existing Variables

When your shell was started, it was given the names and values of many variables. You have been using them in commands such as these:

> **echo $HOME**
> **echo $USER**   (or **echo $LOGNAME**)
> **who | grep $USER**

➥ Ask for a listing of many of the current variables and their values by entering:

> **set | more**
>
> and
>
> **env | more**

The variables displayed are available to you because they are in your shell's memory.

Creating and Changing Variables

The two families of shells each use their own syntax for creating a variable.

1. Depending on your current shell, enter one of the following commands:

   In a **csh** or **tcsh**:

   set *AA*=200

   In a **ksh**, **bash**, or **sh**:

   AA=200

   These commands instruct the corresponding shell to place in memory the variable named *AA* with a current value of *200*.

2. Ask the shell to evaluate the variable in a command line by entering:

   echo *$AA*

   The value of the variable *AA* is output to the screen.

   The shell interprets the **$** character as instruction to locate in the shell's memory a variable that has the name of the character string that follows the $, namely *AA*. Once the variable and value are located, the shell replaces the $*variable-name*, in this case $ *AA*, with the variable's value. After the variable evaluation is completed, the command line reads **echo** *200*. When executing **echo**, the shell passes one argument, *200*, the value of the evaluated variable. The **echo** utility reads its arguments and writes them to standard output, which in this case is connected to your screen.

   A variable's value is not etched in stone.

3. Enter one of the following commands:

   In a **tcsh** or **csh** shell:

   set *AA=wonderful*

   In a **bash**, **ksh**, or **sh** shell:

   AA=wonderful

4. Evaluate the *AA* variable again by entering:

   echo *$AA*

   The new value assigned to the variable is reported.

5. List your current variables:

   set | more

   The new variable *AA* is listed as one of the variables in your shell's memory.

Setting the Value of a Variable to Include Spaces

For programming purposes and user convenience, we often need to set the value of a variable to include characters that are special to the shell, such as spaces. In previous chapters, you created a series of files whose names are used in the next exercise.

1. List your files:

   ls

   If the files used in the next command are not in your current directory, use names of files that are.

2. Enter one of the following:

   In **ksh**, **bash**, or **sh**:

   files='practice west coast respected'

   In **tcsh** or **csh**:

   set *files='practice west coast respected'*

3. With the variable set, ask the shell to evaluate it and list the current variables:

   echo *$files*

   set | more

   The variable *files* consists of several tokens or words separated by spaces.

   A variable of this sort is useful when interacting with the shell.

4. Enter:

   wc *$files*

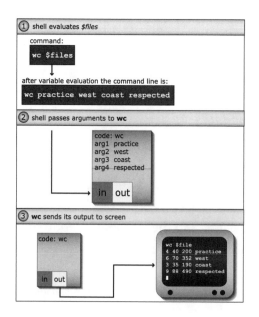

5. Try two other commands:

> **ls -l** *$files*
> **head -3** *$files*

In each case, the shell replaces the variable with its value. Hence, the commands as executed are:

```
ls -l  practice  west  coast  respected
head -3  practice  west  coast  respected
```

The job of the shell is to replace a variable with its value on the command line.

6. Try:

> *$files*

The shell replaces the dollar sign and variable name with the value:

> *practice west coast respected*

The token *practice* is the first one on the line, so the shell interprets it as the utility to execute. When the shell can not locate the utility "*practice*" it displays the error message, "Command not found."

Passing Environmental Variables to Child Processes

Variables created as we just created *AA* are in the shell's memory and are available as long as that shell exists. They are *local variables*; they are not passed to child processes. The shells also allow us to pass user-created variables to child processes, but the mechanisms employed by the shells are different.

Creating a C Shell Family Environmental Variable

In the **csh** and **tcsh** shells, local and environmental variables are separate entities having lives of their own.

1. Make sure you are in one of the C shells.

2. Create or modify the local variable *AA*:

> **set** *AA*=hello

3. Instruct the C shell to create a new environmental variable, *BB*, by entering:

> **setenv** *BB 6060M*

The C shell syntax for setting environmental variables is:

> **setenv** *variable-name variable-value*

Two arguments are given to **setenv**; no equal sign is used.

4. Ask the C shell to list all of its environmental variables by entering:

> **printenv | more**

or

> **env | more**

The variable *BB=6060M* is included in the list. The local variable *AA* is not listed in the output from **env**.

5. Start a child C shell and evaluate the variables. Enter:

> **csh**
> **echo** *$AA*
> **echo** *$BB*
> **printenv | more**

or

> **env | more**

The output includes the value for *BB* but not for *AA*. As the child shell is started, it is given the environmental variable *BB* and its value, but is not given the local variable *AA*. When the child process (and it could be *any* child process) is created, the environmental variables and their values are given to the child process. Local variables are *not* passed to child processes.

6. Start a "grandchild" process:

> **sh**
> **ps**
> **echo** *$AA*
> **echo** *$BB*

Notice how deep we are in shells. A child shell does not have to be the same type to inherit environmental variables. The environmental variable created with **setenv** in the C shell is passed to its child's child, a Bourne shell, **sh**.

7. Exit the current shell and the child C shell, returning to the shell (**tcsh** or **csh**) where you created *AA* and *BB*:

> **exit**
> **ps**
> **exit**
> **ps**
> **echo** *$AA*

The original shell maintains its value for the variable *AA*.

Listing Variables in the *csh* and *tcsh* Shells

We can instruct the C family of shells to list local or environmental variables separately.

1. In your current C family shell, list the local variables:

set | more

The local variable *AA* with a value of *hello* is included in the output of **set**. The environmental variable is not listed.

2. List the environmental variables:

env | more

or

printenv | more

The environmental variable *BB* with a value of *6060M* is output. The local variable is not. When you enter the command **set**, the C shells list local variables. When you enter **env** to a C shell on some systems and **printenv** on others, environmental variables are listed.

Removing Variables in the C Shell

At this point, you have a local variable named *AA*.

1. Remove the local *AA* variable:

echo $*AA*
unset *AA*

2. List the current local variables:

set

AA is not there.

3. Request that the shell evaluate the variable *BB* and then list the current environmental variables:

echo $*BB*
printenv

or

env

The display says that *BB* has a value of *6060M*, which is the value you gave *BB* when you created the environmental variable.

4. Instruct the shell to remove the *BB* environmental variable by entering:

    unsetenv *BB*

5. Confirm that the environmental variable is gone with:

    echo *$BB*

    printenv

or

    env

To remove a local variable in the C shell, enter **unset** *local-variable*. To remove an environmental variable in the C shell, enter **unsetenv** *environment-variable*.

Passing a Variable from an *sh*, *ksh*, or *bash* Shell to a Child

In the **sh** family of shells, there is only one mechanism for creating a variable. Once a local variable is created, though, we can make it available to child processes.

1. Access a **ksh**, **bash**, or **sh** shell.

2. Create two new variables by entering:

    Var2=hello

    LL=Fun

    export *LL*

3. Create a child shell of any kind. Enter the appropriate command for a shell:

    csh or **ksh** or **sh** or **bash**

4. Evaluate the variables:

    echo *$Var2*

    echo *$LL*

The exported variable *LL* is available to the child process; the local variable is not. Using **export** *variable_name* makes a variable an environmental variable.

Modifying an Environmental Variable

We created the *LL* variable in the shell that is this shell's parent. The next steps will modify the value and then examine what happens when a new child shell is started.

1. Modify the *LL* variable's value:

> *LL=evenmorefun*
> **echo** *$LL*

The new value is in the shell's memory.

2. Start a "child of the child" process and evaluate the *LL* variable:

> **sh**
> **echo** *$LL*

The variable is passed with its new value. Once you tell a **sh** family shell to export a variable, the variable is given to all child processes and all their child processes, and so on. All descendent child processes receive the variable and whatever is its current value.

3. Exit from the two child shells, and return to the shell where you created *LL*:

> **exit**
> **exit**

4. Evaluate the variable we have been traveling with:

> **echo** *$LL*

The value of the variable is *Fun*, as it was when you created it in this shell. Child processes do not pass variable values to their parents. Although we changed the value of *LL* in a child shell, it did not report the change to the parent. The parent retains its original value.

Creating and Exporting in One Command

We can create and export a variable at the same time.

1. In a shell in the **sh** family, enter:

> **export** *newvar=enoughalready*

2. List the environmental variables:

> **env | more**

The creation and exporting are accomplished in one command line.

Listing Variables in the *ksh*, *bash*, and *sh* Shells

With the **ksh**, **bash**, and **sh** shells, the **set** command gives you a listing of *all* variables.

1. **set | more**

Variables that are exported and those that are local are both included in the output of **set**.

2. To list only the exported variables in an **sh** shell, try each of the following:

> **env | more**

or

> **export | more**

The **set** command instructs the **sh** family of shells to list all variables, both local and environmental. The **env** command lists only environmental variables.

Removing *ksh*, *bash*, and *sh* Variables

The **sh** family of shells removes variables using the same **unset** command:

1. To remove the environmental *LL* variable in the Korn shell, enter:

> **unset** *LL*

2. Enter:

> **set**
> **env**

LL is gone.

3. Once *LL* is removed, it cannot be exported. It is not available in local or any child shells.

Removing Variables by Exiting the Shell

1. Create a child shell of any kind, for example, a C shell.
2. Set the value of a new variable:

> **csh**
> **set** *college='A great experience'*
> **echo** *$college*

The value of the variable *college* is in the child shell's memory.

3. Exit the child shell and return to its parent, and then evaluate the variable *college* in the parent shell with:

> **exit**
> **echo** *$college*

When a child shell exits, it takes its memory of all variables with it. Parents are not informed of variables set in child processes.

Shell	ksh, bash, sh	tcsh, csh
Create local variable	a=xxx	set a=xxx or set a = xxx
Create environmental variable	b=yyy export b or export b=yyy	setenv b yyy
Remove local (C shell family)	-	unset a
Remove environmental (C shell family)	-	unsetenv b
Remove variable regardless of whether local or environmental (sh family)	unset a unset b	-
List ALL variables (sh family)	set	-
List environmental variables	env	env
List local variables (C shell family)	-	set
Make local into environmental	export	-

Determining the Command-Line Role of a Variable

So far in these examples, the variables were placed on the command line as arguments to utilities such as **echo**. Using arguments with **echo** is a good way to have the shell evaluate variables and display the result. The location of a variable among the other tokens on the command line determines the ultimate role of that variable's value in the execution of the command.

1. Set the value of a new variable to the name of a utility. Enter one of the following commands:

   In a C family shell:

   > **set** *L=ls*

   In an **sh** family shell:

   > *L=ls*

2. Instruct the shell to evaluate the variable using it as an argument by entering:

   echo *$L*

3. Have the shell evaluate the variable when it is the first token on the command line. Enter:

   $L

   The names of the files in the current directory are displayed. When you enter $L and press ENTER, the command line $L is passed to the shell for interpretation. It interprets the **$** as a request to evaluate the variable L. The shell consults its memory and determines that L has a value of the character string *ls*, which is then placed on the command line, replacing the $L token. The $L was the first token on the command line. When the *ls* replaces the variable on the command line, it becomes the first token. Because the first token must be a utility, the *ls* is interpreted as the *ls* utility. The shell executes *ls*, which lists the filenames in the current directory.

4. Change directories and repeat the command from step 3. Enter these commands:

   cd */tmp*
   $L

   The names of the files in the **/tmp** directory are displayed. The variable is again evaluated to be *ls* and the **ls** utility is run, because of the location of **ls** on the command line. The shell keeps the variable names and values in its memory, not in a file. Therefore, regardless of your current directory, shell variables are available.

5. Change back to your original directory.

   The $L variable results in the **ls** utility being executed, because the shell does all the plumbing before execution. If the shell were to look for utilities before evaluating variables, the shell would complain about not finding the utility $L.

6. At the shell prompt, set two variables, each consisting of a string of characters that includes a space.

   In a C family shell, enter:

   set *CC='-l -i'*
   set *DD='practice coast'*

   In an **sh** family shell, enter:

   CC='-l -i'
   DD='practice coast'

7. Confirm the values by entering:

   echo *$CC*
   echo *$DD*

   Now each variable has a value that consists of two strings of characters separated by a space.

8. Employ the variables in the following command lines:

   ls *$CC*

   The variable *CC* has a value of *-l -i* when the shell evaluates it. Thus, after the variable's value is substituted, **ls** **-l -i** is the result. The shell executes **ls** and passes it the two arguments. The output is a long listing (**-l**) with inode numbers (**-i**) included for each file.

9. Extend the use of variables with the following commands:

   echo *$CC*
   echo *$DD*
   ls *$CC $DD*

   A long listing, with inodes for the files *practice* and *coast,* is output. The shell evaluates all variables, creating the command line **ls** **-l -i** *practice coast.*

10. Variable interpretation can be carried to the limit with:

    $L $CC $DD > *$L*

    As a result of this command line, the shell interprets the *$L* variable (created several steps back) as **ls**, the *$CC* as **-l -i**, and *$DD* as *practice coast.* After expansion, the resulting command line is:

    `ls -l -i` practice coast `> ls`

The shell replaces the variables on the command line, then interprets the resulting values as whatever is appropriate for that location on the line.

8.3 Customizing How the Shell Functions

The shell includes a wide variety of customizable features that you can use or not, as you see fit. This section examines how, as a user of the shell, you can modify the path of directories that the shell searches when you issue a command, specify the contents of the shell's prompt, and include instructions in the startup files to tailor how the shell behaves.

Using and Modifying the Search Path

When we issue a command, the shell must locate the code to execute. The directories in the *path* and *PATH* variables are searched for the chosen executable when we issue a command.

↳ Enter:

echo $PATH

Examining Elements of the Search Path in the C Shell

↳ 1. Make sure you are in a **csh** or **tcsh** shell.

2. To examine your current path, enter:

   echo $path

   The output is a series of directories, such as:

   ```
   (/usr/local/bin /usr/X11R6/bin /bin /usr/bin  .)
   ```

   The directories to be searched are separated by spaces. The **.** is the current directory, wherever you are in the filesystem.

   The *path* variable is a local variable. Normally, you assign its value in one of the *startup* files so that its value is available to each shell you create.

   In addition to *path*, the C shell also maintains the environmental variable *PATH*, but does not use it for locating commands. This variable contains the same information as *path*, but in a format that is acceptable to other shells, such as the **ksh**, **bash**, and **sh**. Because *PATH* is an environmental variable, it is passed when you request a child shell in the **sh** family. In the C shells, the two variables are intertwined, in that whenever you change the value of one, the other is automatically updated to reflect the change.

   Whenever we add a new directory of commands or load a new application on a system, the path administrator either puts the new commands in a directory currently in the user path, or changes the path for the users to include the directory where the new commands are located. We will modify the path to include a local directory.

Adding the Current Directory to the Path

If the current directory is not listed among the directories in the path, you can add it.

↳ Enter:

set *path*=($path .)

First, the current value of the variable *path* is evaluated, the space and dot are then added, and this new value is assigned to the variable *path*.

Modifying the Path in the *ksh*, *bash*, and *sh* Shells

Unlike the C shell, the **sh** family of shells maintains only one path variable, *PATH*.

➜ 1. If you are not in a **ksh**, **sh**, or **bash** shell, enter one of them to do the following.

2. In an **sh** family shell, enter:

    echo $PATH

    The format of the shell *PATH* variable is the same as the C shell's *PATH* variable. The directories in the path are separated by colons.

3. Add a new directory to the existing Korn shell path list by entering:

    PATH=$PATH:~/sh-bin

    In this case, you are adding ~/sh-bin to the end of the string of directories in your path.

4. Create a new script in your ~/sh-bin directory and make it executable.

5. Change directories to */tmp* and run the script.

Because the Korn shell actually checks the directories listed in the *PATH* variable rather than referring to a hash table, when we modify the path, the shell can immediately locate the script.

Including the Current Directory in the *sh* Shells' Paths

A colon (:) at the beginning or end of a path string is interpreted by the **sh** family of shells as instruction to search your current directory. You can also place an empty field using two colons (::) or explicitly request the current directory, anywhere in the path, using a dot. If your current directory is to be included in your *PATH* variable, for security reasons it is best to have it listed last, as in:

```
PATH=/bin:/usr/bin:/usr/local::
```

If your current *PATH* does not include the current directory, you can add it.

➜ Enter:

PATH=$PATH:.

The old *PATH* is evaluated. The colon dot is added, and then the resulting construction is assigned to the variable *PATH*.

Creating Personalized Shell Prompts

The shell displays its prompt, we respond, the shell rewards us by doing as we ask, the shell displays a prompt, we respond. Pavlov would be proud. The original prompts were single-character messages: **$** in the **sh** shell, and % with the **csh** shell. Modern shells allow us to customize them extensively. For example, you may want to have the full pathname of your current directory displayed as a prompt. Unfortunately, if you were to set the prompt to include your current directory, when you then change directories, the prompt would indicate you were still in the previous directory. The next sections describe how you can tailor your prompt in the various shells.

Modifying the Prompt in the *tcsh* Shell

The **tcsh** shell provides for quite elaborate tailoring of the prompt.

1. Enter:

   set *prompt*='! %c %% '

   The prompt now includes the current command history number, the name of the current directory, and a percent followed by a space.

2. Change directories to */tmp*:

   The prompt reflects both the new history number and new current directory.

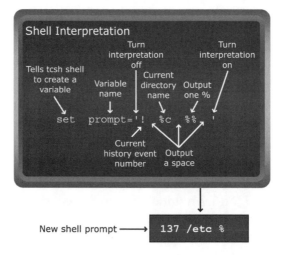

The shell variable *prompt* is evaluated each time the prompt is displayed, and all internal % variables are evaluated at that time. When you change directories, the prompt is reevaluated and the new directory is included in the display.

The **man** and **info** pages for the **tcsh** describe the collection of variables you can use in constructing a prompt.

Modifying the Prompt in the *ksh* Shells

1. Enter the following:

   echo $PWD

   The value of the variable *PWD* is the current directory.

2. In a **ksh**, enter the following:

   PS1='! $PWD $ '
   cd /tmp
   cd

The **ksh** shell uses the value in the variable *PS1* as its prompt. Whenever it is time to display the prompt on the screen, the shell first evaluates any variables in the contents of the prompt variable and then displays the results. The *PWD* has a value equal to the path to the current directory. Every time you change directories, *PWD* is reset. Because the variable *PWD* is evaluated at every prompt display, the prompt includes the current directory. Essentially, any variable can be included in a **ksh** prompt.

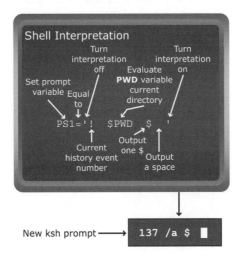

Modifying the Prompt in a *bash* Shell

The **bash** shell, like **tcsh**, provides a wealth of tailoring possibilities.

1. Enter:

> *PS1='\\! \\W $ '*

The prompt includes the current history event number (\\!), the current directory (\\W), the dollar sign, and then a space.

2. To see some of the power of the **bash** features, enter:

> *PS1='\\h \\t \\d \\W \\n \\! bash$ '*

The prompt includes the current host, time, date, and current directory on the first line, followed by the history event number and *bash$* on the second line.

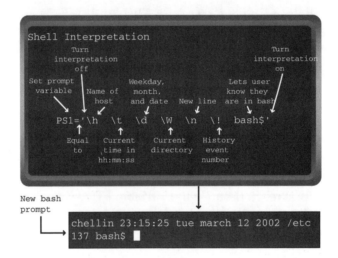

3. Change directories and return home:

> **cd** */etc*
>
> **cd**

4. The prompt variables just used are:

- **\\h** Name of host
- **\\t** Current time in *hh:mm:ss*
- **\\d** Weekday, month, and date
- **\\W** Current directory
- **\\n** New line
- **\\!** History event number

The **man** and **info** pages on **bash** describe the full collection of prompt variables in the section titled *PROMPTING*.

Modifying the Prompt in a *csh* Shell

The **csh** provides a much more limited set of prompt-tailoring options.

↳ Enter:

set *prompt*="! *csh*% '

The prompt includes the history event number, the string *csh* %, and a space.

8.4 Employing Advanced User Features

Built into the shell are several features that make issuing commands more efficient. Previously, we have used history, command-line editing, aliases, and user-created variables to issue command-line instructions more effectively. The shells also provide built-in shell variables, filename completion, and a method for creating a path of directories for file location. Collectively they provide powerful assistance when using the shells.

Employing Shells of Both Families

For the following exercises, we suggest you complete the tasks first using a shell in the C family and then again with a shell in the **sh** family. Choose one of the following approaches:

- If you are using a graphical interface, start two windows. In one window, execute a **csh** or **tcsh** shell, and in the other window, start a **bash** or **ksh** shell. As you complete the exercises in both windows, you can compare how they behave.
- If you are using Linux without graphics, you can use virtual terminals accessible through the F keys. Start a **tcsh** shell in one virtual terminal, and start a **bash** or **ksh** shell in the other terminal.
- If you are not in Linux and using a terminal, you are limited to one shell at a time. We suggest you operate in one shell and complete the exercises; then start a child of the other type and examine the exercises again.

Asking the Shells to Complete Filenames

Because typing command lines with absolute accuracy is difficult to do, a useful feature allows us to give only part of a file or directory name and then ask the shell to complete it. Operation of this feature differs among the shells. The **tcsh** shell, many versions of the **csh** shell, and the **ksh** shell all provide this feature, with some twists.

For these exercises, create three files by entering:

touch *zadigAAA zadigBBB*
ls > *zzzzCCC*
ls -l *z**

The three files are listed.

The next several sections examine the use of file completion in each of the shells.

Instructing the *tcsh* Shell to Complete Filenames

This section examines file completion using the **tcsh** shell. If you do not have access to one, skip down to the following sections that guide you through these exercises using the other shells.

1. Make sure you are communicating with a **tcsh** shell.

2. Inform the **tcsh** shell that you want the *file*name-*c*ompletion feature turned on by entering:

   set *filec*

   When the variable *filec* exists in the environment of the **tcsh** shell, the shell will search for matching filenames.

3. Type the following *but do not press* ENTER:

   ls -l *zz*

4. Instead of pressing ENTER, press TAB.

   The command line on the screen changes to:

   ls -l *zzzzCCC*

   The command in its modified form just sits there. The shell is not executing it yet.

5. Press ENTER to have the command line executed.

   When you enter part of a filename and press TAB, the shell examines the filenames in the current directory, completes the name, and displays it. You can add more to the line, or simply press ENTER and execute it.

6. Enter:

   tr '*a-z*' '*A-Z*' *zz*

and press TAB.

The shell completes the zz filename as *zzzzCCC*.

7. After the filename is completed, add | **more** to the line so it reads:

```
tr  'a-z'  'A-Z'  <  zzzzCCC  |  more
```

8. Press ENTER to execute the command.

Completing Filenames That Have the Same Beginning

When we provide enough of a filename to identify it uniquely, the shell simply completes the name. What happens if more than one name meet the partial name criteria?

1. Enter:

> **ls -l** *za*

and press TAB

The shell attempts to complete the filename by examining the names of files in the current directory. However, the shell cannot distinguish between two existing filenames that start with *za*, namely, *zadigAAA zadigBBB*. At this point, some shells display as much of the name as matches both files. Some shells simply beep or flash; others list the files that match, and then display the incomplete command line and wait for more information.

2. Press TAB again.

If more than one command starting with *za* exists, pressing TAB twice usually presents all the options.

You need to give the shell more characters—enough to uniquely identify the filename.

3. Enter:

> *A*

and press TAB

The command line changes to employ a complete filename:

```
ls   -l   zadigAAA
```

4. Press ENTER to run the command.

5. Attempt to expand a filename that does not exist:

> **ls** *Zx5*

and press TAB.

If no filename in the current directory matches the characters you enter, the shell beeps or flashes.

Completing Utility Names

We can use the filename completion for files, directories, and executables.

1. Enter:

   wh

   and press TAB

   A list of utilities whose names begin with **wh** is displayed.

2. Add:

   oa

   and again press the TAB

The **whoami** utility is executed. Filename completion works when issuing commands.

Filename Completion in the Korn Shell

The filename completion feature of the **ksh** shell functions in the same manner as in the C shells once you turn it on.

1. Start a **ksh** either in another window, or as a child shell.
2. Set the filename-completion variable in the Korn shell by entering:

   set -o *vi*
   set -o *vi-tabcomplete*

3. Go back and run through the same exercise in filename completion with the Korn shell as you did with the C shell.

Filename Completion in the *bash* Shell

The **bash** shell probably includes filename completion by default.

1. Try it:

   ls */t*

   and press TAB

2. If file completion does not work, try:

   set -o *vi*
   set +o *posix*

3. Work through the exercises listed for the **tcsh** shell employing a **bash** shell.

File completion is a useful way to improve effectiveness in a command-line environment.

Filename Completion in the *csh* Shell

Many C shells include filename completion but use the ESC key to trigger completion of filenames.

↳ Go back through the exercises listed as **tcsh**, but use ESC instead of the TAB that is specified in each exercise.

Evaluating Shell Variables

In addition to including the variables examined earlier in all shells, the **bash** and **ksh** shells have built-in variables that are useful in interacting with the shell.

We use the **ps** command to identify the current processes and their parents. These shells also maintain the parent's *PID* in a variable.

↳ 1. In a Korn or **bash** shell, enter:

    echo $$
    echo $PPID
    ps -l

2. The shells keep track of the length of time they have been "alive":

    echo $SECONDS
    date
    echo $SECONDS

The shell maintains a variable named *SECONDS* with a value of the number of seconds since the shell was started.

Execute a child shell and check on its age.

3. In the **bash** shell, another variable allows you to execute any command just before it displays the prompt:

    PROMPT_COMMAND=cal

Every time you enter a command, the shell will run **cal** just before displaying the new prompt.

4. Enter a few commands.

5. To turn the prompt command feature off, enter:

    PROMPT_COMMAND=

Customizing Shell Startup Files

Do you want file completion? A particular prompt? A series of aliases? The designers of UNIX/Linux refuse to make decisions like that for you. Instead, tools are provided that allow you to customize the shell as you see fit. Whenever a shell is started, it reads startup files to see how you want it to behave.

➜ List all the files in your home directory:

ls -a

Included in the output is the set of files with names that begin with a period, the *dot files.* Each dot file is a run control file for a specific utility or shell. We can add instructions to these files to modify the *PATH*, set variables, add aliases, and so on. The various shells read different files.

Customizing the *csh* Shell

When you start a **csh** shell, it reads a system file in the */etc* directory and the *.cshrc* file in your home directory. If you make additions to the end of the *.cshrc* file, you can customize how the **csh** behaves.

➜ 1. Use the editor and make additions to the *.cshrc* file, such as:

> set *prompt*='! % '
> alias cp 'cp -i'
> set *history*=200
> set *noclobber*
> set *ignoreeof*

Whenever you start a new **csh** shell, it reads the *.cshrc* file.

2. Start a child **csh** and examine its variables.

Customizing the *tcsh* Shell

If a *.tcshrc* file exists, the **tcsh** shell reads it. Otherwise, it reads the *.cshrc* file. You could include lines such as the following at the end of a *.tcshrc* file or add them to the *.cshrc* file if there is no *.tcshrc* file.

➜ Use the editor to access the *.tcshrc* file and make additions to the end of the file that include all lines just listed for the *.cshrc* and the following:

> set *prompt*='! %c %% '
> set *filec*

The other variables, aliases, and history settings suggested for the *.cshrc* file can be included here as well.

When you next start a **tcsh** shell, these customizations should be in effect.

Customizing the *bash* Shell

The **bash** shell reads the file *.bashrc* whenever it starts.

⤷ With the editor, create or make additions to the *.bashrc* file:

set -o *vi*
set -o *ignoreeof*
set -o *noclobber*
PS1='\! \t \W \! *bash$* **'**
PS2='-2-$ **'**

When you next start a **bash** shell, these settings should be in place.

Customizing the *ksh* Shell

Usually, systems are set up so that the **ksh** reads the *.kshrc* whenever it is started.

⤷ 1. Use the editor to modify or create the *.kshrc* file and to add lines such as the ones listed earlier for the *.bashrc* file.

In a Linux **ksh**, add:

   set -o *vi-tabcomplete*

Older Korn shells do not have this feature.

2. Start a new **ksh** shell and examine the settings:

   set -o

The settings you listed in the *.kshrc* file should be in effect. If the **ksh** shell does not read the *.kshrc* file, an environmental variable is not set. Do the following:

3. Add the following line to the end of the file *.login* in your home directory:

   setenv *ENV* ~*/.kshrc*

4. Add the next line to the *.profile* file:

   export *ENV=~/.kshrc*

5. Log out and when you return, the Korn shell should behave properly.

The **ksh** shell is programmed to read at startup whatever file is the value of the *ENV* variable. The lines you just added make certain that all shells carry the environmental variable *ENV* as equal to *~/.kshrc*, so whenever you start a **ksh**, it inherits the needed variable and value.

Self Test 2

1. What does the following tell the shell to do?

   wc -l *file[237ACks]*

   _____

2. How do you create a local variable named *tuesday* with the value *8-5* in the C shell? In the Korn shell?

   _____

3. How do you create an environmental variable called *OCT* with the value *NOT PAID* in the C shell? In the Korn shell?

   _____

4. You have a global variable **LEVEL** in the Korn shell with value *one*, and you start a child Korn shell. In the child shell, you enter the command **LEVEL**=*two*. You now start another child (grandchild) shell. What is the value of **LEVEL** now?

   _____

5. How do you enable filename completion in the Korn shell?

   _____

6. You want to find all records containing the string *friend* in some files. You know that the file names begin with *monica*, followed by some character, followed by one number (*0, 1, 2,* or *3*), followed by one other number (*3, 4, 5, 6, 7,* or *8*), followed by more characters. What is the shortest command to find the records?

   _____

7. What does the following accomplish:

   set prompt='! %c %% '

   _____

8. How do we tell the **bash** and **ksh** shells to set the primary prompt?

   _____

9. What do the following accomplish?

   A. **unset** *AA*

   B. **env**

   C. **export**

   D. **echo** *$PATH*

   _____

Chapter Review

Use this section to review the content of this chapter and test yourself on your knowledge of the concepts.

Chapter Summary

- The various shells all accomplish the primary task of interpreting the commands we issue. Each shell speaks a slightly different dialect and may include features that none or some of the other shells provide.
- The shell displays a prompt. After we issue a command line, the shell must first determine whether it concludes with an ENTER key indicating that it is a complete command line. If the line is complete, the line is processed; if not, the shell issues a secondary prompt and waits for additional input.
- Tokens on the command line that must be utilities are identified. The appropriate number of child processes is started, each inheriting the shell's input, output, and error destinations, as well as environmental variables.
- Redirecting input and output from the default (workstation) destination to files and other utilities is one of the functions of the shell. The input, output, and error are initially connected to your workstation and remain there unless you instruct the shell to redirect one or more of them to another utility or to a file.
- Arguments listed in the command line are passed to the appropriate processes.
- With all plumbing completed, the shell locates each utility's code by checking directories in the search path, then instructs each process to execute the appropriate code. Once the child processes are executing the correct code, the shell enters a wait state until all child processes terminate; then it displays another prompt.
- The shell expands command lines in several ways:
  - The **$** indicates that a variable name follows. The shell replaces the dollar sign and variable name with the value of the variable.
  - The shell matches strings with names of files. The shell interprets * as instruction to match filenames, with * matching zero or more of any character, and ? matching any one character.
  - A command line inside back quotes is interpreted and executed as a complete command line, and its output is used to replace the back-quoted command on the original command line.

- Characters inside brackets, [ ], are a list of alternates acceptable for one character position in the matching filename.
- We can create, use, and remove local variables within a shell. Local variables are not passed to child processes. Environmental variables are passed to child processes.
- We can modify the prompt and path, set variables, define aliases, and tailor the functioning of the shell both from the command line and by including instructions in a shell startup file.
- The most recent shells include file completion, which allows us to type part of a file, directory, or utility name; then, when we press TAB or ESC, the shell matches and completes the name.
- Each shell reads a control file as it is initially executed. We can place instructions in the startup files to tailor how the shell functions.

Assignment

1. What command instructs the shell to pass all filenames such as *assign1*, *assignment2*, *assign17*, and so forth as arguments to the **lpr** utility to have them all printed?
2. What must be each token of the following command line?

   _____ _____ < _____ && _____ | _____ `_____` > _____ ; _____

3. If *noclobber* is set on and a user enters the following command, what will the error message be, and why would it be that message rather than one concerning the command? Assume the file *users_on* exists and the utility **datxxx** does not exist.

   datxxx -a *users_on* **>** *users_on*

4. What option do we include when starting a child shell to instruct the shell to output the command line after interpretation and before execution so we can see how it interpreted our instructions?
5. Assume *noclobber* is set on and the files *users_on* and *junk1* both exist. If we issue the following command, does *junk1* get overwritten? Why or why not?

   cp *users_on junk1*

6. What do the following accomplish:

   A. CTRL-Z

   B. **fg**

   C. **wc** *[0-9]

   D. **grep** 'spencer brucker' staff

   E. **export** AAA='Dick McKinney'

   F. **grep** linux * > glmatch **2>** glerr

7. Assume a person enters the following command:

   wc -z *

   The error message indicates there is no **-z** option to **wc**. The user then issues the command:

   echo $?

   (or on older C shells: **echo $status.**)

   What results and why?

8. What are the contents of the variables *PATH* and *path*, and how do the shells use that information?

9. How do you change the prompt for your shell so that every time you start a shell of this type it has your specified prompt?

Project

   A. Read through the **man** pages for the shell you use most of the time. Identify at least two features that were not discussed in this chapter, try them out, and explain how they work.

   B. Issue the following command line:

   sort | **tr -d** 1234 | **sed** s/os/Linux/ | **cut -f1**

   C. Enter a few lines of text that include the string *os* somewhere in the line.

   D. Suspend the process.

   E. Create a file consisting of the output from **ps -l** and **jobs**.

F. Explain why there are several processes and only one job associated with the **sort** command line, and explain why the **PPID**s of the four processes are the same.

G. Bring the job back into the foreground and terminate it.

H. Add to the file *proj-shell* a list of the commands you issued in this project and what each accomplishes.

I. Print out the file *proj-shell* and draw a diagram that shows how many child processes the shell started and what plumbing (argument passing, output redirecting) the shell accomplished for the **sort-tr-sed-cut** command line.

COMMAND SUMMARY

INPUT, OUTPUT, AND ERROR REDIRECTION CHARACTERS	
|	Redirects output from prior utility to next utility.
<	Opens file on the right of symbol and connects it to the input of the utility on the left.
>	Redirects output of the utility on the left into the file named on the right.
>>	Appends output from the utility on the left to the file on the right.
>!	Redirects output of the utility on the left into the file on the right; overrides the **noclobber** feature (C shell).
>|	Redirects output of the utility on the left into the file on the right; overrides the **noclobber** feature (Korn shell).
>&	Redirects the combination of output and error of the previous utility to the file on the right (C shell).
2>	Redirects the error of the previous utility to the file on the right (Korn shell).
2>&1	Redirects the combination of output and error from previous utility to the file on the right (Korn shell).
COMMAND-LINE CONTROL CHARACTERS	
;	Command separator. Executes each pipeline separated by ; as a separate command, although the pipelines are on the same command line.
&	Causes the command to be run in the background.
&&	Executes the pipeline on the right when the pipeline on the left executes successfully.
||	Executes the pipeline on the right when the pipeline on the left does not execute successfully.

` command ` or $(command)	Denotes the beginning and end of the command to be run and replaced by its result prior to the execution of other elements on the command line.
INTERPRETATION CONTROLLING CHARACTERS	
" "	Turns off (and on) shell interpretation of most special characters.
\	Turns off interpretation of the next single character.
' '	Turns off and on interpretation of essentially all special characters.
FILENAME-MATCHING CHARACTERS	
*	Expands to match any number of any character (except . as first character in a filename) to be matched.
?	Expands to match any one character.
[ ]	Defines the list of characters from which one is to be selected for matching.
C SHELL VARIABLE COMMANDS	
set **variable=value**	Initializes or changes the value of a local variable to *value.*
setenv **variable value**	Initializes or changes the value of an environmental variable to *value.*
set	Displays all local variables and their values.
printenv **variable**	Displays environmental variable and its value.
printenv	Displays all environmental variables and their values.
env	Displays all environmental variables and their values.
unset **variable**	Removes a local variable.
unsetenv variable	Removes an environmental variable.

IN THE BOURNE AND KORN SHELLS	
variable=value	Initializes or changes the value of *variable*.
export **variable**	Makes *variable* environmental.
set	Displays all local variables and their values.
printenv	Displays all environmental variables and their values.
env	Displays all environmental variables and their values.
unset **variable**	Removes *variable* whether it is local or environmental).
INITIALIZING SHELL OPERATIONAL VARIABLES	
set filec	Turns on filename completion (C shell).
set -o **vi-tabcomplete**	Instructs the **ksh** shell to complete filenames when user presses TAB.
set **noclobber**	Prevents overwriting of files with redirection (C shell).
set -o **noclobber**	Prevents overwriting of files with redirection (Korn and **bash** shells).
set -o	Instructs the shell to list the current values of shell operational variables.
JOB-CONTROL COMMANDS	
CTRL-Z	Suspends the currently running foreground job.
fg	Brings the last suspended or backgrounded job to the foreground.
bg	Places the suspended job in the background (and will resume running there).
ps	Lists current processes.

Setting and Using Permissions

9

S K I L L S   C H E C K

Before beginning this chapter, you should be able to:

- Create and display files
- Name, copy, and remove files
- Execute basic shell commands
- Redirect input and output
- Access and modify files using an editor
- Use the UNIX directory filesystem
- Create basic shell scripts

O B J E C T I V E S

After completing this chapter, you will be able to:

- Determine the permissions that various kinds of users are granted for files
- Change permissions for files and directories using both numerical and letter specifications
- Specify how permissions limit access to a file
- Specify how permissions limit access to directories
- Change how the system assigns default permissions for new files and directories
- Modify permissions for whole directory trees
- Assign permissions appropriately to achieve security goals

Contemporary UNIX/Linux systems manage files that can vary greatly in their importance—from state secrets to casual notes. To maintain appropriate security, files on each system are given different levels of protection. For instance, if a file contains plans for a new product, then only a few users should have access to read the file. Its availability must be restricted. In contrast, a memo intended for everyone must be accessible to all employees.

UNIX/Linux systems routinely store information in files. They run programs that are in files. How system programs behave is usually prescribed in a control file. Whether or not a user has access to a file is determined by a *set of permissions* for the file. Even workstation terminal displays and other hardware are managed and have permissions as though they were files. By changing a file's permissions, the owner of a file determines which users can read, modify, delete, or execute the file. Fundamental UNIX security for users and for the system is the result of carefully prescribing which users have access to each file and directory. Access is determined by the permissions assigned and the subsequent effect of each permission setting. This chapter investigates how to modify file permissions and explores how these permission settings permit and deny access.

9.1 Describing File Permissions

A person working on a UNIX or Linux system issues commands, enters data, writes programs, changes directories, and obtains information. All these activities are accomplished by accessing files that are utilized in three ways:

- When we examine the contents of a file with utilities such as **more**, **cat**, and **vi**, we *read* the file's contents. The file is not changed, only read. When we use **ls** to list the contents of a directory, we are reading the directory.
- When we have completed editing a file using **vi** and we type **:w**, we *write* the file, making changes. When we enter **who >>** *file*, we add the output of **who** to the file; we write to it. When we add a file to a directory or change a filename, we are writing in the directory.
- When we enter the name of a shell script, we start or *execute* a new child process that reads the command file (shell script) and then runs whatever commands are in it. As you will soon demonstrate, we need execute permission on a directory to change directories to the directory.

The three permissions, read, write, and execute, govern what we can do to files and directories. If a user owns a file, that user may either allow or deny any of the three permissions: read, write, or execute. The owner can modify the permissions on a file for the three classes of users: the owner or *user,* other members of the owner's *group,* and all *other* users (people not in your group).

The first portions of this chapter examine using letters (mnemonics) to modify the permissions for the three classes of users. We then take an in-depth look at using numbers to specify the permissions. The next sections investigate the effects of file and directory permissions on user activities. We then examine how files and directories are assigned their initial permissions. The last section guides you through modifying permissions for all files in a whole directory tree.

Examining the Permissions Field

A great deal of information is packed into the permissions field.

⤷ 1. Reexamine the permissions for all the regular files in your home directory by entering:

> **ls -l ~**

In the permissions field, there are 10 slots for each file. For example:

```
-rwxr-x--x
```

Every slot is occupied either by a dash or by a letter. If the first slot is a -, then the object is a file. If it is a **d**, then the object is a directory. In the last nine slots, a minus sign indicates that the particular permission is denied. If a letter appears in the slot, it indicates that a permission is allowed. The letters you see will usually be *r, w,* or *x,* and for some files you might also see *b, c, l, p, s, S, t,* or *T.*

2. For example, enter:

> **ls -ld /*tmp*

The result is usually:

```
-rwxrwxrwt   /tmp
```

The *t* in the */tmp* directory permissions is a special permission called the *sticky bit,* which requires that a person own a file before being permitted to remove it. How to use permissions other than **r w x** is beyond the scope of this book and is examined in system administration texts.

Directory Permissions

The first slot indicates whether the listing is for a directory, a plain file, or a special UNIX file.

⮡ 1. Again display the permissions for the files listed in your home directory:

ls -l ~

The first character in the permissions field for the file *users_on* is a minus sign, indicating that *users_on* is a regular file. The file *Projects* is a directory, as indicated by the **d** in the first character location.

In addition to including the **d**, this location may also hold a **b**, **c**, **p**, or **l** for some system files. These characters indicate the special nature of the file.

2. For example, enter:

ls -l /dev | more

Note that there is a *c* or *b* at the beginning of many permissions fields, which indicates whether the **dev**ice processes data in units of single **c**haracters or whole **b**locks of data.

File Permissions

The remainder of the permissions field is divided into three sets of three slots each. Depending on how your account is set up, the permissions for *practice* could look like this:

    -rw-r--r--

Following the first dash, there are three sets of three permissions. The first set, *rw-*, determines what you as owner (user) of the file can do with the file. The middle three positions, *r--*, determine the read, write, and execute permissions for users who are members of the same group as the owner. This is done so that people working on the same project can have access to the same files and resources. The last set of three permission slots determines the permissions for users who are not in the owner's group (often called *else* or *others*).

- In this example, the first of these three slots (often called permission bits) contains an **r**, indicating that the owner has read permission and can view the contents of the file. If a minus sign were here, it would indicate that read permission is denied.
- The second slot (bit) contains a **w**, indicating that the owner has write permission and can alter the contents of the file.

- In similar fashion, the third slot indicates whether a child shell can be started to execute the commands in the file. If an **x** were present, it would mean that the owner has execute permission. The dash indicates that the owner does not.
- In this example, the members of the owner's group as well as all other users are granted read permission only.

File Permissions for Group and Other

When you create a file of any kind, you are the owner of that file. As owner, you have the power to set permissions for three kinds of users: yourself (*user* or owner), for the rest of the users who are in the same *group* as you, and for any *other* users who have access to the system (that is, users not in your group).

⤵ Again, display the permissions for the files in your current directory by entering the following command:

ls -l

In the long listing output that appears, the name of the owner and group are the third and fourth fields. (If the group name is not displayed, try **ls -lg**.)

For example, consider the following permissions field:

```
-rwxr-xr--
```

The first slot contains a dash, therefore the object is a regular file. The first three permission bits are filled with **rwx**, so the user (owner) has <u>r</u>ead, <u>w</u>rite, and e<u>x</u>ecute permission for the file.

User	Group	Other
rwx	r-x	r--
The owner of the file	Users in the same group as the owner (rest of group)	Users *not* in the same group as the owner (else)

Other members of the same group as the owner have <u>r</u>ead and <u>e</u>xecute permission, but not <u>w</u>rite permission. They can execute a child process to run the commands in the file. Although they can see the contents the file, they cannot alter them.

All other users have permission to <u>r</u>ead, but not to <u>w</u>rite or e<u>x</u>ecute. Every file has an associated permissions field for user, group, and all others on the system.

Consider the following permissions, and then fill in the missing information.

Permission Field	TYPE	USER	GROUP	OTHER
drwxr-x---	directory	rwx	r-x	---
-rw-rw-r--				
-r-xr-----				

In summary, the three permissions fields have the following meaning:

- *Type*   The first slot or bit describes the file as directory, ordinary, and so on.
- *User*   Bits 2, 3, and 4 determine what the owner can do with the file.
- *Group* Bits 5, 6, and 7 determine what users who are in the owner's group can do with the file.
- *Other* Bits 8, 9, and 10 determine what users who are not the owner nor in the owner's group (other) can do with the file.

Employing Read and Write Permissions

1. Examine the permissions of an old file such as *practice* by entering:

   ls -l *practice*

   The permissions displayed for this file are probably:

   ```
   -rw-rw-rw-
   ```

   or

   ```
   -rw-r--r--
   ```

   The first **rw-** indicates that the current permissions attached to the *practice* file allow you, as owner, read and write permission, but not execute permission.

2. Start editing the file with the visual editor:

   vi *practice*

   You are able to <u>r</u>ead the file. Its contents are displayed on the screen.

3. Make a change in the file by opening a new line and adding text, such as:

   These are two new lines
   I am adding to the file practice in this permissions chapter.

4. Write the file and quit the editor with the **:wq** command.

You are able to make the changes to the file because you have **w**rite permission. To access the contents of a file, you must have **r**ead permission for that file. To make changes or modify a file, you need **w**rite permission for the file.

Changing Permissions for a File to Read Only

As you saw earlier when touring the system, you can restrict access to a file. For example, you (as owner) might want to permit yourself to read a letter but not to change it in any way. To prohibit changes, you remove the *write* permissions for that file.

1. Change the permissions, removing the write permission on the file *practice* by typing:

   chmod -w *practice*

2. Obtain a listing of the new permissions, with:

   ls -l *practice*

   This command line instructs the shell as follows:

chmod	Execute utility that **ch**anges the **mod**e or permission
-w	Remove **w**rite (minus **w**rite)
practice	From the file *practice*

Because you did not specify whether you wanted to modify the user, group, or other, it is removed from all three. The **chmod -w** command is described in the following illustration.

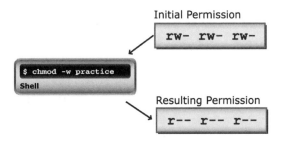

3. Use **vi** to call up the *practice* file again. You can access a file with **vi** because you have read permission.

4. Delete a line.

5. Attempt to write the file with the usual **:wq** command. The resulting error message is something like:

```
File is read only
```

or

```
Permission denied
```

You cannot write the buffer copy of the file that you have modified back to the original file, because you do not have write permission. You still have read permission, so you are able to read the file; but without write, you cannot alter the file's contents.

To return to the shell, you could quit the editor without writing, or write the changed buffer copy to a new file. On many systems, **:w!** forces a write. Because you are the owner of the file, you could change the permissions of the file to permit writing, so the system allows you to insist on writing with the **:w!** command.

6. Quit without attempting to write by typing the editor command:

   :q!

Changing Permissions for a File to Write Only

With one command, you can change the permissions for the *practice* file to add write permission and deny read.

1. Modify the permissions on *practice* by entering:

   chmod -r+w *practice*

2. Examine the permissions on *practice*:

   ls -l *practice*

   The argument **-r** removes <u>r</u>ead from all users. The **+w** adds <u>w</u>rite to your permissions, and depending on how the system is set up, possibly will add this permission to group or other. As you will see near the end of this chapter, the limits established for permissions when files are created also affect permissions granted when we use **+w** and similar instructions.

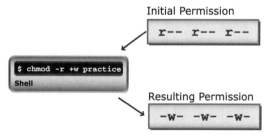

3. Attempt to read the file:

    cat *practice*

    The shell responds with an error message:

    ```
    practice:  Permission denied
    ```

    This error message indicates you do not have read permission on the file; hence, you cannot read its contents.

    However, you still have write permission for the file. It is possible to write to a file, even if you cannot read it. In dealing with sensitive data, organizations often have files that contain data such as a suggestion box or field reports. Users should be able to add information, but not be able to read other people's entries. Usually a script collects the information and writes to the file. No one except the owner is permitted to read it.

4. You can instruct the shell to connect the output of a utility to the end of an existing file. Type:

    date >> *practice*

    This command specifies the output of **date** to be appended to the *practice* file. Because you have write permission for the file, you can add text.

5. Attempt to determine whether the addition was made to the file. Enter:

    more *practice*

    You are not allowed to examine the file, because you do not have read permission for the file. You can add to it; you just can't see what you did.

Adding Read Permission to a File

In the previous exercise, you limited the permission to only write for the file *practice.*

1. Reset the permissions for *practice* to allow reading. Enter:

    chmod +r *practice*
    ls -l *practice*

2. Use **more** to confirm that you are able to read the file.

    The output of **date** is the last line. It was added when you had only write permission for the file.

9.2 Using Execute Permissions with a File

As you saw in Chapters 3 and 6, shell commands can be placed in a file and run all at once. This technique of creating command files, or *shell scripts,* can make work more efficient and reduce errors.

Creating a File of Shell Commands

Shell scripts are created just like any other file, usually with an editor.

1. Ensure that you are in your home directory:

   cd

2. Create a new file named *inform* by entering:

   vi *inform*

3. Place the following lines in the *inform* file:

   ```
   date
   pwd
   echo   You   have   the   following   processes
   ps
   echo   the   process   reading   this   script   has   a   PID   of   $$
   ```

4. Write the file and return to the shell:

   :wq

Telling the Shell to Read a Script

When we enter a command at the shell prompt, the shell interprets the line we enter, executes it, and gives us another prompt. Then we enter another command. At this point, several commands are in the *inform* file. We can instruct the shell to read the file and execute each of the commands it contains.

1. Enter at the (C shell):

   source *inform*

   or (Korn and Bourne shells use the dot as the source command):

   . *inform*

2. The result is that the current shell runs each of the commands in the file as though you just typed them.

3. At the shell prompt, request that your current shell inform you of its process ID (PID):

   echo $$

The **PID** of your current shell is the same **PID** that was reported by the $ $ line in the *inform* script when you executed it. Your current shell executes the commands in the *inform* script when you **source** it.

Running a Script by Entering Its Name

To run a shell script like any other UNIX command, we type its name and press ENTER.

 1. From the shell, type:

>   *inform*

> **N O T E :** If you get an error message that says:
> `command not found`
> it means your path does not include searching for programs in the current directory. Add the current directory to the path (see Chapter 8) or enter the following command to tell the shell that the script is in the current directory:
> **./** *inform*.

2. Either way, when you enter *inform* or *./inform*, you receive an error message such as:

`inform:   execute permission denied.`

Although the file contains valid shell commands, the shell does not execute them, because you do not have execute permission on the file.

3. Examine the permissions of *inform* by entering:

>   **ls -l** *inform*

You have read and write permission only; clearly, that is not enough. Once we write a file full of commands, we cannot execute it by calling its name unless we have execute permission on the file. But we can execute the contents of a script by using the **source** command if we have only read permission. The next few exercises examine what *execute* really means.

Changing Permissions to Make a File Executable

The error message you received in the preceding exercise lets you know that the shell attempted to execute a child shell to run the commands in the file *inform*. When the shell found out that you did not have execute permission, it displayed the error message. This is only a plain, ordinary, nonexecutable file. You need to change the permissions for *inform* to include execute to be able to run the script by calling its name.

1. To make *inform* executable, type:

   chmod +x *inform*

   The **+x** option instructs **chmod** to grant execute permission for the file.

2. Examine the permissions now:

   ls -l *inform*

   There is an *x* in the user permissions field, indicating that it is executable by you. Likewise, execute permission is granted to group and other.

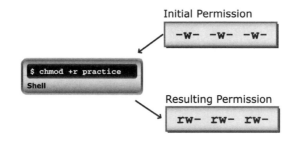

3. Execute the *inform* shell script by typing:

   inform

   or

   ./inform

   You are treated to the display of the current date and time, the path to your current directory, your current processes, and the PID of the shell that is executing the script. All the shell commands that you wrote in the *inform* file are run. The PID of the shell that ran the script this time is not that of your current shell. It has a different PID.

4. Look at the output of **ps** when the script runs. An additional shell (probably an **sh** or **bash**) is included, and its PID matches the one that ran the script.

   When we run a script by entering its name, the current shell starts a child shell that reads the script file and runs the listed commands. In contrast, when we **source** a script, the current shell reads the script file and executes whatever commands are in it. When we source a script, the current shell has to have permission to read the file. When we run a script by entering its name, we need execute permission, and a child shell is started. That is what execute permission governs with respect to files: whether or not we can start a child shell. Read permission is sufficient when sourcing a script because the current shell needs to read it. Because no child shell is started, **x** is not needed. To start a child shell to run a script, the user must have execute permission.

However, when you just executed the script by entering its name, the permissions were **rwx** for you the owner. We have not determined whether execute alone is sufficient.

5. Remove all but execute permission by entering:

> **chmod -rw** *inform*
>
> **ls -l** *inform*

6. Attempt to execute the script:

> *inform*

or

> *./inform*

Permission is denied. Even though you have execute permission for the file, it is not enough. You cannot run the script by entering its name. To issue the script's name is to request a child shell. Although we can start a child shell when we have execute permission, the child shell must read the file to obtain our instructions; hence, we must have read as well as execute permission. To be able to run a script in a child process, the user must have both execute and read permissions—execute to start a child process, and read so the child shell can read the instructions contained in the file.

Determining Who Can Modify Permissions

Throughout these chapters, you have changed the permissions of *practice* and other files. For system security reasons, you can affect only the files you own.

1. Determine who you are by entering the following commands:

> **whoami**

or

> **who am i**

or

> **id**

The output includes your login name.

> **N O T E :** If you are *root*, exit and log back on as an ordinary user; then continue. Doing the following exercise as *root* could damage your system.

2. Determine the current permissions of the file *date* located in the */bin* directory by entering:

   ls -l */bin/date*

   The output shows that although everyone can execute the **date** utility, you are not the owner of the */bin/date* file; **root** is the owner.

3. Attempt to modify the permissions on the system file by entering:

   chmod +w */bin/date*

   An error message indicates that you are not the owner of the file.

4. Enter:

   ls -l */bin/date*

   The permissions are not changed.

Only the owner of a file or directory can modify the permissions that are attached to it. When we own a file, we can modify the permissions that determine what we can do with the file, what the rest of our group can do, and what everyone else is permitted to do with it. If we deny ourselves a specific permission, all is not lost. We can change it.

9.3 Changing File Permissions Using Mnemonics

There are two ways to change the mode or permissions for files using the **chmod** command. One method employs letter arguments for the permissions, such as **-w, +x,** and **-r,** to add or remove permissions. You have already used this method several times. For instance, **chmod +r** *practice* adds read to the existing permissions, and **chmod -r +w** *practice* removes read while adding write to a file.

The mnemonic assignment method allows us to set permissions for each type of user in several ways. The other method that uses numerical arguments will be examined in the next section.

Assigning Specific Permissions

1. Create a test file with:

   date > *permtest*

2. Check the current permissions with:

   ls -l *permtest*

Assigning Permissions to All Users

1. Assign full permissions for the file to all three classes of users:

   chmod a=rwx *permtest*

2. Check the new permissions with:

   ls -l *permtest*

   The command is interpreted as instruction to assign permissions for <u>a</u>ll three permission sets (user, group, and other) and to make them to equal to **rwx**. The **=** is employed as the setting operator, so the assigned permissions are equal to whatever is to the right of the equal sign.

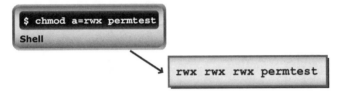

3. Modify all permissions again with:

   chmod a=r *permtest*
   ls -l *permtest*

   Using <u>a</u> specifies that <u>a</u>ll three types of user permissions are set to just <u>r</u>ead.

Assigning Permissions to One Type of User

This approach also permits assignment of permissions to each class: <u>u</u>ser, <u>g</u>roup, or <u>o</u>ther.

1. Try the following:

   chmod ug=rw,o=r *permtest*
   ls -l *permtest*

   The classes <u>u</u>ser and <u>g</u>roup are assigned permissions equal to <u>r</u>ead and <u>w</u>rite, while <u>o</u>ther users are assigned <u>r</u>ead only. A comma separates instructions, and no spaces can be included because it must be one argument.

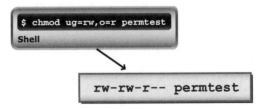

2. Specify each assignment with:

chmod u=rwx,g=rx,o=r *permtest*
ls -l *permtest*

3. Assign the following permissions:

chmod a=rwx *permtest*
ls -l

Denying All Permissions

There are two ways to instruct **chmod** to assign no permissions to a type of user.

1. Enter:

chmod u=rwx,go= *permtest*
ls -l *permtest*

When permissions for a type of user are set to nothing, such as **go=**, no permissions are granted; in this case, both **g**roup and **o**ther are not assigned any permissions, which is indicated by the **---** in the permissions field.

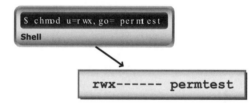

2. Assign full permissions with:

chmod a=rwx *permtest*
ls -l *permtest*

3. Now assign read to **g**roup and deny **o**ther users all permissions by employing the second method:

chmod g=r,o= *-permtest*
ls -l

Group is given read permission, and other has all permissions removed. User is not given any new assignment, so it retains whatever permissions it had before the **chmod** command. We can assign no permissions by including nothing after the equal sign or by using a dash.

4. Explore a little further with:

chmod ug=rwx,o=r *permtest*
ls -l *permtest*

The <u>u</u>ser and <u>g</u>roup permissions are assigned **rwx**, and <u>o</u>ther is assigned <u>r</u>ead.

5. Now try:

> **chmod g=o** *permtest*
> **ls -l** *permtest*

The **group** permission is assigned the permissions currently given to the <u>o</u>ther. Permissions for one type of user can be assigned to another.

6. Enter:

> **chmod u=r,o=** *-permtest*
> **ls -l** *permtest*

User is assigned <u>r</u>ead, and all permissions are removed from <u>o</u>ther. No new assignment is given to **group**, so it retains its current permissions.

Adding and Deleting Permissions

In the previous exercises, you assigned specific new permissions to the *permtest* file that took effect regardless of the current permissions. You can also add or subtract a permission without affecting the remainder of the current permissions.

1. Enter these commands:

> **chmod a=rwx** *permtest*
> **ls -l** *permtest*
> **chmod -x** *permtest*
> **ls -l** *permtest*

2. The **x** permission is removed from all three permission sets. The minus operator is instruction to remove whatever permissions are listed to its right.

3. Modify just one class of permissions:

> **chmod g-w** *permtest*
> **ls -l** *permtest*

The <u>w</u>rite permission is removed from **group**.

4. Enter:

> **chmod u-w,o-r** *permtest*
> **ls -l** *permtest*

In this example, **u-w,o-r** is instruction to **chmod** to remove **w** from <u>u</u>ser and to remove **r** from <u>o</u>ther.

5. Enter:

> **chmod u+wx** *permtest*
> **ls -l** *permtest*

The argument **u+wx** is instruction to add **w** and **x** to <u>u</u>ser.

6. Enter:

> **chmod u-x,o+r** *permtest*
> **ls -l** *permtest*

The **u-x,o+r** tells **chmod** to remove **x** from <u>u</u>ser and add **r** to <u>o</u>ther users.

Permissions can be assigned to <u>u</u>ser, <u>g</u>roup, and <u>o</u>ther, or specific permissions can be added and subtracted from whatever the current permissions happen to be.

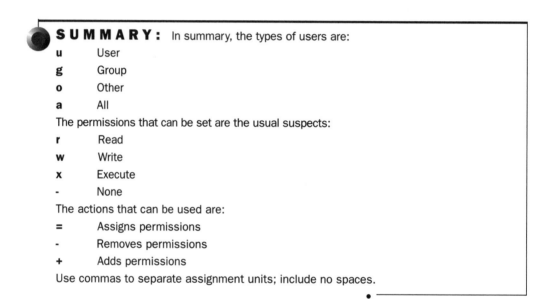

SUMMARY: In summary, the types of users are:

u	User
g	Group
o	Other
a	All

The permissions that can be set are the usual suspects:

r	Read
w	Write
x	Execute
-	None

The actions that can be used are:

=	Assigns permissions
-	Removes permissions
+	Adds permissions

Use commas to separate assignment units; include no spaces.

9.4 Changing File Permissions Numerically

To specify permissions for all three types of users, the other essential method employs numbers that convey the permission information. Once you have mastered the basics, this is the more easily used alternative and is essential for more advanced topics.

1. Examine the permissions of the *inform* file by typing:

> **ls -l** *inform*

2. Type the following:

> **chmod 700** *inform*

3. Examine the permissions now granted by displaying a long listing for the file:

ls **-l** *inform*

The output lists the permissions as:

```
-rwx------
```

This set of permissions indicates the user has full _r_ead, _w_rite, and e_x_ecute permission for the file. The group and other users have no access.

Examining Numerical Permissions for Read, Write, and Execute

We saw that **700** specifies **rwx** for the owner of a file. Other numbers specify all other combinations of permissions.

1. Enter the following:

chmod **400** *inform*
ls **-l** *inform*

Only an **r** is present in the owner's permissions field. The **400** grants _r_ead only to the owner.

2. Change the permission again and examine the results by entering the following commands:

chmod **200** *inform*
ls **-l** *inform*

Only write permission is granted to the owner when the argument to **chmod** is **200**.

3. Now assign only execute permission by entering:

chmod **100** *inform*
ls **-l** *inform*

4. Deny all permissions by entering:

chmod **000** *inform*
ls **-l** *inform*

The basic number permissions you just used are as follows:

Number	Permission
4	read
2	write
1	execute
0	deny all

Using the numerical approach (as in **chmod** *700*) to modify the permissions for a file allows us to specify numerically the exact permissions we want to grant, regardless of the current permissions. The number *700* grants **rwx** to owner and nothing to group and other, no matter what the permissions were before.

Assigning Combinations of Permissions

Users seldom grant only one of the three permissions to a file. Often a combination, such as read and write, is specified.

➥ 1. Change the permissions for *inform* by entering:

   chmod *600* *inform*

2. Examine the resulting permissions:

   ls -l *inform*

   The owner has read and write permissions.

   Combination permissions are specified using the sum of the values for the specific permissions.

Permission		Number
read	=	4
write	=	2
read and write	=	6, which is (4 + 2)

3. Try the following:

   chmod *754* *inform*

   The result is:

   ```
   rwxr-xr--
   ```

   The number *7* sets the permissions for owner to be **rwx**. The number *5* sets the permissions for group to be **r-x**. The number *4* sets the permissions for other to be **r--**.

   This result confirms what we saw previously. Look at the user and group fields. The *7* produced **rwx**, while the *5* produced **r-x**. The numerical difference between *7* and *5* is *2*. The difference in the permissions between *7* and *5* that results is write, which we know is *2*.

   Look at the permissions for other. Clearly, *4* is read. The difference between group (*5*, **r-x**) and other (*4*, **r--**) is *1*, which must be the missing permission, execute.

The numbers *0*, *1*, *2*, and *4* are assigned permission values as follows:

Number	Permission
0	Assigns no permissions
1	Allows execute permission
2	Allows write permission
4	Allows read permission

Identifying All Possible Combinations of Permissions

In the following list, the numbers *1*, *2*, and *4* are used in combinations that add up to produce *3*, *5*, *6*, and *7*. Each of the combinations of the three numbers *1*, *2*, and *4* adds together to produce a number that no other combination yields. All possible numbers from *0* to *7* are uniquely specified.

This set of unique numbers is used with **chmod** to establish the permissions for files and directories.

The primitives (*0*, *1*, *2*, and *4*) can be added together to grant any combination of permissions. The basic permissions for a file are as follows:

Number	Permission
0	Grants no permissions
1	Grants execute permission only
2	Grants write permission only
3	Grants write and execute permission (2+1)
4	Grants read permission only
5	Grants read and execute permission (4+1)
6	Grants read and write permission (4+2)
7	Grants read and write and execute permission (4+2+1)

Thus, combinations of the three numbers *1*, *2*, and *4* can be used to express the eight possible combinations of execute, write, and read permissions.

Each number *0* through *7* translates into a unique set of permissions.

➥ Try each of the following:

chmod *700 inform*
ls -l *inform*
chmod *600 inform*

ls -l *inform*
chmod *500 inform*
ls -l *inform*
chmod *300 inform*
ls -l *inform*
chmod *400 inform*
ls -l *inform*
chmod *700 inform*
ls -l *inform*

4r	2w	1x	chmod value	Resulting Permissions
-	-	-	0	---
-	-	1	1	--x
-	2	-	2	-w-
-	2	1	3	-wx
4	-	-	4	r--
4	-	1	5	r-x
4	2	-	6	rw-
4	2	1	7	rwx

Turning Switches On and Off

Permission bits are either on or off. It is a standard computer operation. The very basis of computer science is the on/off switch. If there is just one switch, only two values are possible: on and off. We can view *on* as having the value *1* and *off* as *0*.

If we have two switches, more values are possible.

If we consider the first switch to represent the value *1* when it is on and the second switch to represent the value *2* when it is on, then the following is possible:

Switch 2	Switch 1	Value
Off	Off	0
Off	On	1
On	Off	2

And if both are on, *2 + 1 = 3*.

Switch 2	Switch 1	Value
On	On	3

Likewise, if there are three switches, the values from *0* to *7* are possible:
We assign a permission to each switch. Because we assign *4* to mean r̲ead, *2* to mean w̲rite, and *1* to be ex̲ecute, then the table looks like this:

4 read	2 write	1 execute	chmod value	Resulting Permissions
Off	Off	Off	0	---
Off	Off	On	1	--x
Off	On	Off	2	-w-
Off	On	On	3	-wx
On	Off	Off	4	r--
On	Off	On	5	r-x
On	On	Off	6	rw-
On	On	On	7	rwx

9.5 Changing Permissions for Group and Other

The numeric values used to set file permissions can be used to specify permissions for any of the three sets (user, group, and other) in the permissions field.

1. Enter the following command to add full permissions for your group only:
   chmod *070 inform*
2. Check the permissions for *inform.* Type:
   ls -l *inform*
   The group permissions include read, write, and execute permission for the group (*7*). Users and others are denied all access (*0*).
3. Type the following command, which grants full permissions to everyone:
   chmod *777 inform*
   ls -l *inform*
   The permissions now show r̲ead, w̲rite, and ex̲ecute for user, group, and all other users.
4. Enter the first **chmod** command that follows to modify the *inform* file's permissions. After the change, examine the results using the **ls -l** *inform* command. Then continue modifying and examining the results through the other **chmod** commands.
   chmod *640 inform*
   chmod *750 inform*

> **chmod** *744 inform*
> **chmod** *732 inform*

With three numbers of values *0* through *7*, such as *750*, you can specify which of three permissions, **r**, **w**, and **x**, are granted to three classes: user, group, and other.

Determining Which Permissions Apply

Permissions are usually most restrictive for other, less so for group, and least restrictive for the owner of a file. If they are not—if group actually has more permissions granted than owner—it raises some interesting questions.

➥ 1. Change the permissions for *inform* to be **rwx** for other, **r-x** for group, and grant no permissions to yourself, the owner.

> **chmod** *057 inform*
> **ls -l** *inform*

The permissions displayed are:

```
---r-xrwx
```

You, as owner, appear to have no granted permissions. But you are in your group. Are you granted your group's permissions?

2. Attempt to execute and read the script:

> *inform*
> **cat** *inform*

You have no access to the file.

The process of determining the impact of permissions for a file or directory begins with establishing whether you are the owner. If the answer is yes, you are granted the owner's permissions as determined in the first three permission bits. The question of what group you belong to—of what the group permissions are— is never raised; you pass the owner test and are given the owner permissions—period. The same thing happens with respect to members of your group. They fail the owner test, but then pass the group test. They get the group permissions. If other users attempt to access this file, they fail to be the owner, fail to be in the group, and are then assigned the "else," or other, permissions.

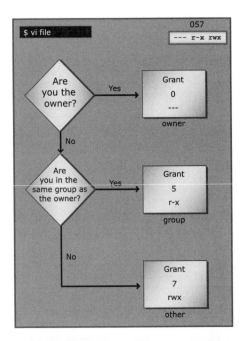

3. Change the permissions back so you can execute the script:
    chmod *754 inform*
4. Run it again:
    inform

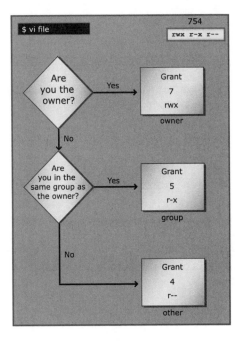

Self Test 1

1. What command outputs a long listing of your filenames in the current directory, including the permissions attached to each file?

   _____

2. What permissions are granted to each class of users for a file with the following permissions?

   r-x------

   _____

3. The file *practice* has no permissions at all. What permission should be assigned to this file so you (the owner) could add text to the end of the file?

   _____

4. Consider a file with the following permissions:

   rwxr-xr-- *scriptfile*

   Who can run each of the following? (Use **y** for yes or **n** for no.)

	USER	GROUP	OTHER
source *scriptfile*			
scriptfile			
echo date >> *scriptfile*			

5. Consider the following conditions:
   - You, the owner, can access the file with **vi** and write changes.
   - The file contains a series of shell commands such as **ls** and **who**. When you enter the file's name at the command line, the commands listed in the file are run.
   - Members of your group cannot make changes to the file, but when they issue the file's name to the shell, the commands in the file do run. Other users can use **cat** or **more** on the file, but when they issue the filename to the shell, the commands in the file do not run.

   What permissions must this file have?

   _____

6. What permission would you *deny* to group and other so they cannot execute or **source** a script?

   _____

7. How can you execute commands in the file *hi* without giving the file **x** permission?

_____

8. How do you identify which objects are directories in the output of **ls** with a long listing?

_____

9. You are in the same group as Sam, Tom, Bill, and so on. The permissions field on a file you own named *answer* is **----r-----**. Who can read the file?

_____

10. There are several commands in the script *inform.* What minimum permissions for the script are needed to run the commands by entering its name?

_____

11. What commands remove **r** permissions and add **x** permissions to the file *inform?*

_____

12. Assume that users *unx0l, unx02,* and *unx03* are in a group and *ora0l* and *ora02* are in another group. Suppose *unx02* has a script file named *inform* containing commands with a permission of **765**. Answer the following questions:
   A. Who can read the file *inform?*

   _____

   B. Who can execute the commands in the file *inform* by sourcing the file?

   _____

   C. Who can execute by entering *inform?*

   _____

   D. Who can change the contents of the file *inform?*

   _____

13. What would the resulting permissions be if the following command were executed?
   chmod u=rx,g=x,o= *inform*

   _____

14. The file *simple* has a permissions field of -rwxr--r--. What command removes **w** from the user and adds **x** to group and other?

   _____

15. In the following table, insert the appropriate **chmod** value or resulting permission.

chmod Value	Resulting Permission
700	rwx --- ---
	r-- --- ---
200	
	rw- --- ---
	--x --- ---
000	
500	

9.6 Exploring the Effect of Granting Different Permissions

In this exercise, you change the permissions on the *inform* file to all possible combinations and examine what you can do to the file as a function of the resulting change in permissions.

1. Change the permissions of *inform* to **rwx** for you, the owner:

    chmod *700 inform*

2. Now attempt to read the script:

    more *inform*

3. Try to add a new word to the bottom of the script file:

    echo *date >> inform*

4. Execute the script:

    inform

5. Have your current shell read and execute the commands in the script. Bourne and Korn shell users use the dot command; C shell users use **source**:

    . *inform*

or

    source *inform*

The **date** command is the last one run, the result of appending the word *date* to the end of the file in the previous step.

6. List the permissions of *inform*:

   ls -l *inform*

   All of these commands were successful with permissions of **rwx**. Put a **y** in each of the boxes associated with each command under the *700* permissions in the following table.

7. Change the permissions on *inform* to *600* with:

   chmod *600* *inform*

8. Issue the commands in the following table to determine whether you can display, modify, and list the file. In each case, enter **y** if successful or an **n** if not.

9. Proceed by changing the permissions on *inform* to *500*, run the commands, and enter **y** or **n** in each block of the table.

10. Proceed on with permissions of *400, 300,* and so on.

	700 rwx	600 rw-	500 r-x	400 r--	300 -wx	200 -w-	100 --x	000 ---
chmod 700 *inform*								
more *inform*								
echo *date* >> *inform*								
inform								
.inform (**source** *inform*)								
ls -l *inform*								

11. Examine the results and consider the following questions:
    - What permissions are essential for executing a script by entering its name?
    - What permission is needed to source a file?
    - What permission is needed to add text to a file?
    - What permission is needed to have **ls** list the file?

Examining the Results

From the previous exercise, we can conclude:

- To access the contents of the file, we need read permission.
- To add content to a file, we need write permission.
- Both read and execute are required to run a script by entering its name. We need execute to start a child shell and then, if the child is to read the script to see what is to be done, we need read.

- When we ask the current shell to read a file and execute its contents—using either the C shell **source** command or Bourne/Korn's dot command—we need only read permission. No child shell is started; the current shell is used. There is no need for execute permission. The current shell just reads the file as though we just typed the commands.
- Regardless of the permissions on the file, we can use **ls** to list the filename and its current permissions.

The following illustration examines the relationship between the current directory, the *inform* file that is listed in the current directory, its inode which is also listed in the current directory, and the data blocks that hold the data of the file *inform*.

Enter:

ls -i *inform*

The **ls** utility does not access the files to produce a listing of the filenames and their permissions. That information is not in the files; rather, the filenames are listed in the current directory along with the file's inode number. The permissions and so on for the file are in the file's index node or *inode*. The inode is read, not the file. Changing the file permissions on a file determines what we can do to the file. It does not impact the current directory nor the inode. The permissions for the file are recorded in the inode.

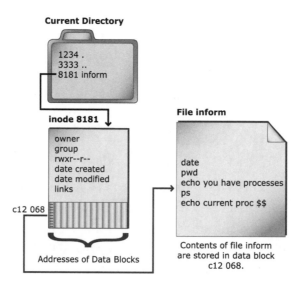

Current Directory

1234 .
3333 ..
8181 inform

inode 8181

owner
group
rwxr--r--
date created
date modified
links

c12 068

Addresses of Data Blocks

File inform

date
pwd
echo you have processes
ps
echo current proc $$

Contents of file inform
are stored in data block
c12 068.

Removing Files

What file permission is needed to remove a file?

↳ 1. Create a junk directory by entering:

   mkdir *Junkperms*

2. Make *Junkperms* your current directory:

   cd *Junkperms*

3. Create a series of files by entering:

   touch *old7 old6 old5 old4 old3 old2 old1 old0*

4. Modify the permissions as follows:

   chmod 700 *old7*
   chmod 600 *old6*
   chmod 500 *old5*
   chmod 400 *old4*
   chmod 300 *old3*
   chmod 200 *old2*
   chmod 100 *old1*
   chmod 000 *old0*

5. Confirm that all permissions are as specified:

   ls -l *old**

6. Now attempt to remove the file *old7* by entering:

   rm *old7*

7. List the files:

   ls -l *old**

   The *old7* file is gone.

8. Continue to attempt to remove each file individually:

   rm *old6*
   ls -l *old**
   rm *old5*
   and so on.

   You are probably asked:

   ```
   rm: remove write-protected file 'old5'?
   ```

9. Answer by typing an **n**.

Whether a user can remove a file is determined by whether the user has write permission on the file. If you grant other users write permission for a file, they can remove the file as well. Without write, you usually cannot remove a file. A special case occurs when a user requests to remove a file that he or she owns, but the user has not granted himself or herself write permission for the file. The owner could add write permission and then remove the file. The **rm** utility saves the step by saying, in essence, "You do not have write permission and cannot remove the file without changing permissions to include write; however, because you are the owner and could change the permissions, I'll remove it if you say so."

10. List your current files:

    ls -l

    All files that initially had write permission were removed.

11. Go back to your parent directory with:

    cd ..

9.7 Modifying Directory Permissions

When you type **ls -l**, the output reveals that directories have the same kind of permissions field as regular files, except there is a *d* in the leftmost position. The owner of the directory has the power to change the permissions, which in turn affect access to the directory in much the same way as the permissions affect file access. The owner determines which users have read, write, and execute access to the directory. Assigning permissions to directories is done with the same letters and numbers that are used for assigning permissions to files.

Directories are special files containing two things for each file or directory listed in them: the name of each file (or directory), and for each, an associated inode number that leads us to the inode for the file. Permissions for directories determine what you can and cannot do to the directory itself. For instance, what permission would you expect is needed on a directory that would allow you to change the name of a file listed in that directory? What permission is needed on a directory to run **ls** to output the names of the files that are listed in the directory? In this section, we examine how to modify directory permissions and what powers are granted and denied with each permission.

Using Permissions to Control Directory Access

The owner of a directory has the power and responsibility for setting the directory access permissions. Directory permissions, like file permissions, include read, write, and execute.

1. Create a new subdirectory, *Mybin*, in your home directory by typing:

   cd

   mkdir *Mybin*

2. Examine the specific permissions attached to *Mybin*.

   ls -ld *Mybin*

   The **d** option instructs **ls** to provide a listing of information about the directory itself, not its contents. Earlier, you examined the total contents of a directory and found two things for each file: a filename and an inode number.

3. Display the contents of your current directory now with:

   ls -i

   The display is a list of the current directory's filenames and associated inodes. This is the total content of the directory—filenames and their associated inodes.

   The directory contains filenames and related inode numbers. The inode contains all the information about a file including permissions, owner, the date it was created, links, and addresses of data blocks on the hard drive where the file's content resides. There is nothing in the file's data blocks except the contents of the file—not even its name. We access the file by first getting its inode number from the directory, then examining the inode for permissions and data block addresses, and finally going to the correct blocks on the drive to access the file itself.

4. Copy the *inform* file into the new *Mybin* subdirectory by entering:

   cp *inform   Mybin*

5. Change to the *Mybin* directory and create eight test files by entering the following commands:

   cd *Mybin*

   touch *old0 old1 old2 old3 old4 old5 old6 old7*

6. Make sure *inform* is executable and run it:

   chmod 700 inform

   inform

7. Return to the parent directory:

cd ..

Listing the Files in a Directory

At the moment, your current working directory is the parent of *Mybin*.

1. Obtain a listing of the files in *Mybin* by entering:

ls *Mybin*

The output on your screen is not the files listed in your current directory, but the files listed in *Mybin*. You can read the filenames that are listed in *Mybin*. The current directory lists itself (the following illustration has *1234*), its parent, and also the child directory, *Mybin*, with an inode of *8555*. To access contents of *Mybin*, the inode accessed first is *8555*, which contains the information about the directory *Mybin*, including the permissions and data block addresses. The data blocks for *Mybin* contain the filenames and inode numbers for the files listed in *Mybin*. To find the permissions for a file such as *inform*, we need to open and read the inode associated with the file *inform* that is listed in the *Mybin* directory.

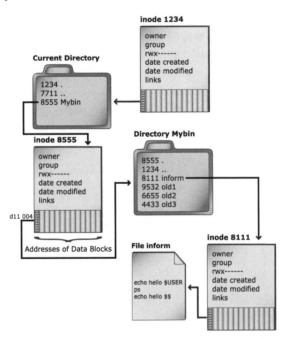

In summary, permissions for the directory *Mybin* are in the inode whose number is listed next to *Mybin* in the current directory. Permissions for files that are listed in the *Mybin* directory are in inodes listed next to the filenames in *Mybin*.

2. Change the permissions of the *Mybin* directory to be only write and execute with:

> **chmod** *300 Mybin*

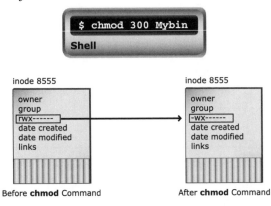

3. Instruct **ls** to list the permissions on the directory *Mybin*, rather than the permissions of its contents, by entering:

> **ls** **-ld** *Mybin*

The permissions are kept in the inode for *Mybin*, which is accessed from your current directory. The output indicates you do not have read permission for the directory, only write and execute permission: **(d-wx------)**.

4. Attempt to obtain a listing of the files in *Mybin*:

> **ls** *Mybin*

Without read permission for the directory *Mybin*, you cannot read the directory's contents; hence, you cannot get a listing of its files.

Denying Write Permission for a Directory

With a file, write permission must be granted before a user can modify the contents of the file. The same is true for directories.

1. Modify the permissions on *Mybin* to exclude write, and examine the results:

> **chmod** *500 Mybin*
> **ls** **-ld** *Mybin*

The directory has only read and execute for the owner; write is denied.

2. Obtain a listing of the files in *Mybin*.

   ls *Mybin*

   You can list the directory's contents because the filenames are kept in the directory, and you still have read permission on the directory. You are reading the directory itself to obtain the list of names of its files.

3. Attempt to change the name of the file *old5* by entering:

   mv *Mybin/old5 Mybin/old5.bak*

   Without write permission, you cannot modify the contents of the directory. You cannot change the name of a listed file, remove a file, or add a new file. To make any of those changes requires at least modifying the content of the directory (that is, writing).

Examining the Need for Execute Permissions

The directory permissions read and write are similar to the same permissions on regular files. The execute permission, however, has a very different impact on a directory than it has on a file.

1. Change the mode of *Mybin* to be read and write only:

   chmod *600 Mybin*
   ls -ld *Mybin*

   Only read and write are permitted. Execute is denied.

2. Attempt to change directories to *Mybin*.

   cd *Mybin*

   The shell returns an error message similar to the following:

   ```
   Mybin: Permission denied
   ```

   Execute permission for a directory determines whether you can make the directory your current directory.

3. Confirm you are still in the parent of *Mybin*:

   pwd
   ls -ld *Mybin*

4. Attempt to read the script *inform*, which is in *Mybin*:

   cat *Mybin/inform*

   ```
   Mybin: Permission denied
   ```

Without execute permission, you cannot **cd** into a directory, nor can you use the directory in a path to reach a file or directory that is listed in it. You cannot read *inform*, because you cannot get through the directory *Mybin* to get to the file. Although you still have read permission on the *inform* file itself, you cannot get through the parent directory to access the file without execute permission on the directory. You cannot get to the file.

> **SUMMARY:** To **cd** to a directory, or to use the directory in a pathname, you must have execute permission for that directory.

Examining the Effect of Directory Permission

In this section, you will examine the effect of assigning various permissions to the directory *Mybin*, keeping track of the results in the following table.

Starting in your home directory, you will assign the first permission to *Mybin* listed at the top of the table and then will try each of the commands listed in the left column. In the appropriate columns of the table, write down whether the command was executed without error, producing the requested information.

	700 rwx	600 rw-	500 r-x	400 r--	300 -wx	200 -w-	100 --x	000 ---
chmod 700 Mybin								
ls -ld Mybin								
ls Mybin								
ls -l Mybin								
cat Mybin/inform								
echo date >> Mybin/inform								
Mybin/**inform**								
who > Mybin/new7								
rm Mybin/old7								
cd Mybin								
if **cd** Mybin works, then... **pwd**								
ls								
inform								
more inform								
cd ..								

↳ 1. Change the mode to the needed permission by entering:

   chmod *700 Mybin*

   Enter a **y** in the table, reporting that you can change the permission.

2. Confirm the permissions for the directory *Mybin* by entering:

   ls -ld *Mybin*

   Enter a **y** in the table.

3. Obtain a listing of *Mybin*'s files by entering:

   ls *Mybin*

   Enter a **y** in the table.

4. From the parent directory, read the *inform* file, which is in *Mybin*:

   cat *Mybin/inform*

5. Add the word *date* to the existing file *inform* (note the double redirection):

   echo date >> *inform*

6. Request that the *inform* script be run:

   Mybin/inform

7. Create a new file in *Mybin* called *new7* by entering the following:

   who > *Mybin/new7*

8. Remove an old file by entering:

   rm *Mybin/old7*

9. Change directories to *Mybin*:

   cd *Mybin*

   pwd

   If the **cd** to *Mybin* was successful and you are in *Mybin,* do the following
   steps. Otherwise, skip steps 10 through 13.

10. List the files in the current directory, *Mybin*:

    ls

11. Run the script:

    inform

12. Read *inform*:

    more *inform*

13. Return to the parent directory:

    cd ..

Continuing the Exploration of Directories with 600 to 000 Permissions

In this section, we examine how the other possible directory permissions (from *600, 500,* and so on down to *000*) impact our ability to perform the actions we just performed when the permissions were *700*.

1. Change the permissions of *Mybin* to *600*.

   chmod *600 Mybin*

2. Repeat the previous exploration steps, using *new6* in step 8 and *old6* in step 9 when appropriate. Write the results in the figure under *600*. Only if step 9 is successful do you include steps 10-13.

3. Continue with each successive permission (and use the appropriate files, that is, *newfile5* and *oldfile5* with parameter *500*) until the table is completed.

4. After completing the exercises for permissions *000* for *Mybin*, return the directory to reasonable permissions so you can access it in the future:

   chmod *755 Mybin*

Examining the Results of Your Exploration

With the impact of the various permissions recorded in the table, we can examine the results. These data tells us a great deal about the impact of permissions on directory access. Consider the diagrams as you review the results. Each section, identified by the command you entered, explores how the permissions impact the running of that command.

ls -ld *Mybin*

This command is a request to list permissions for the directory itself. These permissions are kept in the inode for the directory *Mybin*. The name *Mybin* and its inode number are listed in the current directory. Whether we can be in the current directory to access inodes of its files or go through the current directory is determined by the permissions on the current directory. We are in the current directory, so we must have **x** and can therefore access its inodes. Regardless of the permissions on *Mybin*, we can ask what those permissions are because the permissions for the directory *Mybin* are in an inode listed in the current directory, not in *Mybin,* and in these exercises we are not changing the permissions on the current directory.

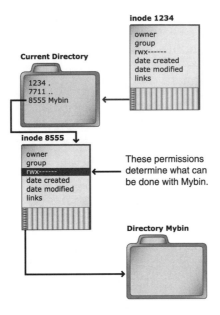

cat *Mybin/inform*

As long as we have execute on *Mybin,* we can go through *Mybin* to reach *inform.* Though we only have **x** on the *Mybin* directory, we can still read the file *inform* because we have **r** permission on *inform.* The **x** on *Mybin* permits us to get to *inform.* What we can do with *inform* is determined by the permissions on that file, not on its directory.

echo *date* >> *Mybin/inform*

We have **x** on the directory so can reach through *Mybin* to the file *inform.* Because we have **w** on the file, we can write to it.

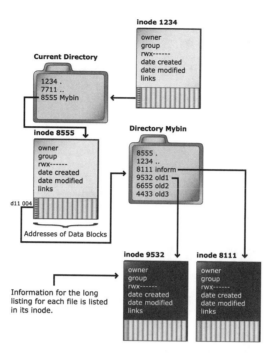

rm *Mybin/old7*

To add or remove a file from the directory, we need **w** to modify the directory's contents and **x** to reach the inode to get data block addresses to release them as we remove the file.

date > *Mybin/new7*

We need **w** to write the name for a new file in a directory, and we need **x** to get through the directory to the inode where we write the addresses for the information about the new file.

SUMMARY: These exercises reveal the following:
—To list the contents of a directory with **ls**, we need read permission.
—To create files in or remove them from a directory (thus, write to the directory file and reach inodes to describe the file), we need both write and execute permissions.
—To make a directory the working directory with **cd**, or to pass through it as part of a search path, we need execute permission on the directory.

Limiting Execute in a Path

Execute permission has important consequences for directories.

↳ 1. Make the permissions **rwx** for the owner of the *Mybin* directory, and then add a new directory named *Testing*:

> **chmod** *700 Mybin*
> **ls -ld** *Mybin*
> **mkdir** *Mybin/Testing*

2. Change directories to *Testing*, add a file there, check your location, and return to the current directory:

> **cd** *Mybin/Testing*
> **date** > *today*
> **pwd**
> **cd** *../..*
> **pwd**
> **ls** *Mybin/Testing*

You are able to change directories through *Mybin* to *Testing*.

3. Change the permissions of *Mybin* to deny execute:

> **chmod** *600 Mybin*
> **ls -ld** *Mybin*

Attempt to change to the *Testing* directory:

> **cd** *Mybin/Testing*

Because you do not have execute permission on the *Mybin* directory, you cannot use it in a path to reach its subdirectory *Testing*. *Testing* and its files are unreachable if there is no execute on its parent. Though the permissions on the directory *Testing* are wide open, you cannot get to it without **x** on its parent.

Granting Execute Permission Only

You have seen that, without execute permission, you cannot change into or through a directory. Is execute enough?

↳ 1. Change the permissions for the directory *Mybin* to be only **x**:

> **chmod** *100 Mybin*
> **ls -ld** *Mybin*

2. Attempt to change directories to *Mybin,* get a listing of its files, and then change directories to *Testing* and get a listing there:

> **cd** *Mybin*
> **pwd**
> **ls**
> **cd** *Testing*
> **pwd**
> **ls**
> **cd** *../..*

With only execute permission on a directory, you can **cd** into it, but you cannot get a listing of its files. You can also change directories from it to a subdirectory. Once in the subdirectory, the permissions on that subdirectory are in effect.

When I was 13, my mother once asked if she could get some of her things out of a family closet that was in my room. I replied that it was the holiday season, and I was making presents in my bedroom. I didn't want anyone looking around in there. Mom said she wanted to get into the closet, not my room. I said, "But Mom, you have to go *through* my room to get to the closet." She replied, "I'll go through your room *blindfolded.*" Once she was in the family closet, she could turn on the light, take the blindfold off, and get what she needed. I granted her execute but not read or write permission to my room. Once she passed through my room into the closet, where she had full **rwx** permission, she could do as she wished.

Establishing Directory Permissions for Group and Other

The permissions on directories are specified for user, group, and other, in the same fields of the long listing that are associated with file permissions.

1. Restore full permissions to owner for *Mybin* by typing:

> **chmod** *700 Mybin*
> **ls -ld** *Mybin*
> **ls -l** *Mybin*

With the present permissions, no ordinary user except the owner of the directory can obtain a listing of the files in *Mybin* using **ls**. (Of course, the super user *root* can access a directory regardless of its permissions.) Members of the group and others cannot **cd** to *Mybin* or use that directory in a path to access any files in it or below it—regardless of the permissions granted for the individual files.

2. Allow all users in your group to have execute permission to your directory *Mybin*. Enter:

   chmod *710 Mybin*
   ls -ld *Mybin*

   This command changes permissions to allow the owner total access to the directory. Members of the group cannot run **ls** or create files in the directory. However, they can **cd** into it. Other users who are not in your group are denied all access.

3. If you have **root** power and know how to add a user, add another user, then log in as that user and try to access the directory.

4. If you logged in as a different user, log out and log back in as yourself.

5. Allow your group and others to change directories into *Mybin* and to obtain listings of files. Enter the following:

   chmod *755 Mybin*
   ls -l *Mybin*
   ls -ld *Mybin*

The **chmod** program modifies the permissions for files and for directories in exactly the same way. In a numerical argument such as *754*, the first number (*7*) assigns permissions for the owner/user, the second number (*5*) assigns group permissions to users who are in the same group, and the last number (*4*) assigns permissions to other users.

9.8 Changing Permissions for Files in All Subdirectories

Thus far, you have changed the permissions for individual files. The **chmod** utility can be used to change the permissions for *all* files in a directory and even for all of its subdirectories.

1. Issue the following commands to change to your home directory and then to create a subdirectory that contains several files, another subdirectory, and additional files:

   cd
   mkdir *DIR-A*
   ls -ld *DIR-A*
   cd *DIR-A*

> **touch** *A AA AAA monica*
> **ls -l** *
> **mkdir** *DIR-B*
> **ls -ld** *DIR-B*
> **cd** *DIR-B*
> **touch** *B BB BBB olenka*
> **ls -l** *
> **cd**
> **ls -l -R** *DIR-A*

The resulting files and directories are shown in the following illustration. The new directory, *DIR-B*, contains a series of files with limited permissions. *DIR-B* is listed in the *DIR-A* directory, which is listed in your home directory.

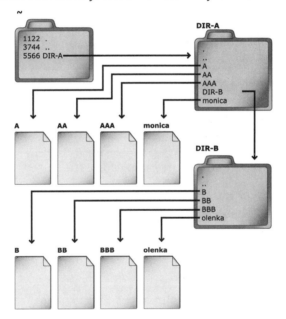

2. Change the permissions for *all* the files in *both* directories by issuing one command:

> **chmod -R** *777 DIR-A*

3. Check the permissions of the directories and files:

> **ls -ld** *DIR-A*
> **ls -l** *DIR-A*
> **ls -ld** *DIR-A/DIR-B*
> **ls -l** *DIR-A/DIR-B*

The **-R** option to the **chmod** utility is instruction to start at the named directory and <u>R</u>ecursively descend through the directory tree to change the permissions for all the files and directories it encounters.

Self Test 2

1. What are the minimum permissions that allow the user to read and have the current shell execute commands in a file?

   _____

2. What minimum numerical permission do you need to execute commands in a file by entering the filename as a command?

   _____

3. The file *inform* has a numerical permission of **754**. Consider the following questions:

   A. Who has what permissions?

   User:_____

   Group:_____

   Other:_____

   B. Who can change the permission of the file?

   _____

   C. Who can change the contents of the file?

   _____

4. What is the minimum permission required to go through a subdirectory to access one of its files?

   _____

5. What information is kept in a directory?

   _____

6. What minimum permission(s) for a subdirectory do you need to list the contents of the subdirectory?

   _____

7. What minimum permission for the current directory do you need to be in the directory and list its contents?

   _____

8. What minimum permission for a subdirectory do you need to create files in the subdirectory?

_____

9. What minimum permissions for the file or directory are needed to do the following successfully?

A. cat *Mybin/inform*

*Mybin:*_____

*inform:*_____

B. date > *Mybin/newfile*

*Mybin:*_____

C. echo *date* >> *Mybin/today* (*today* already exists.)

*Mybin:*_____

*today:*_____

D. touch *Mybin/hello* (**touch** creates a new file, *hello.*)

*Mybin:*_____

E. rm *Mybin/hello*

*Mybin:*_____

*hello:*_____

F. ls -l *Mybin*

*Mybin:*_____

G. ls -ld *Mybin*

*Mybin:*_____

10. Fill in the missing data in the following table:

chmod Argument	Resulting Permissions
777	
	r-xr-xr--
640	
400	
	rwxr-xr--

9.9 Identifying Other System Permissions

When cruising around the filesystem, you will sometimes see permissions **s** and **t** for files, rather than **r**, **w**, or **x**. The **s** and **t** permissions can only be set by the super user, not by ordinary users. This section introduces these remaining two permissions. For a detailed account of these super user permissions, consult the **man** section on **chmod** in Section 2 of the **man** pages, or look in a good system administration text.

Running Programs as Root

The executable *passwd* file is a program that users run to change their passwords. The binary is located at */usr/bin/passwd* or */bin/passwd*. Encrypted passwords are kept in the password file */etc/passwd* or in */etc/shadow*, depending on your system. Ordinary users do not have write permission to these password files.

1. Enter the following commands:

   ls -l */etc/shadow* (You may not have this file on your system. It is used in more secure installations.)

   ls -l */etc/passwd*

   The super user, *root*, is the owner and has write permission. Ordinary users do not have write permission. Even though you lack write permission to the password files, you have probably run the *passwd* program to change your passwords, thus changing the contents of one of these files.

2. Examine the permissions in the password-changing program file:

   ls -l */usr/bin/passwd*

   On a network system, examine the permissions for */usr/bin/yppasswd*. The output includes one or more unusual permissions:

   ```
   -r-s--x--x   3   root   94208   Jun 29 1995   /usr/bin/passwd
   ```

This output indicates that the file's owner is *root*. The owner has read permission, and also has an **s** instead of an **x** in the execute field. Group and other each have execute permission, but not read. The **s** in the owner field indicates that when anyone who has permission to execute this program executes it, the program runs as though *root* is running it—that is, with the identity of *root*, not the identity of the person who actually requested that the program run. When an ordinary user runs *passwd*, the **s** tells the system that while running the *passwd* program, the user has *root*'s identity. Because the *passwd* changing program runs as *root*, and because *root* does have write permission for the *password* data file, any user running *passwd* has the power to change the user's password in the protected file. This is called *set user ID*.

Setting Group ID

Often programs on systems need to be available to any member of a specified group. A member of the group owns the programs, but other group members have execute authority. If the administrator wants other users not in the specified group to run the specific program, the set group ID is turned on for that program. If the execute permission slot for *group* for an executable program contains an **s**, then others with execute permission for the program run the program as though they were a member of the group, though they obviously are not. Often system administrators limit certain programs to be executable only by *root* and *root*'s group. On Linux, many games and some other programs (such as **gataxx**, **kdesud**, **gnibbles**, and **slocate**) have set group ID set. When regular users have other permission execute these programs, they do so as though they were a member of *root*'s group.

Requiring Ownership to Remove a File

Directories can have special permissions.

Assume the permissions in a directory are **rwxrwxrwx**. If another user creates a file in the directory, you could remove the file because you have write and execute permission in the directory. The */tmp* directory is wide open to all users. We can all write create and remove files from */tmp*.

⮑   Check the permissions on the */tmp* directory:

ls -ld */tmp*

In this case, the output is:

```
drwxrwxrwt        10   root   root   4096   June 23   07:31    /tmp
```

The last permission bit is a **t**, which changes the rules. A **t** in the last permission slot for a directory limits who can remove files. Even though a user has write permission on the directory, that user can not remove or change the name of files unless they are the owner. This is called the *sticky bit set.* When the sticky bit is set on a directory, only the owner of a file can delete or change the name of the file in that directory. We cannot remove each other's files.

9.10 Setting Permissions When Files and Directories Are Created

In UNIX, we create files in three ways: We copy an existing file into a new one; we use a utility such as an editor or **tee** to create a file; or we specify that the output of a utility be sent to a new file, using redirection in a shell command. When we run **ls -l** after creating a new file, the new file has permissions already set, without our ever specifying them. We are not consulted first; the initial permissions are automatically assigned to the new files and directories.

Examining the Default Permissions

Thus far in this chapter, you have examined how to change the existing permissions to new permissions on files and directories. This section investigates how the initial settings are established.

Earlier in the chapter, you created the command file *inform*. The operating system initially set the permissions for you, the owner, as read and write. At that point, you were not able to execute the file. At creation, permission settings were included for other users who were members of your group and for all others. These default permission settings are determined by the **umask** value.

As you will see, the **umask** is so named because its value determines which permissions are *masked* from being set.

1. To ensure that you can access the files used in the following exercises, check to make sure you are in your home directory:

   cd

2. Obtain the current setting of **umask** by entering:

   umask

   A number such as **22** or **022** is displayed.

This **umask** setting determines the value of permissions for new files as they are created. Changing the **umask** has no effect on an existing file. The **umask** setting is initially determined by default on the system, but can be modified from the shell command line, or through entries in a user's startup files. For some hollow reason, especially in late October, people often enter **unmask**, but the command is **umask**. (True, it happens.)

Specifying Default Permissions for Directories with umask

To explore how directory permissions are affected by **umask**, the following exercises guide you through changing **umask** values and creating new directories to see the effects.

➥ 1. Create a new, empty directory for these next exercises and make it your current directory:

   mkdir *DIRS*
   cd *DIRS*
   pwd
   ls

2. Determine the current **umask** value:

   umask

3. You are about to change the value of the **umask**. First, write down the present value so that you can change back to it later.

   Original **umask** value: _____

4. Reset the **umask** to *000* by entering:

   umask *000*

5. To confirm that you have changed the **umask**, type:

   umask

   The **umask** is now set at *000*, which may be displayed as *0*. (It doesn't make much difference whether a checking account balance is *$0.* or *$0000.*)

6. With the **umask** at *000*, create a new directory and determine its permissions:

   mkdir *DIR000*
   ls **-ld** *DIR**

   The output is:

   ```
   drwxrwxrwx  DIR000
   ```

The permissions of the directory are wide open—readable, writable, and executable by everyone.

When the **umask** is set to *000*, nothing is masked out, and all permissions are granted for new directories.

The next illustration describes the situation when **umask** is *000*. No doors are closed. Because no permissions are masked, all nine permissions are granted to the new directory.

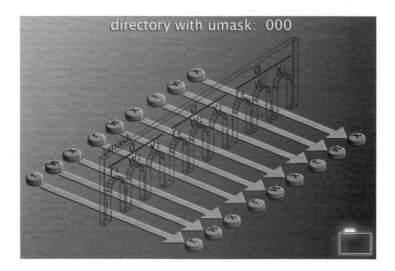

Creating a Directory with Write Masked

A directory created while **umask** is *000* has full permissions granted to user, group, and other.

⤷ 1. Change **umask** to be *022* and request confirmation:

   umask *022*
   umask

2. With the **umask** at *022*, create a new directory and examine its permissions:

   mkdir *DIR022*
   ls -ld *DIR**

   This new directory, created while the **umask** is *022*, has permissions of:

   ```
   drwxr-xr-x
   ```

   The owner has **rwx**, the group **r-x**, and others **r-x**. What permissions are missing or *masked*? Nothing is masked from the owner, *0*. Group is missing write permission (*2*), and other is missing write (*2*). The missing or masked permissions are *022*.

   The directory *DIR000* retains its full permissions. It was created while the **umask** was *000* and is not affected by the change of **umask**. The **umask** determines the permission when files and directories are created, not after. Once they are created, we change permissions with **chmod**.

   The following illustration summarizes how permissions are determined for a new directory when the **umask** is *022*. The two doors, **w** for group and **w** for other, are closed.

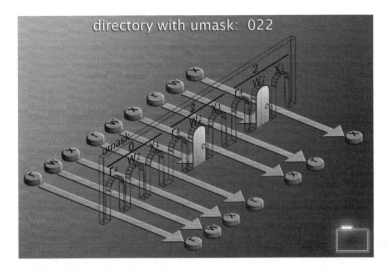

directory with umask: 022

Permissions masked when the **umask** is set to *022* are as follows:

- *0* Nothing is masked from the *owner's* permissions.
- *2* The permission write is masked from *group*.
- *2* *Other* is also missing write permission.

umask	Owner	Group	Other	
000	rwx 421	rwx 421	rwx 421	Directory permissions granted if nothing was masked.
022	0 ---	2 -w-	2 -w-	Permissions masked by **umask** at current setting.

Masking Different Permissions for Group and Other

In the last exercise, when a new directory was created, the write permission was masked for group and other, because there were 2s in the second and third fields of **umask**.

1. Change the **umask** by entering:

   umask *037*

2. Create another directory:

   mkdir *DIR037*

3. Check the directory's permissions:

   ls -ld *DIR**

This time the directory's permissions are:

```
drwxr-----DIR 037
```

The *owner* has full **rwx**, the *group* has just read, and *others* are granted no permissions. The directory's permissions are **740**: read, write, and execute for the owner, and read for the group. With the **umask** set at **037**, no permissions are masked for the owner, write and execute (**2+1=3**) are denied to group, and all (**4+2+1=7**) permissions are denied to other users.

The following illustration summarizes how permissions for a new directory are determined when the **umask** is **037**. Although all permissions are possible for a directory, the mask doors of 0, 2 + 1, 4 + 2 + 1 are closed.

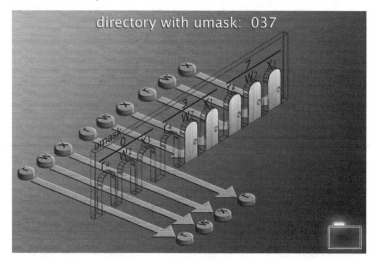

directory with umask: 037

4. Change the **umask** to each of the following values. At each **umask** value, create a directory, and then examine the permissions for that directory.

umask value	Resulting Directory Permission
023	d _ _ _ _ _ _ _ _
066	d _ _ _ _ _ _ _ _
027	d _ _ _ _ _ _ _ _

Because nothing is masked for user (owner), and directories are created with full permissions if nothing is masked, the user gets **rwx**. Group has a mask of **2**, hence the **w** is masked, so group gets read and execute permission. Other has a mask of **3**, which masks **2** (**w**) and **1** (**x**), so the only permission granted is read, **4**.

In the following illustration, all permissions are "launched," but the umask doors *0* for owner, *2* for group, and both *2* and *1* for other are closed. The resulting permissions are **rwxr-xr--**.

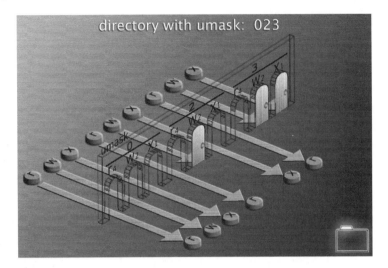

directory with umask: 023

> **SUMMARY:** If the **umask** is set to *000*, no permissions are masked, and any directories created have full **rwx** permission for all users. A nonzero in any field of **umask** specifies the permissions that are *denied* to the owner, members of the group, and others, depending on which field is not zero. The **umask** values and resulting permissions are as follows for each of the three fields in the following illustration:

Umask Value	Result
0	Denies no permissions hence, grants all three permissions, **rwx**.
1	Restricts execute permission only, granting **r** and **w**.
2	Restricts write permission only, granting **r** and **x**.
3	Restricts write and execute permission only, granting **r**.
4	Restricts read permission only, granting **w** and **x**.
5	Restricts read and execute permission (4 + 1), granting **w**.
6	Restricts read and write permission (4 + 2), granting **x**.
7	Restricts read, write, and execute (1 + 2 + 4), granting no permissions.

Identifying File Permissions with Nothing Masked

A particular **umask** setting results in different permissions for files than it does for directories.

1. To examine the resulting *file* permissions when nothing is masked, change the **umask** value to *0* by typing:

   umask 000

2. Create a file named *file000*:

   date > *file000*

3. Check the mode of *file000*:

   ls -l

   At this point, the file is readable and writable by everyone.

   When the **umask** is set to *000*, nothing masked, the default permissions for a new file are *666* (readable and writable by owner, group, and others). Even though the **umask** is set to *000*, nothing masked, when files are created, they do not have execute permission. No one, not even the owner, is granted execute permission for a file until it is specifically added using the **chmod** command.

Denying Write Permission for New Files

The **umask** is used to mask permissions for new files in the same way it masks directory permissions.

1. Set the **umask** to *022* by entering:

   umask 022

2. Create another file called *file022* and check its permissions:

   touch *file022*
   ls -l

   The permissions are read and write for owner, and read alone for group and others (*644*).

   When the **umask** is set to *000* and you create a file, the file's initial permissions are as open as possible without granting execute permission (*666*). When you reset the **umask** to *022* and create a new file, the new file has permissions of *644*. The write (*2*) is masked or denied for group and other.

The following illustration summarizes how initial permissions are granted to files when the **umask** is *022*. Only read and write are possible, to be limited by closing **umask** doors.

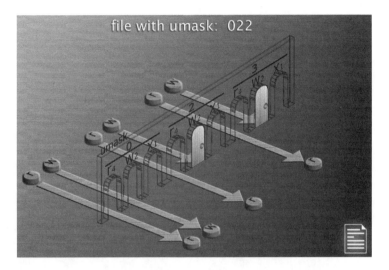

File Permissions When Execute Is Masked

At file creation, execute is never granted to a file. If **umask** also *masks* execute, what is the result when files are created?

1. Set the **umask** to *023* by typing:

    umask 023

2. Create another file named *file023* and check its permissions:

    touch *file023*

    ls -l

The new file created while **umask** is *023* has permissions of:

```
-rw-r--r--
```

This result is exactly the same as when the **umask** was set to *022*. The only difference between the two is that *023* calls for masking the execute permission for other users. Because files are never granted execute permission at creation, it makes no difference whether the **umask** masks or doesn't mask execute for files.

The following table and illustration summarize how permissions are granted to a new *file* when the **umask** is masking execute. At file creation, execute is not granted; hence, there is no permission to mask. Masking execute permission for files is irrelevant.

umask	Owner	Group	Other	
000	rw 42-	rw 42-	rw 42-	File permission granted when nothing is masked.
023	0 ---	2 -w-	21 -wx	Permissions masked by **umask** at current setting
	42 rw-	4 r--	4 r--	Resulting file permissions

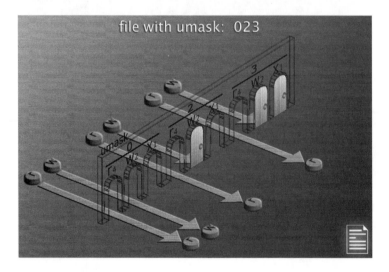

file with umask: 023

Predicting Permissions for Files

In this exercise, you change the **umask**, calculate the permissions for a file, and then check the permissions.

1. Set the **umask** to *037*:

     umask *037*

2. Create another file named *file037*:

     touch *file037*

3. In the following table, write down the permissions you expect *file037* to be granted at creation:

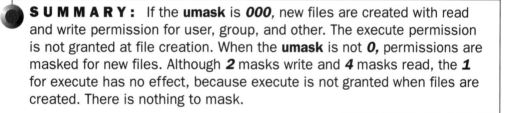

umask	Owner	Group	Other	
000	rw- 42-	rw- 42-	rw- 42-	File permissions granted when nothing is masked
037				Permissions masked by **umask** at current setting
				Resulting directory permissions

4. Check the new file's permissions against what you wrote in the table. Type:

ls -l *file037*

ls -l

5. The file's permissions are read and write for owner, and read for group (**640**). The **umask** works as expected: the file is not writable or executable by the group; nor is it readable, writable, or executable by others.

> **S U M M A R Y :** If the **umask** is **000**, new files are created with read and write permission for user, group, and other. The execute permission is not granted at file creation. When the **umask** is not **0,** permissions are masked for new files. Although **2** masks write and **4** masks read, the **1** for execute has no effect, because execute is not granted when files are created. There is nothing to mask.

Predicting Permission for Files and Directories

Because file and directory permissions are affected differently for the same **umask**, it is useful to compare the results.

In this next exercise, you will predict and compare permissions for files and directories using the **umask** values specified in the next table.

1. Predict the permissions for a file and a directory when **umask** is **022**.

2. Modify **umask** and create a directory to verify your prediction.

3. Predict each **umask**'s effect; verify by changing the **umask** and creating directories and files.

Resulting Directory Permissions	umask	Resulting File Permissions
drwxrwxrwx	000	rw-rw-rw-
	022	
	023	
	033	
	037	
	077	
	777	

9.11 Examining the Impact of *umask* on Other Operations

The value of **umask** determines the initial permissions when files and directories are created. It also impacts permissions when files are copied and when we make global permission changes using the mnemonic arguments to **chmod**.

Inheriting Permissions When Files Are Copied

Clearly, the **umask** affects permission when new files are created, but does it affect all new files? Whether the **cp** command retains permissions when files are copied depends on the version of UNIX you are using.

1. Set your **umask** to *077*, return to your home directory, and create two files:

    umask *077*
    cd
    touch *newfile077*
    who > *who-file077*
    ls -l **077**

Notice that, at this point, new files are created with no permissions granted to group or other.

2. Earlier in this chapter, you created a new file, *inform,* in your home directory that contained several shell commands. You made it executable and then executed it. Change the permissions for the *inform* file:

    chmod *755 inform*
    ls -l *inform*

3. Make a new file by copying the *inform* file:

> **cp** *inform inform1*
> **ls -l** *inform1*

Because you have read permission for *inform,* you can copy it into *inform1.* However, *inform1* has one of the following permissions:

```
rwx------
```

or

```
rwxr-xr-x
```

If your version of the **cp** command simply copies the permissions when it copies a file, the resulting permissions are **rwxr-xr-x**. In this case, **umask** is not consulted, and permissions are copied when **cp** copies a file.

If the resulting permissions for *inform1* are **rwx------**, then when **cp** copies files, it begins with the original file's permissions, then copies them up to whatever **umask** allows.

4. Try the following:

> **umask** *013*
> **chmod** *777 inform*
> **ls -l** *inf**
> **cp** *inform inform3*
> **ls -l inform3**

The permissions on *inform* are **rwxrwxrwx**, the **umask** is *013*. When **cp** copies the file, the permissions are copied as well, except that **umask** limits x for group and **wx** for other (*013*), resulting in **rwxrw-r--** for the file.

5. We can instruct **cp** to copy permissions when making a copy of a file, by entering:

> **cp -p** *inform inform4*

The **-p** option on some systems tells **cp** to copy permissions, ignoring the **umask** when it copies a file. On other systems, the default **cp** copies exact permissions.

If you do want to have **umask** take effect regardless of the original permissions when making a duplicate file, you should use **cat**.

6. For instance, copy the file *inform* to a new file named *inform5* using the **cat** utility. Enter:

> **cat** *inform > inform5*

7. Examine the permissions:

> **ls -l** *inform5*

The new file has the permissions determined by the **umask**. In this instance, you instructed the shell to redirect the output of **cat** to a new file. The shell follows **umask** instructions when creating files.

Limiting Permissions Granted with *chmod*

When we change the permissions on a file using the mnemonic arguments, we can make assignment changes to all users.

1. Enter the following commands:

   umask 000

   chmod a=rwx *permtest*

   ls -l *permtest*

   All three types of users are granted all three permissions.

2. Remove write from all users with:

   chmod -wx *permtest*

   ls -l *permtest*

   The resulting **r--r--r--** permissions reflect that write and execute were removed from all (globally).

   Adding permissions globally is affected by the **umask**.

3. Enter:

   umask 077

   umask

   chmod +wx *permtest*

   ls -l *permtest*

   The resulting permissions are:

   ```
   rwxr--r--
   ```

   Even though you instructed **chmod** to add write and execute globally (to all three kinds of users), they were only added to the owner. The **umask** value (*077*) masks all permissions for group and other at the moment. Only the user can be given added permissions globally.

4. Enter:

   chmod a=rwx

   ls -l *permtest*

   We can still add permissions beyond the **umask** when we assign them specifically. When we make global additions using the mnemonic arguments to **chmod**, the permissions are added up to the limit set by **umask**.

5. Before continuing with the upcoming Self Test section, go back to the earlier section "Identifying File Permissions with Nothing Masked" and locate the original **umask** value that you recorded. Reset the **umask** back to that value. Or, just log off and log back on.

Self Test 3

1. What command sets the **umask** permissions fields so that no one other than the owner can write to the file, but everyone can read the file?

   _____

2. What command sets the **umask** permissions fields so that the owner can read, write, and **cd** to directories and everyone else can only **cd** into them?

   _____

3. If **umask** is **022** and the permissions on a file named *scriptA* are **rwxr-x----**, what are the resulting permissions for files or directories when you enter the following commands?

   A. touch *abc*

   _____

   B. mkdir *def*

   _____

   C. who >> *ghi*

   _____

   D. cp -p *scriptA scriptB*

   _____

   E. wc *scriptA >> wcA*

   _____

4. If **umask** is set to **000**, who has what permissions for newly created files and directories?

	USER	GROUP	OTHER
files			
directories			

5. The **umask** is set to **067**. Now you create a directory *Club* and a file *members* under the directory by typing:

   mkdir *Club*
   who > *Club/members*

What are the resulting permissions for *Club* and *members*?

6. The permissions on a file *oldstuff* are **rwxrwxrwx** when the owner changes **umask** to *077*. What are the permissions for *oldstuff* after the **umask** is changed? *Club*:

_____

members:

_____

7. Consider the following scenario:

    umask 022

    date > *today_date*

    cat *today_date*

    umask 777

    cat *today_date*

Will the second **cat** command be successful? Why or why not?

Chapter Review

Use this section to review the content of this chapter and test yourself on your knowledge of the concepts.

Chapter Summary

- For a file, read permission is needed to access the file's contents with a utility, write is needed to make changes in the file, and execute is needed to start a child shell to run the commands in the file
- The contents of a directory must be read by **ls** to list the filenames; hence, read permission is needed.
- To add a file, remove a file, or change a file's name in a directory, the user must have write and execute permission in the directory—write permission to modify the directory contents, and execute permission to access the inode to modify information about the file.
- To **cd** into a directory or include the directory in a path, the user must have execute permission.
- Two methods are available for changing the permissions of files and directories: with letters (**chmod +x** *filename*) and numbers (**chmod 700** *filename*).

- If the file is a script, execute permission is necessary to start a child process, but that is not sufficient. The child shell must also be able to read the file to see what to do, so permission to read must also be granted.
- Files and directories are granted initial permissions at creation determined by the **umask** setting at the time that the file or directory is created. Changing the **umask** has no effect on current files or directories, but determines the permissions for new files/directories.
- When files are copied, permissions are copied as well up to the limit of the **umask**, or are copied exactly, ignoring the **umask**, depending on your system.

Assignment

1. Fill in the missing data for the following:

Argument to *chmod*	Resulting Permissions
a=rw	
	rwxrw-r- -
750	
644	
	r-xr-xr- -
u=rw,g=u,o=	

2. We can list the contents of a directory, and we can **cd** to it, but we cannot add any files to it. We are not the owner, nor in the owner's group. From that data, what do we know about the permissions for the directory?

3. If the owner of a file can read it and enter its name, the shell runs it as a program, but the owner cannot make changes to the file, and no other users can access the file at all, what permissions are on the file?

4. The **umask** is set to *027* when a new file and a new directory are created. What permissions do each have?

5. The **umask** is set to *027* and *file-jessica* has permissions of **rw-rw-rw** when a copy is made by issuing: **cp** *jessica mckinney*

   What permissions are granted for the new file?

6. If you want the permissions for a directory to be **rwxr-x---**, what numerical and what mnemonic argument to **chmod** could you enter to get the desired results?

7. If you want to be able to run a script named *scr-proj*, but you want no one else to be able to run it, which of the following could you use and why?

   A. chmod *744 scr-proj*

   B. chmod *710 scr-proj*

   C. chmod *007 scr-proj*

   D. chmod *544 scr-proj*

   E. chmod *500 scr-proj*

   F. chmod *700 scr-proj*

   G. chmod *711 scr-proj*

   H. chmod u=a,g=,g= *scr-proj*

8. How can you change the permissions of all files in the directory *Mybin* to be **rw-r----- ?**

   Why is **chmod**, not **umask**, used in all the commands listed in question 7?

9. Project

   A. Set the **umask** for *000*.

   B. Create three new files named *s1, s2,* and *s3*.

   C. Set the **umask** for *027*.

   D. Create a new directory named *GroupStuff*.

   E. Copy all files with names starting with the letter *s* from your current directory to *GroupStuff*.

   F. Explain why the permissions are set they way are in the *GroupStuff* directory.

   G. Create a new directory named *VeryPrivate*.

   H. Make permissions such that no one but you has any access to the directory.

   I. Copy some of your scripts into the *VeryPrivate* directory.

   J. Create a file that contains the long listing for the directories *GroupStuff* and *VeryPrivate* as well as all the files each contains. Even though files in *VeryPrivate* have permissions granting access to group and other users, why can they not access them?

Answers to the Table in "File Permissions for Group and Other"

PERMISSIONS FIELD	TYPE	USER	GROUP	OTHER
drwxr-x- - -	Directory	rwx	r-x	- - -
-rw-rw-r- -	File	rw-	rw-	r- -
-r-xr- - - - -	File	r-x	r- -	- - -

COMMAND SUMMARY

source *filename*	Runs a script in the C shell.
. *filename*	Runs a script in the korn or bash shells.
whoami	Displays the information about who you are and your current login name.
chmod mode *filename*	Changes the permissions on *filename* to those represented by *mode.*
chmod -w *filename*	Removes the write permissions for all classes of users.
chmod +x *filename*	Adds the execute permissions to all classes of users.
chmod a=rwx *filename*	Changes all permissions for all classes to read, write, and execute.
chmod u=rwx,g=rx,o=r *filename*	Changes permissions to read, write, and execute for user; read and execute for group; and read for others.
chmod u=rwx,go= *filename*	Changes permissions to read, write, and execute for user, and removes all permissions for group and others.
umask mode	Changes the default permissions for newly created files and directories. The initial permission value is equal to **777** masked by *mode* for directories, and a permission value equal to **666** masked by *mode* for plain files.
u	User
g	Group
o	Other
a	All
r	Read
w	Write
x	Execute
-	None
=	Assigns permissions
-	Removes permissions
+	Adds permissions
Mode Summary	
4	Allows read permission for the designated user.
2	Allows write permission for the designated user.
1	Allows execute permission for the designated user.

Controlling User Processes

O B J E C T I V E S

After completing this chapter, you will be able to:

- Display information about processes
- Identify parent and child processes
- Terminate processes
- Suspend and activate processes
- List background, foreground, and suspended jobs
- Manage jobs

At any moment, one to several hundred users can be logged on to the same Linux or UNIX system, each accomplishing different tasks. One user may be editing a file in one window and searching the Web in another. At the same time, other users are performing system administration tasks, updating different database applications, sending mail, creating Web pages, programming a new game, or creating special effects for the next film. Even in a single-user system, a person can be running programs in the background, in the foreground, and possibly in different windows or login terminals. In addition to all the user activity, the system itself is also running tasks, handling central processor scheduling, reading and writing to the disk, sending mail, printing jobs, and completing other system functions. When UNIX was designed, multitasking such as this was a main objective. The goal was to allow several tasks to be accomplished at essentially the same time. This multitask nature of UNIX and Linux is central to both its success and its complexity. Having the system do several things essentially at once is efficient, although keeping all the activity straight can be a nightmare.

This chapter investigates how the hardware and software execute utilities, and how to monitor and control separate tasks. These skills are essential, not only for the system administrator, but for users and programmers as well.

10.1 Processing Processes

Because UNIX and Linux provide numerous users the opportunity to run many different programs at the same time, managing those tasks is essential. Every running program is a separate entity, called a *process*. When we request that the shell execute the utility **date**, a process is started that follows the instructions in the file */bin/date*, the code for the utility **date**. Each process is reading instructions, accessing computer memory, possibly reading from input, evaluating arguments, performing calculations, and writing to output. A *process* consists of several components working together, including the code, data, CPU activity, memory, input, output, and error handling. Each process on the system has its own unique process ID number. It also has in its memory the ID of the process that started it, its parent process. Instructions and data are available and in memory. Some processes take only a short time to complete; others run continuously. All processes, however, go through a life cycle that begins when they are started and that ends when they exit.

When any user logs on to a system, a shell process is started. We enter commands to the shell. The shell interprets the commands that we type, executes the utilities requested, waits, and then after the utilities are finished, asks what we want to do next.

Obtaining Detailed Information on System Processes

Many processes that maintain the system's functionality (printing, accepting logins, serving web pages) are started when the system is booted, and remain active until we shut down the system. In previous chapters, you used **ps** to display information concerning processes that you own. You can use **ps** to examine all processes running on your system, regardless of who owns them.

➥ 1. Enter the following commands:

> **ps -aux | more**
>
> **ps -ef | more**

One or both of these command lines probably results in a long list of all the processes currently running on the system. The output is a series of lines like the following:

```
USER       PID %CPU %MEM   VSZ  RSS TTY      STAT START   TIME COMMAND
root         1  0.0  0.0  1412   72 ?        S    Apr23   0:04 init
root         2  0.0  0.0     0    0 ?        SW   Apr23   0:00 [keventd]
root         3  0.0  0.0     0    0 ?        SW   Apr23   0:00 [kapm-idled]
root         4  0.0  0.0     0    0 ?        SWN  Apr23   0:00 [ksoftirqd_CPU0]
root         5  0.0  0.0     0    0 ?        SW   Apr23   0:04 [kswapd]
root         6  0.0  0.0     0    0 ?        SW   Apr23   0:00 [kreclaimd]
root         7  0.0  0.0     0    0 ?        SW   Apr23   0:00 [bdflush]
root         8  0.0  0.0     0    0 ?        SW   Apr23   0:00 [kupdated]
root         9  0.0  0.0     0    0 ?        SW<  Apr23   0:00 [mdrecoveryd]
root        13  0.0  0.0     0    0 ?        SW   Apr23   0:03 [kjournald]
root        88  0.0  0.0     0    0 ?        SW   Apr23   0:00 [khubd]
root       555  0.0  0.0     0    0 ?        SW   Apr23   0:00 [eth0]
root       632  0.0  0.1  1472  156 ?        S    Apr23   0:02 syslogd -m 0
root       637  0.0  0.1  1984  164 ?        S    Apr23   0:00 klogd -2
```

The output lists the ID of each process, what code it is running, who the owner is, and other data.

We can request that **ps** list only the processes owned by a particular user.

2. List all processes that you own:

> **ps -u *$USER***

This **–u** option instructs **ps** to list all the processes owned by whatever <u>u</u>ser is listed as the next argument. Information about processes running in any terminal owned by the user is output.

3. List the systemwide processes again and examine them carefully:

ps -aux | more
ps -ef | more

Several of the processes belong to *root*. Because the system administrator, *root,* is the owner of system scripts and files, the user *root* owns the system processes generated at system startup.

4. Enter:

ps -u *root* **| more**

The wealth of processes started when your system booted up, and owned by the user *root*, are described.

Identifying Processes Connected to a Terminal

If you are using a graphical environment, processes that you own are employed to manage the various graphical components. If you are on a terminal or interacting through a terminal window, all current processes started through this terminal can be identified. Most user processes need to read input from the keyboard and write output to a terminal display. Thus, most user processes must be informed of the *tty* or port to which they are attached. This data is stored with each process and is displayed as part of the output of the **ps** command.

1. Start a process, having it execute in the background by entering:

sleep *1000* **&**

2. At the shell prompt, determine what terminal port you are using:

tty

The output is something like */dev/console* or */dev/tty09* or */dev/pts/04*.

3. Use the portion of the *tty* output after the */dev/* for your *port* in the following:

ps -t *port*   (where *port* is like *console, tty/09,* or *pts/04*)

The output probably shows the running processes, your shell, a process running **sleep**, and the process running the **ps** utility. If you are running the graphical interface or have logged in more than once, there may be more processes. The output is probably like the following:

P I D	T T Y	T I M E	C M D
8464	pts/04	00.00	**bash**
9312	pts/04	00.00	**sleep**
9627	pts/04	00.00	**ps**

4. Using the output displayed on your terminal from the **ps** command, fill out the following chart for your shell, the process running **sleep**, and the process running the **ps** utility:

PID	TTY	TIME	CMD
			sleep
			ps

In this exercise, you recorded three pieces of information for each process:

- The *PID* or *P*rocess *ID*entification number. As each process is created, it is assigned a unique *PID*, beginning with 0, at system startup. If 1,207 were the *PID* of your **ps** process, it might or might not be the 1,208[th] process started on your system since the last time the system was rebooted. *PID* numbers do not simply increase forever. Each system has a maximum process identification number. When this number is reached, the numbering starts over again from the first available number greater than 1. As a result, a process with a lower PID may have been started after one with a higher *PID*.
- The *CPU* time that the process has consumed so far. Because systems are quite fast, this is often zero.
- The *CMD* or command code that the process is executing is listed in the fourth column. These are the names of the utilities associated with each of the processes you have running.

On most systems, when you run **ps**, one of the processes listed is **ps**. When the **ps** utility is running, it lists all the processes that are running at that time. Thus, it lists itself.

5. Run the **ps** utility again using your port data to list processes attached to your terminal, and fill out the following chart based on this new output:

    ps -t *port*   (where *port* is like *console* or *tty09* or *pts/04*)

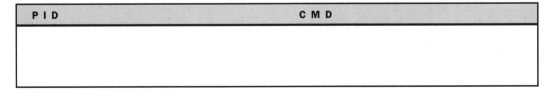

PID	CMD

6. Compare the *PID*s for the shell process in this table and the previous table.

It is the same *PID*, and, therefore, the same shell process as before. You did not exit the shell; it is continuing to wait on your every need.

Compare the *PID*s for the **ps** process in the two tables. They are different because when the first **ps** completed its work the first time, it output its results and exited. The second instance of executing the **ps** utility is a whole new process; hence, it has a new *PID*.

When a user enters a utility name at the shell prompt, a process is created to carry out the instructions contained within the utility code. The process completes its task, writes its output, and dies. If the user then enters the same command name again (as you just did with the **ps** command), a new process is created with a new *PID*.

When we enter a command line at the shell prompt and press ENTER, the shell starts a new child process, completes redirection of input and output, passes arguments, and finally instructs the process to execute the appropriate code for the program that was specified in the command line. We start child processes all the time: **vi**, **cat**, and **who**, for instance, are utilities that are run in child processes. When we start a child shell by entering **tcsh** or **bash**, a child process is started that runs the shell code. The shell is just another program or utility. When a utility such as **vi** is being executed by several users (or several times by the same user), each execution of the program is a separate process.

Starting a New Shell Process

Most processes live a short, happy life executing a utility. They perform their functions and then die.

↳ **1.** Log out and then log back on.

2. After logging back on, identify your current port:

   tty

3. After you have logged on again, get a list of the processes you are running:

   ps -t *port*   (where *port* is like *console*, *tty09*, or *pts/04*)

The *PID* of your current shell is different from the *PID* of your previous login shell, which you noted in the previous tables.

This is a new shell process. It has a new *PID*. When you logged out, you exited the old one. The shell process that you are now using was created when you logged on.

4. Start a child shell, determine its port, and examine the currently running processes:

   sh

   tty

   ps -t *port*   (where *port* is like *console, tty09,* or *pts/04*)

5. Ask your current shell for its *PID*:

   echo $$

   Every shell maintains a variable that contains its *PID*. It is the value of the variable $$.

   The parent shell is still alive, and so is the child. You are communicating with the child shell.

6. Exit the child:

   exit

When you enter the command **exit** or press CTRL-D, the shell process finally does what all processes do when they reach the end of a file or receive an **exit** command: it exits (terminates, or dies).

Obtaining Detailed Data about User Processes

The **ps** utility provides a great deal of information about the status of processes and their relationships.

⮑   To generate a long listing of your current processes, enter:

ps -l   (minus *el*)

The output is a long listing of information about all your current processes, looking much like this:

```
 F S    UID   PID  PPID  C PRI  NI ADDR    SZ WCHAN  TTY            TIME CMD
100 S   1004  7719  1320  0  69   0    -   629 wait4  tty3       00:00:00 bash
000 S   1004  7746  7719  0  72   0    -   639 wait4  tty3       00:00:00 sh
000 R   1004  7758  7746  0  76   0    -   816 -      tty3       00:00:00 ps
```

Following are descriptions of some of the fields in this display. The **man** pages provide information about **ps** on your system and are an essential resource.

• **Flags (F)**   This field contains a number indicating what Flags or options are set for the process. For this purpose, the only meaningful number is the one that indicates that the process is in memory. Which of your processes is in memory? Certainly **ps** is—it must be in memory when it is running, and it must be running while it is performing its function. Probably the shell that is running—**bash**, **tcsh**, **csh**, or **ksh**—is also in memory.

- **State (S)** The State field contains an uppercase letter indicating the state of the process. The most common states are sleeping (**S**) and running (**R**). Other states are idle (**I**) and traced (**T**) for suspended processes.
- **Size (SZ)** The SiZe field contains a number that indicates the size of the process in memory. Depending on which system you are using, the process size may be given in kilobytes, blocks, or pages.
- **Command (CMD)** This label refers to the actual command being run by the process.

Identifying the Genealogy of Processes

A process is much more than a series of instructions for the CPU to follow. Important data is associated with each process, including the workstation (*tty*) to which it is attached, a list of open files to which it can write, and other pertinent information. When you create a process, it inherits most of this information from its parent process.

1. Enter the following commands to explore how processes keep track of their parents:

   ps -l
   sh
   ps -l

2. Using the new subset of fields displayed by the **ps -l** command, fill in the following chart:

PID	PPID	TTY	CMD
			_____(shell)
			sh
			ps

   Essentially, each process is created, or spawned, by a previously existing process—its parent process. Each process knows its own *PID* and the *PID* of its parent. Specifically, in the table you just created, the *PPID* (**P**arent *PID*) associated with the **sh** process is identical to the *PID* associated with

sh's parent—that is, whatever shell process (**csh**, **bash**, or **ksh**) you were in when you started the **sh**. The shell process executed the **sh** and therefore is the parent of the **sh** process. When we ask a child for the name of his or her parent, we get the same answer as when we ask the parent for his or her own name.

Processes inherit data from their parent process. When you log on to the system, the login program starts up your first process, which is usually the shell process. From then on, every utility or executable filename that you type in is executed by a process that is a child (or *n*th grandchild) of your shell process. Because each new process that is created is a child process, it inherits data (such as *tty*, user ID, and the current directory) from the parent process. Variables that are exported are passed to the child shell.

Ending Foreground Processes

Generally, once a process is under way, it runs until it is finished, unless you issue a keyboard interrupt, log out, or instruct the process to die.

Identifying the Interrupt Setting

One of the important settings for your terminal is the *interrupt*, which tells processes to exit. Usually, the interrupt is set to CTRL-C, but it may be set to another key sequence.

▶   Display the setting for your system:

stty -a

The output is a long list of settings for your teletype input device. Well, in the 1970s it was a teletype machine, today it is a terminal and keyboard. The signals the terminal and system use for communication are displayed in lines such as the following.

```
intr = ^C; quit = ^\; erase = ^h; kill = ^U; eof = ^D; eol = M-^?; eol2 = M-^?;
```

One of the settings is probably:

```
intr = ^C
```

This indicates that whenever your terminal sends a CTRL-C signal, UNIX/Linux interprets it as the *interrupt* signal.. If you have some other value set for `intr`, use it in the following exercises instead of CTRL-C.

Interrupting a Process from the Keyboard

We can end running processes by issuing a signal.

⤷ 1. Start a process by entering:

>   **sleep** *100*

>   The program is running in the foreground; you are not presented with a new prompt. At this point, you could wait nearly two minutes (100 seconds), or you could tell the shell to issue the interrupt signal to the process.

2. Press:

>   CTRL-C

>   The **sleep** process dies and the shell asks what's next.

3. Ask for the exit status that the process running **sleep** sent to the your shell as it exited:

>   For the **sh** family of shells and recent **csh** family shells:

>   **echo** *$?*

>   For older **csh** family of shells:

>   **echo** *$status*

The shell interprets the variable *?* or *status* as the value of the exit code of the last process. The status reported is probably *130* or *1*, indicating that the process did not end successfully, but was terminated.

Comparing the End-of-File Signal with the Interrupt Signal

The interrupt and end-of-file signals both bring many utilities to a close. However, they are not the same.

⤷ 1. Start a utility with the keyboard as input:

>   **wc**

2. Enter a few lines.

3. Then, on a new line, indicate that you are through entering data by pressing the end-of-file character:

>   CTRL-D

>   The output of **wc** is displayed, reporting the number of lines, words, and characters that you entered as input.

4. Run **wc** again, but do not issue an end-of-file character; instead, enter an interrupt as follows:

wc

A few lines of text

CTRL-C

After receiving the interrupt CTRL-C, the process exits, the shell prompt is displayed, but no output is generated by **wc**. When we issue a CTRL-D, we are saying, "end of file, there is no more input, do your counting and report." In contrast, the CTRL-C interrupt signal tells the process to stop all operations, die, and be gone. No output is generated; the process just croaks.

Telling a Process to Quit

Another keyboard signal that users can employ to stop a foreground process is *quit*.

1. Start a foreground process:

   sleep *300*

   The **sleep** process is running in the foreground. No new prompt is displayed.

2. Instruct the process to *quit* with the CTRL-backslash:

   CTRL-\

   The **sleep** process quits; a new shell prompt is displayed. The *quit* signal destroys the process and sometimes makes a copy of the CPU memory associated with the process at the time of its hasty exit. This copy is called a *core* file.

3. List your files and remove the *core* file if it is there:

   ls

   rm core

The *interrupt* (CTRL-C) and its stronger brother *quit* (CTRL-\) are available to users to force a process running in the foreground to exit.

Ending Background Processes

When a process is running in the foreground, we can issue interrupt and quit signals from the keyboard. If a process is running in the background, what is the impact of the interrupt and quit signals?

Interrupting and Quitting

Start another process.

1. Enter:

   sleep *500* &

The **&** appended to the command line tells the shell that the command should not be run as the current job, but rather should be executed in the background while the shell attends to other tasks that we request.

2. With the **sleep** process running in the background, enter:

> **ps**

3. Attempt to issue the *interrupt* and *quit* signals:

> CTRL-C
>
> CTRL-\
>
> **ps**

The *interrupt* and *quit* signals from the keyboard have no impact on the process. We are not able to send keyboard signals to a process unless it is running in the foreground.

Killing a Background Process

We can terminate processes running in the background.

1. Examine the output from the last **ps** and identify the *PID* of the **sleep** process.

2. Kill the **sleep** process using its *PID* as the second argument in the following:

> **kill -2** *PID*

The shell responds with

```
[1]   Interrupt    sleep 500
```

indicating that the process ended as a result of an interrupt.

The **kill** command sends one of several *signals*, which are like bad news telegrams to processes. For instance, we can kill many processes running in the foreground by entering the keyboard interrupt character, CTRL-C. We can achieve the very same result by sending *signal 2* (**kill -2** *PID*) to the process. In fact, the keyboard interrupt character CTRL-C just sends *signal 2* to the foreground process that is attached to your terminal. When you press CTRL-C with no process in the foreground, the shell process itself gets the *interrupt*. Wisely, the shells are programmed to *catch* the interrupt signal and to do nothing special with them. Upon receipt of a signal, a process may be programmed to forestall its demise by catching the signal, or it may follow the signal's instruction and exit. Not all utilities can catch signals.

The **-2** option to **kill** instructs it to issue the *interrupt* signal to whatever process is associated with the argument *PID*. We can also enter instructions to **kill** to send the same *quit* signal to a process as we send from the keyboard with CTRL-\.

3. Start another process, identify the *PID*, and kill it with the *quit* signal as an argument to **kill**:

> **sleep** *600* **&**
>
> **ps**
>
> **kill** *-3* *PID*   (the *PID* of the sleep process)

The shell confirms the process was ended with a *quit*.

The CTRL-\ from the keyboard sends the same *quit* signal to the current foreground process that **kill** *-3* sends to any process identified by its *PID*.

Listing All Signals

Although users need only a few signals, the system employs a large variety.

The signals that we mainly use are:

Signal *1*	Hangup; closes process communication links.
Signal *2*	Interrupt; tells process to exit.
Signal *3*	Quit; forces the process to quit.
Signal *6*	Aborts the process.
Signal *9*	Kills the process; cannot be caught.
Signal *15*	Software terminate (default signal for **kill**); tells the process that the application it is running must exit.

When you need to kill a process, start with **kill** and no argument, which is the same *-15*, and then increase the power with *-2*, then *-3* and *-6*. If nothing else works, enter **kill** with a *-9* argument. Signal *9* is special; the process cannot catch it. So unless another process is involved, the process ends. However, you should always try one or more of the other signals first, because processes need to go through some cleanup procedure before they exit. Sending them signal *9* prevents processes from performing the cleanup operations.

We can list all the available **kill** signals for the current system.

➡ Enter:

> **kill** *-l*   (minus *el* for <u>l</u>ist signals)

Terminating a Process That Is Not Responding

Sometimes a process gets hung up, fails to respond, and is not affected by interrupt and quit signals. There is a temptation to head for the three-finger salute.

CTRL-ALT-DELETE. Don't. In UNIX and Linux systems, processes get hung, not the system.

1. Start a long process in the foreground:

   sleep 1000

   For this exercise, we will pretend that the process is not responding to the usual interrupt and quit signals. Because it is running in the foreground, we cannot run **ps** to determine the *PID*. Nor could we run **kill**, if we knew the *PID*. The goal is to gain access to a shell that can be used to determine the *PID* of the runaway **sleep** process and then **kill** the process. Three choices are available.

2. Start a new terminal by doing the one of the following that is appropriate:
   - If you are in the graphical environment, click the shell icon.
   - If you are on a UNIX system with many terminals attached to the server, log on to another terminal.
   - If you are on a Linux system, you can employ a virtual terminal. Press CTRL-F3 and log in again.

3. Identify your current terminal port at the new login or terminal:

   tty

4. List your processes:

   ps -u *$USER* | more

5. Identify the *PID* of the runaway **sleep** process and use **kill** to terminate it.

This approach of establishing a new shell to determine the *PID* of errant processes and then dealing with them protects the system from harsh shutdowns caused by pressing CTRL-ALT-DEL.

10.2 Managing Jobs

A command line that instructs the shell to start several processes with output from the first connected to the second, and so forth, is often called a *job*. All modern shells allow us to start, suspend, make active, and kill all processes associated with a job.

Part of effective process management is the ability to switch from one task to another. Suppose you need to print a file, but you're in the middle of writing a long letter with the editor. When you're running one program, you cannot start a new program without terminating the first program, unless you are in a graphical environment or are using virtual terminals. You could **kill** the editing session, or you could finish the letter before printing the file, or you could open a new window or virtual terminal. In most environments, you can suspend one program without ending it to start another program.

Suspending a Job

First we need to check what CTRL keys your shell in interpreting as instruction to suspend a process.

↳ 1. Enter:

    stty -a

The display is the list examined earlier that describes the CTRL key settings that the terminal and shell use for communication. Among the lines in the output are the following:

```
intr = ^C; quit = ^\; erase = ^h; kill = ^U; eof = ^D; eol = M-^?; eol2 = M-^?;
start = ^Q; stop = ^S; susp = ^Z; rprnt = ^R; werase = ^W; lnext = ^V;
```

In particular, you probably have the following on one of the lines:

```
susp = ^Z;
```

Don't attempt to use this CTRL key until we provide instructions in the next steps. However, if your system uses a different CTRL sequence for *susp,* use whatever is listed in the following exercises.

Begin by starting a process to edit a new file.

2. Enter:

    vi *joy*

3. Type a line such as the following:

    Bill Joy has made enormous contributions to our field.

4. Return to command mode of the editor by pressing:

    ESC

5. While in command mode, press:

    CTRL-Z

The shell responds with the message:

```
[1] Stopped
```

or

```
[1] Suspended
```

This output includes *[1]*, which is the number the shell is assigning to the job that you just suspended by pressing CTRL-Z. The shell then displays a new prompt showing it is ready for new instructions.

6. List your current processes:

   ps -l

The **vi** process is still there, although you are not actually editing the file at the moment. The process that is running **vi** is now *suspended* (the technical term is *Traced [T]*, and it appears as the status code **T** in the output).

Bringing a Suspended Job Back into the Foreground

You are sitting at your desk reading a book. The phone rings. You insert a bookmark in the book, put it down, and answer the phone. You don't put the book back on the library shelf or give it back to its owner and lose your place. With a bookmark in the book, you can return to the exact place you left off when you are ready to continue. By keeping the book around and using a bookmark, you are really suspending the job of reading the book. Picking the book up and starting again is bringing the reading process into the foreground, making it active.

Likewise, we can request that a suspended UNIX/Linux job be made active again.

1. Enter:

   fg

   The **vi** process editing the file *joy* becomes active, exactly where you left off before you suspended the process. The **fg** command without an argument brings the last suspended job into the <u>f</u>oreground.

   Add some more text.

2. Return to command mode and then suspend the **vi** process again:

   ESC

   CTRL-Z

   ps

Identifying Jobs That Are Running or Suspended

You just started **vi** in the foreground and then suspended it. Start the following jobs in the background.

⤷ 1. Enter:

    sleep *1500* *&*

    A message similar to the following is displayed:

    `[2] 11407`

    and the shell prompt reappears.

2. Enter:

    sleep *60* *&*

    A message similar to the following appears:

    `[3] 11422`

    The bracketed numbers [2] and [3] are the *job numbers* for each background job. Following the job number is the *PID* for the process.

3. Start a process in the foreground and suspend it with:

    sleep *20*

    CTRL-Z

4. Now list the current processes:

    ps -u *$USER*

    The **ps** utility displays information about each individual process. Another utility lists the jobs that are running or suspended.

5. Enter:

    jobs

    The **vi** job is listed as job *[1]* and is "Stopped" or "Suspended." The **sleep** jobs *[2]* and *[3]* are running, even though they are in the background. In less than a minute, the **sleep** *60*, job *[3]*, will be finished and will exit. The last **sleep** that was suspended (or stopped) is not running, but it is not killed, either. The system keeps track of where the program stopped its execution (bookmark) and can restart it at the same point later. The process consumes no computer time while it is suspended.

6. Start another job, suspend it, and examine the job list:

    vi *newfile*

    CTRL-Z

    jobs

The **jobs** program lists all background and suspended jobs and their status.

Comparing Jobs and Processes

The **jobs** program lists all jobs that are either suspended or in the background in the current shell.

1. At the shell prompt, enter:

   grep *the* | **tr** *'a-z' 'A-Z'* | **uniq** | **sort**

   Because only one argument is passed to **grep**, it is interpreted as the target search string. No filename argument is provided, so **grep** reads from input connected to the keyboard. Whatever you enter is searched by **grep**, passed to **tr**, then passed to **uniq**, and finally passed to **sort**, which displays its output on the screen.

2. Enter the following text, being sure to include all the *the* strings.

   ```
   what is this?
   the cat
   FATHER
   THE cat
   the dog
   father
   The dogs
   ```

3. Instruct the shell to suspend the whole job by pressing:

   CTRL-Z

   The shell responds with the suspended information either on one line or across several:

   ```
   [3]  Stopped   grep  the  |  tr  'a-z'  'A-Z'  |  uniq  |  sort
   ```

   At this point, you have, either running or suspended, two **vi**, one long **sleep,** one suspended **sleep** (unless you are very speedy, the **sleep** *60* has surely exited), and the processes in the recently suspended **grep** job.

4. Confirm by listing the jobs:

   jobs

   A list of jobs appears, similar to the following:

   ```
   [1]  -     Stopped    vi joy
   [2]        Running    sleep 1500

   [3]        Stopped    sleep 20
   [4]  .     Stopped    vi newfile

   [5]  +     grep the | tr 'a-z' 'A' 'Z'| uniq | sort
   ```

The output shows that the whole **grep** command line probably is job *[5]*. The **jobs** command is a shell built-in command. It lists all jobs that are running in the background or that have been suspended. The **jobs** output is divided into four columns: the job number, the order (the + marks the lead job, and the – marks the second job), the status (running in the background or stopped), and the command being executed.

5. Examine your current **jobs** and processes using the <u>l</u>ong listing to get the *PID*s and *PPID*s:

   jobs
   ps -l

   The single job [5] that started with **grep** is seen as one job, and this job consists of many different processes. Every job can include one to many processes. If the job is more than one process, pipes connect them. Note that all the processes associated the **grep** job, have the same parent *PID*—your current shell.

Bringing a Suspended Job into the Foreground

When we start a job, it is either in the background or the foreground. We can suspend a foreground job. We can also make a suspended job the foreground job or change it to the background.

While your job is suspended, you can give any instructions to the shell that you wish. You can edit files, run other utilities, or even edit other files.

1. Check the date and time by typing:

   date

2. Restart your **grep** job again by typing:

   fg

   The system responds with:

   ```
   grep the | tr 'a-z' 'A-Z'| uniq | sort
   ```

   You are back at the same place, entering data to be read by **grep**. The job is back in the <u>f</u>oreground.

3. Enter another line to **grep**, such as:

   When will the output be displayed?

4. On a new line, end the input with the end-of-file marker:

   CTRL-D

The output is a unique, uppercase, sorted list of the lines you entered containing the string *the*. The whole collection of processes is suspended and brought into the foreground.

5. Bring the next suspended job into the foreground with:

   fg

6. Dispose of the job with **:q!** if it is **vi** or CTRL-C if it is a **sleep** process.

7. Continue bringing each suspended **sleep** job to the foreground:

   fg

8. End each job appropriately.

The **fg** command brings the most recent (lead) job into the foreground.

Recalling the Most Recent Jobs Specifically

So far, you have manipulated only the lead job, the most recently issued. We can access the other jobs without killing the lead jobs in succession.

1. Make sure you have several jobs pending by typing:

   sleep 200 &
   sort | grep 'a-z'
   CTRL-Z
   sleep 150
   CTRL-Z
   vi *practice*
   CTRL-Z
   jobs

   The **vi** *practice* job is the most recently suspended job, and it is marked with a plus sign. The **sleep 150** job is the next most recently suspended and is marked with a minus sign.

2. Previously, you brought the lead job into the foreground by typing **fg**. This time, bring the lead job specifically into the foreground by typing:

   fg %+

   The %+ argument to **fg** in the command line specifies the lead job. Because **vi** *practice* is the lead job, it is brought to the foreground and is now the current job.

3. Add a few lines of text.

4. Escape to command mode and suspend the **vi** process again by entering:

   CTRL-Z

5. Check the job status:

   jobs

   The lead job **vi** *practice* is again marked with the plus sign, and the previous job is marked with the minus sign.

6. Move the previous lead job into the foreground by entering:

   fg %-

   The %- is the symbol for the job started before the lead job. In the example, the suspended **sleep** *150* job is listed above (before) the lead job. This command tells the shell to bring it into the foreground.

7. Resuspend the current job by pressing:

   CTRL-Z

8. Enter:

   jobs

   Note that **sleep**, which was the second lead job, is now the lead job (marked with a **+**). This is because it was the last job suspended.

Recalling Jobs from the Jobs List

We can specify any job on the job list and bring it into the foreground.

1. Have the shell display a list of the current jobs. Type:

   jobs

   The output is a listing of all of your stopped or background jobs.

2. Place the job listed as having job number 2 in the foreground by entering:

   fg %2

   The %2 specifies the job with the job number 2, which is brought to the foreground.

3. Resuspend the job by pressing:

   CTRL-Z

4. Similarly, bring the fourth job to the foreground. Type:

   fg %4

   Job number *4* is brought to the foreground.

5. Suspend it again by pressing:

    CTRL-Z

    Another way to bring jobs to the foreground is by using the job name instead of its number.

6. Enter:

    fg %sort

7. Resuspend the job by pressing:

    CTRL-Z

    You can even use the first letter of the job name.

8. Enter:

    fg %v

    The suspended **vi** job is now brought to the foreground. If you have more than one job that begins with the same letter, add one or more characters in order to differentiate the job you desire to bring to the foreground.

9. Resuspend this job by pressing:

    CTRL-Z

Killing a Particular Job

Earlier, we killed the current foreground job using CTRL-C (the interrupt signal), and killed specific processes using the *PID* as an argument to the **kill** command. In this section, we examine how to terminate or kill stopped jobs and jobs running in the background.

1. Find out what jobs you have pending by typing:

    jobs

2. Kill the most recent job in the job list by entering:

    kill %+

3. Examine the list of jobs again:

    jobs

    The job probably exited; if not, increase the power of the **kill** signal with *-1* or *-2* and so forth.

    Another way to kill a job is by using the job number.

4. To kill job number 2, type:

    kill %2

    A message is displayed that indicates that the job has been killed.

To avoid killing the wrong jobs, first check the currently running jobs, using the **jobs** command then use **kill** to terminate the appropriate job.

5. Try this now. Type:

    jobs

6. Kill one of the other jobs, using its job number as the # in the following:

    kill -1 %#

    You can also use the initial part of the command line of a suspended job to kill it by typing:

    kill %*sort*

> **C A U T I O N :** In general, to kill a particular job, you use the command **kill %***job_number* or **kill %***command.* You may kill the wrong job if you are not particularly careful. If you run **jobs** to determine the rank or job number of the job you want to kill, and the **+** job is running in the background, that job could finish before you enter the **kill** command. If this happens, you may kill the wrong job.

10.3 Exiting When Jobs Have Been Stopped

Job control is a very useful method for managing processes. Because background jobs and stopped jobs remain invisible to you until the jobs either write to the terminal or are finished, you might forget that processes other than the current one are running. UNIX job control provides a method of warning you of stopped or running background jobs when you attempt a **logout** or **exit** of the process.

1. Type the **jobs** command to make sure there are jobs running in the background or stopped.

2. If you do not have any stopped jobs, add:

    vi *testfile* **&**

3. Issue the command to exit your shell:

    exit

    The shell responds with an error message:

    ```
    There are suspended jobs.
    ```

    or

    ```
    There are stopped jobs.
    ```

    In addition to the issue of stopped jobs remaining in the queue, you have not exited the shell. The assumption is that you have forgotten about your stopped jobs, so you are informed that there are stopped jobs, and the current shell remains active.

> **CAUTION:** This gives you a chance to decide whether to kill any of the unresolved jobs. Text editors and database programs are good examples of programs you do not want to kill. However, if you were able to log off without resolving these programs, they would continue. When you logged on again, you would not be able to access the process from your new shell. You would then have to kill the process and lose any work done.

4. Check your jobs now by typing:

   jobs

5. If you don't care whether the jobs continue running, you can ignore them and exit anyway by typing **exit** again:

   exit

When you make this second request, the shell exits even though there are stopped jobs.

Self-Test

1. A user enters **who**, and the output of **who** is displayed on the screen. What process is the parent of **who**?

   _____

2. A user enters the command:

   grep *class* **/etc/passwd** | **sort** | **tr** *'a-z'* *'A-Z'*

   A. How many processes are started?_____

   B. How many jobs are started?   _____

3. Let's say you start a foreground process that appears to be taking too much time. You decide to terminate the process. What do you enter to kill the running process?

   _____

4. If there is no response to the attempts to send interrupts or quits to the process and the terminal appears to be locked up, how could you determine the *PID* of the wayward process?

_____

_____

5. Once you determine the *PID* of the process in the previous question, how do you kill it?

_____

6. Suppose that you enter the following sequence of commands to your shell:

> **who >** */dev/null* **&**
> **sleep** *100* **&**
> **vi** *practice*
>
> CTRL-Z
>
> **jobs**

What is the output of **jobs** and why?

_____

Chapter Review

Use this section to review the content of this chapter and test yourself on your knowledge of the concepts.

Chapter Summary

- Any program running in a system is being executed by a process that reads the appropriate code and accomplishes the tasks.
- All processes have their own unique process identification number (*PID*), the *PID* of their parent (*PPID*), an owner, group, memory, code, input, output, error, and, if attached to a terminal, its *tty* port.
- A process follows its instruction code to conclusion and then exits or terminates unless it receives a signal to exit prematurely.
- A command line that is entered consisting of one process or a series of processes connected by pipes is a *job* and can be managed as one entity.
- If the job is running in the foreground, we can terminate it by issuing an interrupt (CTRL-C) or a quit (CTRL-\).

- A job is executed in the background when the **&** is placed at the end of the command line. A background job continues to run but accepts no keyboard input. Keyboard interrupt and quit signals do not reach a background job. We must terminate them by using the **kill** command with either the process ID or the *%job_number* as an argument, or by bringing them into the foreground where interrupt and quit are effective.
- A job can be suspended so that it remains intact, but no processing takes place. It is simply bookmarked until it is brought back into the foreground for continued execution.
- We can kill or terminate jobs and processes by sending them signals of various meanings. The **kill** command terminates processes identified by either their process ID or job number.

Assignment

Fill-in.

1. What series of commands starts a child **csh** shell, determines the current port, and then examines the processes currently running on that port?

   _____

2.

   A. What signal quits a process?_____

   B. What signal interrupts a process?_____

   C. What are the differences between the two?_____

   D. When should you use **kill -9**?_____

   _____

   For the next three questions, refer to the following listing:

   ```
   [2]         Stopped    sort /etc/passwd
   [3]    -    Stopped    vi .cshrc
   [4]    +    Stopped    more .login
   [5]         Running    find / -name foo
   ```

3. What command would you use to bring the **vi** editor to the foreground?

   _____

4. What is the command you would use to kill the **more** process?

   _____

5. What is the command you would use to get this listing?

   _____

6. Consider the following scenario: You log on to your system on *tty23*. The system starts a **csh** for you that has a PID of *1056*. Then you start a shell script (the script is executed by a **sh** with a PID of *1080*) that in turn executes **who** (a PID of *2020*).

   A. What is the PPID of the **who** process?

   _____

   B. What is the PPID of the process executing the script?

   _____

   C. With information provided, can you determine with what *tty* the **who** process is associated?

   _____

Project

A. Create a file called *root-proc* containing a list of processes owned by root, sorted by process ID.

B. Create a file called *my-proc* containing a list of all your current processes, sorted by process ID.

C. Log off, then log back in.

D. Create a file called *root-proc2* containing a list of processes owned by root, sorted by process ID.

E. Create a new file called *my-proc2* containing a list of all your current processes, sorted by process ID.

F. Compare *my-proc* and *my-proc2*. What differences do you find? Why?

G. Compare *root-proc* and *root-proc2*. What differences do you find? Why?

COMMAND SUMMARY

ps	Lists processes that you own.
ps -l	Generates a long listing of your processes.
ps -f	Outputs a full listing of processes that you own.
ps -u *login*	Lists processes that are owned by the user whose login ID is login.
ps -t *nn*	Lists processes that are associated with the workstation tty.
ps -ef	Prints information about all processes.
ps -aux	Prints information about all processes.
kill *PID*	Terminates a process by sending a Software Terminate signal.
kill -1 *PID*	Hangs up communication links to a process.
kill -2 *PID*	Ends a process by sending a Process Interrupt signal.
kill -3 *PID*	Brings a process to a conclusion by issuing a Process Quit signal.
kill -6 *PID*	Instructs a process to end by issuing the Abort Process signal.
kill -15 *PID*	Instructs a process to end by issuing the Software Terminate signal (default).
kill -9 *PID*	Kills a process. This is usually the last form of kill to try. It usually cannot be ignored, but may not allow the utility to clean up.
CTRL-C	Kills the current foreground process by sending the interrupt signal.
CTRL-	Kills the current foreground process by sending the quit signal.
CTRL-Z	Suspends the current job.
fg	Brings the most recently stopped job into the foreground.
fg %+	Brings the most recently stopped job into the foreground.
fg %-	Brings the stopped job listed before the most recent into the foreground.
fg %*job_num*	Brings the job with number job_num into the foreground.
fg %*command*	Brings the job with name command into the foreground.
jobs	Prints a listing of all of the stopped and background jobs under control of the current shell.
kill %*job_num*	Kills the job with job number job_num. Without an argument, kill terminates the most recently stopped job.

Locating, Printing, and Archiving User Files

O B J E C T I V E S

After completing this chapter, you will be able to:

- Split a large file into several small pieces and reassemble the file
- Locate files by using name or other characteristics in the filesystem
- Copy files to floppy disks and retrieve them
- Send files to specific printers and remove them from queues
- Create and manage archives of directories and their files

As we use Linux and UNIX systems to accomplish work, we often create large files that we have to manage. We need to split files into smaller pieces, copy individual files or whole directory trees to backup media or archives, and locate or recover lost files. This chapter examines how to accomplish those tasks.

11.1 Creating a Long File

To complete the exercises in this chapter, you need to have a text file that is at least 200 short lines long. The content is not important, the length is.

1. Create a new file containing a list of the names of the files in your home directory:

    ls -R ~ > *longfile*

    To make the file longer, the next command takes the first 25 characters from each of the lines in your *practice* file and adds them to the end of *longfile*.

2. Enter the following, which uses double-redirects to add to the file:

    cut -c 1-25 *~/practice* >> *longfile*
    more *longfile*

    The first 25 characters from each line in the *practice* file in your home directory are read and added to the end of *longfile*.

3. Add the names of the files listed in */bin* by entering the following:

    ls */bin* >> *longfile*

4. Examine the file, determine the number of lines, and keep adding the filenames listed in */bin* until *longfile* is at least 200 lines long:

    more *longfile*
    wc -l *longfile*
    ls */bin* >> *longfile*
    wc -l *longfile*
    ls */bin* >> *longfile*

5. Instruct **cat** to add numbers to the left of all lines in a copy of the file:

    cat -n *longfile* > *nlongfile*
    more *nlongfile*

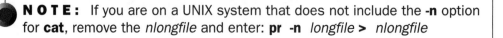

> **N O T E :** If you are on a UNIX system that does not include the **-n** option for **cat**, remove the *nlongfile* and enter: **pr -n** *longfile* > *nlongfile*

The file is now reasonably long and has a number at the beginning of each line in the file.

11.2 Splitting Long Files

Sometimes a file is too long to fit on a floppy or to be processed by a utility. We could use **sed** to break the file into pieces and then invent a naming scheme for the parts that could be used to reassemble the pieces quickly. Or we could use **split**. Let's use **split**.

Creating a Directory to Do Splits

The current directory contains many files. By creating a new directory and placing a copy of the long file there, we can see the small files generated.

1. Create a new directory so we can play with **split** more easily:
     mkdir *SplitDIR*
2. Copy the long file you just created into the new directory
     cp *nlongfile SplitDIR*
3. Make *SplitDIR* the current directory:
     cd *SplitDIR*
4. Count the elements of the file:
     wc *nlongfile*

The total number of lines, words, and characters in the file is calculated and output to the screen.

Splitting a Long File into Pieces

The contents of any long file can be read and broken into a series of small files.

1. We can employ **split** to read *nlongfile* and break up the contents. Enter:
     split -20 *nlongfile lf+*
2. Examine the contents of the current directory with:
     ls
     ls *lf**

The directory now contains a series of files with filenames such as *lf+aa*, *lf+ab*, *lf+ac*, and so forth. The file was **split** into files of 20 lines, with each piece named *lf+* and two letters of the alphabet.

3. Examine the pieces:

> **more** *lf+aa*
> **wc** *lf **

Each file, except for the last one, has 20 lines in it. The first 20 lines of the *longfile* are in file *lf+aa*, the next 20 in *lf+ab*, and so forth. The original file remains intact. Its contents were read and written to several files.

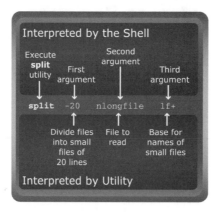

We now have a copy of the file split into pieces of specified size. Each piece has an extension starting with *aa* and going through the alphabet as far as needed to hold a copy of the whole file.

Reassembling the Pieces

A copy of the original file is now residing in a series of short files. We can use **cat** to read all the small files and output data that matches the original file.

1. Enter:

> **cat** *lf+** | **more**

The output is the contents of the original file, with its lines in the proper order.

The last part of the filenames that **split** added, such as *aa* and *ab*, are in ASCII order, the same order the shell uses for the filenames when it replaces the * in the command line.

2. Remove the pieces and then split the file into much smaller units:

rm *lf+**
split -5 *nlongfile slong*
ls *slong**
wc *slong**

The *nlongfile* file is divided into small files of five lines each, each file with a name beginning with *slong* and ending with *aa* through *az*, then *ba* through *bz*, and so on.

3. Enter:

cat *slong** **|** **more**

The file's pieces are read and assembled into the right order.

Very long files can be split, placed in media with limited file size capacity, transferred elsewhere, then reassembled in a target environment.

11.3 Locating Files with *find*

As you create more complex directory structures, it becomes easier to lose files. Fortunately, UNIX provides a utility that searches through directory trees to find missing files based on several criteria such as the file's name, owner, size, age, or permissions assigned.

Locating Files by Name

Files named *practice* are located in several of your directories. All of the files named *practice* can be located using the utility that searches.

Ask **find** to locate each file with the name *practice* by entering:

find ~ -name *practice* **-print**

The **find** utility may take some time to complete its work. As **find** is examining directories, it reports to your workstation screen both its output and any error information that is appropriate. You may see the pathnames of files named *practice*, as well as information about which directories you cannot examine because of their assigned permissions.

The preceding command line is interpreted as follows:

COMMAND/ ARGUMENT	INTERPRETATION
find	Instructs the shell to execute the **find** utility, which searches a target directory and all of its subdirectories.
~	The first argument specifies the target starting point directory—in this case, your home directory. After searching through the target directory, **find** searches all subdirectories listed in your home directory. This recursive examination continues until all files and directories below the target directory are examined.
-name *practice*	Instructs **find** to locate all files with the specified name *practice*.
-print	Specifies that the full pathname of each occurrence of the file(s) matching the selection criterion should be output to your screen, unless you redirect it elsewhere. In this case, *print* just means to output, not actually print on the printer.

Locating Files by Owner

The **find** utility is used to locate files based on a variety of criteria. We just found files that had the target name. We can also instruct **find** to select all files owned by a specified user.

Creating a Directory and Files to Locate

This section will guide you in creating several files in a directory in the *tmp* directory so we can search for files based on ownership.

1. Determine whether you have a directory in */tmp* named the same as your user login name:

   ls -ld */tmp/$USER*

2. If a long listing for your directory in */tmp* is displayed, make sure you have full permissions (**rwx**) for the directory.

3. If you do not have a directory in */tmp* of your login name, create one:

   mkdir */tmp/$USER*

4. Make sure you are in your home directory:

   cd

5. Copy three of your files to the directory you created in */tmp*:

   cp *practice names.tmp users_on* */tmp/$USER*

6. Create a subdirectory of your directory in */tmp*:

>**mkdir** */tmp/$USER/Hall*

7. Add two files to the new directory:

>**ls** > */tmp/$USER/Hall/candlestick*
>**date** > */tmp/$USER/Hall/colmustard*

You now own several files located in */tmp*'s subdirectories.

Locating a User's Files

Instruct **find** to identify files owned by you by entering:

>**find** */tmp* **-user** *$USER* **-print**

The paths to all files in the target */tmp* directory and all its subdirectories that you own are displayed. In addition to the files you just placed in */tmp*, there may be others you or your processes created there. Certainly the two files and directory are there: evidently, *colmustard* did it with the *candlestick* in the *Hall*. In general, this command instructs **find** to display all files belonging to the identified user that are located in the directory tree that has */tmp* at the top.

The elements of the preceding command line are interpreted as follows:

COMMAND / ARGUMENT	INTERPRETATION
find	Instructs the shell to run the **find** utility.
/tmp	This first argument to **find** instructs **find** to start its search in the */tmp* directory and search all directories below that.
-user	This option instructs **find** to search for files by the owner (user) associated with the file, not by name or any other criteria.
$USER	The shell replaces *$USER* with your login name and passes that name as an argument to **find**. This argument directly follows the **user** argument and is interpreted by **find** to be the user whose files should be located. All files belonging to this user in the directory tree starting at */tmp* are located.
-print	Once files are located, this action takes place. The path to the selected files is output.

Putting *find*'s Output in a File

In the previous exercise, the **find** utility completed a search of the directory tree below */tmp* and displayed the output on the screen. Often we need to obtain a list of all files owned by an employee (or ex-employee) and save the list. Because **find** is a utility, we can redirect its output to a file or to another utility such as the printer.

➥ 1. Instruct the shell to redirect the output of **find** to a new file:

   > **find** */tmp* **-user** *$USER* **-print** > *my-tmp-files*

2. After **find** completes its search, examine the output file:

   > **more** *my-tmp-files*

The *my-tmp-files* contains a listing of the pathnames for the files you own in */tmp* or any of its subdirectories. We redirected the output, not error, so any error messages went to your screen and not to the output file.

Using Error Redirection with *find*

When we search for a file with **find**, the screen often fills with many error messages, prohibiting us from further work. We can redirect all error output from jobs running in the background.

➥ In an **sh** family shell, enter:

   find **..** **-name** *temp* **-print** 2> */dev/null* 1> *mytemp* **&**

The **find** utility looks for all files named *temp* in all directories starting with your parent directory. If a *temp* file is found, its full pathname is placed in the *mytemp* file.

In this case, output, called **1,** is redirected to *mytemp,* and errors, called **2,** are sent to the "bit bucket in the sky," */dev/null*. All systems have a */dev/null*, which accepts any input we give it, but never writes it anywhere. When we want output neither saved nor on the screen, we redirect it to */dev/null*.

Locating and Acting on Files by Owner

In addition to writing file names to output, you can instruct **find** to remove located files, change file permissions, or employ essentially any shell file-manipulation command.

➥ 1. Enter:

   find */tmp* **-user** *$USER* **-exec** **head** **-2** {} \; **-print**

The execution of this command results in the printing of the first two lines of all files belonging to the selected owner that are located in the directory tree with */tmp* at the top.

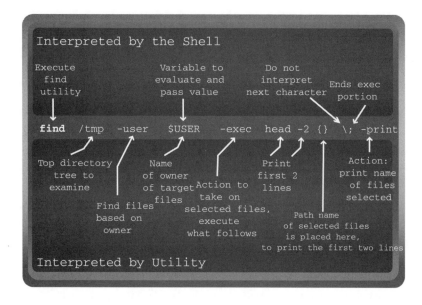

The preceding command line is interpreted as follows:

COMMAND/ ARGUMENT/ OPTION	INTERPRETATION
find	Instructs the shell to run the **find** utility.
/tmp	Instructs **find** to start its search in the **/tmp** directory and search all directories below that.
-user	Instructs **find** to search for files by owner.
$USER	The shell interprets **$USER**, replaces it with its value—your login name—and passes the login name as an argument to **find**. This argument directly follows the **-user** argument and is interpreted by **find** to be the user name whose files should be located. All files belonging to this user in the directory tree starting at **/tmp** are located.
-exec	Instructs the shell to execute the command that follows on all files located.
head *-2*	Instructs the shell to run the **head** utility with a *-2* option.
{}	Placeholder for the located filename(s). **find** substitutes each filename that meets the selection criteria into the command following **exec** at this location. Hence, each located file becomes an argument to **head**, and the first two lines from that file are displayed.

COMMAND/ ARGUMENT/ OPTION	INTERPRETATION
\;	Tells **find** where the **exec** command ends. A semicolon (;) is always required to identify the end of the **-exec** portion of the **find** command. The backslash before the semicolon is required to tell the shell not to interpret the semicolon. If there were no backslash, the shell would interpret the semicolon as a command separator and run everything up to the semicolon as one command.
-print	Instructs **find** to output the path to all files that meet the search criteria.

The **find** utility, with the **-exec** option, is used to execute any command utilizing the filename(s) that are selected.

2. As another example, enter:

> **find** /*tmp* **-user** *$USER* **-exec ls -lFi {} \; -print 2>** /*dev*/*null*

All files owned by you in the directory tree starting with /*tmp* are located, and the long listing of information about each file is displayed. Error messages are redirected away from your screen to /*dev*/*null*.

Locating Additional Options

The **find** utility is used to create backup copies of all files owned by a user, to locate large, old, unused files, and so on. As usual, the **man** and **info** pages detail these and other options and features of the utility.

┗▶ Examine the **man** pages for details on how to use the following options:

atime *4*	Locate files that were created longer ago than a specified number of days.
perm *644*	Locate files with a specific permission.
size *+50*	Locate files larger than a specified number of blocks.
type *f*	Locate files of a given type.

Acting on All Files in a Directory Tree

Although **find** is often used to locate files that match certain criteria, it can also be used as the agent to go through a directory tree recursively and execute another utility on all files.

⮡ Enter the following command, which integrates several of the concepts examined earlier in this section:

find . -type f -exec wc {} \; 2> *⁄dev⁄null* **| more**

The output consists of the results of **wc** examining the contents of all files in the current directory and all subdirectories.

find	Instructs shell to execute the **find** utility.
.	The shell passes dot as first argument to **find**, which interprets it as instruction to start the search with the current directory and recursively examine all subdirectories and their subdirectories throughout the whole tree.
-type	Instructs **find** to locate files only of the type listed as the next argument.
f	Instructs **find** to locate files of the type <u>f</u>iles not directories.
-exec	Instructs **find** to execute the following command on all files that match the search criteria (all regular files in this case).
wc	Specifies the command to execute on each selected file.
{}	Placeholder in the command line where **find** is to put the absolute path for each file that matches the search criteria. Each file is passed as an argument to **wc**.
\;	The semicolon marks the end of command to be executed. The backslash instructs the shell not to interpret the semicolon, but to pass it to **find** uninterpreted.
2>	Instructs the shell to redirect the error (**2**) from the process running **find** to whatever file is listed as the next argument.
/dev/null	Specifies the file to receive the error from **find** process.
|	Instructs the shell to redirect the output from **find** to the next utility.
more	Specifies the utility to receive output from **find.**

The **find** utility is a powerful search tool. It allows us to search through specified directory trees, based on a variety of criteria, and then perform actions on the located file.

11.4 Printing Your Heart Out

One of the first devices attached to an early UNIX system was a printer. No matter how electronic our age becomes, printers continue to be essential. This section examines the various options available to tailor printing of files and output from previous utilities in a pipeline.

Printing a File

You have been sending files to the printer using either the **lp** or **lpr** commands in previous exercises. The **-d***printer* and **-P***printer* portions of the following commands request a specific printer. If you have access to a printer that is named, type one of the following commands (substituting the name of your printer for *printer*).

> **lp -d***printer practice*

or

> **lpr -P***printer practice*

In the following exercises, we will specify only **lp** or **lpr**. If you need to designate a printer, add the **-d** or **-P** options.

Printing the Output of a Pipeline

As with most other UNIX utilities, you can connect the output of another utility to the input of the print utility, using a pipe. Here are two examples.

We can print the contents of the current directory without first creating a file. Have the shell connect the output of **ls** directly to the input of **lp** or **lpr**.

1. Type one of the following commands depending on whether **lp** or **lpr** is running:

> **ls | lp**
> **ls | lpr**

The output of the **ls** utility is sent directly to the **lp** or **lpr** utility, which sends the data to the printer exactly as if that output had been stored in a file. If your system has the online UNIX manual, you can obtain a hard copy of the manual pages describing any utility.

2. Type one of the following commands:

> **man wc | col -bx | lp**
> **man wc | colcrt | lpr**

The **col -bx** and **colcrt** utilities remove control characters that are of value to terminals but make reading a printed version difficult.

Printing Multiple Copies

Suppose you need a copy of your *numbers.tmp* file for several of your colleagues. You can send the file to the printer once for each copy you need, but a more efficient way is to issue a single command line asking for multiple copies.

⌐▸ For example, request five copies of a file by typing one of the following command lines:

lp -n5 *west*

The option **-n5** tells **lp** to print five copies of the file.

Or type:

lpr – #5 *west*

The option **– #5** instructs **lpr** to print five copies of the file.

Adding a Title Line to the Banner Page

Each of the jobs you just printed probably was preceded by a *banner page*, also called a *burst page*, containing information about the printer and about the user issuing the print request. If you want, you can add a title line to this banner page.

⌐▸ Add your title and print the *numbers.tmp* file again. Type one of the following commands:

lp -t'*numbers file***'** *numbers.tmp*

or

lpr -P*printer* **-J'***numbers file***'** *numbers.tmp*

The formats of the two print commands are as follows:

lp -d*printer* **-t***title* *filename*

or

lpr -P*printer* **-J'***title***'** *filename*

If the *title* contains any special characters that the shell would interpret, include single quotes as in the preceding example. Notice there is no space between the **-t** or the **-J** and the *title*. When using a title that includes spaces, be sure to surround the title with single quotes.

Checking the Status of Print Jobs

On some systems, print jobs are sent faster than the printer can produce the output. Each new job is added to the list of jobs to be done (the *queue*). UNIX lets us check for specific print job, or all jobs from all users in the printer queues.

The *spooler* is the program that administers print requests. This program receives print requests from multiple users and sends jobs one at a time to the printer. The spooler makes it possible for the system to process simultaneous print job requests from several users.

When you type a print command followed by a printer designation and filename, the spooler processes your request, assigns a request number to the job submitted, and queues the job for printing at the specified destination. If the printer you specify is free, the print request is passed to the printer, and the file starts printing. Otherwise, the job must wait for the printer to be available.

You can search the printer queue for the status of any job you send (printed, printing, or waiting).

1. Send the file *practice* to the printer, using the print command appropriate for your system. Your file *practice* is now queued for printing, waiting for its turn to be printed.

2. Examine the queue by typing one of the following commands:

   lpstat

   or

   lpq **-P***printer username*

   where *username* is the login name of your current account, and *printer* is the selected printer.

If few people are using the printer, your print job is printed immediately upon request. There would be no trace of it in the output of **lpstat** or **lpq**.

Canceling a Print Request

Just as you can send a request to a printer, you can also cancel that request.

1. From the command line, type one of the following commands:

   lpstat **-t**

   or

   lpq **-P***printer*

2. Enter the following command to remove jobs from the queue:

   cancel

   or

   lprm

If you are using a Linux system, all printing jobs owned by you are removed from the queue. If you are on a UNIX system, you need to include the **-u** option to indicate jobs owned by you, the **u**ser.

The programs that manage print queues are the *print spoolers*, **lp** and **lpr**. We use the **lp** and **lpr** commands to add print jobs to queues, to display status information about queues, and to remove print jobs from queues.

Examining the Manual Pages for Spooler Information

The two utilities **lp** and **lpr** include many useful options that are described both in the **man** pages.

Examine the **man** documentation and locate the option that turns off printing of a banner and header. Try it out.

Locate another interesting option among the many options available.

11.5 Archiving Files

As we use a Linux or UNIX system for more important work, the need to put copies onto transportable media grows. We often want to drop a file onto a floppy to take it to a meeting, back up important work for safety, create an archive for historical purposes, or transfer data to a new environment. Two archiving approaches are examined here.

Archiving Files on Floppy Disks

Most Linux systems provide or have access to a set of programs called **mtools**, which facilitate copying files to the floppy drive without going through the process of mounting the drive, a topic examined in "Managing and Administering a Stand-Alone System," found in Chapter 13. The **mtools** are examined in these exercises.

1. Locate a floppy formatted in DOS.
2. Put the floppy in your Linux system's floppy drive.
3. Make sure you are in your home directory by entering:

   cd
4. Request a list of files that are on the floppy by entering:

   mdir

If a brief list of the disk's contents is displayed, you have **mtools** available. Continue. If you see an error message that **mtools** is not found, skip this section and locate someone to help install **mtools** if you are on Linux. See the **www.muster.com** site.

Copying a File to and from a Floppy

⤷ **1.** Enter:

mcopy *practice a:*

This command instructs the shell to run **mcopy** and give it two arguments: a filename from the current directory, and the *a:*, which is an agreed-on name for the floppy.

2. List the contents of the floppy:

mdir

A copy of the file *practice* is listed as residing on the disk.

3. Change directories to another directory, such as:

cd *~/SplitDIR*

ls

4. Copy the *practice* file from the floppy to the current directory with:

mcopy **a:***/practice* .

ls

The file *practice* is copied from the *a:* drive to the current directory.

Copying All Files

We can select all files from a directory and copy them to the floppy.

⤷ Enter:

cd

mcopy * *a:*

mdir

As many files as could fit on the floppy are copied from the current directory.

Removing Files from a Floppy

⤷ **1.** List the files on the floppy:

mdir

2. Select several files to remove, and use their names in the following:

mdel *file1 file2*

3. To remove all files from the floppy, enter:

   mdel *

   mdir

4. To remove directories from a floppy, enter:

   mdeltree *directoryname*

Formatting a Floppy Disk

Additionally, we can format a floppy in DOS format using the command **mformat**, which formats the *a:* drive.

A copy placed on a floppy with **mcopy** is just a copy of the file. Attributes such as permissions are not included in the copy. When you copy a file from a floppy, the permissions for the newly copied file may not match its original permissions. Instead, when we use **mcopy** we are creating a new file on the system and the rules for default permissions apply.

Creating Archives with tar

One of the workhorse archiving utilities is **tar**, originally a <u>t</u>ape <u>ar</u>chiving program. It has been so reliable that it is used extensively to make archive files on most systems. The advantage of a **tar** archive over a floppy disk copy is that a **tar** archive retains file attributes such as permissions.

Creating an Archive

Files are listed in directories, and have permissions, ownership, and other characteristics. We can use **tar** to create a single file, called an archive, that contains all the files in a directory tree and all the information about each file.

1. Make sure you are in your home directory:

   cd

2. Create a **tar** archive of the files in your home directory by entering:

   tar -cvf *archfile.tar* .

   This command instructs **tar** to <u>c</u>reate an archive in <u>v</u>erbose mode (it displays all filenames being archived), then use a <u>f</u>ile to hold the archive. *archfile.tar* is the filename.

   The dot (.) is the source directory, in this case your current directory, from which all files will be archived.

   The extension *.tar* is not required for the archive file, often called a **tar**ball, but it's a good idea to use the extension so that you can easily identify your **tar** files.

3. List the contents of the **tar** archive with:

   tar –tf *archfile.tar*

   The <u>t</u>able of contents from the <u>f</u>ile is displayed.

Extracting the Files from an Archive

Once a **tar***ball* is created, it can be moved, mailed, or placed on portable media, and later the contents can be extracted.

1. Create a new directory and make it your current directory:

   mkdir *Backups*
   cd *Backups*

2. Move the archive to the current directory:

   mv *../archfile.tar* **.**

3. Extract the directory tree from the archive:

   tar –xvf *archfile.tar* **.**

   This command is instruction to e<u>x</u>tract the structure from the archive in <u>v</u>erbose mode, from a <u>f</u>ile.

4. List the files:

   ls -l

   All the files listed in your home directory are not copied to this directory. The **tar** archiving and retrieval process maintained permissions, directories, ownership, and so forth for the files.

5. Return to your home directory:

   cd

   We often employ **tar** to create an archive of a project directory tree, a user's home tree, or a whole file system. The archive can be stored on permanent media, sent to a remote machine, or just used to move a structure from one location in a system to another.

Self Test

1. What command prints the file *nlongfile*?

   _____

2. What command instructs **find** to locate all files named *core* anywhere in your home directory and its subdirectories, and then remove the files?

   _____

3. What command sorts the output of **ps -aux** and divides it into a series of small files, named *ps-aa*, and so forth, each file containing 10 or fewer lines?

_____

4. What is the difference between copying all the files from a directory to a floppy using **mcopy** and creating a **tar** image of all the files in a directory and putting it on a floppy?

_____

Chapter Review

Use this section to review the content of this chapter and test yourself on your knowledge of the concepts.

Chapter Summary

- The **split** utility reads the contents of any ASCII file, divides the contents into units of a specified number of lines, and then creates a series of small files to hold the pieces. The created files are given names that all have the same root, but end in a progression of *aa*, *bb*, *cc*, and so forth as is needed.
- The **lp** and **lpr** utilities manage files directed to the printer. They maintain a print queue, accepting print jobs from all users, then they send jobs one at a time to the printer. We can select printers, request titles on banner pages to be printed on files, remove jobs from the queue, and print multiple copies.
- In UNIX and Linux, the **find** utility searches through a directory tree for all files based on specific criteria and then takes action on each identified file. The selection criteria includes the name of file, the user who is the owner, permissions, size, and the various dates associated with files. Once files are located, the possible actions include outputting the path to the located file or taking any system utility action on the file by employing the **-exec** option.
- The **mtools** utilities facilitate copying files to and from the floppy drive using a DOS-formatted floppy. We can list the contents of a floppy with **mdir** and copy files each way with the **mcopy** command. We can also format a disk with **mformat**.
- An archive of a directory tree or a file that includes all information about the file (permissions, owner, and so on) is made using the **tar** utility. We can create an archive, list its contents, and extract files from the archive.

Assignment

<u>Fill-in</u>.

1. What command splits the file *july_birthday* into smaller files containing 13 or fewer lines and with base names of *na*?

2. What command prints out two copies of the manual pages for **wc** with all control characters removed?

3. How would you identify all the files on the system owned by the user *w-blank* and have the list written to a file called *wade-blank* in your home directory?

4. How would you copy the file *july_birthday* from the current directory to the floppy disk?

5. You just sent a long file to the printer and you realize it was a mistake. How can you cancel the job?

6. Explain the relationship between a print job, a print spooler, and a queue.

Project

    A. Create a **tar** archive of all your files starting at your home directory.
    B. Locate a floppy and format it
    C. Copy the **tar** archive to the floppy.
    D. In */tmp*, under the directory of your name, create a directory called *Backups*.
    E. Copy the <u>tar</u>ball from the floppy to the *Backups* directory.
    F. Extract the files from the <u>tar</u>ball to the *Backups* directory.
    G. Have **ls** do a recursive listing of your directory in */tmp* and redirect the output from **ls** to a file.
    H. Print the file.

COMMAND SUMMARY

PRINTING COMMANDS

lp *-dprintername* *filename*	Requests that the file *filename* be printed on the destination printer *printer*.
lp *-dprintername* *-nnumber* *filename*	Specifies number of copies to be printed, where *number* is the number of copies desired.
lp *-dprintername* *-ttitle* *filename*	Specifies that *title* be printed on the banner page.
lpstat	Produces a report on the status of all your print requests.
cancel -P *printername* *jobnumber*	Cancels the specified print request (whether printing or not), where *printername* is the printer and *jobnumber* is the ID of the requested job.
cancel *printername*	Removes all of the user's jobs that are being printed on *printername* (requires the **-u** option in UNIX).
lprm *printer*	Removes all the user's jobs that are being printed on *printer*.
lpr *-Pprinter* *filename*	Requests that the file *filename* be printed on the destination printer *printer*.
lpr *-Pprinter* *-#number* *filename*	Specifies the number of copies to be printed, where *number* is the number of copies desired.
lpr *-Pprinter* *-Jtitle* *filename*	Specifies the title to be printed on the banner page.
lprm *-Pprinter* *jobnumber*	Cancels the print request if it is not printing.

COMMAND SUMMARY FOR *split*

split *-#* *targetfile* *outname*	Instructs **split** to read *targetfile* and divide the contents into files of **#** lines named *outnameaa*, *outnameab*, and so on.

COMMAND SUMMARY FOR *find*

-print	Outputs the path to all matched files.
-exec	Runs whatever command follows **-exec** on the command line for each matched file.

-user *username*	Locates files owned by user *username*.
-atime *#*	Locates files older than a specified number of days.
-perm *755*	Locates files with specific permissions.
-size *+#*	Locates files greater than a specified size of # blocks.
-type d	Locates files of a specified type.

COMMAND SUMMARY FOR *mtools*

mdir	Lists contents of floppy in drive *a:*.
mcopy	Copies file(s) to or from drive (*a:*) to or from a directory.
mformat	Formats a drive in DOS format.
mdel	Deletes files from a floppy.

COMMAND SUMMARY FOR *tar*

c	Creates an archive.
v	Instructs **tar** to be verbose and display the name of each object as it is read or written.
f	Instructs **tar** to read from or write to a file.
x	Extracts data from an archive.
t	Reports on the table of contents of an archive (contents).

Accessing and Exploring Graphical Desktops

UNIX and Linux support both graphical and character-based terminals. Although interacting with a system by typing commands is an effective means of communicating our intentions to the system, some applications are more easily managed through a graphical environment. A complete graphical desktop that utilizes a mouse, menus, icons, and all the usual functionality is available in several flavors. Two of the most popular are GNOME (GNU Network Object Model Environment) and KDE (K Desktop Environment). At least one of these two graphical desktops is available in nearly every Linux version. They can also be downloaded for free from *www.gnome.org* and *www.kde.org*.

The underlying code and structures in all the desktops are the same, but they present different functionality, look and feel, and default programs that are included by default. The **X** Window system is the collection of files and programs that enable particular desktop window managers such as GNOME and KDE to operate. This chapter examines how to access, use, and customize the most popular graphical desktop environments.

12.1 Starting the X Window System from a Terminal

If you log on to your system and a graphical environment is displayed, then skip this section and begin with the next section, 12.2, *Exploring the Graphical Desktop Environment*.

When you log in, if a character-based terminal is started without a graphical environment, you may be able to start a graphical environment from the character-based terminal. If you are on a Linux system, follow the instructions listed first. If you are connected to a UNIX computer, follow the instructions that are described second.

N O T E :   If the following instructions do not launch the graphical desktop environment, the **X** Window system is probably not installed on your computer. Sorry, but this chapter only works if you have a graphical environment installed. Fortunately, the rest of the book explores the system by issuing commands to a terminal or terminal window rather than employing utilities from the graphical desktop.

Launching the X Window System from Linux

At a command prompt of a terminal screen on a monitor connected to a Linux system, enter the following:

startx

The **startx** command **start**s the fundamental graphics program, the **X** Window system, and it then launches your account's default window manager. A desktop such as that shown in Figure 12-1 is started, complete with icons, a menu bar, and an active mouse.

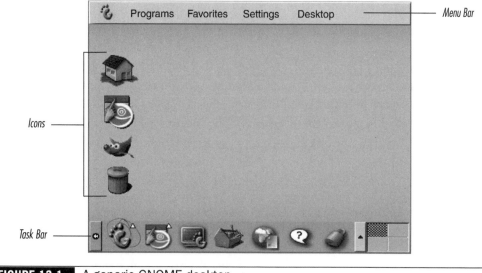

FIGURE 12-1   A generic GNOME desktop

If you now are interacting with a graphical desktop similar to Figure 12-1, proceed to section 12.2. If the shell reports that the **startx** utility is not found, **X** Windows is probably not installed.

Launching the X Window System from UNIX

If you are using a graphical monitor, but it is functioning only as a character-based terminal in UNIX, you may be able to start the graphical programs.

1. In a UNIX environment, enter:

   xinit &

   The **xinit** command starts the fundamental graphics program, the **X** Window system, which runs any one of several window manager and graphical desktop applications. It may read a configuration file and start other programs or it may allow you to specify which you would like to run.

   If **xinit** does not work, you probably do not have access to the graphical environment and will have to be content using the character-based terminal. If you receive an error message like:

   ```
   Fatal Server Error: Server is already active for system
   ```

   the **X** Window system has already been started and is currently working.

   After you have started an **X** Window session using the **xinit** command, you may see a full graphical desktop environment with icons and a menu bar or you may see a plain graphical screen with just a terminal window, probably located in the upper-left. If you have icons and a full graphical environment, proceed to the next section, 12.2.

   If the display is a very plain graphical screen with a small terminal window, you need to choose which desktop you want to execute. Usually, several are available.

2. Move the mouse into the small terminal window and click it to make the window active.

3. At the prompt in the terminal window, enter:

   gnome &

   You may receive an error message indicating that this particular graphical interface is not available. If so, enter:

   kde &

   This command tells the **X** Window system to run the **K** Desktop Environment (KDE).

If it is not available, enter:

mwm &

which starts the Motif Window Manager.

Or enter:

blackbox &

blackbox is a very efficient, relatively small desktop program.

If one of the desktops is running, proceed to the next section.

12.2 Exploring the Graphical Desktop Environment

The exercises in this section introduce the major features of GNOME and KDE. Because there are many variations among the various releases of the graphical user interfaces, we can not provide exact step sequences that will work in every case. This exploration of the major desktop environments describes the central features. You may need to explore a bit to locate some of the features or applications described.

The GUI interface, as shown in Figure 12-1, usually consists of three or four major parts:

- A desktop, which is the blank screen. The desktop holds the other parts and has some powers.
- Various icons sprinkled about the desktop area. These icons access programs.
- A taskbar or dashboard at the bottom of the screen. This bar contains icons for specific features.
- Possibly a bar of menus at the top of the screen. This menu bar contains drop-down menus for applications.

Navigating the Task Bar

The *Task Bar,* which looks somewhat like the dashboard of a vehicle, usually appears by default at the bottom of the desktop.

⮎ 1. Move the mouse pointer over each icon in the *Task Bar.* Do not click, just rest over each one.

Each icon's title is displayed.

In the GNOME interface, the various icons allow us to access the *Main Menu, Terminal Emulator, Documentation (Help)*, and a web browser. See Figure 12-2.

The KDE interface includes many of the same features as buttons or icons: *Terminal Emulator, Help*, and a web browser, as well as some differently named buttons that have similar types of functionality as GNOME offers, such as *Start Application*. In any GUI environment, the taskbar contains a wide variety of configurable settings and features.

 NOTE: When your desktop first appears, there may be a window already open entitled Start Here. This window includes many icons that contain frequently used menus and directories, as well as a file manager and web browser. See Figure 12-3.

2. If you have a Start Here window, close it by clicking the *X* in the upper-right corner of the window.

Starting a Terminal Emulator

The taskbar usually contains a way to start a terminal window.

1. Locate the following button that looks like a terminal on the taskbar:

2. Click the *Terminal Emulator* or *Console* icon.

A new terminal window is started on the desktop. If a *Tip* window starts in the middle of your terminal window, kiss it goodbye with the *X* in the upper-right corner.

multiple desktops

 **FIGURE 12-2** The taskbar

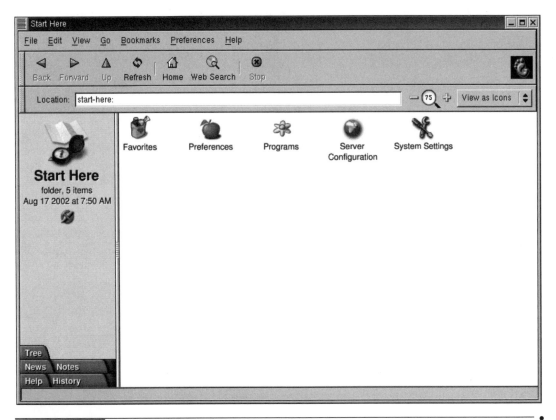

FIGURE 12-3 The Start Here window

3. To make the new terminal window the active window, click on white space inside its main area.

4. Enter a command such as:

   date

   and press ENTER

   The shell is running, and it is interpreting commands.

5. To end this terminal session, type the following:

   exit

Increasing the Font Size of a Terminal Window

When using a desktop, we can create multiple terminal windows on the screen to work in two or more environments at the same time.

If the text appears small, we can start a terminal window with a larger font.

1. Start a default terminal window by clicking the *Terminal* icon on the *Task Bar*.
2. At the shell prompt, enter the following:

   xterm -fn r16 &

   A second terminal window with a larger type size is started.
3. Exit the new terminal:

   exit
4. Increase the font size even more.

   xterm -fn r24 &

When we start a terminal window, a default font is used unless we employ **-fn** to specify a font name. The fonts **r16** and **r24** are usually available and reasonably large.

Employing Alternate Desktops

The *Task Bar* usually contains four clustered square buttons that are often labeled *1, 2, 3,* and *4,* and sometimes are just four squares. See Figure 12-2. The top left button of the four is probably highlighted, indicating that it is currently active.

1. Click one of the other three buttons that is not highlighted.

   An alternate desktop is displayed.
2. In this second desktop, start a default terminal by clicking on the *Terminal* icon in the *Task Bar*.
3. Determine who is logged on to your system at the moment by entering:

   who

   Your original log in and each graphical terminal are seen as separate logins with their own ports.
4. In the *Task Bar,* click the top left of the four buttons to return to the original desktop.

   The large font terminal is in one desktop, a default terminal in another. The four desktops give you four places to work, all in the same login session. We can use the desktops to work on different projects without having to put applications away. We can start terminals in one desktop, run other applications in a second, and so forth.

5. Move among the desktops by clicking various boxes in the *Task Bar*.

Accessing Applications through the Main Menu

The essential features of desktops such as GNOME and KDE are the same. However, depending on which desktop you are using, the appearance of the *Task Bar*, the names of the particular buttons, and the locations where configurable settings are stored may differ from those discussed here.

Usually on the left end of the *Task Bar* is an icon that brings up a main menu of applications.

1. Locate one of the following on the *Task Bar*:

If you are using GNOME, it is the footprint on the far left:

Main Menu

If you are using KDE, it is the gear with a *K* on the left end:

Start Application

2. Click the menu icon one time.

Each of these buttons produces a pop-up menu that provides access to various programs, utilities, settings, applets, and other system menus.

Launching the Calculator

A full-powered button calculator is an essential feature of a graphical environment.

1. Locate the calculator in one of the following menu selections:

Main Menu | *Programs* | *Utilities* | *Simple Calculator*

(In the *Main Menu* is another menu named *Programs*, in it is *Utilities*, and so forth.)

or

Main Menu | *Office* | *Calculation*

Main Menu | *System Menus* | *Office* | *Calculation*

Main Menu | *Utilities* | *Kcalc*

Explore various menus until you find the calculator.

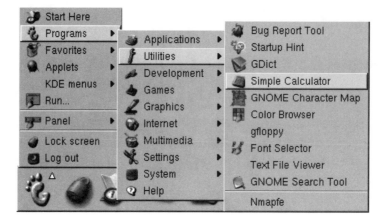

2. When you locate the calculator, click one time on the menu option to start the calculator.

It is now on the desktop.

3. Perform a calculation by checking on the keys of the calculator.

Employing a Spread Sheet

Many applications can be launched or executed through this set of menus. A workhorse is the spreadsheet programs.

1. In the *Task Bar* open one of the other three desktops by clicking on one of the other squares.

2. Locate a spreadsheet program in one or more of the following:

   Main Menu | Programs | Applications | Gnumeric
   Main Menu | Applications | Gnumeric
   Main Menu | Office | KSpread

3. Perform a calculation and then close the spreadsheet.

Using the Calendar

A standard program we all need maintains our appointments.

1. Examine the calendar programs:

   Main Menu | Program | Applications | ical
   Main Menu | Office | ical
   Main Menu | Office | Korganizer

2. Close the applications or minimize them when you have completed your exploration.

Maintaining an Address Book

Several programs are available that keep our address book information orderly and available.

   Main Menu | Utilities | KAddressbook
   Main Menu | KDEMenus | Utilities | KAddressbook
   Main Menu | Programs | Applications | XimianEvolution

Tracking Time

Most graphical environments include a tool that users can access to keep track of their time on projects and other completed work.

1. Launch the tool at one of the following:

   Main Menu | Programs | Applications | Time Tracking Tool
   Main Menu | Applications | Time Tracking Tool
   Main Menu | Utilities | Karm

2. Make an entry billing for your time today, then exit.

Processing Words

The graphical desktops provide mouse, menu-driven word processor programs that feel familiar.

➥ 1. Locate one of the following:

Main Menu | *Programs* | *Applications* | *AbiWord*
Main Menu | *Programs* | *Applications* | *gedit*
Main Menu | *Office* | *Kword*
Main Menu | *Programs* | *Applications* | *gedit*

2. Create a short document, then save and quit the editor.

Relaxing in the Game Room

No system can claim to be graphical without games. Unless they were not installed, several real time stealers are available.

➥ Explore the following:

Main Menu | *Programs* | *Games*
Main Menu | *Games*

The Main Menu or Start Application option organizes many applications and critical system functions on your machine into a set of menus. The applications available to users can be easily accessed. However, you must be logged on as the superuser *root* to configure the administrative features.

Moving, Resizing, and Iconifying Windows

The window manager interprets mouse clicks and drags in the usual ways. For instance, we can move windows to different places on the desktop.

➥ 1. Move the mouse pointer to the top of the window frame of a window resting on the desktop.

2. Left-click and hold down the mouse button, then drag the window to another location on the desktop.

We can move windows anywhere on the desktop.

Additionally, we can reshape the size of windows.

3. Locate a handle on the side and corner of the window.

4. With the mouse pointer on a handle, left-click and hold down the mouse button and move the mouse.

   The window is resized.

   Windows can also be minimized.

5. Click the minimize button (which looks like an underscore) at the top-right of the window.

   The icon of the window is placed in the center of the *Task Bar*.

Obtaining Help

A *Help* or *Documentation* browser is an interface to the various forms of documentation on the computer as well as the Internet.

1. Move the mouse over the icons in the *Task Bar* to locate the icon labeled:
   Help
   or
   Documentation

2. Click the icon.

3. Scan the information provided and get acquainted with the Help resources available to you.

   Your window appears similar to Figure 12-4.

4. Examine some of the help resources.

5. When you are finished browsing these Help descriptions, close the window by clicking the X in the upper-right corner of the Help window.

Connecting to a Web Browser

A web browser is usually included on the *Task Bar*. Occasionally, it is on the desktop in the form of an icon, sometimes in both places. Usually **netscape**, **galeon**, or **mozilla** is available.

1. Locate the browser on the *Task Bar* or in the *Main Menu* and click its button. See Figure 12-5.

   We can customize the various adjustable browser settings by using the *File*, *Edit*, *View*, and *Search* drop-down lists on the *Menu Bar*. Using the window handles, we can also reshape the window or minimize it to rest on the *Task Bar*.

2. Type in the following address in the URL window to explore our site:
   www.muster.com

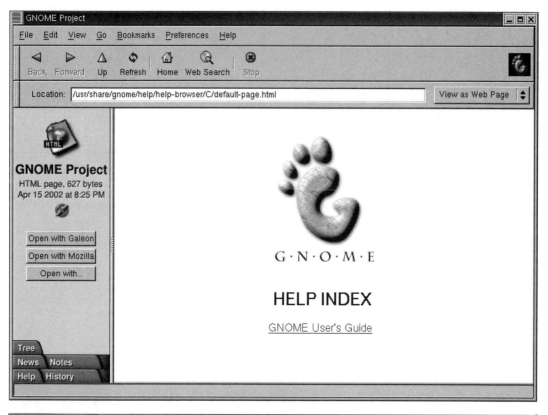

FIGURE 12-4 The Documentation (Help) Window

3. To close your browser window, click the *X* in the upper-right corner of your browser window.

Starting Programs with Icons

There are various icons you might see resting on the desktop (by default). All icons can be customized or removed altogether. Certain old favorites include a trash disposal icon, a web browser, and maybe an icon for your home directory.

1. Explore the desktop icons by clicking on each one to verify what it accomplishes.
2. Click the *Trash* icon.

   Inside the *Trash* will be items awaiting deletion. Their presence in the *Trash* indicates that putting them in the trash is not an irrevocable decision. You can restore a particular item by dragging it back onto the desktop.

FIGURE 12-5   Exploring the web browser

3. To delete a file from the system permanently, open *Trash* and select:

File | Empty Trash

The *Trash* is taken out, and all items that were in the *Trash* are now really gone.

Using the Menu Bar

A menu bar may be at the top of your screen. Not all graphical interfaces include menu bars because they do not possess any functionality that is not provided elsewhere. Rather, the menu bar functions like a quick reference location for frequently used applications, configurations, and even your favorite web sites.

1. If you have a menu bar, locate and click *Programs* on the menu bar.

A list of topics such as *Applications*, *Utilities*, *Development*, *Games*, *Graphics*, *Internet*, *Multimedia*, and various others appears on a drop-down menu. These are exactly the same topics found in the *Task Bar* listed under Main Menu.

2. Try to locate the settings for your CD player. Usually, this is listed under the menu topic *Multimedia*.

3. Locate and click *Favorites* on the menu bar.

If you have saved any pages as Favorites in your browser, they will appear for quick reference.

Customizing the Desktop Environment

The desktop is the aesthetic centerpiece of the graphical environment. It's here that icons languish and loll in the lap of freedom from work, and application windows claim real estate when running.

Modifying the Desktop Appearance

We can easily change the color and theme of the graphical desktop.

1. Move the mouse to an area on the desktop where no window or icon is resting.

2. Right-click the desktop.

A menu appears.

3. Select *Change Desktop Background* or *Configure Desktop* (or maybe *Configure Background*) from the pop-up menu.

From this menu, you can choose your desktop theme, color, and wallpaper.

4. Explore the remainder of the options of the *Main Menu*. From these menu options, we can select a default such as the word processing editor. We can control system operations, select a screensaver, and launch hundreds of programs.

5. When you are finished reviewing the menu options, close the window by clicking the *X* in the upper-right corner.

Adding Shortcuts to the Desktop

You can also create shortcuts on the desktop to frequently used programs.

1. From the main menu, go to:

   Programs | Utilities | Simple Calculator

2. When your mouse is directly over *Simple Calculator* on the pop-up menu, left-click the mouse and drag your pointer to the desktop to the right. See the depiction in Figure 12-6.

The shortcut to the calculator is now residing on the desktop.

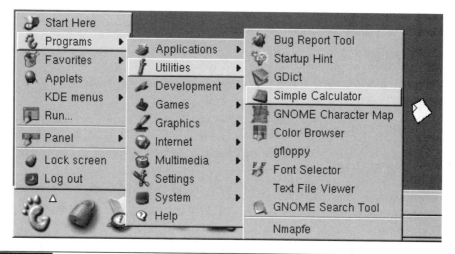

FIGURE 12-6 Creating a shortcut on the desktop

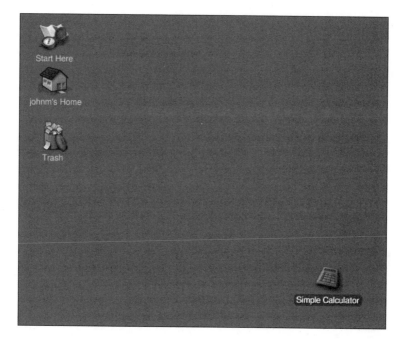

Exiting the Session from the Desktop

You can exit the desktop session in a variety of ways.

↳ 1. Locate and click one of the following buttons on the **Task Bar**:

If you are using GNOME:

Main Menu

If you are using KDE:

Start Application

You may choose simply to select **Lock Screen**, which keeps alive your current session, but requires anyone wanting to use this computer first to provide the current user's password in order to "unlock" the screen.

2. To exit your session, choose ***Logout*** from the pop-menu.

3. You might also try to log out from your system by using the menu bar, or by right-clicking the desktop and then selecting ***Logout*** from those pop-up menus.

Self Test 1

Answer the following questions, and then check your answers using the information within the chapter.

1. What command in Linux launches the graphical environment?

_____

2. How do you access help?

_____

3. How do you minimize a window? How do you bring it back to the desktop?

_____

4. What is the role of the four square buttons on the dashboard?

_____

Chapter Review

Use this section to review the content of this chapter and test yourself on your knowledge of the concepts.

Chapter Summary

- In UNIX and Linux, the **X** Window system provides users with a full graphical environment.
- Various desktops, each with their own look and feel, are available. The most popular are KDE and GNOME.
- Login accounts can be configured to start up in the graphical or terminal mode. If after our login we are communicating with a character screen in a monitor, we can probably start an **X** Window session and subsequently a desktop. If we are in the graphical environment, we can start a terminal window that is character-based.
- In the graphical desktops, the dashboard, or *Task Bar*, provides a series of menus and icons for easy access to programs.
- An active desktop permits us to move, resize, and iconify windows as well as access desktop menus for customizing the environment.

Assignment

Fill-in.

1. What command allows you to open a new terminal window session without ending your current session?

   _____

2. What are three ways to open a browser window during a graphical session?

   _____

3. What are two ways to exit a graphical session?

   _____

4. How can you create a shortcut for the calculator function on your desktop?

   _____

5. Using the Help browser, determine how to make a chosen desktop environment the default.

   _____

COMMAND SUMMARY

startx	Initiates an **X** Window session in Linux.
xinit	Initiates an **X** Window session in UNIX.
gnome	A popular and common graphical user interface, often represented by a foot.
kde	Another frequently available and often used graphical user interface.

13

Maintaining and Administering a Linux System

S K I L L S   C H E C K

Before beginning this chapter, you should be able to:

- Log on and off a UNIX/Linux machine
- Issue commands to the shell that include variables, arguments, and redirection
- Examine and modify files using the **vi** editor
- Employ basic file management utilities to create, copy, move, and remove files
- Navigate around the filesystem
- Correctly enter *root*'s password

O B J E C T I V E S

After completing this chapter, you will be able to:

- Identify the major responsibilities of a system administrator
- Start up and shut down the system, and change the system's state
- Add user accounts and change user passwords
- Archive and back up data
- Install application packages

The administrator of a Linux PC system is responsible for installation, operation, maintenance, repair, and security for the system. Problems can arise when we fail to accomplish needed tasks or when we make mistakes while performing certain duties. In this chapter, we first examine the significant powers of the system administrator, then we explore the management of users, filesystems, startup and shutdown, processes, and archiving data.

This chapter is an introduction to Linux/UNIX system administration. Topics are briefly introduced, basic commands examined, and fundamental operations explored. The goal is to provide you with the skills needed for basic operation of a PC running Linux. To advance beyond the basics examined here, consult a system administration text or class.

13.1 Introducing Super User Powers

The super user has enormous power both to enhance and to destroy the integrity of a UNIX or Linux system. When a person is the super user (*root*), he or she essentially can read, change, or remove any file, start or stop any process, and manage all equipment. Much damage has been inflicted on many systems because the administrator made ill-advised requests as the super user, and unfortunately the requests were followed by the system. Many administrators have thought they were in a user's home directory and when attempting to remove the user's files, issued a command to remove the current directory and all its subdirectories. Unfortunately, because they were actually at the top of the filesystem, *root*, they removed the whole system.

Logging on as Super User

The user name or login name of the super user is *root*.

1. At the login screen, log on by entering the user name *root*.
2. Provide the super user or *root* password that you assigned in the installation. After login, your prompt is probably a pound sign (#), which is the traditional super use or *root* prompt.

3. Check your identity:

> **id**

Because you are the super user, your user id *uid* is *0*.

4. Determine the super user's home directory:

> **pwd**

The super user's home directory is one of the following:

On a UNIX system:

> */*

On a Linux system:

> */root*

In UNIX, the top directory in the filesystem, the */* directory, is also *root*'s home directory. In Linux, *root*'s home is a directory named *root* that is listed as a subdirectory of the */* directory.

5. List the contents of the */* directory:

> **ls /**

On Linux there is a directory named *root* listed in */*, on UNIX there probably is not.

6. Ask your current shell for the value of the variable *USER* by entering:

> **echo $USER**

The user name is *root*.

7. Log out of the system:

> **exit**

Becoming the Super User after Logging in as a User

Any user can also start a super user shell process, if they can provide the correct password for *root*.

1. Log in to your own account as a regular user, (not as the super user, *root*).

2. Check on your current user identification by entering:

> **id**

The screen displays the user ID number and name, which match your user account.

3. As a regular user, examine the permissions for a system file and attempt to read it with:

   ls -l */etc/shadow*
   more */etc/shadow*

   On most systems, the *shadow* file contains login names and encrypted passwords for all users on the system. The file is accessible only by *root*, which is the owner, and by members of *root*'s group. For password security, we mere mortals cannot even read the file.

4. Identify the current directory:

   pwd

   You are in your home directory.

5. Obtain the value of the *USER* variable:

   echo $USER

   The shell has your user name for its value of the *USER* variable.

Starting a Super User Shell with Full Environment

There are two ways to start a shell with super user powers: One takes on the power and environment of *root* (variables and home directory), the other takes on the powers but not the environment.

1. Become the super user by typing the following command, which includes one argument, the dash:

   su -

2. Answer the password request by typing in the password for *root*.

3. Check your identity by typing:

   id

   Your **uid** is *0*. You are now the super user. If we enter the correct *root* password, the <u>s</u>ubstitute <u>u</u>ser command starts a child process owned by root. As super user, we can also substitute user to *any* other user by entering that user's login name as an argument to **su**. Because we are the super user, we are not asked for the user's password. (As *regular* users, we can also use the **su** command to substitute to any other user; however, we must then provide the other user's password.)

4. Confirm your location and *USER* value:

   pwd
   echo $USER

The super user shell when started with a dash argument has *root*'s identity and full environment, including the home directory and the value of the **USER** variable. With (**su -**), we have the same powers and environment that we have when we log in as *root*.

5. Attempt to view the *shadow* file with *root*'s powers:

    ls -l */etc/shadow*
    more */etc/shadow*

    As *root* we can examine the file because we are now the owner.

6. Exit the super user shell and return to your login shell by entering:

    exit

7. Confirm your identity:

    id

Becoming Super User While Retaining the Original Environment

We can also start a super user shell that has *root*'s power but not its environment.

1. Enter the following (there is no argument):

    su

2. Check your identity by typing:

    id

    Your **uid** is *0*. You are again the super user.

3. Examine the environment:

    pwd
    echo *$USER*

    The super user shell, when started without a dash argument, does have *root*'s identity and therefore **root's** powers, however, it retains the *original* user's full environment, including current directory, home directory, and the value of the **USER** variable.

4. Again attempt to examine the *shadow* file:

    more */etc/shadow*

   You can see the contents of the file because you have the super user identity powers, even though you do not have its environment.

Identifying Super User Powers

Whether we log in directly as *root*, we use the **su -** command to take on *root*'s identify and full environment, or we just become the super user without the super user environment using the **su** command, our powers are quite extensive.

As super user, we can:

- Read any file
- Write to any file
- Remove any file
- Execute any file that has at least one **x** permission set for any type of user
- Change the permissions of any file
- Change the group ownership of any file
- Change the owner of a file
- Add or remove users
- Reassign users' home directories
- Back up files
- Change any user's password
- Move any files or directories

The *root* user is the definition of the 600-pound gorilla that can sit wherever he or she wishes.

Because of the powers associated with the super user account, commands used by regular users have much greater impact when issued super user. Table 13-1 summarizes several often-used super user commands and their effects. Be careful out there.

COMMAND	EFFECT
su *otheruser*	Adopts the identity of any specified *otheruser*, but you stay in the current directory and retain your current user environment. As the super user, when you substitute one user with another user, you do not need the password of the other user.
su - *otheruser*	Starts the child shell as the user *otheruser* and takes on the full environment of the *otheruser*. If you are the super user, you do not have to provide *otheruser*'s password.

TABLE 13-1   Beware the Power of the Super User

COMMAND	EFFECT
su	Makes you the super user, retaining your original environment.
su -	Starts a child shell as the super user, taking on ***root***'s identity and environment.
exit	Exits the current shell, returning to the parent shell.
id	Displays the ID of the current user.
passwd *user1*	Allows the super user to change the password of *user1*. Only the super user can change the password for another user.
./*file1*	Starts a child shell to execute commands in *file1*. Because the super user usually does not have the current directory in its path, the super user must execute scripts not in the path by specifying its location (in this case, the current directory). The super user can execute any file that is executable for anyone.
rm *file1*	Removes the file *file1*. The super user can remove any file regardless of the permissions associated with it.
cat *file1* **more** *file1*	Displays *file0*. The super user can display any file regardless of its permissions.
cat *abc* **>!** *file1*	Writes the file *abc* to the file *file1*. The super user can write to any file regardless of its permissions.
cat *xyz* **>>** *file2*	Appends the file *xyz* to the file *file2*. The super user can append to any file, regardless of its permissions.
touch *file3*	Creates *file3* if it does not exist. The super user can create a file regardless of the permission on the directory where it is listed.

TABLE 13-1   Beware the Power of the Super User *(continued)*

The need for a super user arises from security considerations. For example, what happens when a user forgets the password for his or her account? Someone needs the power to mess with the password file. Not everyone, however, should be able to modify the file that controls all user access.

➥   Exit the super user shell:

    exit

Whenever you have finished performing super user duties, you should exit from super user so that you do not inadvertently alter important system components.

> **CAUTION:** There is a temptation just to become the super user and do all work as that user. All power is granted, anything can be done. Don't do it. Instead, log on as a regular user, and do everything you can as a regular user. When you need super user powers, start an **su** or **su -** shell and accomplish the task, then immediately exit the super user shell and continue working as a regular user until you again need superpowers. Superman does not walk around in those ridiculous tights all the time. As Clark Kent, he wears a business suit. When there is a locomotive to be stopped, he just enters a phone booth and changes clothes. Then, when he no longer needs superpowers, he quickly changes back to Clark Kent. We should follow his super example.

13.2 Exploring System Files, Processes and Features

A functioning system consists of many running processes, often employing data located in system files and directories. The particular collection of processes determines how the system behaves. This section examines system processes, system files, and the resulting system features.

Examining System Processes

A functioning Linux or UNIX system consists of not only the processes that users start, but many processes that are begun when the system is booted. A process is started at boot that manages the queue for printing, another provides the login prompt at a terminal port, another process keeps the system log, and another makes sure processes that should be running are replaced if they exit. Any user can list the processes currently running.

1. As the regular user, view all the system processes currently running:

   ps aux | more

   or

   ps -aux | more

   The **aux** options instruct **ps** to list all processes, including those not run from the terminal (<u>x</u>), and to include the name of the <u>u</u>ser who owns the processes.

The processes with a *?*, listed under *TT* (for controlling *tty*) column, were not started by a user at a terminal. They are owned by *root* and were started by the system startup scripts.

2. Locate a process named **mingetty** or **getty**. These processes have a terminal *tty* as an argument. Each **getty** program displays the word "login" on the screen of one *tty* and waits for a user to respond.

One of the system programs is named **init** and has a *PID* of *1*. This program reads a file that contains a list of all the system processes that should be running, and if one of the processes exits, **init** starts a new one to replace it.

If a system is running as a web page server, a process such as **apache** is running.

These programs that run constantly are often called *daemons* because in mythology there were two kinds of lesser gods: the evil *demons*, and the helpful guardian spirits, the *daemons*. These daemon programs, started when the system is booted, perform a wide range of housekeeping, serving, programming, and helpful administrative functions.

Listing Processes Including Parent PID

The **ps** utility includes options.

1. Breeze through the possible **ps** options in the manual:

   man *ps*

   Among the options are:

l	A long listing of information, including parent process ID.
a	A listing of all processes.
x	A list that includes processes that were started from startup scripts, not from a terminal.

2. Continuing as a regular user, list all of the system's processes, including their parent process IDs, by entering:

   ps -lax | more

All processes listed as owned by user *0* are owned by *root*. If a program has a *PPID* of *1*, it was started by *init* when the system was booted.

Examining the System Directories

Many files containing system data and programs reside in the *root* directory.

1. As a regular user, make the *root* directory your current directory and list its contents:

   cd /
   ls -Fl

   Each of the directories in the *root* directory is owned by the super user and has a role in making the system function.

2. Examine the *bin* directory with:

   ls -C *bin* **| more**

   Many executable files (utilities) reside in the */bin* directory.

3. List the contents of the *boot* directory:

   ls -l *boot*
   file *boot/*

   The modules, drivers, and kernel are in the */boot* directory.

4. List the contents of the *dev* directory:

   ls -C *dev* **| more**

   All the devices that could be attached are listed as files in the */dev* directory. The device *fd0* is the floppy drive.

5. Examine the contents of the *etc* directory with:

   ls -C *etc* **| more**

   The */etc* directory lists a host of system control files.

6. Use **more** to examine each of the following files:

/etc/crontab	The system consults this file and runs specified jobs automatically.
/etc/group	This file contains a list of groups that are currently defined on the system.
/etc/hosts	The names of all currently defined host systems on the network are listed. At minimum, the local host is present.
/etc/motd	Any text in this file is displayed after login is completed as the message of the day. Putting announcements in this file is a way to communicate with all users.
/etc/passwd	This is the controlling file for users. Every user has a one-line entry that defines *username, uid, gid, home directory,* and *startup program.*

/etc/rc	Script read by system at startup that starts the initial setup of the system and controls processes when system changes state (see the next section on startup files).
/etc/redhat-release	This file contains the name and release number for the installed version of Red Hat.
/etc/shadow	This file contains login names and encrypted passwords for all users. Only the super user can read this file.

7. List the contents of the *lib* (libraries) directory:

   ls *lib*

   The system programming libraries are housed in the */lib idirectory.*

8. In Linux, enter:

   ls -l *proc*

   This directory contains live information about processes currently running. Each process ID is listed and is a directory that contains information about each process.

9. Examine the directory named *root* that is listed in the */* directory:

   ls *root*

   The user *root* has a home directory on Linux that is the */root* directory.

10. List the contents of the *sbin* directory:

   ls -C *sbin* **| more**

   System administration utilities are listed in */sbin* so it can be included in the super user path, but not in the path for regular users.

11. As a last place to visit, examine the *var* directory:

   ls *var*

   The */var* directory contains files that various programs use to maintain or record information. The system log files are here and need to be monitored regularly.

12. Examine the log files with:

   du */var/log*

   The current size of the directories and files is reported.

   The */* directory contains system directories and files that are essential to system operations. It is best to explore this directory as a regular user, not as super user, so you do not accidentally harm the system.

Viewing Mounted Filesystems

One way to set up a system is to put the whole filesystem on one disk partition. Another way is to divide it up into different partitions that can be managed independently. On UNIX/Linux systems, all disk storage is integrated into a single directory hierarchy by *mounting* different partitions or even drives onto the main or *root* partition.

 As a regular user, list the disks and disk partitions, along with where they are attached to the directory hierarchy, by entering:

mount

This command generates a **mount** table similar to the following:

```
/dev/sd0a  on /   type  4.2  (rw)
/dev/sd0g  on /usr  type  4.2  (rw)
/dev/sd0h  on /home  type  4.2  (rw)
```

The **mount** utility, when run without any arguments, simply displays a list of the mounted filesystems and their mount points. The filesystems are referred to by the names of their hardware device, and the mount points by directory names. In the preceding example, */dev/sd0g* is a hard drive partition and is mounted on */usr*, and */dev/sd0h* partition is mounted on */home*. When the system is booted, the **mount** command with appropriate arguments is included in the startup scripts so the needed filesystems are mounted to create a functioning system.

13.3 Managing System Startup and Shutdown

We often shut the system down to perform maintenance, add new equipment, cope with an emergency, or simply conserve energy when the system will not be used for an extended period of time. The procedures for starting up and shutting down a UNIX/Linux system are automated but require some administrative intervention. We need to issue the correct commands and push the right buttons.

Shutting a System Down and Starting It Up

Shutting down a Linux system requires some special attention. For example, it is never a good idea simply to flick off the power switch when you want to shut your Linux system down. Linux keeps various system files and processes running, such as the disk memory buffers. If you suddenly reset the system or shut the system off, the filesystem(s) may become corrupted. During a controlled shutdown, Linux carefully puts all its toys away and then sings goodnight. Most modern systems keep sudden-halt damage to a minimum and run cleanup programs at startup, but we should always use controlled shutdowns before turning the power off.

There are a number of commands available to shut down a Linux system. The following are the safest, most recommended methods.

1. Become the super user with the full environment by entering:

    su -

    and provide the password.

2. Make certain both the floppy and CD drives are empty.

3. As the super user, enter:

    shutdown -h *+30*

    This command instructs **shutdown** to wait 30 seconds, then **h**alt the system. The **shutdown** utility accomplishes a number of tasks. Any other users logged on are notified of the impending shutdown and told to log off. User programs such as **vi** are instructed to put files away and exit. No other users are permitted to log in. Then, after a 30-second pause, system processes are terminated in an orderly, controlled fashion. Finally the system is turned off or halted.

4. After the system reaches a complete halt, start it up again by pressing the "on" button.

    The system starts up by executing all the needed startup system programs and then displays the login banner.

5. Log back in as *root*.

6. This time ask to have the system shut down without a pause and then reboot, rather than halt:

    shutdown -r *now*

    The **-r** is instruction to **r**eboot, and the *now* results in no time delay before the shutdown commences.

7. The system shuts down then immediately begins a reboot.

    Most Linux distributions also support a CTRL key command that performs a shutdown. The definition for the three-finger salute is in a system file.

8. Enter:

grep -i *del* */etc/inittab*

Most Linux systems include the entries:

```
#What to do when CTRL-ALT-DEL is pressed
ca::ctrlaltdel:/sbin/shutdown -r -t 4 now
```

This *inittab* entry has a name *ca* that defines pressing CTRL-ALT-DELETE as entering the **shutdown** command.

9. If this entry is in your */etc/inittab* file, then enter:

CTRL-ALT-DELETE

The system reboots.

Rescuing with a Boot Disk

Hard drive failures occasionally happen. A rescue boot disk usually can allow your system to reboot when it cannot boot on its own. Almost all Linux distributions prompt you to create an emergency boot floppy during installation. In Appendix A, when installing the system, we create a boot disk.

1. Locate your boot disk.
2. Shut down the system.
3. Insert your Linux boot floppy into the floppy drive and start your computer.

The boot floppy contains only the Linux kernel, which is just enough to get the system started again. Once the Linux system is up, you will have to use the distribution's disks, such as the CD-ROMs at the back of this book, to repair any damage.

Recovering If Super User Password Is Unknown

The boot floppy is also the way to rescue a system if you forgot the root password and you installed with minimum security.

1. Shut the system down again.
2. Put the boot disk in the drive.
3. Turn on the power.

After a few seconds a prompt appears:

```
boot:
```

4. At the boot prompt, enter:

linux *single*

The system boots up and you are logged in as *root* without providing the needed password. At this point, the system is in a state called *single user mode*. Only the super user is logged on. No one else can log in. Only essential features are available.

In this single user mode, you could change *root*'s password if necessary. You are *root*, alone on the system. You could perform any other needed system maintenance function or make system modifications.

5. Remove the floppy from the drive.

6. Use **shutdown** to reboot the system.

When the system reboots normally, it is in the full multiuser state that you are used to.

Because the installation was completed with classroom minimum security considerations, this approach works. In a production environment, we password-protect the single user mode entrance that you just used.

Changing the State at Startup

At all times, Linux is in one of several *states*, namely:

0	Halt. In state *0*, the system is off. To go to state *0* is to do an orderly shutdown.
1	Single user mode. Only the *root* can be logged on. Minimal resources are available. This is the state for system maintenance.
2	Multiuser mode. Other users can log in, and network functionality is available except that the system does not serve or accept Network File Systems (NFS).
3	Multiuser with NFS.
4	Not defined. The local administrator can create and employ this state to meet local needs.
5	Same as state *3* except the login screen is the graphical window, and users are placed in the graphical environment after login.
6	Reboot. To change to state *6* is to reboot the system.

When the system is booted, it automatically goes to one of the states 2 through 5. When you logged in using the boot disk and the **linux** *single* command at the boot prompt, the system came up in state *1*, single user mode.

As system administrator, you can change not only the current state (see the **man** pages concerning **init**), but you can also change which state is the default state reached when the system is booted.

The definitions for the various states are in a system file in *letc*.

↳ 1. Examine the *inittab* file with:

   more */etc/inittab*

   Partway down the file is the list of states and their definitions, *0* through *6*. Just below the state definitions is the line:

   ```
   id:3:initdefault:
   ```

   This line controls which of the init states the system goes to when it is booted.

2. Quit **more**.

3. Become the super user.

4. With super user powers, make a copy of the *inittab* file:

   cp */etc/inittab* */etc/inittab.BAK*

   It is wise to make copies of system files before making modifications.

5. Edit the */etc/inittab* file:

   vi */etc/inittab*

6. If the graphical windows system is available on your system, modify the *initdefault* line so it reads as follows:

   ```
   id:5:initdefault:
   ```

7. Write the file, then quit the editor.

8. Reboot the system.

   When your system boots up, the graphical login window is displayed. It is booting to state *5*.

9. Log back in and reset the *initdefault* value to its original state.

13.4 Managing Users

One of the most demanding aspects of administration can be user management. We add users, supply passwords when they are forgotten, modify the environment, and remove users.

Adding Users

The central user-access control file is the password file.

 1. Examine your current password file by entering:

> **more** */etc/passwd*

Every user who has access to the system has a single line entry in the */etc/passwd* file on the local system or on a server if Network Information Services is active. To add a user, we must accomplish several tasks: make a new entry to the password file, create a home directory, grant proper ownership of the home directory and startup files, and then usually supply a password.

2. Gather your super-human powers:

> **su -**

A script provided with Linux accomplishes the needed steps for adding a user.

3. Enter the following, where *newuser* is the new login name for a new user you want to create:

> **useradd** *newuser*

or

> **adduser** *newuser*

After creating a new user, the program exits.

4. Now assign a password to your *newuser* account:

> **passwd** *newuser*

5. When prompted, enter a new password. Then, when prompted, confirm the password by entering it again.

N O T E : You must create a user before you can assign a password.

6. Examine the modified password file:

> **more** */etc/passwd*

The *newuser* login name and account data are added to the */etc/passwd* file.

7. List the home directories:

> **ls** */home*

The new user has a place to play.

Including Startup Files When Adding Users

Congratulations, you just gave birth to a new user. Pass out cigars and complete the following exercises to examine how to configure the startup files for new users.

1. Change directories to the home directory of the user you just created:

   cd *~newuser*

2. List all files in the current home directory:

   ls -a

   Default startup files are included when we create a new user. Of course, we can modify the default files.

3. Change directories to the location of default files and list its contents by entering:

   cd */etc/skel*

   ls -a

   All the currently defined default files are listed here in the **skel**eton directory.

4. Use **more** to examine some of the files:

   more *.bash_profile*

   At this point, you can make changes to the existing files, add new files, or even delete files from this directory.

5. Create a new file in the *skel* directory called *Welcome* and put a welcome greeting in the file.

   The contents of the */etc/skel* directory (dot files, regular files, and directories) are copied to the home directory of any new user created using **useradd** or **adduser**.

6. Add another user to your system and check the contents of the new user's home directory.

Adding and Changing Passwords

As super user, we can create new passwords for new users and modify passwords for existing users. The process is exactly the same. Assume *newuser* forgot his or her password. Only the encrypted version is on the system in the */etc/shadow* file and there is no "unencrypt" utility, so you can't tell *newuser* what the old password is.

Because we cannot provide the user with the old password, the only choice is to use super user powers to assign a new password for the user.

➥ 1. To modify the password of an existing user, enter:

 passwd *newuser*

 You are prompted:

 ```
 New password:
 ```

 2. Enter the new password and press ENTER.

 You are then prompted:

 ```
 Re-type new password:
 ```

 3. Follow its lead and retype the new password.

 The password is now changed. As super user, we can change a user's password because the **passwd** program does not ask the super user for the user's old password, just the new one. It's nice to be 600 pounds.

 4. Exit the super user shell.

13.5 Backing Up User Data

Storing copies of files and directories on a storage medium such as diskette or tape is an essential system administrator duty. Sometimes we need to clear old system files. It is a good idea first to archive (store) them on a storage medium so that they can be restored in case they are needed later.

Compressing and Uncompressing Individual Files

We usually need to compress large files before we can effectively e-mail them as attachments or store them on media. We can use several utilities to compress large individual files.

➥ 1. As the regular user, not *root*, return to your home directory:

 cd

 2. Locate a big file:

 ls -Ss

 The option **S** is interpreted by **ls** as instruction to sort by files by size, and the **s** option is instruction to include the sizes in the output.

3. Enter the following command, where *bigfile* is the name of a large file in your current directory.

   gzip *bigfile*

   The <u>G</u>NU utility for compressing or <u>zip</u>ping files is **gzip**.

4. Verify the new size of the *bigfile*:

   ls -l

   The filename has changed to *bigfile.gz,* and the file is significantly smaller.

5. Copy the zipped file to one of your subdirectories, such as:

   cp *bigfile.gz Projects/*

6. Change directories to *Projects* and list its contents:

   cd *Projects*

   ls -l

7. Uncompress *bigfile.gz*:

   gunzip *bigfile.gz*

   The <u>G</u>NU <u>**unzip**</u> utility uncompresses the file.

8. Verify the size of the file after uncompressing:

   ls -l

The file extension *.gz* is removed, and the file is back to its original size. The **gzip** and **gunzip** utilities compress and expand individual files.

Creating and Using *tar* Archives

One important part of maintaining a filesystem is archiving directories and their files, including permissions and other file data, onto removable magnetic media. This exercise explores archiving a file onto the regular disk.

➥ 1. Create an archive of your regular user home directory tree by entering the following commands:

   id

   cd

   tar cvf *home.tar.image* .

   The name **tar** is derived from <u>t</u>ape <u>ar</u>chive. This command packs the contents of a directory and all its subdirectories and files into a single file, retaining file information such as permissions. The **tar** utility does not expect a dash before its options. The **tar** options employed in this command are **cfv** for

<u>c</u>reate a <u>v</u>erbose archive (display the name of each file affected) and put the archive in a <u>f</u>ile.

2. Examine the directory entry for the archive file with:

    ls -l *home.tar.image*

3. List the file and directory contents of the archive by entering:

    tar tvf *home.tar.image*

    Output the <u>t</u>able of contents, <u>v</u>erbosely, from a <u>f</u>ile.

    At this point, you could **zip** the file and send it to another system, put it on a floppy and load it onto another computer, or file it away. This next exercise will put a copy of your whole home directory tree and files in a new directory.

4. Create a directory to hold a copy of your home directory tree:

    mkdir *Home-copy*

5. Move the **tar** archive file to the new directory by entering:

    mv *home.tar.image Home-copy*

6. Change directories to *Home-copy* by entering:

    cd *Home-copy*

7. E<u>x</u>tract the files from the archive by entering:

    tar xvf *home.tar.image*
    ls

    A copy of your home directory tree is placed in the current directory. The archive file is read and the data extracted. The file remains in the directory after extraction.

8. Return to your home directory:

    cd

Compressing an Archive

We can use **gzip** to compress **tar** images. We can also use **tar** to compress large files or directories in a single step.

➥ 1. Create a compressed archive image of your home directory by entering:

    tar czvf *home.tar.image.smaller* .

    With the **z** option, the **tar** utility creates an archive and compresses it in one step. Likewise including the **z** in th extraction command extracts files from a compressed archive.

2. Verify that the size of the file is smaller:

   ls -l *home.tar.image**

3. Remove the archives by entering:

   rm *home.tar.image**

   The *tar.image** files are removed.

13.6 Installing Application Packages from the CD

Linux includes a powerful package manager that is used to build, install, query, uninstall, update, and verify individual software packages on a system. The software, developed by Red Hat, is called **rpm** for r̲edhat p̲ackage m̲anager, and is available on most Linux systems.

An RPM package consists of an archive of files, plus package information including name, version, and description. The features provided by RPM are many, making software maintenance easier than was possible with **tar/zip** packages.

Mounting the CD

Installing software packages is the most frequently employed operation for RPM. Software can be installed from the net or from CD. This exercise installs a package from the Red Hat CDs provided at the end of this book.

1. Become the super user:

   su -

2. List the devices currently mounted on your system:

   mount

   Unless you have a disk in the CD, the CD is not listed on the table of mounted devices displayed on the screen.

3. Insert Disk 2 of the Red Hat Linux 7.3 installation CDs.

4. Examine the mounted filesystems again:

   mount

   When you put a CD in the drive and close it, the system automatically mounts (makes available) the CD on the */mnt* directory.

5. Change directories to */mnt* and list its contents:

   cd */mnt*
   ls -F

   A directory named *cdrom* is listed in the */mnt* directory.

6. Change directories to *cdrom*:

   cd *cdrom*
   ls -F

   The CD is mounted on the directory *cdrom*, which is listed in *mnt*. When we list the contents of the */mnt/cdrom* directory, we see the contents of the topmost directory on the CD itself. After we mount a drive on a directory in the root filesystem, we can access that mounted drive by changing directories to the directory where it is mounted.

   Among the directories listed in the *cdrom* directory is one named *RedHat*.

7. Change directories to *RedHat* and list its contents:

   cd *RedHat*
   ls -F

   The directory *RPMS* contains the packages.

8. Change directories to *RPMS*, and list its contents:

   cd *RPMS*
   ls
   pwd

9. Count the number of packages in this directory:

   ls | wc -l

   Many hundreds of packages are included on the distribution. Among them is the Linux version of the **ksh**, which has a different name.

Installing the Korn Shell Package

1. List the packages that have names starting with *pd* by entering:

   ls *pd**

   The package with the name and numbers like *pdksh-5.2.14-16.i386.rpm* is the <u>p</u>ublic <u>d</u>omain <u>ksh</u> package. It is in the *RPMS* directory on the CD. The task is to read it from the CD and install it on the hard drive. Code, **man** pages, even the proper entry in the system files are all installed using one utility in a single command line.

2. Install the Korn shell RPM package by typing:

rpm -ivh *pdk**

The <u>r</u>edhat <u>p</u>acket <u>m</u>anager installs the Korn shell from the CD to your hard drive.

3. After installation is complete, exit the super user shell:

exit

4. Take the new shell for a spin:

ksh

ps

echo $$

The current shell is a **ksh**.

5. Examine the **man** pages:

man *ksh*

6. When you are finished playing with the new **ksh**, exit.

13.7 Installing a Printer

Printers can be attached to the local system, or can be attached to a different system on the network and accessed across the network. This set of instructions guides you through installing a local printer.

There are many different kinds of printers available today, each behaving differently. In UNIX and Linux, driver programs interpret standard signals (for point size, font, indent and so forth) to the appropriate signal for each particular printer. In addition to attaching the correct driver, printer installation requires creating a queue to manage the order of printing, and starting a process to handle the queue when users start making print requests.

1. To begin the printer installation, safely shut down your system:

shutdown -r *now*

2. Physically attach a printer to the computer.

3. Reboot your system.

4. Log in as a normal user.

5. Start the printer configuration tool by entering:

   printconf-tui

   Because you are logged on as a normal user, you're politely informed that to run the **printconf-tui** utility, you must be the super user. You are asked for the correct password.

6. At the prompt, enter the super user password.

   The **print**er **conf**iguration tool for **t**erminal **u**ser **i**nterface determines what printer is attached, what interface programs are needed, and what capabilities the printer possesses.

   The Linux print database is initialized and the *Printer Configuration* window is displayed.

> **N O T E :** Use TAB and the direction arrows to navigate between text boxes and buttons in these windows.

7. Press TAB, until the *New* button is highlighted and then press ENTER.

   The *Create a New Print Queue* window is displayed.

Creating a Print Queue

1. If every user could send information to the input of the printer at the same time, the printer would print out a word salad. Instead the system starts a printer daemon program, called a *spooler*, that accepts jobs from users and puts them on a queue. The print queue is a list of jobs from different users that are waiting to be printed. The spooler sends jobs one at a time to the printer so they are worked on sequentially, instead of all at the same time. Using the arrow keys, select *Local Printer Device*.

2. Using the TAB keys, navigate to the *Queue Name* text box.

3. Assign a name to the print queue you are creating such as:

   myqueue

> **N O T E :**   If you have a network printer, Use Unix Print Queue and enter the UNIX network printer server name or IP address and its desired queue.

4. Using the TAB key, select the *Next* button and press ENTER.

   The ***Setting Up a Local Printer Device*** window is displayed.

   The system should automatically detect your printer device.

5. With the correct printer highlighted, press TAB to select the *Next* button, then press ENTER.

   The ***Queue Driver*** window is displayed.

   The program examines the printer database and automatically locates which queue is appropriate for your model of printer.

6. Using the TAB key, select the *Next* button and press ENTER.

   The ***Create a New Queue Window: Name and Type*** window is displayed.

7. Verify that the device and driver information for your printer model is accurate.

8. Using the TAB key, select the *Finish* button and press ENTER.

   A menu list of available printers and print queues configured for your system is displayed. Probably, unless you are on a large network, there will only be one printer listed. (However, if there are several listed, choose *Default* to make your new printer setup the default queue.)

9. Using the TAB key, select the *Exit* button and press ENTER.

   You may be prompted by a pop-up window asking you to confirm that changes or additions to the print configuration files have occurred.

10. If this window appears, use the TAB key to select the *Yes* button and then press ENTER.

11. Print a text page to verify the printer installation was successful:

    lpr *any-small-file*

NOTE: If you want to reach the printer tool from the graphical desktop, choose the footprint menu button on the taskbar, then ***Programs*** | ***System*** | ***Printer Configuration***. You can also open a terminal window and run **printconf-gui**.

13.8 Maintaining a Secure System

Valuable data is stored on UNIX/Linux systems. Programs, resources, communications, text, and other data must be available, uncorrupted, to appropriate users, and unavailable to inappropriate users. In a bank, we know when something is stolen, because it is gone. In the computer world, if someone makes a copy of important data, it is stolen, yet is not missing. As administrators, our task is to protect the data from being read or copied by unauthorized users.

Likewise, failing to maintain proper security can lead to a problem of inaccessibility: an authorized user attempts to access data and it is either gone, altered, or not available. Our job is to protect data from harm and make sure it is available to those who have the right to access it.

Keeping a Physically Secure System: Employing Basic Protection

The physical components must be protected. Power cords must be placed where people will not step on or pull them. Magnetic media (disks and such) must be secure and protected from exposure to destructive magnetic fields, spillage of liquids, and excessive exposure to direct sunlight. A user leaving his or her logged-on terminal unattended could lead to unauthorized disclosure of data, corruption, or deletion or creation of unauthorized access doors.

Physical security means protecting hardware: terminals, printers, the CPU, magnetic media, and so on. Obviously, data security is dependent on the security of the hardware. Someone who obtains a hard disk or magnetic tape can then gain access to the data stored on it. If a computer becomes incapacitated, access to its data is eliminated. Even though the main purpose of data security is to protect access to information, we must also consider the security of the hardware. Access to the servers should be controlled with locked doors, possibly video monitoring, and room logs. Backups should be kept offsite, in a fireproof safe. Network cables should be inspected regularly.

Software Security

Unfortunately, many system administrators are not able to use directory and file permissions to secure data adequately. Although file permissions are essential, employing directory permissions to prohibit all but essential users from accessing a directory tree is the strongest defense. Carefully organize the permissions granted, **umask** setting, ownership of system files, group memberships, and accessibility to system resources.

Historically, the largest security issue is user passwords. In this text, we describe the method of developing passwords from the first letter of each word in a meaningful sentence. The resulting passwords look like randomly generated passwords, but are memorable to the user. Avoid issuing difficult passwords, people forget them and write them down.

Self-Test 1

1. What command lists all system processes?
2. As super user, what do each of the following accomplish?
   A. **passwd** richard_dorothy
   B. **su -**
   C. **adduser** dougbennett
   D. **shutdown -k now**
   E. **tar cvf** *etc-archive* **/etc**
   F. **printconf-tui**
3. What is the contents of the */etc/skel* directory?
4. What are the following *init* states?

   0 _____
   3 _____
   5 _____
   6 _____

Chapter Review

Use this section to review the content of this chapter and test yourself on your knowledge of the concepts.

Chapter Summary

- The system administrator is responsible for the hardware, data, applications, users, and security of the system.
- The account *root* has super user powers permitting wide access to the system, data, and resources. The super user can modify or delete any file owned by any user with any permissions, and can execute any executable program; add, delete, or modify any directory, program, or peripheral; modify system files and scripts; change the state of the system; and shut it down.
- The super user can add users using a script, or by making appropriate entries in the needed files.

- Any user can become the super user if he or she can provide the super user password.
- Many processes are started when the system boots, usually by the **init** process, which is informed if the process exits. If so, **init** starts another process executing the same code.
- A system can be in one of six states, including halted, single user, multiuser, a locally defined state, graphical login, and reboot.
- Many system control files are located in the *letc* directory. They provide startup information to the system, to processes, and to user programs. Thus, the files in *letc* tailor the way the system works.
- The super user can modify the *letc/skel* directory to modify the startup files placed in the home directory of any new user.
- Partitions on hard drives can be mounted onto the *root* partition of a system so that various parts of the drive (or other drives) can be accessed through the filesystem.
- Utilities are available to compress and uncompress files and to create and extract archives of directory trees.
- The Red Hat package manager facilitates installation, update, and removal of application packages to the system.
- Peripherals such as printers can be installed through administration tools available on the system.
- Security of systems is essential. System security consists of several components: We must protect the system from intentional and accidental corruption by employing permissions of files and directories, thoughtful passwords, and maintaining physical security of the system. We must keep track of the system's operations so that disks do not get full, adequate memory is available, and applications are functioning.

Assignment

Fill-in

1. List and describe three important responsibilities when administrating a system as *root.*

2. Why must such extreme caution be used when operating the system as super user?

3. What series of commands would create an archive of the *root* directory, compress it, and save it to a floppy disk?

4. Compare and contrast two methods of shutting a system down properly. When would each be used?

5. What command works in conjunction with a boot disk and allows you to boot into single user mode where minimal resources are available?

6. Which of the following results in the same super user powers?
    A. Log in as a regular user, enter **su**, and provide the correct super user password.
    B. Log in as a regular user, enter **su -**, and provide the correct super user password.
    C. Log in as a regular user, then enter the command **cd /**.
    D. Log on as user *root*.

7. Assume a user on your system forgot his or her password. Where is the encrypted version of the password on the system? What steps would you take so the user could access the account?

Project

A. Write a script named *sps* that when run lists all processes on the system in sorted order with their parent process ID as the primary sort field, and the process's PID as the secondary sort field.

B. After thoroughly testing the script, put the script in a directory named */usr/local/bin* on your system.

C. Try the script as a regular user from several different directories.

D. Print out the contents of */usr/local/bin* and the contents of the script. Explain how the script works.

E. Make the following changes in the */etc/skel* directory:
- Add the following lines to the *.vimrc* file (create the file if it is not there).

  map *g 1G*

  set *number*
- Modify the *.bashrc* file to include two interesting, useful aliases.
- Modify the *.bash_logout* file to display a friendly goodbye message at logout.

F. Create a new user and confirm that all *skel* files were copied.

G. Add text to the file */etc/motd* that describes the system and its uses.

H. Print out the contents of the new user's *.bashrc, .vimrc, .bashrc* files and the system's */etc/motd* file.

COMMAND SUMMARY

SUPER USER SHELLS

su -	Starts a child super user shell with full root environment.
su	Starts a child super user shell maintaining the user's environment, not the super user's.

PROCESSES

ps -aux	Lists all processes including user names.
ps -lax	Lists all processes including **PID**, **UID**, and **PPID**.

SHUTTING SYSTEM DOWN

shutdown -h now	Shuts the system down immediately, and halts.
shutdown -r +20	Shuts the system down after a 20-second delay, then reboots.

Adding Users

adduser *username*	Creates a new user named username and copies all default files from **/etc/skel**.

FILESYSTEM MANAGEMENT

mount	Lists all partitions currently mounted on the system.
gzip *filename*	Creates a compressed version of the file filename with a **gz** filename extension.
gunzip *filename*	Uncompresses the file **filename.gz**.
tar cvf *filename directory*	Creates an archive of the files and directories in the tree starting at directory and names it filename.
tar xvf *filename*	Extracts all files and directories from the archive filename.
rpm -ivh *packagename*	Extracts all files and directories from the rpm archive packagename and installs them on the system.

PRINTER MANAGEMENT

printconf-tui	Starts the printer management tool in the character-based terminal user interface.
printconf-gui	Starts the printer management tool in the graphical user interface.

Installing
Red Hat Linux 7.3

Linux is available either via the web or through the CDs provided by its distributors. The Red Hat version is included with this text. This appendix will guide you through your initial installation of Red Hat 7.3 on a PC.

Preparing to Install Red Hat Linux

7.3 is available on Red Hat Linux the CD-ROMs located at the back of this book. Red Hat is a fully functioning operating system that implements all the features of UNIX along with many added applications and administrative programs. Two CDs provided at the end of this book contain the Linux distribution created by Red Hat for use on X86 equivalent systems. The underlying code for all Linux systems is the same. Each distributor adds value by creating an installation program and including system administration tools. This chapter guides you through an installation of the basic programs required for a server system. After you have completed the installation outlined in this chapter, you should have a fully functioning system that can be used to complete all exercises in this book.

> **CAUTION:** Don't put the CD in the system yet. This first section identifies the information you need to achieve a successful installation and determine whether you have appropriate hardware, and sketches out the installation process.

Determining Whether the System Hardware Is Adequate

Literally thousands of components are presently available for building an X86 PC system. Some hardware, especially on older systems, can be incompatible with Linux. Red Hat Linux 7.3 should be compatible with most hardware in systems that were factory built within the last two years. However, hardware specifications change almost daily, so it is hard to guarantee that your hardware will be 100 percent compatible.

We suggest you obtain a list of all components of your system, including manufacturer, model number, and any variables such as onboard memory. You can either locate the data from the manufacturer's documentation, or open the box and look at the components. We suggest you attach the list to the outside of the case for easy reference.

It is worth taking a moment to check the component list against the most recent list of supported hardware. Red Hat maintains a list at:

http://hardware.redhat.com/hcl/

Describing the Hard Drive Contents

Often the PC hard drive is divided into several large sections or *partitions*. On some systems, one or more partitions hold all the programs and data for one operating system (such as Windows) and other partitions hold the programs and data for another operating system such as Linux. Such a setup is called *dual boot* because it can be started up as either kind of system. If it boots and accesses the Windows partitions, it is a Windows machine. If it accesses the Linux partitions, it functions as a Linux system. A hard drive consists of many chunks of space of a specific size, often 1,024 bytes. These data blocks hold data. The thousands of data blocks and related structures are formatted when the drive is formatted and the operating system is installed.

Creating a Linux-Only System

It is possible to install Linux in a dual boot environment where Linux co-resides on the disk with other operating systems such as with Microsoft Windows. In a dual boot setup, the user powers on the system and is asked whether to boot Linux or another OS. The disk space used by Linux must be separate from the disk space used by any other OS installed on the system, such as Windows, OS/2, or even a different version of Linux. Each OS is installed on one or more partitions of the hard drive.

This appendix provides instructions that guide you through setting up a Linux-only system. All existing programs and data on the computer hard drive will be lost when the drive is formatted. If you ultimately want a dual boot system, you should first back-up the user files and locate the other operating system's installation media. After you have installed Linux successfully, you can go back and install the alternative OS in dual boot mode. We suggest you add a second hard drive and install Linux in that space. You could also use one drive, employing something like Partition Magic to confine the alternative OS to a portion of a shared drive, and then install Linux on the remainder of the drive.

In this installation, at least two partitions will be created and dedicated to Red Hat Linux. We must create one partition called / and another called *swap*.

Before you start the installation process, one of the following conditions must be met: Your computer must have enough *unpartitioned* disk space for the installation of Red Hat Linux, or you must have one or more partitions that may be deleted, thereby freeing up enough disk space to install Red Hat Linux.

During the installation process, you must decide whether to:

- Overwrite the entire hard drive (all preexisting installations) with Linux (this is the option used in this set of instructions).
- Overwrite only the previously designated Linux partition with this version of Linux, presuming you have two operating systems in a dual boot configuration (Windows and Linux, for example).
- Overwrite none of the currently existing partitions and instead install Red Hat Linux 7.3 on another drive or on the free disk space that is available on the current drive.

These instructions guide you through deleting all data and programs on a disk, and installing only Linux on the current drive.

Identifying Needed Hard Disk Space

This chapter's installation establishes a server configuration. A server installation includes all the needed programs for a user and for serving files, web pages and so forth. Server installations do not require extensive customizations of your system's configuration.

The following are the minimum recommended disk space requirements for a server installation where only one language (such as English) is installed:

- Server (minimum, no graphical interface): 1.3 GB.
- Server (choosing everything, no graphical interface): 1.4 GB.
- Server (choosing everything, including GNOME and KDE): 2.1 GB (the instructions guide you through steps making this choice).
- If you plan to choose all group packages, as well as select additional individual packages, you should probably allow yourself 4 GB of disk space.

Locating Additional Help

You can find online help and Red Hat Linux documentation in both HTML and PDF formats at:

http://www.redhat.com/docs

For additional information on downloading and installing Red Hat Linux, refer to:

http://www.redhat.com/download/howto_download.html

Locating Needed Information before Beginning the Installation

The following items and information must be obtained prior to starting the installation:

- The CDs located at the end of this book
- A blank, IBM-formatted floppy disk to be used for the creation of an emergency boot disk
- A good password for *root*
- A user name and password for your account on the system
- If you are attaching the system to a network, specific information about your network

Locating Information for DHCP Connection

If you will be attaching the system to a network that provides assigned IP addresses from a DHCP server, you will need to obtain the following information from the system administrator, teacher, or service provider:

- Hostname: _____
- Gateway: _____
- Primary DNS: _____
- Secondary DNS: _____
- Tertiary DNS: _____

If your network uses static IP addresses you will need:

- IP address for this system: _____
- Netmask: _____
- Network: _____
- Broadcast: _____
- Hostname: _____
- Gateway: _____
- Primary DNS: _____
- Secondary DNS: _____
- Tertiary DNS: _____

When the preliminary information is gathered, you are ready to start.

Installing Linux on a PC

This chapter uses the CD-ROMs at the end of this book to perform a local CD-ROM installation of Linux.

Starting Installation

To begin, the system must be off. If the system is on, you could go through a controlled shutdown procedure to avoid damaging any open files or filesystems. However, if you are going to replace whatever there is on the disk anyway, it is okay to simply turn off the power.

➥ 1. Start by making sure the power is off, and have the first CD ready to insert in the CD drive.
   2. Make sure that the monitor is on and that the keyboard and mouse are plugged in.
   3. Turn the power on and immediately insert the first CD-ROM.

   The machine should boot into a text-based installation screen.

> **NOTE:** Until you make the final commitment to install Linux, you can always shut the system off and start over. For instance, if the system boots into Windows, shut it down and start over. If it still boots in Windows, check the order of startup in the BIOS to make certain the CD is read before the hard drive.

Selecting an Installation Method

At the text-based Welcome Screen, you are presented with several choices concerning how this installation is presented to you.

The default boot method, which employs a graphical user interface to guide you through the remaining steps, is highlighted and is the default choice.

➥ 1. Press ENTER to accept the default graphical choice.

   Alternatively, the default boot will proceed after a one-minute timeout.

   The *Red Hat Linux window* is displayed.
   2. At the *Red Hat Linux window*, locate the box in the lower-right corner and click *Next*.

If you have used a graphical user interface (GUI) before, you are familiar using a mouse to navigate the screens, click buttons, or enter text fields. You can also navigate through the installation using the TAB and ENTER keys.

> **CAUTION:** Unless a dialog box is waiting for your input, do not press any keys during the installation process. Doing so may result in unpredictable behavior.

> **TIP:** Once the installation program is loaded into memory, you can obtain information about the installation process and consider various options in detail by pressing F1 through F6. For example, press F2 to see general information about the online Help screens.

Selecting a Language

The *Language Selection window* is displayed. English should be highlighted by default.

 Verify that English is highlighted and then click *Next*.
The *Keyboard Configuration window* is displayed.

Selecting a Keyboard

The installation program should identify your keyboard by default.

 Verify and proceed by clicking *Next*.
The *Mouse Configuration window* is displayed.

Identifying the Mouse

If the connector your mouse plugs into is round, it's a PS/2 or bus mouse; if it is rectangular, it's a serial or USB mouse. Be sure to check.

 Select the appropriate mouse option and click *Next*.
The *Install Option window* is displayed.

Selecting the Installation Configuration

There are several different configurations that can be installed on a system, including a workstation configuration, a server configuration, and so forth.

↳ Click the radio button next to the *Server* icon and then click *Next*.

The ***Choosing Your Partitioning Strategy window*** is displayed.

Partitioning the Hard Drive

At this point, you could decide on the appropriate sizes for each partition, or you can let the installation program create a partition scheme. Unless you are experienced and have a particular reason to tailor the configuration, allow the program to assign partition values.

↳ 1. Click the radio button next to *Have the Installer Automatically Partition for You*. Then click *Next*.

The ***Automatic Partitioning window*** is displayed.

2. Click the radio button next to *Remove all partitions on this System* and then click *Next*.

If you previously had an OS installed on your machine, a pop-up warning window appears asking whether you're sure you want to remove all previous partitions and overwrite them with the new installation. All data previously on the computer will be lost!

3. Click *Yes* to proceed with the installation.

The ***Partitions window*** is displayed.

4. Accept the default partition settings by clicking *Next*.

Examining the Server Configuration

The server configuration sets up your system in specific ways. Partitions are created, programs are installed, and startup scripts are modified to have the system behave as you request. The following partitions are defined:

- A swap partition is created. The size of the swap partition is determined by the amount of RAM in your system and the amount of space available on your hard drive. For example, if you have 128 MB of RAM, then the swap partition created can be 128–256 MB (twice your RAM), depending on how much disk space is available.

- A 384 MB root partition is created and named */*.

- A partition is created for */usr* (the exact size of this partition is dependent on your available disk space).

- A partition is created for */home* (the exact size of this partition is dependent on your available disk space).
- A 256 MB partition is created for */var*.
- A 50 MB partition is */boot*, in which the Linux kernel and related modules are kept.

This disk partitioning scheme results in a reasonably flexible system configuration for most server tasks.

At this point, the ***Boot Loader Installation window*** is displayed.

Deciding How to Boot

When you later install a dual boot system, ***GRUB*** or ***LILO*** will be employed to give you a choice of operating systems at boot time. Even though this first installation is a Linux-only system, a loader is needed.

 Select

Use GRUB as the Boot Loader and click *Next*.

The ***GRUB Password window*** is displayed.

The GRUB *Password*

Because you want to be able to pass options to the kernel, do not password-protect the ***GRUB*** boot loader.

 Just pass to the next window by clicking

Next.

The *Network Configurations window* is displayed.

Configuring the Network

If you are not connecting the system to a network, leave the information on the Network Configurations window blank and proceed to the next section.

 1. If your network uses a DHCP server to assign IP addresses, enter the following information on the eth0 tab:

```
Hostname:
Gateway:
Primary DNS:
Secondary DNS:
Tertiary DNS:
```

If your network uses static IP addresses, provide the following information on the eth0 tab:

```
IP Address:
Netmask:
Network:
Broadcast:
Hostname:
Gateway:
Primary DNS:
Secondary DNS:
Tertiary DNS:
```

2. Click *Next*.

The Firewall Configuration window is displayed.

Selecting Firewall Protection

Unless your instructor tells you otherwise, keep the system fairly open so you can connect to other classroom systems.

↳ Select the radio button *No Firewall* and then click *Next*.

The *Language Support Selection window* is displayed.

Choosing a Supported Language

↳ Verify that *English* is selected and then click *Next*.

The *Time Zone Selection window* is displayed.

Selecting the Correct Time Zone

A map of the world with dots for cities is presented.

↳ 1. Click on the map of the globe near where you live to bring up your time zone.

2. Click on the time zone in which you live and then click *Next*.

The *Account Configuration window* is displayed.

Adding a Password for root *and User Accounts*

The *Account Configuration window* asks first for your password for the user *root.* Even though this is a practice system, create a good password. Be certain to employ both cases and some characters that are not *0–9* or *a–Z*. Using the first letter from the words in a sentence creates a good password. For example, the password *Li$50@mls* is a solid password and reasonably easy to remember because *L*inux *i*s *$50* @ *m*y *l*ocal *s*tore.

↳ 1. Enter a *root* password and then confirm (retype) the password.

   This window also allows you to add user accounts.

2. Click *Add User*.

3. Add a one-word (no space) user name for yourself, using your name. For example, Dave Liebman could enter:

   ```
   User Name: dliebman
   ```

4. Add a full name for the user:

   ```
   Full Name: David Liebman
   ```

5. Assign a password for the new user:

   ```
   Password: ********
   ```

6. Confirm the password by retyping it:

   ```
   Confirm: ********
   ```

7. When finished, click *OK*.

   The new user is now created.

8. Repeat steps 2 through 7 to create a user named *guest1* with a reasonable password.

9. When finished creating users, click *Next*.

   The Selecting Package Groups window is displayed.

Selecting Graphical and Application Packages

Several graphical desktops, all based on the X Window system, are available.

↳ 1. Select *GNOME, KDE,* and *Classic X Window System*.

   If you have a large amount of disk space, you may want to select packages for SQL or Web Server. You can select as many packages as you wish as long as there is enough space on your hard drive.

2. When finished selecting, click *Next*.

   The *Video Configuration window* is displayed.

Configuring the Video System

Your system's video hardware should be automatically detected.

↳ Verify and then click *Next*.

   The *About to Install window* is displayed.

Actually Installing the Code

> **C A U T I O N :** This is the last point at which you can abort the installation process without modifying the current system. The installation program will begin to overwrite any preexisting partitions and data when you confirm that you want to continue the process.

 1. If you want to install a system using the data you just provided, click *Next*.

A series steps take place that format the filesystems and install packages. The remaining installation process takes from 20 minutes to hours approximately, depending on the speed of your system's processor and the amount of memory available. For a while, watch the screen as it announces which packages are being installed. Think of a special holiday with many presents and being seven years old.

After half the installation is completed, you are prompted for disk 2.

2. Remove the first disk, install the second, and press *OK*.

Enjoy the trivia questions.

Creating a Boot Disk

In an emergency, a floppy disk that contains a boot image allows us to rescue the system. You are given the opportunity to create a boot disk.

 1. At the Boot Disc Creation window, insert a blank, formatted floppy disk into your floppy drive.

2. Click *Next*.

The drive spins and a boot disk is created.

The Monitor Configuration window is displayed.

Configuring the Monitor

The installation process should automatically detect your monitor type and specifications.

 Verify that this is the case and then click *Next*.

The Custom X Configuration window is displayed.

Selecting a Graphical Desktop

The various desktop options are presented.

1. Select *GNOME* as your default desktop environment (you can change this setting later).
2. Select *Text or Terminal Window* as your login type and then click *Next*.

Rebooting

1. Remove the boot floppy.
2. Remove the CD from the CD drive.
3. Press ENTER to reboot your system.

After you reboot, you are presented with a text login window. Congratulations.

Testing the System

1. At the login prompt, log in using the user name that you used when you created your account.
2. Start the graphical environment with:

   startx &

   The graphical desktop should be displayed.

Summary

- Installation of Linux using the CDs provided with this book consists of providing information about the network, local time zone, and type of installation desired, and confirming the hardware that the program detected.
- The procedure consists of filling out data and making choices. Then, when all information is provided, the installation takes place.
- The installation results in a PC functioning as a Linux workstation, including a graphical desktop.

Index

INTERNATIONAL CONTACT INFORMATION

AUSTRALIA
McGraw-Hill Book Company Australia Pty. Ltd.
TEL +61-2-9900-1800
FAX +61-2-9878-8881
http://www.mcgraw-hill.com.au
books-it_sydney@mcgraw-hill.com

CANADA
McGraw-Hill Ryerson Ltd.
TEL +905-430-5000
FAX +905-430-5020
http://www.mcgraw-hill.ca

**GREECE, MIDDLE EAST, & AFRICA
(Excluding South Africa)**
McGraw-Hill Hellas
TEL +30-210-6560-990
TEL +30-210-6560-993
TEL +30-210-6560-994
FAX +30-210-6545-525

MEXICO (Also serving Latin America)
McGraw-Hill Interamericana Editores S.A. de C.V.
TEL +525-117-1583
FAX +525-117-1589
http://www.mcgraw-hill.com.mx
fernando_castellanos@mcgraw-hill.com

SINGAPORE (Serving Asia)
McGraw-Hill Book Company
TEL +65-6863-1580
FAX +65-6862-3354
http://www.mcgraw-hill.com.sg
mghasia@mcgraw-hill.com

SOUTH AFRICA
McGraw-Hill South Africa
TEL +27-11-622-7512
FAX +27-11-622-9045
robyn_swanepoel@mcgraw-hill.com

SPAIN
McGraw-Hill/Interamericana de España, S.A.U.
TEL +34-91-180-3000
FAX +34-91-372-8513
http://www.mcgraw-hill.es
professional@mcgraw-hill.es

**UNITED KINGDOM, NORTHERN,
EASTERN, & CENTRAL EUROPE**
McGraw-Hill Education Europe
TEL +44-1-628-502500
FAX +44-1-628-770224
http://www.mcgraw-hill.co.uk
computing_europe@mcgraw-hill.com

ALL OTHER INQUIRIES Contact:
McGraw-Hill/Osborne
TEL +1-510-420-7700
FAX +1-510-420-7703
http://www.osborne.com
omg_international@mcgraw-hill.com